T0354303

MOUNTAIN OF TEARS

A Novel of the Making of a United States Marine

LEO LEPAGE

authorHOUSE®

AuthorHouse™
1663 Liberty Drive
Bloomington, IN 47403
www.authorhouse.com
Phone: 1 (800) 839-8640

Published by AuthorHouse   07/27/2015

ISBN: 978-1-5049-2641-6 (sc)
ISBN: 978-1-5049-2640-9 (e)

Library of Congress Control Number: 2015912097

Print information available on the last page.

ABOUT THE AUTHOR

The author is former Marine and retired Sergeant
from the Hartford Connecticut Police Department.
He has published two books regarding his H.P.D. Career.
The Badge, The street and The Cop
as well as
The Forgotten Memories of the Blue Soldiers.

DEDICATION

To my mom and dad

Leo and Marie

Who by example

Stirred the stew of life

Honor, integrity, accountability

and responsibility

Loving God fearing parents

I will never forget you

A Note of Thanks

To all the Officers and Noncoms I served with,
living and dead, a profound thank you. Your skill
and dedication prepared me for manhood.

To all Veterans no matter the uniform. You served the colors
with dignity and courage went in harms way. I hope this book
rekindles memories both good and bad. Never forget, you earned
the right to walk proud. You have my respect and gratitude.

To Chief Bernie Sullivan, Retired Chief Hartford Police,
who encouraged and continues to do so. To keep on writing.
Thanks skipper for your continued support and friendship.

To Captain Donald Gates, Former Marine and Retired Hartford
Police Department, who also kicked my butt to stay the course.

To Lieutenant Nathaniel Davis (Boo) retired H.P.
D. and former paratrooper who's knowledge and
skill was a needed asset. Thanks Boss.

To those who currently serve the flag and keep
The Hun at bay. Thank you and God bless.

To my loving wife and soul mate Lisa, who labored long and hard by my side in completing this work. There are no words to describe her love, patience and understanding. For during her time, she glimpsed a part of Hell during this travel.

To Joe Hunt, my scratching post who listened patiently and as a brother shared in the emotions.

To all our beloved troops who gave their all. May the hand of God bless and welcome you. May you rest in peace. Only the dead have seen the end of war. The adage, "All gave some, some gave all, reads so profound and true.

To those who stood by my side in this endeavor, thank you. There are so many, I know I've deleted. It was not with malice only an old brain that at times misfires. From the heart, thank you.

To all who read this novel both critics and allies. Thank you and stay well.

Semper-Fi!

PROLOGUE

The writer was proud, fortunate and privileged to have served in what I believe to be the finest military institution in the world, The United States Marines Corp. Which as we know, prides itself on discipline, esprit de corps, honor, integrity responsibility and accountability.

The Marine Corps sells itself to potential recruits as an institution whose members are bound together by mission and purpose. The motto "Semper Fi," expresses a commitment to perpetual loyalty that is derived from love. Marines are not always shy about owning up to this attachment for this attachment arises in training and combat. For some it becomes a feeling they cannot lose and do without. It sustains them and comforts them in their affliction.

The brave men and women who don the green have always faithfully marched into harms way and continue to do so. Marines possess a fierce loyalty, to the commander in chief, the colors and that of our great nation. The eternal motto of "Once a Marine, always a Marine," it is embossed on one's soul. It is imperative that we always remember that yes they are warriors, but boys of common virtue called to duty, brothers and sons, friends and neighbors, husbands and fathers. It's as simple as that.

To my brother and sister Marines, past, present and future

"SEMPER-FI"

LITTLE FAWN LAY IN BED. Her small frame contorted and ravished with pain. Sweat glistened on her petite body. Soft moans of anguish emitted from her dry cracked lips. She was with child and the time was at hand. Alone and forlorn in her humble room, she called to the Great Spirit to assist her as she delivered a new life into the world. Her spirit was distraught, overflowing with guilt and shame, for her child would never know the father. On a cold winters night lonely, her soul depressed she'd succumbed to the weakness of the flesh and had bedded with a transit stranger who just rode off into the sunset never to be seen or heard from again. Through tear filled eyes she caught a glimpse of her father, who stood straight and tall in the bedroom door. Through bleary eyes she observed the passive look on his face. His dark angry eyes bored into hers. She had shamed him and had brought dishonor into their lodge. Two wolves remained silent and showed little remorse or compassion regarding her suffering. Within his proud heart, he felt the Great One acting out his revenge on the ravaged soul lying in her bed of torture and would account for her great sin alone and tormented.

Little fawn experienced extreme pressure within the womb. Excruciating pain took hold. Thrashing to and fro she pushed with fading strength attempting to expel this painful pressure from her petite body. Grasping for breath, she struggled with the last of her failing strength, affecting a powerful thrust. Blackness engulfed her.

The soft cries coming from the bed announced the arrival of a new soul into the world of life.

Two Wolves moved to the bed. Standing serene and quiet, he gazed down at the small oozing body of new life before him. Scurrying to the side of the bed, he quickly severed the umbilical cord. Tenderly he brought his grandson to his breast. Tears like rain caressed his cheeks and gazing at the small frame of his daughter, he caught a flicker of a smile in her amber eyes. Grasping her tiny hand he whispered in a hoarse voice, I love and forgive you. Tears trickled down her face and in a spasm she fell back on the pillow. Gasping she took a deep breath, slowly exhaling, her body fell limp and quiet. Her spirit had joined those of her ancestors.

Two wolves stood mute. Soft cries from his grandson purged his soul. Gazing at a lone rose lying on the night table, tears cascaded down his checks matching the rain pelting the cabins tin roof. A bolt of lightning lit the night sky and its power casting the humble dwelling in a splendor of golden hue. In this moment Two Wolves hoisted his grandson high in the air. In a powerful voice he called to the Great Spirit. From this day, this life I hold in supplication to you will be known as John Broken Rose. Life was given at the cost of my daughter. Great One welcomes the soul of Little Fawn into the lodge of her ancestors. Bless the spirit of this man child. May he grow strong as the bear and wise as the owl? Enlighten me, Two Wolves, so that I and the creatures of the forest teach him and point the way.

Pulling the man child close to his breast, Two Wolves, whispered softly, it is written you will grow to be a fine tuned warrior. You will walk the path chosen by the Great One. You will tread in the footsteps of our ancestors.

Two Wolves laid Little Fawn to rest in a small knoll caressed by lilies of the valleys. Her final resting place was surrounded by tall scented pines a short distance from the cabin. While he stood over her grave, he began chanting an ancient Indian prayer to the Great Spirit imploring the Great One to welcome his daughter's spirit into the peaceful land of the ancestor's long gone. Standing alone in quiet solitude, his thoughts drifted to another time, when his wife of forty years, Little Robin went to that quiet place to frolic with spirits who greeted her soul with joy, and lead her to the promised peace.

Tears lined his cheeks as he turned walking slowly and erect heading toward the cabin where the cries of Broken Rose had shattered the peaceful stillness. The soft cries of the child, a beacon too Two Wolves, that hunger caused him to fuss for nourishment.

Two Wolves, wise in the journey of life, knew he inherited a powerful responsibility. In dreams he saw the image of a warrior. One who would strike fear in adversaries. The Great Spirit had directed him to embrace his grandson. To nurture him, enlighten strengthen him, in preparation for the great adventure. His was the responsibility to mold this future warrior in the likeness and skills of the ancient ones. A mark had been branded on his soul, stamped to his heart, thus ensuring he would persevere guiding his grandson by pointing his spirit on the byway of life that would please and eventually lead him to caress the Great One.

Rain continued to deluge the area for several days. Two Wolves sitting quietly in front of a log fire spent time reflecting. His thought processed in over drive. Broken Rose lay peaceful in a deep sleep. Two Wolves could hear the wind rustle through tree tops. The smell of the forest pine permeated the air filling the small cabin with the gift of its fresh aromatic scent. The days turned into weeks leap frogging into months. Neighboring tribe's women lovingly assisted in the nurturing of Broken Rose. Broken Rose grew healthy due to their tender attention.

As the years passed, the young brave displayed a strong curiosity and interest in those who shared his world and delighted in the creatures which abounded in the surrounding forest. Time refuses to stay still. Years came and went, thus on a clear spring day, Two Wolves staring at Broken Rose, like a ram rod sapling had grown into a young manhood. Ah, thought Two Wolves the time to speak is at hand. The moment is ripe to become his teacher and prepare him for his destiny. For Two Wolves knew it was his responsibility to guide him in the ways of our people. Let the morning sun light his way, May the Great One embrace his heart and spirits.

Seated by the warm fire, Broken Rose gazed at his grandfather. Listened attentively as the old warrior spoke eyes boring into the crackling fire, the old man began, "Today my son, we begin your great journey through life. You will discover great and wondrous things. You will learn the secrets which guide the creatures of the forest. How they are magnificent hunters, survive hot summers, and bitter winters. These wondrous creatures will embrace you and share their instinct for survival. Man cannot duplicate these instincts, but you my young warrior shall inherit this gift from them. You must strive to unlock the mystery of life. Discover its secret and unravel its mystic. You must possess the honor bestowed to you by our brave ancestors, for you have been chosen to resurrect their powerful ways of the hunt and life's challenge to survive. Let the Great One breath wisdom, courage, and honor in to your spirit. Always be mindful that man is the true animal and the one predator that for whom some unknown foolish reasons kill his own. You will learn to trust your instincts and yours alone. Soon my son we enter the mighty, where in I, Two Wolves, will introduce you to the ways of the great bear, the cunning of the mountain lion, and the stealth of the snake. You will match the vision of the great sky warrior, the majestic eagle. You will adapt the wisdom of the wise old owl. You will be sleek as the fox, and like the wolf you will hunt alone and mistrusting. You will inherit the speed and quickness of brother deer. From the lion you will learn the skill of the run and adopt his ability to strike swift and fatal. My son must take time and patience. You must work to earn the respect and friendship of these great creatures. Tonight you must pray to the Great One and call to the spirits of our ancestors. Tomorrow when the sun peeks from the horizon we began the quest that will mold you into the complete warrior. This you will do and bring honor to our people."

Morning came quickly. The sun burning bright cut through the grayish haze rising from the forest bed. Its brilliant rays revealed the carpet of snow which had canvassed the earth in the quiet of the night. The white tarp spread miles before them. Clothed in heavy deerskin, Two Wolves and Broken Rose entered the forest. Its majestic oaks and tall pines as powerful sentinels marked their path. It was within this country side that Two Wolves strove to unravel its secrets ensuring that Broken Rose would ingest the knowledge which abounded within its womb. In silence they began the journey. Chirping birds announced their arrival. The wind howled singing its powerful tune. The sun warm on their faces propelled their track forward. The tracks of the forest creatures pointed the way. Within this canopy of green a soft gentle breeze engulfed them. It was as a whisper from the Great One. If one listened, he could hear and feel that the Great Spirit had granted his blessing and breathed fire into the heart and soul of Two Wolves, for his was the awesome task to guide and teach, the mentor, to Broken Rose.

Now deep within the forest, Two Wolves halted turning slightly; he faced his 12 year old grandson. "Ah-ha, he thought, "now it begins," he spoke softly. Broken Rose, "heed what you see here, the mighty oak, the scented pine, bramble bush, Mother Earth. Inhale these senses. Feel the power of the forest. Absorb its strengths. Embrace its soul, for this is the place ancestors' spirits. Roam free, listen to the wind, which carries voices from the past. It can warn you of danger. Place your ear to earth. It too telegraphs messages. Implore your eyes and ears to be sharp as the fox. Know that brother wind carries the scent of wood smoke and the sweat of man. The cologne he wears and his cooking fires, rotted food and carcasses, even one's voice carries in the wind. Embrace Mother Earth, she relays the snap of a twig, the foot falls of man or beast. Study the heavens and observe how friend sun roams east to west. Hone to the stars. Learn their identities and they will guide you in darkness. The sudden silence of birds will warn you of the presence of man or beast. These are things you must know. One day they will save you from certain destruction. Maintain a pure heart. Keep your mind clean and avoid evil spirits for they cloud the mind. Control lust for the flesh. Avoid tobacco for it imperils breath and the ability to run quick as the deer. Be mindful of your surroundings. Be slow and deliberate in movement. Listen to the creatures of the forest. Befriend them and earn their trust. Once you had succeeded, you will be accepted. Remember, they too can be lonely. They will embrace you and guide you through and around danger.

Remember, Broken Rose, the forest can and will sustain you provided you study and learn its secrets. One should never hunger or thirst or be cold or without light. You are surrounded by nature's spirit and she will provide food, fuel, and water and the ways and means to survive. Discipline your mind and body so they mesh as one. Tone your body. Labor and sacrifice will render a solid physique and clear mind, a pure spirit. Soon you shall thread life's byways alone. Be prepared to face danger, hatred, greed, lust, hypocrisy. These demons will pock mock your path and being of strong spirit cast them aside.

My son you must steel yourself for your moment with destiny. The Great One has chosen you to go forth as his warrior. Prepare! Lead a life of self-imposed discipline and prevail in this hallowed endeavor."

As the hands of time ticked away, Two Wolves continued his intense training of Broken Rose. He taught him to blend with the forest. Months flitted by the tentacles of time turned into years. The old man taught his grandson the method of the silent kill with a knife and bow. Endless hours spent in mastering the skill and secrets of these weapons. He would position Broken Rose in the center of a small meadow blindfolded and would have him circle him in the foliage, tossing rocks into the bushes. It was left to Broken Rose to point his bow and the twang of the release would reveal if he'd fired in the right direction where the rock had come to rest. Endless hours were spent in this exercise. Countless errors recorded. But, Ah, the young warrior's senses now nurtured and nourished began to blossom. Success soon followed, ears fine-tuned, strokes in the proper area were now prevalent.

Two Wolves no longer deceived him. For Broken Rose, his hearing was as radar. The first training session was digested and the keen sense of ear perfected. Now the language of the blade was explored. Two Wolves would swing a rope through the air while Broken Rose stood tall and quiet in a meadow. Blindfold in place, hearing again was the key in this exercise. He would concentrate on the sudden change of air ways about him. Broken Rose, soon came to swipe at the exact moment severing the rope while air borne. Months of sweat, frustration, and failure, led to success. He'd learned the kill zones with which to launch. The silent kill, quickly and efficiently, on man or beast. Memorizing which organs were vulnerable and where a lethal thrust would cause instant death.

Now the big challenge presented itself. Two Wolves studied and caressed the rifle as he presented same to Broken Rose. Whispering softly, he spoke, "to master this weapon you must master the art of breathing and the slow steady squeeze to the trigger. You must forge your body to become as one with the weapon. Let it become an extension to yourself."

Broken Rose accepted the rifle and it appeared that it instantly molded with his being. They together were as body and soul, one entity. Broken Rose practiced the art of the shoot endlessly. He could hit a fly in flight. Two Wolves observing in the distance was content. The boy was a natural—thank the gods. Training continued. There was reprieve from the exhausting regimen.

Two Wolves continued his illustrations and harsh teaching of Broken Rose in the art of fighting hand to hand. He taught him the where and how to cripple or maim his enemy. The eyes, nose throat solar plexuses, kidneys, shortened blows were practiced. The hands, as his brothers, mastered, had become an extension of the body. Now he was able to effect death to an unseen enemy with the speed of the cobra. Like the bow, knife and rifle, his body was a weapon.

After 6 years in the forest, Two Wolves and Broken Rose had forged a bond and were as one. Two Wolves, satisfied, Broken Rose would emerge as the complete warrior, turned and headed home. Seeking refuge and comfort in the sanctuary of his humble cabin. The modest dwelling stood on a small hill overlooking the gurgling waters of a small stream. Constructed of logs, it contained four large rooms. They were heated by a wall fireplace situated in the north wall of the kitchen. A country porch lined the outside of the cabin. It was here on this porch, while Broken Rose lay in peaceful slumber, that Two Wolves exited the comfort of his living room and his desire to sit in his old rocker, had propelled him to seek refuge so as to reflect on things long past. While photos of his life danced before him, the hand of the Great One reached out and brushed the forehead of the old man. Two Wolves whispered his thanks for the gift of life and slumped deep into his old rocker, gasped once, twice, then stillness. His spirit, like the morning mist rose from his body, soared ever upward. Two Wolves had now reunited in the lodge of the ancestor's. The sun peeked over the horizon and the cabin now bathed in warm sunlight, stood still in the morning mist. Morning birds chanted a mournful song. The fragrance of lily's and pine purified the air. Like a sigh in the wind, Two Wolves had gone the way of the warrior. His spirit did not look back.

Broken Rose pushed open the porch door. Looking to his right, he glimpsed the form of Two Wolves seated in his old rocker, stilled and quiet, as his pipe lying alongside him on the floor. Broken Rose approached and sank to his knees. Tears welled in his eyes, transfixed; he uttered an old Indian prayer. Gazing into the heavens, he whispered, so long grand-pa, may our ancestors welcome you. May the Great One bless you and give you peace and comfort.

Broken Rose stood at the foot of Two Wolves grave which rested between the graves of his wife, Little Robin and his daughter, Little Fawn. Tears streaming down his face, he whispered words of love and gratitude. Kissing the graves, he rose quickly. Turned and walked briskly to the cabin. Gazing fondly at the dwelling, he struck a match tossing same into the peat moss he'd stacked around the cabin earlier that morning. He stood perfectly still as the match flared. A small fire erupted its tentacles and spread quickly. Soon large fires danced about the cabin. It fed on oxygen and fuel; it soon engulfed the cabin with awesome power. In minutes the cabin burst into complete flame, like a wounded animal, it creaked and groaned as it succumbed to its fate.

Broken Rose stood tall, silent, as tears welled in his eyes and then slowly ebbed down his cheeks, with the tears glistening in the glow of the fire as they fell quiet to mother earth. His heart was heavy with grief and his soul hollow and without light. He felt alone, abandoned and the fear of the unknown anchored him in place. All that he had cherished and loved was no more. Tongues of fire leaped into the air. The crackle and groans of his beloved refuge roared as in pain and collapsed in ash and embers. Clouds of dark smoke enveloped the sky. His vision blurred from tears and the sting of hot ash. Falling to his knees, he moaned in anguish. His soul tormented by the spectacle of his boyhood refuge smoldering in the morning wind. Falling to his knees he raised his arms in supplication, voice trembling, gazed into the smoke filled sky. Softly he prayed, oh Great Spirit, mother, grandfather, I Broken Rose, son of Little Fawn, Grandson of Two Wolves, will not fail you, nor bring dishonor to the lodge of our ancestor's. You have gone the path of the old ones and now share the pipe of peace with them. Give me strength to prevail. Guide my footsteps so that I find peace as the setting sun. Lift the pain from my spirit so that I do not despair but mostly, strengthen my heart; steel my body so that I honor you as the true warrior.

He stood staring mutely. Memories of youth flashed in front of him. He'd never known his mother never felt her touch. Never breathed her scent, yet because of his grandfather, Two Wolves, he had felt her spirits presence all of his days. Bowing his head, he whispered a tearful goodbye. As he turned to leave, he touched his heart, oh spirits departed, those who I love, your memory will walk with me all of my days. You will be as my heartbeats that spew forth life.

He turned and not looking back entered the forest. He walked slowly for his heart was heavy, as thoughts filled of days now departed. The birds greeted him with a chorus of sweet tunes, which filled him with warmth and some comfort. As he moved stealthy through the forest, he noted the tracks of creatures who inhabitant this wondrous place. There, leading into a clump of pines, the sign of deer and to his right, by a gurgling stream, that of a she wolf and her cubs. As he passed a mighty oak, he smiled as he observed the territorial markings of the great bear embossed in her bark as a warning to others of his species. Clothed in a buckskin jacket and dungarees, he carried his meager possessions in a deerskin satchel, on his left hip. He felt the security and power of the ivory handled hunting knife given him by Two Wolves, Moons ago. His jet black hair was neat and clean, with a lone braid dangling down to his shoulder blades. He moved silently as a cat. His path marked by soft scented pine needles. Overhead two red tailed hawks soared. Ah, they hunt for breakfast. He spoke softly, hoping the spirits of ancestor's walked beside him.

He followed the sun and his feet propelled him in a westward direction. Two Wolves had often told stories to him regarding the town of Indian Ville, the object of his trek. He'd hastened his pace, knowing he had a long road to travel. In his lives pouch, he carried several days of provisions, comprising of dried venison, berries, corn and a modest supply of flat bread. He smiled inwardly, food was no problem for the forest and woodlands skirting the highway would amply supply his needs. As the sun began sun rose high in the sky, he began to run. Oh how he loved to run. He felt free and strong like a young buck. Since many moons ago, he found he could run many miles and was never winded. Two Wolves had trained him well. Running up hills and mountains, sometimes with a heavy log carried on his shoulders, his legs were as pistons and his heart and lungs were strong and pure. He continued his run for two hours. Coming to a halt at a stream of the two tall trees, named for the majestic pines that reached to the clouds, he drank of the streams clean sweet water, then sat back resting against the back of a to tall pine, feasted on venison, berries, and a handful of dried corn. He watched a rabbit scurry by. A red fox is in hot pursuit. "Ah," he laughed this time the rabbit eluded the fox, disappearing into bramble bushes. But alas he shouted, "Beware! The fox now knows your trickery!"

Rising, he rearranged his satchel and threw it over his shoulder and sprinted through the stream continuing his march to Indian Ville. The sun sank slowly. He knew day was winding down. He'd spotted a small knoll spouting a small stream off to his right. "Ah, this is good. This is where I will bed for the night." Gathering dry wood, he soon had a warm fire glowing. He'd constructed a bed of pine needles and leaves for a bed. He had consumed two flat breads and

venison for his evening meal. Assured he'd stocked enough firewood
for the night, with a full stomach, he prepared to settle for the night.
Broken Rose added a generous amount of wood to the fire and he lay
on his make shift bed, covering him with a deer skin blanket taken
from his satchel. His hunting knife by his side, he lay back and fell
into a deep sleep.

The tarp of darkness settled over his small camp. The glow of
his fire warmed and comforted him. The music of birds roused him
from sleep. Daylight seeped into the forest. He quickly added wood
to his dying fire. Rummaging in his satchel, he breakfasted on berries
and flat bread. Relieving him-self in a nearby bush and then doused
the fire with water from the stream. Broken Rose inhaled the pure
scented air as he stepped briskly into the steam crossing to the far
side where he continued his journey once again in the thick forest. He
began to jog, and would pace himself conserving his strength. The
signs of the wind and sun enlightened him that he would reach the
edge of this forest by sunset. His mind was clouded, yes his destiny
was that of a warrior, yet he would be entering a new and strange
world. He'd never left the forest for his schooling and training was
done on a reservation. Once Two Wolves had brought him to its edge
where they quietly stared at the white man's highway. This is where
the strange horseless machines traveled its artery.

His spirit was confused. Yes he was excited, yet apprehensive.
He was embarking on an unknown adventure. As he ran, words of
Two Wolves spoken long ago, settled in his heart. "Always listen to
the voice of the wind and the whispers of the forest. Be aware of your
surroundings and on that day you begin your quest in the midst of
those of pale skin. Silence your tongue. Make your ears sharp and
hear what they say. Listen and always listen. Speak little and look into
the eyes of your fellow warriors. They are the windows to his soul.
Do not show fear or weakness. You are of the lodge of true warriors.

Never reveal your intentions. You are of true and pure blood. And remember, pray to the Great One, so that he walks by your side."

His walk was brisk. He had ceased jogging for the moment electing to conserve energy. He entered a small meadow enclosed by the rapture of numerous mountain laurels and their fragrance emitting sweetness in the air. He'd known he was approaching this place as brother wind had carried the aroma of the spirit flowers to his breath. Entering the meadow he heard the guttural growls of a creature off to his right. A high pitched cry froze him in his tracks. Perfectly still, he watched as the sleek mountain lion approached, circling cautiously and sniffing the air inhaling the scent of this man creature which stood before him. The powerful creature drew closer. His growls, carried on the wind, were low and threatening. He bore his fangs menacingly. Broken Rose shanked his knife slowly, heart racing, he prepared for combat with the powerful creature, now only yards distance. Suddenly the creature halted and his head rose high. The lion had captured Broken Rose's scent. Soft cries of pleasure now poured from deep in its throat. Broken Rose stood confused. Then a huge smile lighted his sweat soaked face. Eeha--Eeha. It is you. It is my brother Scar. Oh Scar, how good to greet one another. Scar bounded into him. His momentum knocking Broken Rose to the leaf covered ground. Scar licked and pummeled him, happiness in its dark eyes. Broken Rose sighed and laughed with pleasure as they frolicked in the grand meadow. Man and this powerful creature of the forest reunited, sharing emotion, strength and joy.

John Broken Rose now sat stroking scars back and head as the great cat licked its paws. Twilight had descended and they bedded down together by a small rambling stream. A small fire warmed them from the night chill. Broken Rose had shared his meal with scar. They devoured dried venison and lush berries. As the tarp of night engulfed them, Broken Rose reflected, returning to the past of many moons, when he and Two Wolves had rescued this powerful creature as a lion cub. His mother lay dead, killed by crazed grizzly.

Next to her lay the bodies of scars two sisters. Decimated in the grizzly's attack. Two wolves had beaten the huge bear creature into retreat using the glow and heat of a fire stick. Both the old warrior and young brave carried the injured boy lion to their camp refuge a sanctuary at this moment which was a deep cave forged by mother nature and low on the mountain.

Time and patience, saw the healing process begin with the kindness and understanding. The boy lion healed and grew strong in the process. He bore the mark of the grizzly deep on his left flank and upon consulting the spirits, the name scar was chosen and given.

Broken Rose became as a brother to scar. He watched in wonder as he grew strong and developed quickness of feet with speed that matched brother wind. His sense of scent on the hunt carried for miles. He studied this creature determined to learn, to emulate his skills and strength. They frolicked in the forest, hunted together, shared their kills, slept side by side on the forest floor, climbed the great mountain and from its zenith marveled at the power of the Great One stretching for miles.

Before them, Broken Rose gathered strength from the Spirit of Brother Scar. From him he mastered the art of stealth and patience, inherited speed, the art of the scent, the use of his surroundings with which to deliver the coup to grace to unsuspecting prey. He delighted in the taste of raw meat. He was rich in that now that he possessed the spirit and skills of the man warrior and that of brother lion. Alas, the time came that each would follow his own path. Scar on a soft summer night, roared as he entered the forest. It was his farewell. Two Wolves and Broken Rose uttered eeha, eeha, may the spirits guide and protect you through the journey of life. That was moons ago. Now here reunited they shared a bond only the true hunter understands.

Broken Rose stayed for a week relishing the rekindling of this bond of man spirits and creatures. As he sat quietly before the dying embers of their morning fire, Broken Rose knew this day they would part, perhaps forever. For this was his only source of comfort and he knew that he would long for the day to frolic once more where the free spirits roamed. Scar sensed his grief. Nudging him with his powerful head, slowly they trudged through the forest. Silence paved their way. Only the chatter of numerous birds, as they approached, engulfed them.

All too soon they stood at the edge of the forest. The white man's highway looked large and foreboding. Before them, horseless machines frittering through and from caused scar to growl his displeasure. Broken Rose, his spirit filled with emotion, stroked the head of his mentor and friend. "Scar my powerful brother, you must return to your wooded world where your spirit and heart roam free and brave. May the wind always caress you? May the sun warm your sleek muscles? May you live long and true? May the spirits grant you off spring that carries your strength and wisdom? Go now my friend, go and breathe the breath of life in happiness and freedom. For now, I Broken Rose will step into an unknown world." He watched as scar loped into the forest. The great cat turned and howled and was gone.

Broken Rose stood alone. The world he'd known and loved had faded into a deep void. Now his adventure would direct a new unknown existence. He'd felt safe and secure at home in the forest. He knew little of that which lay before him. Looking to the sky, "Two Wolves, I need your strength. I miss your wisdom and guidance. Do not forsake me at this hour. Let your spirit walk with me. Give me the courage of our ancient warriors. The wisdom of your past for I am alone and weak. Make pleas to the Great One to fill me with the resolve to overcome my fears." As he stood alone and isolated, the dread of departing the land of the ancients filled his soul with grief. Suddenly the sun burst through the clouds. Its rays shrouded him with brilliance. The forest grew still and quiet as a voice bellowed from within the cloud. "John Broken Rose, take heed! Remember the code of honor of our people. I am always with you." The voice faded into a whisper, "The ancient ones bless and walk with you." The sky grew dark and the sun hiding behind the clouds so as not to display its grief. Creatures of the forest watched with pride and sadness as Broken Rose turned and bellowed to the sky. "I, Broken Rose, grandson of Two Wolves, son of the ancients, go now to do honor and glory to my people!"

He strode slowly toward the pale face asphalt pathway. The sounds and smells of the horseless machines were new to him. His spirit filled with fear, confusion and interest. John marveled at the size and speed of these iron machines. He choked on the clogged air and wondered why smoke flowed from the rear of these strange creatures. He remained still by the side of the road in awe and wonderment. As iron machines whizzed by him, he caught glimpses of people staring at him through the machines windows and heard strange music blaring from several. "Eeha—Eeha, my spirit talks, it is time to begin." He glanced at a large green and white sign housing the words I-286 East, Indian Ville, 35 miles. Smiling to himself he sighed. The way of the warrior is marked but as the flattened rock will be hard. So be it. He mused and began to jog, heading east. He was shredding his youth. Leaving that sanctified place where he'd grown tall and strong. Now he thought, as he continued to jog, I follow the breath of life and go where it leads and do what I must to fulfill the dream of Two Wolves and forge my destiny.

Staff Sergeant Ed Manuel felt elated cruising along eastbound on I-286 in his 52 Ford. It filled him with euphoria and he loved this car. He'd inherited it when his father died prematurely of a massive stroke two years before. "Ah, pop was a good guy," he mused. "Lost him to quick, part of you goes when a parent passes." He switched radio stations and was satisfied when he heard the familiar twangs of Hank Williams bust from the console. That's another downer; guy was fantastic, dies at 29. Shit, had it all, too much booze is what they say. His travels were to bring him to Indian Ville where he was to address students on the glory of the Marine Corps and the merit and satisfaction of hitching up. He mused ah shit I'm a lifer and love it. These kids today, don't no. No some want the challenge or the hardship it takes to wear this green suit. This drive was a God-send. For it allowed him time to think and practice his speech. Times were tough. Recruits were hard to wheel-in. Life was to good and soft in the outside world. Why give it up, these kids feel there is one reward to this thinking, the ones we do get are the best.

Cruising along at 55 M.P.H., He spotted a lone figure jogging by the roadside just ahead. Damn, that guy's got balls. Spooky at hell out here, not a soul or dwelling in sight and looks like rain, fuck wonder where he's headed. Oh yeah there's the first drop of rain a coming. Oh, hell, I'm right on him, may as well have company and someone to shoot the shit with.

He pulled the vehicle to the side of maybe two car lengths ahead of the jogging Broken Rose. Slowing his gait, Broken Rose approached cautiously. He shifted into a defensive mode for he was unsure what the paleface in the funny machine wanted. Be mindful of your surroundings, trust no one. The familiar warnings of Two Wolves stamped in his consciousness, as he came along side this thing of metal with wheels for feet. A voice rang out from within, "hey pal, where you headed, need a lift?" Broken Rose ceased his run, stared long and hard at the speaker. His mind in overdrive, he'd never spoken to a pale face before, at last he was able to stammer. "I'm going to Indian Ville." Manuel grunted, "Hells, bells that is where I'm headed. Come in get on in. You'll be getting a shower soon if you don't." Broken Rose was undecided. He didn't like the machine. But he kept starring at the green uniform. Many pieces of colored ribbons adorned his left breast. Broken Rose looked to the sky and felt the coolness of rain cleanse his face. Now he stared into the green clad man's eyes searching his soul. "Are you a warrior?" Manuel taken aback replied, "I guess you could say that, been in some fights, I have. Come on, I've got a schedule to meet. I don't bite, just being friendly. I thought you could use a break. It's up to you either way I'm a going and I can't dawdle here all day."

He stood by the strange machine staring at this pale face in green, unsure, undecided, but the figure seated behind a strange wheel. Emitted a warriors scent. Broken Rose fingered his knife and was startled as the door near him opened. "Come on, get in, it's beginning to rain and I've got to move on, your call. Coming or not?" Broken Rose was curious and the machine intrigued him. He slipped into the contraption and sat facing front. "Close the door piped Manuel." He looked about in panic, "Uh, how close door?" He asked. Manuel exasperated pointed at the handle, "then pull it towards you. Jesus, haven't you ever ridden in a car?" Broken Rose eyes downcast, replied, "No never, seen from afar is all. This is what is called, car?" "Hell yes," admonished Manuel, astonished at this stranger's ignorance. Manuel shifted into low gear, pulling back into the traffic lane. Few vehicles were on the road for the hour was early and traffic would pick up as they neared Indian Ville. "So what's your interest in getting to Indian Ville?" inquired Manuel. "Oh, I go to join warrior tribe. This is my destiny for grandfather-train-me for this." "Really, where is your grandfather?" "Grandfather goes to lodge in sky, one moon ago, I alone now. My spirit roams alone."

Manuel studied the well-muscled youth and he'd aroused his interest. "You mind if I ask you a question?" Broken Rose signed, "Is alright, yes ask." "Well, what do you mean by warrior tribe?" "I wish to be warrior, seek honor and glory for the ancient ones. Keep warrior flame burning and alive. May I ask question?" "Go ahead," uttered Manuel. "Are you a warrior?" He smiled, "I like how you put, well yes, and I'm a Marine, been one for 15 years." Broken Rose was attentive. "You are Marine Chief?" "No, no, no, I'm a nom com, platoon sergeant. Right now I'm assigned recruit duty." "Let me ask you, you lead men?" "Oh yes, but I answer to ranking officers."

"You are a warrior tribe?" "Well, we're not a tribe as you know it. Let's say we're a fraternity, a brother-hood, we fight for country and to keep our honor clean." "Grandfather, he told me about Marines and advised I should join your tribe, uh, brotherhood, you can help?" Manuel was impressed so far with this young buck sitting next to him. "Maybe I can, tell me how you lived, survive the years in the forest?" "Grandfather teach, the use of the bow, the silent kill with knife, hunt and kill much deer, live on venison, berries, corn wild plants, good life much food, clean water." "Sounds awesome, did you even shoot a rifle?" "Oh yes, many, many times, easy to kill, no need to close." Manuel felt excitement course through his veins. Premonitions flooded his conscious here was a golden specimen. Seldom did one of his character or makeup come forward. "Hey, what's your name queried Manuel?" "Name, John Broken Rose, me Cheyenne. Followed the trail of the ancient ones." "Well, John Broken Rose, I believe I can help you. You wish to enlist in the Corps?" "What mean enlist?" It means join us, be one of us." "Yes this is my destiny mapped out by the Great Spirit and grandfather, Two Wolves." "Well, John, just sit tight, we'll point you in the right direction. The Marine Corps will share in your destiny.

John listen up, here me out, I'm in route to Indian Ville as you know, there's a good reason. I'm scheduled to speak at the high school there, addressing the senior class. See if I can net some fish for the corps, you know get guys to enlist. Why don't you come along? Listen, you'll get an idea what the corps is all about. When I'm finished we'll head to Boulder City. That's where my station is. We'll get you signed up and squared away. Then it's off to the recruit depot, the Rock, Paris Island. What do you think, you game?"

Broken Rose grunted an approval while his mind a whirlwind gazing out the window at the passing scenery. He marveled at the speed of this horseless carriage. He noted many more were ahead and behind them. He was apprehensive. He left the serene beauty of his boyhood forest and now he was heading into a new and strange world. Pictures of his youth flashed by and the hours spent with Two Wolves preparing for his destiny lit up his soul. Now, he thought, the adventure begins. Soon I will join the tribe of this warrior seated beside me.

Broken Rose sat mute and alone in the rear of the auditorium. He watched as Staff Sergeant Manuel resplendent in forest green. His left breast gleaming with ribbons strolled tall and proud to the podium. Listened attentively as the sergeant's deep baritone voice resonated throughout the auditorium. "Ladies and gentlemen good morning I'm Staff Sergeant Manuel of the United States Marine Corps and I've been in service for fifteen years. I stand before you to educate and hopefully enlighten you on the merits of the corps.

Founded in 1775, at a place called Tun's Tavern for The Marines pride themselves on discipline and es spirit DE corps. We have fought in every war in every climate and place. Our battle streamers are many and flutter with pride and glory on their standards. For instilled in our souls is the motto God, Country, Corps. We are loyal to the Commander in Chief, each other and country. Marines are stationed throughout the world safe guarding our embassies, the poor and impoverished, in short we chase the bullies who prey on the weak. Marines are with the fleet at sea and also soars the heavens like the great bald eagle. The roll call of those who have given their all through the decades is endless. Often we are summoned to put out fires of conflict throughout the globe. The slogan first to fight is embossed throughout the islands of the pacific. Within the hymn of The Marines Corps the verse, "First to fight for right and freedom then to keep our honor clean," it defines what we are about.

I dare say it's no easy task to be a marine. Training is difficult and intense. Discipline is the key to our success. It is instilled at a price of blood, sweat and tears. It is embossed in our very soul, for without it, survival in combat is nil. You will be harassed, ridiculed, badgered. You will be led by example and forced to do the impossible. The words, "I can't," are nonexistent in the corps. Marine training is not for the weak or timid souls, rather the stout of heart. It's a challenge for those of you who are gutsy and seeking fulfillment and adventure, may wish to consider. Looking beyond you, I see the stars and stripes displayed so proudly in her standard. It can't be and never will be wrong to serve and protect her. Thank you for your courteous attention and I profoundly hope some of you will join our brotherhood. I bid you adieu, with the eternal words of our corps, Semper-Fi- *always faithful.*"

As the student body filed from the auditorium, Broken Rose met up with Sergeant Manuel engrossed in a conversation with a tall dignified man surrounded by several of the schools staff. "Oh, this is Mr. Rizzo, Principal here at Indian Ville High. He's just invited me for refreshments. You know coffee, sandwiches, that sort of thing. Would you care to join us?" Broken Rose acknowledge the group with a nod. "Uh, no sergeant, if you wouldn't be offended, I'd like to check out the town, never seen before. Never walked beside buildings and things I would like to see. Hope you are not angry." "No, no go ahead. Meet here say in an hour. That's enough time for you." "Oh yes is plenty, with a soft wave Broken Rose broke from the group. Exiting the main entrance, he was dazzled by bright sunlight. He stood quiet, allowing his vision to adjust to the bright sunlight. Within minutes he found himself on the main thoroughfare. A small green sign caught his attention. Approaching the words Indian Ville, population 5,500, "ah," he thought, not so big. The wild ones live free within a stone's throw. Continuing his stroll, his head bobbing side to side, he was alert and intense. Several people had passed and there was no exchange of courtesies for he was too engrossed in his travels looking for a general store. But just ahead, across the street he observed a hardware store and a small pharmacy. Traffic was light and he was bemused by the restrictions placed on one's movements by these buildings and houses all about him. He was a free spirit and had run free with the creators of the forest all of his days. He approached a quaint diner and stood at the window peering inside. He laughed as he noted patrons dining. "Hum," he thought, these people no hunt; eat what strangers place before them, can't be good, no cooking fire, no wind at your back, no scent of pine, no creatures to share your meal, no song of birds. Ah, Eeha, Eeha, my body walks here, but my spirit roams with my friends in the forest." His curiosity satisfied, he turned heading toward the high school. His heart heavy, this was not his world. Continuing his march as the words of Two Wolves stirred deep in his spirit. Remain quiet, listen, watch and learn. He would hear these words again and again.

Sergeant Manuel was waiting in front. As Broken Rose approached, Manuel gestured to his vehicle. Both sprinted to the old Chevy. Once settled inside, Manuel turning towards Broken Rose, asked, "How was your stroll through town?" "Oh was alright, but I Broken Rose, could not, would not wish to live so confined. One must run free. Feel the spirit of the wind on his face. Race the creatures of the great forest. No would not live with buildings barring the freedom to run like the deer. Flutter like the butterfly. I answer you." Manuel was quiet. Already he'd formed a strong impression of this man that was here seated beside him was indeed a true warrior. The corps would teach him weaponry and tactics. Heart and drive were already embossed in this man's character. Manuel stirred behind the wheel, "Well John, in your travels you'll most likely see much bigger buildings. There are cities as big as, maybe bigger, than your beloved forest. You'll see wonders you wouldn't believe. Don't let it throw you. In time you'll learn there are other avenues in life. You don't have to embrace those avenues just tolerate them. Anyway we're heading to Boulder City. Thought we would stop overnight at a motel. I'm familiar with. It retains a good eatery so we can chow down and get a good night's rest. Sounds okay to you?"

Broken Rose staring out the window spoke in a whisper, "why motel? Sleep as prisoner. Are you not warrior? Do you not feel the need to feel the nights creatures breathe their howls and call in the night? Me, Broken Rose prefers to sleep in woodlands. In my life's pouch, are dried venison, ripe corn and sweet berries and we found refuge by fresh water, sleep to the tune of night birds, stare into good wood fire, and share the protection of the dark as two warriors?" This sound much better to Broken Rose. You marine warrior, share stories of honor and courage, while brother fire warms and lights our way brings peace to our spirit."

Manuel sat mute, deep in thought. "Wow, this guy is going to be one hell of a marine. I can feel it, taste it. He's mesmerizing and is home in the forest. Hell, the boon-docks will be a piece of cake to him." Turning to face his new warrior friend, Manuel signaled a hand OK. "Yeah sounds good. I've a change of utilities in my trunk. You have enough chow for both of us." Broken Rose laughed softly, Eeha, you warrior must know woods, provides food, streams, fresh water and fish. One never starves or thirst in the woodlands for there the spirits of the ancients. Both man and creatures roam free and peaceful."

Sitting warm and content by their campfire, Broken Rose broke the silence. "Well, how you like my motel? Nice to be free in spirit world, is it not? "Manuel chuckled, "Well John, you kind of put my back to the wall. I couldn't let the corps down and let you out tough me. But yeah, this is peaceful, no question." They'd completed their meal of venison, corn, and berries, as they settled back, Broken Rose gazing at the starlet sky asked, "Tell me about the Marine Corps." "Well, John, you heard my address to those high school kids. It's a gutsy outfit. You earn the tittle of Marine through guts, blood, tears and sweat. Don't misunderstand the other armed forces, are fine and their ranks overflowing with good dedicated brave merits warriors, but as I stated on a whole no one matches our discipline. I believe

the others would agree. We have a special brotherhood. Marines respect each other. They know the price and heartache. They paid to earn the tittle. Our history is full of pride and courage. You'll soon experience what it takes to wear the green. Anyway John, this jarhead is tired and it is time to cop some Zs. In the morning you'll be sworn in and by midday your or your way to hell, Paris Island. You'll enter that gate one man and come out another. But you'll have your wish. You'll belong to one hell of a fighting outfit. Goodnight John."
"Goodnight," whispered Broken Rose He sat quiet and straight in the glow of the burning fire. In the distance the yip-yip of a coyote on the hunt violated the quiet. Broken Rose smiled inwardly, for he knew the coyote had let him know of their presence. "Ah," he thought. My creature brothers will assist and guide me in the warrior's way. As his eyes grew heavy with fatigue, the North Star shone bright. "Eeha-Eeha" he whispered. "It points the way to the Great Spirit and the ancient ones cast their wisdom and strength in my footsteps and may their shadows stand and walk beside me always."

The sun peeked over the horizon. Night creatures scurried to their lairs and day creatures stirring preparing to battle nature for survival. Birds bid the world a good day. Their sweet musical chirps rising in crescendo throughout the woods. Broken Rose long awake nudged Manuel softly. "Rise and shine old warrior for it is another day to serve the corps and mankind." Manuel rose quickly, glanced at his watch, and reached for his overnight bag. The fire now fed by Broken Rose, cast a glow of splendor about the area the orange flame a beacon to predators to beware. Manuel heated water in a tin cup and shaved briskly. Sprinting to the Chevy, he retrieved his greens, donning same in a military mode. They breakfasted on flat bread and berries, doused the fire with water and dirt then headed to the rusted old Chevy.

The sun cast a golden hue on the landscape around them. Both breathed in the sight and fragrance of the woods and marveled at the peace and beauty that for the moment embraced them. Manuel keyed the ignition and in a plume of dust they entered the freeway. The ride to Boulder City was made mostly in silence and small talk ensuing only sporadically. Both tuned to their own quiet thoughts. An hours ride and Boulder City loomed before them. Manuel turned down exit 35 and in minutes had parked in front of a small office. The words Marine Corps Recruiter posed in large black lettering across the window. Two other marines were in attendance. Both sipping hot coffees, they gazed with non-interest at Broken Rose. Both busy with folders laid out neatly on their desk tops. Manuel read the oath of allegiance to Broken Rose who with right hand rose to the heavens, repeated word for word.

The oath completed both men stood smiling. "Well, Broken Rose, here's a government envelope. Inside your ticket to hell, as well as, money chits for meals because you're out of berries," He chuckled. "Your train departs in a half hour, headed? Why I don't know to New York. From there you'll make the trip south to South Carolina. You'll be alone till you hit New York. Then other sad sacks will hookup with you, any questions?" Broken Rose stood tall and poised. "No my destiny was forged long ago by Two Wolves as you know. I'm set and thank you. I hope we meet as warriors together when the moon is high in the sky." Manuel was touched. He liked this Indian boy who stood solemnly to his front. Extending his hand, Broken Rose grasped same in a powerful grip. Manual whispered, "Good luck kid. Keep your head down." Releasing his grip, he grasped Broken Rose by the arm and walked him to the door; pointing south he uttered, "See that yellow building? That's the train station. Your ride is already there. On your way, and give them hell. Broken Rose without a word turned and headed toward the station and destiny.

His journey on the train was uneventful. He seldom vacated his seat basking in such luxury only to relieve him-self or take meals at the government expense via his meal chits. He sat quietly starring out the window as passing scenery while numerous towns and modern

cities lined his travels. He marveled at the huge structures that
loomed high in the sky. Words on pictures had not prepared him for
the hypnotic landscape that greeted him. As the train entered New
York, he was enthralled by the breath taking cement forest that lay
before and about him. Never had he seen so many people scurrying
to and fro to who knew where. His heart pounded, and his mind in
turmoil. To him this was a terrifying world. Horseless carriages were
everywhere and endless in parade. Noise he'd never heard offended
his ear drums. Sweat formed on his forehead and armpits. He felt
alone and anxious, while his mind flashed back to his beloved forest
for its solitude and beauty where all he had known. The rapture and
splendor of his creatures that he had come to love made his heart
feel empty. His soul wailed in pain and hysteria. Oh Two Wolves,
strengthen me. I grow weak and I fear this place. Please grandfather;
chant the recreate prayer to The Great One that I do not succumb to
fear and bring shame and dishonor to our humble lodge.

Bowing his head, he slumped in his seat as the train entered
Grand Central Station and lurched to a grinding sudden stop. He
remained seated waiting till his car had expelled its passengers.
Then Rose exited down the small metal stair case. He was propelled
forward by crowds of people. Panic enveloped him briefly for a
moment, but his boyhood training took hold and self-discipline rose
to the occasion. He found a space by a graffiti painted wall, retrieved
a manila folder which contained his orders from his deerskin satchel.
He studied the contents. He had to make his way to Penn Station.
This Iron Horse would carry him to his destination. This was strange
ground to him for he was at home in the forest and knew how to
read it. He knew its secrets and lay of the land. Here there was only
cements and endless people exiting the station. He stood transfixed
and enthralled gazing at buildings that reached to the heavens and
kissing the sky. He wondered that if he were to climb one and stand
at its top if he would reach the Ancient Ones. Confused and full of
anxiety, he thought," must find this Penn station." Glancing about

he saw a blue uniform. He'd familiarized with a uniform thanks to Manuel. But this uniform was different. "All blue, oh, well he must be warrior;" he approached the uniformed figure shyly. "Excuse me, can you help me?" A friendly face stared at him. "Sure mac, what do ya need?" "Penn station, where Penn Station? Need iron horse, go to Paris Island, need to get there quick. It goes soon." Officer Fran Dakin N.Y.P.D. laughed heartily at this characters use of words. "Oh, well what the hell, New York lures em all. Okay kid, head east to 50th St. Just keep walking you'll run smack into it can't miss it. What'd you do join the marines?" "Oh yes, I become green warrior." Dakin roared. "Well kid good god damn luck. I've been out of the corps going on four years. Brother you're in for--r a shock. Ha, Ha, Ha. You won't know what hit you." "Excuse, you green warrior?" Dakin grew serious, "was maybe, still am cause I'm a cop. Don't you know that?" "No never saw cop, none in forest I grow in." Dakin studied the youth before him, "hey kid, really best of luck, you'll get an education now for sure. Do me a favor? Don't let this world out here ruin you. Best be on your way and one marine to another Semper-Fi." Broken Rose watched as Officer Dakin turned and headed into the throngs of human creatures.

Broken Rose gazed eastward and began his track towards Penn Station. He was both in awe and bemused by the crowds of people. All seemed in a hurry scurrying in an out of the numerous stores. He copied that of those around him waiting patiently on the curb of intersections. His interest centered on the objects swaying in the air that blinked red, yellow and green lights. These devices, he mused, controlled the endless flow of the horseless carriages and that of pedestrians. "Eeha," he thought, "there are more people than that of the Great Herds of buffalo, and he'd witnessed the great run of those beautiful beasts as a young boy. But Two Wolves, his grandfather, had told him that palefaces had all but eliminated the great herds. He gasped as a huge bird like machine emitting powerful noises flew by overhead. He'd inquired of a passerby about this great creature.

The man stood mute for a moment then responded angrily, "it's a fucking plane, what are you an asshole?!! Don't fuck with me!! Then sauntered off muttering "Fucking nuts everywhere in the city!" Broken Rose smiled shyly and continued toward his objective. All the while thinking plane, a plane, be quiet, listen and learn. He walked slowly pacing himself studying the numerous vendors lining the streets. They hailed their wares loudly and most seemed to be serving various food stuffs. What he saw and smelled quite different from the foods he knew. His life pouch was near empty. As he walked he munched on what few berries and corn he possessed. But the small fare satisfied him for the moment. His sense of hunger fulfilled, he felt he was nearing his goal as the throngs of people grew larger. He was anxious to find his iron horse. He was seeking quiet and solitude and the peaceful bliss of being with one self. He wanted to escape the herd of humans which pushed and shoved seeking anyways or means to get to their objectives.

Suddenly without warning he was there. The large sign hung high above him announced Pennsylvania Station. Large revolving doors greeted him. He pushed through and stood transfixed aware he was in a huge lobby with pedestrians everywhere. Heart pounding, he stood confused, alone and fearful. He knew he had to find the iron horse, but how? "Eeha," he would have to ask. Now he knew he must learn and accept this strange new world, be quiet, listen and learn. Ah yes, he would learn calling on the breath of the Great Spirit and the wisdom of Two Wolves to do so. He moved forward deeper into the concourse. The multitude of people heading in all directions dazzled him.

As he stood staring he felt a hand on his right shoulder, turning he was looking into the dark eyes of a youth about his age wearing a blue jacket with a large white A embroidered on the left breast. "Hi, sorry to startle you, saw your manila envelope. See I've got one too. He held it high. Thought hell, maybe this guy's headed where I am.

So I'll ask. You wouldn't be going to Paris Island by any chance?" Broken Rose smiled weakly, yes I go there, be warrior, you too? "Damn that's cool. Yes I am. Oh, I'm Lee LeSage." He extended his right hand. Broken Rose confused, grasped it, the hand shake firm and short. "Well that's two of us so far," uttered LeSage. "Listen we've ten minutes to make the train. Best we get going." Broken Rose calm and excited, you know how, uh, get to train?" "Hell yeah, we board on track 11 heading for Washington DC. Let's roll. We'll just make it." Both broke into a sprint. Entered a door marked to trains and were greeted by cement piers and numerous lines of tracks. Several passenger trains were standing idle at selected piers with their engines hissing steam. "Ah", growled LeSage "there's our ride on track II, right over there. Passengers are boarding her now. So we're on time. Come on my friend, let's hop aboard and get settled."

Climbing aboard they were forced to traverse two cars in order to fined two empty seats. Moving quickly, brushing aside several traveler's they plopped into their seats located in the rear of the passenger car. Both displayed excitement, curiosity and fatigue. They'd had a long day and a long trip ahead of them. Engaging in small talk they were joined by a third party as the two seats facing them were vacant. A tall black male sat slowly facing them. His eyes like coal bore into them. "Hi, I'm Jake LeBron; think we're en route to the same finish line. See your envelopes, here's mine. Headed for P.I, hope you don't mind I join you. LeSage and Broken Rose nodded approval with smiles. Broken Rose had never been this close to a black man. He studied him carefully, measuring him, white men had hurt him.

As the clicky clack of the train lulled them they shared small talk, each giving summations of their lives, likes dislikes, dreams, successes and disappointments. LeSage and LeBron enthralled with the solitude and wilderness of Broken Rose. They devoured his way of life and the teaching and wisdom of the great one, exploited him on his experiences and bond with the creatures of the forest.

They are young men from different walks of life, one white, one black and one Indian, slowly were bonding. The train sped south along the way at various stops, other recruits boarded. In Philadelphia one tall handsome youth entered and headed to the only seat available which was shared by Broken Rose, LeSage and LeBron. The lone figure approached. "Hey guys, mind if I sit? This is the lone seat available." All three nodded approval. "Thanks. My name is Lance LaPore, What's yours?" As LaPore sat, three pairs of eyes bored into him as he fiddled in his seat seeking a comfortable position; all of a sudden the train lurched forward, the engines wheels biting into the rails seeking traction, successful to the train gathering speed. It's mournful whistle in the night as a warning to vehicles and pedestrians of its approach. Four young men who traveled different bi-ways in life shared idle chatter about their various likes, fears and their past way of life and upbringing. All heads leaning towards one another in order to hear the choir sing of a car full of cocky youths seeking adventure creating noise that resounded throughout the compartment. Young men with personnel reasons for enlisting and thus perhaps, placing themselves in harm's way. Here was a youth who'd been a high school dropout. There was a youth who'd impregnated his girlfriend electing to escape and avoid responsibilities. Yonder seated across the aisle a young man forlorn and edgy. He'd been charged in a in a serious crime in his home town. The judge gave him an offer. He couldn't refuse, jail or the Marines. On it went virile young men from all walks of life coming together, farmers, city boys, workers and shirkers all seeking direction in their youth. The atmosphere within the Pullman was that of a carnival, little did these youths realize that in time they would be molded into a crisp, disciplined, cohesive unit.

Broken Rose stared out the window gazing at passing scenery. As they passed through towns and villages the engines whistle would shatter the silence rousing some who'd been catnapping. Some muttered oaths and a deluge of cursing coursed through the car. Smokes were fired up and soon thick gray smoke clouded the interior. Coughing and snoring and the passing of gas orchestrated the night. Broken Rose deep in thought gazed at his three new found friends dead asleep. He was bewildered by the shenanigans occurring around him. Struggling to understand how white men could act as a wild herd gone mad. Slowly the ruckus ebbed and then silence. Dozens of young men in the golden flower of youth sat quiet in the dark each alone with his thoughts and fears. The motion of the Pullman and the humming of the wheels lulled Broken Rose into sleep mode. Soon his eyes grew heavy and he drifted into the peaceful void of sleep. As he did, the words of Two Wolves came softly. Remain silent, Listen, watch, and learn. Smiling inwardly, he was soon asleep. The dream was short but direct. Two Wolves came to him, "Broken Rose, he commanded, "you have learned and mastered the ways of the creatures of the forest. So must you master the ways of those around you and as a warrior that of your enemy. Always keep bright eyes, quiet tongue and clean mind. I am always with you." As the image faded he was abruptly roused from his sleep by the booming voice of the conductor, "Baltimore next stop in five minutes!"

LeSage, LaPore, and LeBron stirred in their seats, stretching and yawning, they took in their surroundings. "God damn," exclaimed LeBron. "This fucking car smells like a shit house. Jesus, open some windows! Son of a bitch, I'm hungry! When the fuck, do we get to use these worthless pieces of shit meal chits. Probably ain't worth shit. LeSage smiling, maybe we'll get a layover. Shit they gotta know we're hungry. Yeah, piped up LaPore, "ain't a dining car here either," whined LeBron. Mother fuckers, they gonna starve us to death. "God damn, I needs my vittles to keep me going. Broken Rose smiling reached for his life's pouch and pulled out a blue bulging cloth wrapped in deer skin. What the fuck that shit shouted LeBron, Broken Rose pulled out several pieces of dark dried meat. He stared hard at LeBron, "is dried deer meat, very good you try. Make stomach happy and quiet your spirit." "Man, I ain't eating that shit. How the fuck old is it? Looks like it's been dead as long as my grand pappy been." "Hey," LaPore said, "LeBron, try it you might like it and it's better than some of the shit you ate in Brooklyn." "How you know?" "It's good! Shouted back, LeBron "I don't, but I am ready to eat shoe leather. So looking at Broken Rose "Thanks my brother taking a modest bite "Ah, not bad, not bad. Hey, LeBron if you don't want yours, give it here." LeSage studying the dark meat gingerly took a nip, sat back letting his taste buds decide for him. "Hey, Broken Rose, not bad, and thank you." LeBron pulled his portion in close. "Okay you mother fucker, I'll swallow the piece of shit but I'm not chewing. They all laughed and dove heartily at their unexpected breakfast. Broken Rose shared what was left of his corn and berries. Rationing it fairly as they chewed the train slowed to a crawl. The conductor in a sing, song, twang announcing, "Washington, Washington Station."

The train crawled to a stop and its engine hissing steam. Passengers disembarked in an orderly manner disappearing into the large concourse each going their separate ways some ending their journey others just beginning. The four rose from their seats. The Pullman had expelled its human cargo, and the passengers were informed there would be a four hour layover. They romped through the concourse. Bright sunlight greeted them as they stepped into the street. Washington DC, their nation's capital loomed large and inviting before them. Hearts beating with excitement, the foursome headed east after a short trek, they stumbled onto an old all night diner. The patriot refuge, as it was named, looked inviting. Cooking odors emitted a friendly atmosphere. They approached quietly and then entered. The walls were adorned with numerous patriotic photo's which hung from the painted walls. The American color's hung proudly from the ceiling located just above an old jukebox. Several patrons glanced their way showing no interest and just returned to their meals. LaPore nudged Broken Rose, "never been in one of these chow boxes, eh John." "No, never was, first time, and is nice, maybe food be good. Maybe serve critter heart?" "I don't think so John; it's time you move on. Find out what white man's fare is all about. You'll have to sample it one day or another and it might as well be now." LeBron eyed LeSage, "Fuck I'm hungry, man!" Best they accept our meal chits, because I'm broke. Brother, mother fucken broad I shacked up with night before I left cleaned me dry. Hope the bitch gets crotch rot." LeSage laughing, "No sweat Jake, I'm sure they'll accept out chits. If not I've got you covered."

The four headed to a window booth. Once settled, they gazed at passing traffic and the huge buildings standing as sentinels off in the distance. "You know," said LaPore, "that's an awesome sight. Kind of gives you goose bumps. I mean here we are in our nation's capital. It's kind of beautiful." "Shit, uttered LeBron, it's a waste land, houses all them mother fucking hypocritical politicians. It's like being in a rose bush with a skunk looks nice till the little prick sprays your ass, then you up to your ears in stink that what this capital be like, for sure." "Aw come on, retorted LaPore ain't all that bad. Shit some of them prissy gotta be okay." "Say what," LeBron spoke hoarsely, "they all shit man, all shit, think of themselves and big businesses. Little guy means nothing. Never has, never will. You'll see LaPore, one day you'll see. Look fancy buildings, imagine what they're like inside those shit for brains only obtain the best. They've the good life. Yes sir, all the frills and thrills. You and I well, we service those bastards. Anyways, I'm getting a burger well done with onions, fries and a chocolate milk shake can't handle a vanilla to fucking white for me." He laughed heartily.

Broken Rose stared at LeSage, "what you think I should get Lee all strange to Broken Rose? Help me out please." "Well John, I think a burger rare with fries will suit you. I think you'll like a milkshake, possibly strawberry. Go for it bro. I'm sure you'll like it. Order it plain, you're not ready for all the sides yet. Go slow, grow into it, okay?" "Is okay Lee, that's what I'll do, thank you. What's a burger?" "It's beef John, cow beef, you'll find it suitable, trust me."

A middle aged waitress came and took their orders then sashayed down the aisle to complete that task with the short order cook. LeBron smiling stated," wow she got an ample ass that bitch be fulfilling, god damn that's certain." All four laughed. Loud laughter earned them curious glances from diners. As their laughter died out, the waitress returned with their orders. LeBron, LeSage, and LaPore wolfed their meals quickly. Broken Rose reluctant at first ate slowly, savoring this strange meat, is good he thought. He found the meal to be tasty and filling. The waitress accepted their meal chits smiling as she sauntered away. "Okay you guys," utter LaPore, what's next? We still have three hours." Exiting the diner, they observed a large blue, red, white bus idling in a spaced sign proclaiming tour lines see your capital city. Two hour tour, exchanging glances they mutually agreed to join the line of tourists entering the bus.

LeBron stared at LeSage, Man I got no bread. They wants three bucks, shit, I'll wait hear. LeSage chuckled, "no sweat I told you you're covered." They chose seats in the rear. Relaxing as the bus moved into traffic. Small talk broke the silence of the ride. They passed the capital, the white house, the bus driver's monotone voice booming over the intercom pointing out the various landmarks. They entered Arlington Cemetery and the bus was cloaked in a respectful silence. Row after row of white oval stones stretched before them. The garden of stone seemed endless, not a voice or a mumble or a whisper could be heard only the sighs and the trickle of tears streaming down many checks would one's senses decipher. They exited the bus at the tomb of the Unknown Soldier. The tourists stood mute at a respectful distance. All stood in awe at the crisp military bearing of the sentry guarding this fallen hero. The crack of his heals as he marched halted and completed an about face.

The tour ended at the Iwo Jimi Monument. They stared in wonder at this structure of wondrous granite. Studied the details, the veins protruding from forearms and the faces locked in the grimace of mortal combat old glory flattering in pride high above as though peering down with honor and sadness at these brave men who held her aloft.

The ride back to the bus stop was made in solitude. All four deep in thought. They were about to serve their country. Would they measure to the task? Time would be their judge and witness. Returning to the rail terminal they boarded their Pullman observing that a score of enlistees were present. Luckily they were able to salvage their original window seats took comfort in their new found friendships. Hopefully they'd remain together.

As the train prepared for departure, the recruits were startled when four green clad figures entered their Pullman. Red and gold arm bands with MP embossed adorned their left arms. The car grew silent as a tall lean figure mounting three red chevrons addressed them in an authoritative voice. "Listen up ladies! I'm Sergeant Ryan U.S.M.C. from this point on you will conduct yourselves with dignity. You are now the property of the United States Government. Thus, if you slip out of line, your ass will be mine. We are here to babysit you till you complete your march to P.I. We are not aboard to hassle you. The smoking lamp is lit at all times, unless you piss me off. We are not here to socialize or frolic with you. Bear in mind that you belong to the corps act accordingly and we'll get along just fine. We should arrive at P.I. tomorrow at about 13:00 hours. For you dopes that means 1:00 o'clock. You'll sleep aboard this luxury rolling hotel. Ask me no questions, just behave and control yourselves. That said you won't even know we're aboard unless you act like a herd. That is all." The four green figures disappeared strolling erect and proud exiting the car.

LeBron shattered the silence, "damn man those dudes be sharp. See all the shiny ribbons on their chest. Fuck they look lean and mean. That one black dude, he be eye balling my black ass. Shit, don't need a brother stomping on me." "Ah," chimed in LeSage your exaggerating. He was eyeballing everyone, not just you Jake your being paranoid." Broken Rose in a soft whisper, "they'll warriors, green clad warriors, what I'm going to be. What you're going to be, the ancients spoke today with the sign of these warriors. You noticed there were four. Well we're four. The old ones have blessed us. Have marked our path and we will warrior as brothers, you and I. He stretched his hand forward. Holding steady as his three new found comrades placed theirs one on top of the other upon his. "We are as one," he proclaimed we are brothers." Softly he chanted an old Indian prayer then pulled his hand back slowly. Smiling, he uttered, "Time for rest." Night had spaced its tarp unnoticed. The Pullman's lights dimmed to a soft glow. The car grew quiet only the sound of someone experiencing a broken dream pierced the stillness. Night had spread its tarp blanketing the countryside in darkness. Only the twinkling of lights off in the distance acted as a beacon as they passed towns and villages.

Little conversation made as the four drifted back through the hands of time. Memories of home and happy times engulfed them. The car remained peaceful and tranquil as the train sped south during the night. Slowly the sun poked its majestic power rising in the east. They peered out the window marveling at the beauty of Virginia's landscape. Box breakfasts were distributed to these future warriors who wolfed their fairs down hungrily. The meal completed the buzz of numerous conversation resonated throughout the car. Periodically one of the MP's made an appearance. Satisfied all was well, he departed exiting the Pullman to check out another. LeBron was in a hyper state bored with just sitting. "Man I feel boxed in. Shit, this hour I be walking Brooklyn Streets looking for some easy cash. Shit there was always a dumb tourist you could rip off on an easy snatch and grab in one of those mom and pop stores could steal a car here and there to fuck was like peeling open a can of spam. Fucking judge made me join this outfit. Mother Fucker probably masturbates under his robe." LeSage eyeing LeBron, "so you were a street thug preying on innocents. Now you stupid fuck you will be protecting them. What an irony from thief to potential hero. "Ah, fuck you Lee, what you was an athlete? Coddled is what you were, spoiled, protected, have no street sense. Shit, Brooklyn eats you up." LeSage laughed, "Maybe just maybe, but often the prey out foxes the predator. Best you remember that."

LaPore joined the debate. "LeBron how much street smart you got? You got nabbed and here you are en route to the rock, same as us. You might want to consider that. Maybe you get away ninety nine times but on the hundredth you're collared." LeBron snarled, "Yeah, you white boys think alike, could be your right because here I am sitting alongside ya. Oh well, fuck it, beats Ryker's Island that's for damn sure." Broken Rose had listened attentively never injected a word. Looking at LaPore, he queried, well, we know LeBron here was a thief and LeSage an athlete, what about you my friend what's your spirit been through?" LaPore stifled a chuckle, "oh, long story. I was adopted as a baby, never knew my mum. My adopted parents were gentle and kind, but were killed in an auto accident when I was ten. Anyway, I ended up in an orphanage for the last eight years. I parted company with that institution three weeks ago. Shit, no family, no friends on the outside, didn't know shit from shebang so here I am bullshiting with my three bro's, only family I got. Hope we stay together."

LeSage staring at LaPore, "that had to be rough Lance. I think you have all our respect and yes we are your family." LaPore embarrassed looked at Broken Rose. Come on there, Red-man what's your history. Broken Rose gazing out the window whispered his response. Me Indian raised by grandfather, two Wolves in the great forest, trained to be warrior. Lived and played with the creatures that lived there.

Learned their ways and secrets now learn ways and mysteries of this new world. I too have no family all with Great Spirit, but I have many friends. Friends like brother wolf, sister fox, the snake that slithers quiet and deadly. My friend in spirit and body old mountain lion, the great bear and my musical birds, the beauty of the deer and they all guard the great forest and await my return." Broken Rose gazed somberly at his friends, "no more to tell, is what it is." The booth went quiet, LeBron, LeSage, and LaPore reflecting on Broken Rose's words.

The mood in their booth had grown solemn, each withdrawn to his own reflections. The train continued its journey. The hooting of its whistle as it chugged through small towns jolting them back into reality. They wondered what fate awaited them. Would they succeed? Soon, very soon, they would find that adolescence would be shed with blood, sweat, and tears they would embrace manhood.

The door to the car burst open, the voice of the conductor announcing stop "Raleigh, North Carolina, two hour layover, arriving five minutes." He strolled through the car briskly disappearing through the door to continue informing others in adjoining cars.

The train slowed to a crawl and then came to a sudden stop. No one moved, two MP s had entered, "Okay girls you got two hours, get some chow and ogle whatever broads you see, cause where your heading you won't see smell or touch pussy for months. Best you behave and get back here on time. Now get the fuck out of those seats and skedaddle. Keep your cocks in your pants unless you have the habit and jack-off. Go girls, may I remind you to grab plenty of chow cause next stop ain't till you see South Carolina. Long ways off, best you move, this train of fools don't wait!"

Stepping from the train they found the terminal crowded with traveler's an MP watched their movements. His web gear glistening pure white in the dim lights. The forty five holstered at their side displaying a menacing power. LeBron broke the silence. "Shit I gonna talk to that fucker, get some dope on where we're headed." Ah, I wouldn't," said LaPore. "Fuck man he ain't God," with a smirk he headed toward the green clad figure. Coming alongside LeBron hissed, "Hey man what's happening, what's this Boy Scout all about. Lay it on LeBron man. Spit it out." The marine corporal side stepped to LeBron's left his eyes dark and brooding peered from under his visor. His voice came in a low menacing growl. "Look shit for brains and listen up! One, you address me as corporal. Two, you don't talk to me period. Three, you'll find out what Boy Scouts means. Four, now move your black ass out of my face before I use you as a swab and field day this terminal! Go get the fuck out of my face!" LeBron frozen in his tracks turned abruptly and sprinted to his three allies. "Man that mother fucker ain't friendly at all. Told me to get my ass out of his face shit, what we get into. Huh, looks like we are in a world of shit up to our asses." LaPore chuckling, "I warned you, you'll learn. Don't fuck with these guys. They've been where it's at."

The four buds moved off the train and spotted a pizza shop. Their taste buds came to appetite attention. Gazing at Broken Rose all three echoed each other. "Time you try pasta our Indian friend. There are a lot of morsels you'll love and this is one of them." They sat at the counter. LeSage ordered for himself and Broken Rose electing to go with cheese topping no frills. Broken Rose munched slowly, sipping a soft drink smiling he uttered. "Is good, pale face eats well. Broken Rose like food so far LeSage laughed, "Okay John, but remember the fare won't be like this at P.I." Broken Rose smiled remaining quiet. Be silent, listen, watch, learn, and be mindful of your surroundings. The words echoed in his spirit a reminder from Two Wolves.

They decided to remain in the terminal browsing in a gift store then a quaint book store LaPore and LeSage each purchasing novels. LeBron hoisted playboy under his shirt. Broken Rose had moved off, they found him staring at an Indian figurine. A war bonnet donned his head. He held a bow in his right hand the arrow in the left. Broken

Rose muttered softly "is good sign sent from the Great One shows his pleasure. Ah, yes it is the warrior's way. The path has been open and shown to me. You my friends will be warriors as well. The spirits know this and grant their blessings." No one spoke mesmerized by the appearance of the warrior figurine and words of Broken Rose.

Once again they boarded their train and were fortunate to secure seating together. Their stomachs full of pasta. They sat back in semi contentment with the nagging worry of what lay ahead always festering. The train slowly chugged from the station gaining speed as it broke free on open track. Hills and knolls pock marked the landscape farms seemed in abundance. The sun cast its shadows on the landscape. Nervous conversations dominated the Pullman. All aboard apprehensive with what unknown fate awaited them. As night descended the car grew quiet and an eerie stillness was present within. There were arguments two rows down from them. Nerves frazzled and drained. The harsh reality of the unknown had descended on these youths seeking manhood. Soon they would arrive at their destination. This knowledge frightened some while others transfixed with mixed emotions as well as a salad of excitement, mistrust and fear. The MP's refused to converse with them, thus the unknown ruled the time. They resigned themselves to the old adage, time would tell. And so these young souls settled in their seats some praying, some cursing some doubting but all hoping their future would shine light and bright. They'd left the security of home and the care of their parents. Most experienced the hardship of exams at school, some elated to escape the tentacles of a home without love. Some like LaPore willing to embrace the corps as its only family in their hearts and souls all they would experience hardship and sacrifice. They'd enlisted knowing this, one thing was certain, there was no turning back.

Their journey continued through the Blue Ridge Mountains and endless plains. It propelled them through scenes of villages and towns. Each mile brought them closer to what destiny had chosen for them. They'd grown close these four and a bond established. Fate had brought these young men together. Now they would walk as one side by side. They'd bared their souls to each other and vowed to go it as brothers. Broken Rose alone remained awake. His three comrades had drifted off to sleep. He stared out the window catching glimpses of lights in isolated homes. "I am ready," he thought. "I've trained for the moment at hand and have steeled my body. I have offered my spirit to the Great One and now I must follow the path of the ancients. In my dreams I hear the howl of the wolf. The growl of the bear, the hiss of the snake, the yip of the fox, they have shared their instinct and cunning with me. They tell me I, Broken Rose, will prevail. I will make my mark as a green warrior. This I vow with my sweat, my blood and my tears. I offer my life my spirit to the ancients so that they will breathe strength and wisdom into my spirit."

"Yama see, stopping at Yama see," the conductor's voice spit the word out with malice and his smirk displaying a secret knowledge as to what awaited the rows of youthful men sitting before him. Softly he uttered "use the rear door please and step cautiously. Your green hosts await you." Filing from the Pullman, they were greeted by scores of green uniformed figures. One a tall sergeant bellowed, "all right herd assemble before me over here and shut the fuck up and listen! I'll only say this once! You'll spend the night in the receiving barracks located behind me. There are racks and sandwiches waiting on you. I strongly suggest you eat, shower and hit the sack; reveille is at 04:00 that means your soft lazy civilian asses fly out of bed at 4:00 am. Buses will be waiting and will be your transportation to the Island. There's to be no grab assing or fucking around. You've no time. The three corporals behind me will sort you into your barracks, okay! Move your scrawny asses!"

Eighty men followed the corporal's orders, forty to a barracks. Broken Rose LeSage, LaPore and LeBron remained together. They scrambled into a barracks, each grabbing horse cock sandwiches and

41

all they were allotted, all the while the corporals screaming epithets and orders. They downed their fare with cold milk and were led to showers. Once completed, they were instructed to pick up bed gear and hit the sack. They had fifteen minutes but were not allowed to talk. Finally, they stood in front of two twin bunks. A lean black corporal eyeballed them solemnly. "Okay camel fodder, hit em and keep your mouths shut and hands off your dicks. Oh and by the way assholes welcome to the corps."

Bright light flashed overhead, an authoritative voice screaming "Get out of the racks! Do it now, girls! I won't say it again! Hit the deck, which to you poor excuses for humans! Floor! Move! Move! Stand in front of your bunks!" Bleary eyed souls stood mute and disheveled. "Okay, shit stains! You've fifteen minutes to shit, shower and shave!" When dressed there are more sandwiches for your breakfast! Your ass is now the corps and it say's eat! You'd better! You're in for a long day and may or may not get noon meal! Hop to and do it quiet, no bullshiting! If I catch some asshole talking, trust and believe his ass is mine!"

Eighty swing dicks shared showered and relieved themselves and filed out of the head. Some squeamish they'd never showered naked with anyone in their lives. Marine NCO's pushed and shoved the line of confused recruits towards a table packed high with sandwiches. The contents unknown, forced to wolf down their chow and they were ferried to waiting buses. With the aid of curses, shouting and blasphemous oaths from NCO's they piled into the buses. An eerie silence descended as the engines revved to life. The large green buses engines roared as they hurtled forward in the morning darkness. Fog and a mist like rain shrouded their journey. Eighty hearts skipped beats sweat formed on foreheads and armpits. The men questioned whether it was the heat or fear, maybe a little of both. In silence the behemoth carriers sped toward their objective. The cloud of anxiety permeated the interiors. Some whispered to mates seeking their thoughts. There were no answers.

In no time at all, bright lights like a beacon hone into view. A large gate entry, a marine sentry resplendent in uniform, waved them to a stop. Just above him in large lettering, "Welcome to Paris Island Marine Corps Recruit Depot." The buses waved on by the sentry roared through. The sentry yelling, "You'll be sorry!" Unknown to the souls within they'd entered the gates of Hell.

The green carriers halted in front of a large white building marked receiving station. Within the buses the human cargo sat in stony silence. LeBron turned to LeSage, "men what the fuck happens now?" The words weren't out of his mouth when a huge figure entered. His greens pressed to perfection, campaign hat tilted so that his eyes like coal simmered in the semi darkness. "All right people! He screamed, "Get off this bus and move your scrawny asses! Assemble in front of the building! Jacking his thumb rearward, place you're fucked up feet in those printed footprints on the asphalt! Move you low life maggots! Move! Move son of a bitches! What a herd of Shit!" The recruits stumbled into the semi darkness, scrambling to plant feet correctly. The large figure joined by three comrades shouting profanities all the while.

Settle down assholes and listen tight! From this moment on I am your mother, your father, even God! The only thing I am not is your shack up! Forget that broad back home. Some spoiled football hero is probably banging her as we speak. Here, the first words out of your ugly mouths are SIR, always SIR! Looking at you pieces of shit I wonder what the fuck I've got here! Looks like I've a herd of homos, dick lickers, cunt lappers, jack offs all rolled into one. I tell you now, you will think of nothing but the Marine Corps! You'll eat; drink sleep, shit, piss, Marine Corps! Also I emphasize, there is only the color green! I don't give a fuck if you're white, black, purple, and yellow whatever the fuck, Marine green is all you need to recognize! Mommy is no longer going to coddle your asses! Now, there are rules, and then there are mine! You do not kill a sand flea, they are Marine pets! They've been here since the beginning of time! His voice rising, do not even walk on my Marine grass or I'll have your ass! Again whoever you pass on this base, be it man or beast it is SIR to you! You people are lower than whale shit! I don't believe I've ever had such shit assembled before me in all my time in the corps! God must hate me! He sent me society's garbage! He's testing my soul! I'm supposed to make marines out of this cluster fuck! God please, God strengthen me!"

"All right, you herd of turds! You've received your welcome! If you need to know, I am Staff Sergeant Baker, your senior DI! These three slaves to my right are my assistant drill instructors, turning his address, to the buck sergeants. All right take over get them settled in and squared away. Abruptly he turned and disappeared into the morning mist.

The three junior DI s were on them like flies on shit. Yelling and shoving the recruits every which way. Sergeant Haunchmaker took the lead, "All you fuck faces! You will line up according to height! You tall dicks to my left, and the feather merchants to my right, take a good look at the ugly faces on each side of you! Memorize them! They will be your asshole companions the rest of the way. Now do it!" Bodies scrambled in the semi darkness, Fear and adrenaline propelling them to assemble correctly. Now and then a DI would yank a body out of line, shoving him into the proper height range.

After twenty minutes of mass confusion the DI's studied their artistic arrangement. Satisfied, Sergeant Tonny screamed, Jesus Christ, what a Chinese fire drill! All right ladies! Turn to your right! When I say forward march, step out with your left foot. I had better not catch one of you girl's eye balling me! No talking! Eyes straight ahead! All right you sick excuse for humans, forward march!

In a semblance of order, they marched to the supply depot with a cold misty rain lining their way. En route, the DI kept admonishing them accusing them of being soft, weak, jack-offs, and homos. They were human garbage here to be recycled. At last they reached the current destination shivering in the chilling rain. They halted by fours they were ushered into the depot where four marines in utilities stood behind high counters. One by one, they moved down the line. All the while the marines screaming, "Head size! Shirt size! Shoe size! Trouser size! Jacket size! Sir 6 7/8, size 72, size 29, medium. This was repeated eighty times for each mans size.

The recruits showered with utility covers, piss cutters, barrack caps, tropical uniforms, and khakis, forest greens, boots high and low cuts, skives, foot locker, sea bag, helmet, web gear canteen, weighed under a ton of government issue. They were marched in double time to their home for the next sixteen weeks. Bullied into tossing their gear on a chosen rack and the rest of the recruits rushed outside where the hollering and screaming continued in a frenzy. The DI's caroused, pummeled kicked and tossed bodies threw and fro. Confusion ruled the day and the recruits disorientated tired; hungry were now led to the PX. They acquired personnel supplies, like shaving cream, razors, soap, toothpaste, and informed these articles would be deducted from their pay. Outside they were forced to stand at attention for forty five minutes while rain pelted them mercilessly. The DI shouting, "God is cleansing your bodies of civilian puke!" Finally he gave the command, "right face!" They double timed to their barracks where they were ordered to shed their civilian attire and don green utilities. "Five minutes, assholes that's what you get!" screamed the DI. "Oh you poor sad fuckers," he raved. See the government mail boxes at the foot of your racks? Well dick heads! They're not tchotchkes, place those vermin filled civilian rags in them. And if you can, include your home address so we can get rid of that diseased shit! Do it quiet and get your pathetic asses outside. You've five minutes!"

The DI's in a foul mood glared as the recruits stumbled and skidded into assembly. "Fucking Chinese marines will have your fat asses for breakfast one day!" They bellowed "ASSEMBLY!" The DI stepped to their front. "All right you beauties listen up! Tighten those ass checks and here what I say! From this point on you'll be known as platoon 75! Right now you're a herd, but we'll correct that real quick. PLATOON 75 ATTENTION!" He roared. Eighty bodies stiffed, "LEFT FACE! God damn it, people step out on your left foot. You march like a bunch of drunken sailors. He began to sing song the cadence known only to marines. El-left—El left---El left, two, three step to your left, two three step to your left. The sun had embraced the island. These recruits stood out. Their new utilities acted as a beacon to the saltier platoons which they passed on the march.

A large building loomed before them. "Okay, freeloaders, this is the mess hall form a single line get your asses inside and remember what you take you eat. Best you understand that right away. No talking, no one sits till the last man fills the table. Hold your trays in front of you. The last shit brain will order ready seats, then seats. Then you commence filling your flabby bodies. I best see no fuck ups, Go!" They stepped single file into the mess hall. They dined on mashed potatoes with some unknown meat gravy poured over them. Thick bread and milk and there was no desert.

The platoon stood in formation as senior DI Baker eyeballed them. Turning to his assistants he bellowed, "They look like a bunch of African head hunters! Get these assholes motivated! They just ripped Uncle Sam off for eighty meals!" Turning back to the platoon, he growled! "When you're called to attention we'd better have eighty pairs of heels click like thunder! Get them out of my face! Get them over to the indoctrination center! Damn, I'm going to vomit my meal! I'm looking at an apparition from Hell! A bunch of soft ass civilians in marine utilities! Jesus H Christ, time to retire! We're getting animal shit! The corps must, have to, consider us miracle workers!"

Near exhaustion, their nerves frayed they were once again standing ridged in line. Several other recruit platoons shared the sweltering heat. Reluctantly waiting their turn to be indoctrinated into the corps, papers needed to be signed and insurance beneficiaries had to be listed as well as next of kin addresses, etc., etc.

After nearly three hours of waiting, the last soul exited the center. Sergeant Emanuel called them to attention and gave the command, "left face!" Then in a loud voice, "let's see what you rejects are made of! Double time, Oh! Move it! You look like a gang of defective sperm!" The recruits groaned inwardly. Fatigue had them in its grip. Bet there would be no mercy here. The corps was no walk in the park. They were fast learning this. The sprint to their barracks distance wise was two miles. Emanuel never faltered calling cadence in double time mode. At last within three hundred yards of the white structure, he yelled "platoon halt!" Electing to march them the rest of the way, with a smirk, glaring at the sad sacks, who stood mute, confused, frightened, and exhausted to his first test inflicted on them. "You pieces of shit loathe me! You run like fat ass girls! Look at you, half of you puffing your guts out. Your bodies are soft filled with society's great disease, the soft life! Well, we'll soon correct that! You're here to be marines, we shall see! You'll pay the price to wear this uniform, in blood, sweat and tears; some of you pudgy brats will be cashed out, no doubt, those who succeed will know a pride and fulfillment only a marine experience! Okay fall out enter our hooch and stand at attention in front of your racks! Move! God Damn it! No walking! Run your asses in there! You think your home! Go! Go! Get out of my sight!"

The recruits stampeded into the barracks. Confusion reigned as they sought their racks. LeBron and LeSage shared a double berth, LaPore and Broken Rose next to them. They'd not uttered a word to each other the entire day. Hassled, driven, there's been no time. LeBron glancing at his three comrades and uttered softly, "man, what the fuck this ain't no military institution, it be a mother fucking insane asylum! You see those eyes glowing at you from under those smokey hats God damn. They be the devil's eyes. Those fuckers are wide eyed crazy! Man, crazy! They're under a rock!"

Emanuel entered the squared bay. Roaring, "SHUT THE FUCK UP AND STAND TOO AND LISTEN UP! I won't repeat. Get it the first time. The room your in is called a squad bay. The toilet is the head and the floor is the deck. The wall is the bulkhead and your bed is the rack. Most important when someone enters this squad bay, other than a recruit, someone had better yell attention on deck. That means you drop whatever you're doing until given the command to carry on. You do nothing without a blaring permission from your drill instructor. And remember, the first words out of your mouth are SIR! Now shit birds, I'm giving you a break. Sit easy. You've 10 minutes till evening chow."

After evening chow, Emanuel marched them back to the barracks. Dismissed from ranks they poured into the barracks. Where for two hours the DI instructed them in the marine way of making their racks, and the proper way to store gear, and clothing in footlockers. Now he stood ram rod straight at the head of the squad bay. "All right turds, you have one hour to talk and get to know each other. No hollering or grab assing just quiet talk. Do it!" He strolled out the hatch to his quarters.

LaPore, LeBron, Broken Rose, and LeSage sat in at semi-circle. Individually the conversation began as a bitch session. They wondered what the fuck they had gotten themselves into. It ceased when Broken Rose raised his hand. His face tilted upward. "My friends," he began, "life is like a spun thread. It's how you complete the spin that marks your path forward to fulfill your destiny. The thread can be strong or weak. It's how you handle it, so it is with life. The thread is your life line. Treat it with respect. Protect it with honor, pride, integrity, accountability and responsibility. Do this and you enter the lodge of your forefathers with clean hands and straight eyes."

In twos and threes, idle conversations in hoarse whispers permeated the squad bay. It was a welcome reprieve from the torment experienced this first day. The hands of time do not remain still. Sergeant Emanuel burst into the squad bay. "Tension on deck!" screamed recruit, Ron Lecker. The roar of eighty pairs of boots snapping together roared through the barracks. "Jesus Mary and Joseph and the poor fucking donkey," muttered Emanuel, "you stooges learn fast. All right, listen up. It's shower time. I want you germs scrubbing all that civilian sweat off your revolting bodies. If I get a whiff of civilian sweat when you've finished I will personally disinfect that body or bodies with Lysol and a Brillo pad. You will not infest my corps with grime from that shit world out there. Now move your sad asses! Lights out in fifteen minutes and whoa, as you were I don't remember dismissing you. Reveille is 0530 and you'll fall in outside on my command at that time. Uniform of the day is utilities. Sorry no more dungarees, we hit the parade ground for our morning run, works well for your constitution. Then we return, shit shower, and shave and head to morning chow. Tomorrow we begin close order drills. Alright, hit the shower! Don't let me catch anyone grab assing. Go! Go! Go! Aw fuck, what are you all without brains. Remove your clothes first, fucking idiots," as he strolled from the squad bay. Some were already headed for the head and were ripe from sweat, weak from mental and physical fatigue. They looked forward to a night's sleep.

They're shower's complete, the recruits stood at attention in front of their bunks as Sergeant Emanuel conducted a hygienic inspection. Checking finger nails toe nails and looking for impurities caused by improper care in the civilian world. Completing his inspection Emanuel stood by the squad bay hatch. "All right river rats, lights out and get in the racks. Eighty souls leaped into their assigned racks as the jolting of springs wore down. Emanuel bellowed, "good night flower children and I'd better not catch anyone choking the chicken!"

They were clothed in eighty despairing souls at last alone in the comfort and privacy of this private refuge. It would be their only source of peaceful respite for the next sixteen weeks. Most fell asleep almost at once. Their bodies succumbing to the physical torment inflicted on that horrific day. Broken Rose lay quiet; he sensed the gloom and despair which filtered through the quiet night. He closed his eyes, and an image of Two Wolves flashed before him. He reflected on those peaceful moments when they shared bread and breathe of life. He wondered about his mother. Saddened that their spirits had not meshed together and he'd never known her smile or the softness of her voice. Never felt her tears, whether happy or sad moisten his body. Broken Rose was denied the gentle touch of a loving mother. He had never shared his secrets or fears except in his dreams. He had never looked into her eyes, the windows to her soul, thus he had never known of her hopes and dreams. He thought how he envied the creatures of their forest as they passed. The young one's tolling behind their mothers, secure and safe from predators and the elements. Moisture clouded his eyes a single tear trickled down his cheek. He would call to her in his dreams. He'd learned long ago to just close his eyes and she would be there.

Moans and soft sobs ebbed through the night. Slowly, under the tarp of darkness, calm settled on the squad bay. Broken Rose whispered a silent chant, allowed the peaceful splendor of sleep to embrace him. Bright light and the booming voice of Sergeant Emanuel jolted them from tranquil sleep. "All right shit stains! Hit the Deck! Reveille! Reveille! Time to earn your pay and serve the corps! Fall in outside in five minutes. And I fucking well mean five to the fuckers who are not motivated with the program!"

A light drizzle greeted the recruits as they stumbled sleepy eyed into formation. Emanuel eye balled them sternly. "Platoon ten—shun! Right face! Hup, two, three, four! Hup, two three, four! You're left, your left, right, left!" They marched to this sing song cadence and were led to the wide expanse of PI's parade ground. To the naked eye it appeared endless. Emanuel led them on to the well-groomed parade ground. He commanded, "DOUBLE TIME MARCH!" The platoon as one stepped out quickly. Emanuel sprinting beside them mindful there'd be stragglers. Hearts began to pound sweat formed and dripped from foreheads and faces. The run was endless. The weak and out of shape began to falter and finally fall to their knees in exhaustion. Critics would say new fodder should be broken in slowly but Emanuel knew this is not the Marine Corps way. It is imperative to flush the weak and out of shape early on and tender strict regimens to the sick, lame, and lazy, to motivate them into marine physical shape. Emanuel was mortified out of a platoon of eighty only twenty five completed the five mile run. "Jesus, he muttered, what's happened to this country. With so many of these youths that are so fucked up and out of shape. We're becoming a nation of sleep fucks. Sergeant Baker's gonna be pissed. By God, we've our work cut out for us. That's for sure." Morning chow consisted of eggs and creamed beef and toast. The coffee was strong but stuck to the innards one's body got a jolt of energy from the thick caffeine.

The day was spent learning close order drill. Hour after hour, they marched through and fro. Left oblique's, right oblique's, to the rear march. The DI's were all over them. Straighten your shoulder's lean back, strut, strut, and strut. By mid-afternoon, they were marching in unison. Baker looked at Emanuel, "fuck at least they're marching like a platoon." "Okay Bob, get em back to the squad bay. Get em settled in studying the manual till chow. We'll run em through this same drill tomorrow." "Aye mon commandant, can do, see you later Jim." Staff Sergeant Baker started off, with his dark eyes eyeballing his platoon, "out of shape fuckers, we'll square you away, trust and believe."

The next three days were repetitive. Close order drill, dress right, straighten those hips, stomach in, chest out, lean back, strut, strut, strut. They ate drank and slept with the cadence of drill sergeants. The DIs swarmed over them, slowly but surely the platoon was becoming a cohesive unit. It was the marine way to brow beat them. Instill in these young minds they were the best and yes eventually the extreme discipline of the corps reaped dividends.

The big day arrived. They were marched to the armory where the m-1 Garand was issued them. They called off the serial number of their individual weapon and at port arms double timed to platoon formation. Sergeant Baker stood tall and lean. His eyes bore into his platoon. "You shit stains have just been issued the finest rifle in the world. You will treat it with respect. You will cuddle it. It is an extension of your body. Your rifle is your lifeline. Care for it with tenderness and one day it will save your life. Embrace it as you would your girlfriend. It is not a gun it is a weapon. If I even hear one of you monkeys refer to it as a gun, you can believe your ass will be mine! Today Sergeant Hanchenmaker will begin instruction in the manual of arms. Pay attention and get it right. We've no time for fuck ups or stupidity. You will learn to field strip that weapon and reassemble same blind folded. Remember a marine with his rifle is a killing machine. That's what we're all about. Now slop heads, you heard me. Now learn to be lean and mean." Sergeant Baker turned and briskly marched off.

Sergeant Hanchenmaker barked "PLATOON ATTENSION!" Rifles at their sides, he pointed when I say right shoulder arms, bring that weapon to your right shoulder and nowhere else. The entire day was spent absorbing the manual of arms, port arms; present arms, etc., etc. As the sun settled low in the sky, the platoon was marched to the barracks. Driven into the squad bay where they stowed their weapons and then marched to evening chow.

After chow, they were instructed how to clean and field strap their weapon. This was repeated again and again until the recruits had a feel for their weapons. After all, it was their life line and most of the recruits had never even held a weapon in their young lives. Night spread its peaceful refuge. Lights out the recruits lay quiet each with their own thoughts. Now and again a muffled sob echoed through the squad bay. Voices whispering in the dark, they been on the rock for two weeks and unused muscles barked to their displeasure. But these boys were learning the warrior's trade. Already their civilian mode had disappeared. They found themselves like a young plant blossoming into the warrior mindset. Forget about that high school dance or the frappe at the corner drug store, they'd been issued a rifle that won the 2nd world war. They were indoctrinated in the fighting history and legend of the Marine Corps. Tomorrow they would commence close order drill with their weapons. Unknowingly they were shedding all semblance of their civilian past.

Days turned into weeks. The platoon now marched and performed the manual of arms with precision. They'd been instructed in judo the art of hand to hand combat. Battled and blooded each other with the punji stick. Their day's beginning punctually at 0530 with the labored run on the parade ground. They shed their civilian flab which prevented them from completing the five mile run. This was accomplished with the assistance and threats of their parental guardians the Dis. These dedicated instructors were hard yes, but their code and motto was to train men to survive combat. They left no stone unturned and would show little or no compassion. They could ill afford to be lax. The corps was a fighting unit not a drum corps. The heartbeat of the marines is discipline and pride and they would drive a wedge into the recruit's soul to accomplish that goal. The DI was a marine who'd trained long and hard to instruct future marines.

He'd be there done that and was morally determined to pass that knowledge along in order that his green warriors would survive, the horrors, loneliness, fear and confusion of combat. The Dis creed, let no man's ghost say, "If only my training had been harder drove them to instill the tough fiber of discipline into their recruits. It obsessed their very souls.

Weeks of training showed a new found crispness in the platoon. They marched with precision were now molded into a cohesive unit. Body flab melted away. Lean hard muscles replaced the soft civilian tissue.

"Alright platoon! Stand by for rifle inspection!" barked Sergeant Baker. "Second and third ranks one step to the rear, MARCH!" he commanded. "Inspection commenced as the DI's came eyeball to eyeball with a recruit. He instantly came to port arms. Hit the bolt to his rifle exposing the empty chamber. The weapon was torn quickly from the recruits grasp. The DI twirling the weapon and checking same for dust particles, rust, and any organisms that may have inhabited said weapon. Sergeant Baker faced LeSage who brought his weapon to part arms. As the DI reached for the weapon, LeSage prematurely loosened his grip. In horror, LeSage grimaced as the weapon fell to the ground with a thunderous crash. For a moment there was an eerie stillness. Sergeant Baker glanced at LeSage. He began to quiver, spittle formed on his lips. "My God!" he screamed. "Look what you've done! You've assaulted your weapon! You've caused injury and indignity to it!" The Sergeant was in an unbelievable frenzy. Yelling and screaming at the top of his lungs. "You little prick! You're a communist who's infiltrated my corps. You're a devil from Hell sent to destroy my soul! You piece of donkey shit! You make me want to vomit! God hates me!! That's why he sent you here! How the fuck can we win another battle with assholes like you! Get on your knees now! Cradle that weapon caress it! Beg for its forgiveness! Sooth its pain! You shit stain! Check its pulse and see if it's breathing! Do it!

Do it! The platoon stood in silence as LeSage on his knees, gingerly retrieved his fallen weapon. God damn it, you puke shit for brains, run that weapon over to sick bay. It's screaming in agony. Crying for help! My heart is breaching! You low life fucking dickhead! Do it now! GO! GO! GO!"

LeSage at port arms double timed to sick bay. Crashing through the hatchway, a startled corpsman stared wide eyed at the sweating marine recruit standing before him. "What's your problem lad?" shouted the corpsman. "Sir, I've injured my rifle and my drill instructor ordered me to have it checked for injuries." Corpsman O'Neil looked away. A smile on his face, he knew the drill and would ride along with the DI's harassment. "Place that weapon on the examine table," he ordered then stood away. "Sir, yes Sir, LeSage acknowledged and gingerly placing his weapon on the appointed table." The corpsman began probing the weapon and running his hand along the stock. Then stood back a little and said "your weapon has a severe bruise to the stock right side. I'm going to apply a dressing. You will change same once a day understood?" "Sir yes Sir, replied LeSage.

The platoon was preforming close order drill when LeSage came into view at double time. Staff Sergeant Baker halted the platoon as LeSage came to a running stop facing him. Baker's eyes scanned the weapon. A large white gauze dressing adorned the stock. "You fuck! Look at that poor weapon! Look what you have done! Turing to the platoon, he shouted, "Take a good look! This camel dung assaulted a marine issued M-1 Garand! This is an unforgivable act! Despicable! Turning back to LeSage, "You moron! You will sleep with this weapon! You will nurse it back to health! Every night before taps, you will pray on your knees begging its forgiveness! You will relieve its pain and you had better not let it become depressed! Get back in ranks! You piece of shit and handle that weapon carefully!"

Staff Sergeant Baker exploded into the squad bay. "Attention on deck!" Bellowed recruit Larson, "Well no fucking shit," hissed Baker. Alright you turds, time for lights out. LeSage you low life shit. Are you caring for our injured weapon?" "Sir! Yes Sir!" screamed LeSage. "You little prick on your knees and we want to hear you pray for that abused weapon! Do it now!" LeSage dropped to the deck and on his knees he began to pray. "Louder!" screamed Baker. "I can't hear you! In a high pitch voice, LeSage began, "Dear Lord, please bless this poor injured weapon that I so neglectfully caused injury to. Please heal its wounds. I beg for forgiveness and I apologize for my sloppiness." "Alright! Bellowed Baker, enough! You shit brats, hit the racks!" The men scrambled arms and legs flailing into their bunks. Baker strolled to LeSage's bunk, "you prick! Give that rifle more mattress room. Cover it with the blanket. You can see it has a chill! You're a numb nuts, LeSage. That rifle had better not have a fever in the morning. Kiss it good night and sooth it with soft words. I better see that rifle showing signs of healing at reveille. Good night assholes. Think of chesty in your dreams."

The squad bay went dark. Men fatigued and exhausted would sleep deep and each with his thoughts and fears. In the still of the night, LeBron peeked over the rack into LeSage's space. "Hey man, you gonna fuck that piece tonight?" He chuckled as LeSage retorted, "Fuck you LeBron." "Hey man, whispered LeBron, these mother fuckers, they be crazy, we all gonna be mental before they be finished." "Sleep tight my man, tomorrows another day."

Sudden light flared and the voice of Sergeant Baker boomed throughout the squad bay. "Rise and shine camel dung time to serve the corps. Hit the parade ground and LeSage, front and center!" LeSage scurried quickly and stood at attention facing his DI. "Well otter shit, how's your weapon?" LeSage in skivvies brought his weapon to port arms. Baker eyeballed the M-1 Garand lovingly. "Hold it tight shit for brains," and he then stroked the injured weapon tenderly. "Well, your ugliness there's no fever. Did it sleep well?" "Sir Yes Sir!" "Idiot, you will care for that weapon with your life until further notice you will carry it with you everywhere. When you eat, shit, sleep, it's to be forever by your side. You will be as one. That weapon will be treated with love and respect. You will care for it as you do your puny cock! Understood?" "Sir, Yes Sir!" "Get out of my face! GO! GO! GO!"

At morning chow LeSage was forced to stand facing the seated platoons with his rifle at port arms. He explained how he had injured his trusted friend and had betrayed it and had caused it physical and mental anguish to a loyal weapon that was meant to preserve his life. The mess hall greeted him with stony silence. He had committed the unpardonable sin. Several DI's passed him by; as they did they uttered words of disdain. "Camel Dung, Shit Stain, Cow shit, fuck lips, gook lover." On it went. LeSage stood quiet and remorse radiating from his pale face. A cry from the rear of the mess engulfed him. Apologize, apologize! Staff sergeant Baker ram rod straight echoed the call. Apologize to all present and especially to that injured weapon. LeSage bellowed loudly, "I do apologize! I am a sinner and will care and protect my rifle with my life."

Seated in the squad bay that evening, Broken Rose broke the silence addressing his comrades; he whispered softly, "there is a lesson to be learned from LeSage's torment. A warrior must first and foremost preserve his weapons. Love it, trust it and in the heat of battle it will not fail you. You all think the Dis are going south, but they are training us to be warriors. That is our quest. Grandpa Two Wolves always said, "Be silent, listen, watch, learn." He is right. If we are to be warriors, we must learn the way, for one day, we will face the bear." LeBron chuckled, "Tonto, sometimes you're out there. You know up in the clouds somewhere." Broken Rose stared long and hard into LeBron's eyes reaching into his soul. "My brother, one day you will find that these warrior teachers, who did battle,

had it right. That's why they instruct, not some palace guard type."
LeBron stood, "Tonto, and they branded you with that name, why
do you think you're so right all the time?" Two Wolves taught me to
live with mother earth and all she embraces. Be it man or beast, one
must know his surroundings. He must be always alert and prepared.
He must never be surprised."

The platoon now in its 12th week broke from the daily routine of
close order drill. The day had arrived to qualify with their weapons.
It was a welcome respite; for the DI's let up somewhat on the harsh
regimen of training rather they wanted the platoon in a relaxed
mode, for this was what it was all about, a marine, and his rifle and
qualification was imperative. Snapping in was a painful exercise.
Muscles seldom used screamed their displeasure. Marines fire, from
the prone sitting, kneeling and standing positions. Dry firing is
repeated relentlessly until they are ready for the live range, "Already
on the left, already on the right, already on the firing range. The
range instructor's voice resonated up and down the line. With a clip
of eight rounds, lock and load, ready on the firing range, commence
firing, commence firing." The line exploded with the discharge of
weapons. Off in the distance the silhouette of targets rising up and
down. The shooter and instructor waited for results from marines in
the gun pits signaling with a Maggie drawers or a white disk for bull
eyes. For three days the marines practiced firing. On the fourth day
it was crunch time, you fired for qualifications.

Along the way several bodies from the platoon simply disappeared,
gone in the night. Like a light breeze they drifted off. These were
the weak, the misfits, like weeds they were separated from the corps.
Those who remained were molded into the making of marines. Their
civilian identities and thinking stripped from their souls soon they
would enter into the green warrior brotherhood.

Platoon seventy five was fast whipped into shape. Molded into the precise machinery that was the corps. A well-oiled fine-tuned mechanism trained to kill. Yes, the DI's continued to render harsh discipline. The familiar cry of drop and give me twenty five resounded about the parade ground. Often a blow to the solar plexus roused a recruit from his stupor. However, in spite of occasional lapses, the platoon now marched and drilled as a cohesive unit. Pride and determination propelled them forward to the day they would earn and be blessed with the title marine.

Then it happened, on a hot sultry day, while the platoon stood at parade rest, an unwanted sound expelled from within the ranks. Staff Sergeant Baker charged into the platoon squaring off eyeball to eyeball with Private LeBron. Dark menacing eyes glared into LeBron from under the DI's campaign hat. Private LeBron. He screamed did you do what I think I saw! Did you just murder a sand flea?!!" Baker howled with anger. "Jesus H Christ!! You did! Its body is decomposing on your black ass cheek! Son of a bitch, you traitorous swine! You low life puke! After all you've been told you executed a marine pet! You piece of snake shit! Private LeSage, double time into the barracks and bring a towel! Do it now! Move lizard lips! GO! GO! GO!" LeSage double timed into the barracks and brought a towel back to the platoon and halted in front of Sergeant Baker "Sir, Private LeSage reporting with towel, Sir!" Baker quivering with anger, "no shit fuck lips!" Carefully remove that carcass from this piece of shit's cheek. Do it respectfully or I'll have your fucking ass down in the grass six feet below!" LeSage dabbed at LeBron's cheek. "Sir, I've the carcass in hand." "Is he dead shithead? Check his vitals." LeSage confused stared at the crushed remains of the sand flea. "Sir, the victim is indeed expired. No sign of pulse or respiratory function." Baker howled in grief, we've a fucking murderer in our ranks!" LeSage and you LaPore escort the remains to the squad bay and stand by for further orders!" "Sir, Yes Sir!"

The platoon stood in front of their racks as Sergeant Baker entered the squad bay carrying a wooden match box. He marched briskly to the center of the barracks with a mournful wail he gazed down at the remains of the deceased sand flea. "LeBron!" he screamed, "Front and center!" Private LeBron moved quickly and stood at ram rod attention to the front of his DI. "You communist son of a bitch!" roared Baker. Gingerly and with respect remove that body from the towel and place it inside this box. LeBron gently lifted the dead flea's remains, respectfully placing same within the match box which had been lined with cotton. "Close the box fuck head! Place it on this foot locker and get the fuck out of my face!"

LeBron did as ordered and sprinted back coming to attention in front of his rack. At a given signal Sergeant Daniels and Hanchenmaker entered the squad bay each in possession of a tenniel candle. They slowly and respectfully wrapped the match box in black crepe paper and covered the footlocker located in the center of the aisle with a Marine Corps blanket. Then carefully placed the small make shift casket at the center. Both snapping to attention and rendering a hand salute. Baker scanned the platoon. "When you pieces of shit arrived on my island you were told, no ordered never to slap at or kill a sand flea. They are one with us. They had a duty to perform and this unfortunate son who lies in state paid the price. He made the supreme sacrifice in carrying out his mission who was to seek out an expose one who was weak and undisciplined. Private LeBron is a murderer. Oh, he'll never be tried but he will be labeled as a killer for the remainder of his tour on this island of joy." Baker was livid, "you jack offs will switch off all night standing guard over this dead hero. This squad bay will be given a field day commencing now. As other platoons will be in attendance to pay their respects to this lonely soul lying in repose among all you shit heads."

Candles were lit and flared brilliantly at both ends of the make shift bier. Through the night members of platoon seventy five were forced to kneel and pray for the heroic flea's soul. Early the next day, the first of sister platoons marched in single file paying homage to the little black box sitting alone and forlorn on a Marine Corps towel. As the solemn recruits passed they were strained to glimpse a dejected Private LeBron kneeling before the bier. Hands clasped behind his back, head bowed. A sign sat in front of him. The words printed in scarlet and gold. I am a murderer. I took the life of this career sand flea who gave his all. I will one day answer to my God for this heinous crime.

At 0900 hours the platoon was marched to the swamp halted and given parade rest. Privates LeBron and LeSage escorted the small black box placing same carefully on the ground. Then each member of the platoon was directed to dig a grave six by six by four. Two hours later the grave lay open. The small black casket was lowered by a string slowly into the ground. The grave was recovered as once again members of the platoon shoveled dirt into the lonely grave. A bugler summoned from the band played taps. The platoon stood crisp presenting arms. The ceremony over, they were given the command "order arms, right face, right shoulder arms," and quickly marched off. One lonely figure remained. Private LeBron had been ordered to spend the night at the grave site and to watch for cracks on the make shift grave stone were etched the words, "here lies in honor and glory one small sand flea killed in line of duty by one of its own."

The next morning the platoon marched to the cadence of Sergeant Baker to the bronze statue of Iron Mike a magnificent statue depicting a first world war Marine in combat regalia. Baker halted the platoon and kept them at attention. A soft breeze whistled through the air. Carried by the wind, one could almost hear the words of Iron Mike's ghost. "Duty, Honor, Pride, Integrity, Responsibility, Accountability." The platoon stood quiet even the birds ceased their musical chorus. Respectfully listening as LeBron on his knees prayed to Iron Mike for forgiveness pleading loudly so that all could hear for mercy on the soul of Sam the sand flea, as he'd been designated that he had so ruthlessly executed.

Sergeant Baker terminated the ritual bellowing, "LeBron return to ranks!" he then gave the platoon at ease. "Listen up turds, and Listen well, I seldom explain my actions, but feel you must ingest the lesson at hand. Here you may all think what shit for brains LeBron did was trivial. NO! Roared Baker, in the bush that slap would carry on the wind a sharp enemy would hone in on the sound. The movement of his hand would be seen by concealed adversaries. Good men would die. For their position would have been exposed because of lack of discipline. You've only two weeks left on this forsaken island. Learn from this. You may suffer discomfort even pain but discipline is the watchmen of death.

The rest of the day was spent drilling and executing the manual of arms. Under a blazing sun the platoon was marched back to their barracks. After evening chow, the platoon was allowed two hours of leisure time to read and write letters. Broken Rose, LaPore, LeSage and LeBron sat in a tight circle. LeBron as usual lamenting how the DI's were fucked up and demons from Hell, mother fucker's embarrassed me and made me look like a fucking asshole. Shit, all that over a fucking bug. Broken Rose sat quiet and in a soft voice directed at LeBron stated, "no my brother, it's not about a bug. It's like the Sarge said, it's about us, the future in the woods. You'd die for such action. Come on man. We're training for combat to be warriors, not Sunday strollers." The four buds grew quiet and the soft mummer of other recruits flowed through the squad bay. At 2100 hours they hit the showers and then practiced rack drill as Baker screamed over and over, "get in the racks, to slow, get out of the racks!" This continued for ten minutes until Baker had satisfied his appetite for amusement. "Okay ladies, no grab assing and no playing with your cocks. Tomorrow is camera day and we get our platoon picture taking. Let me hear it say it loud, as one." The platoon bellowed, "Semper-Fi—Semper Fi, do or die!" "Not bad girls, you're getting better."

The squad bay was suddenly cloaked in darkness. Young men lay beneath their blankets. They'd cashed in their youth and were fast becoming green clad warriors. Sundays were usually a day of reprieve, a respite from the rigors of boot training. Sergeant Baker had from the beginning brow beat his platoon into attending religious services. He threatened KP for those who declined the solitude of a religious experience. Thus his platoon was always one hundred percent in attendance. Thus showers of praise were bestowed on Baker by the Chaplin who was ignorant of the DI's sneaky method.

The four buds sat in their usual circle after services cleaning weapons and shooting the shit. LeBron scanned the squad bay always on the alert for the DI s. "The coast is clear," he began, "that mother fucker Baker, he be crazy man. Loony like a rabid coon, shit, look what he did on that Elliot's Beach march. Has us pitch pup tents then when we're in the fart sack, he be throwing boulders, screaming artillery barrage! Could have crushed some dude's skulls, dark and raining and we're all diving in the bush. That fucker has gone south, man. His brain fried, kaput, finite, whatever. The fuck, then that night, we gets back and he rousts us out of the racks at 0300 hours and herds us out to the parade ground in our skivvies and puts us at fucking attention facing the lights of Beauford yelling and screaming, "my bitch is over there, probably fucking some squid, cause I've got to babysit you pieces of shit!" "Man that's just wrong, that fucker is under a rock and it's getting bigger.

All four laughed, they were relaxed and knew they were short timers on the island. Graduation was one week away. They felt pride in themselves and had handled everything thrown at them. They had learned that Marine training was soaked in harsh discipline and its purpose to break and weed out the weak. Well they'd not bent or broken. They were confident and mentally disciplined for the next phrase of training. A TR advanced training regiment, Camp Lejeune, N.C. The final weeks passed quickly and the recruits fine-tuned in the art of manual of arms, close order drill, studying the bible the Marine Corps manual. Each day was repetitive with the DI's seeking a polished finished product.

Night spread its tarp over the island. The recruit's final day of boo\t camp completed. Each lay in his rack reflecting. They were no longer boys. They'd sweated, bled, cried; shed all semblance of civilian identity. The next day under a Carolina sun they would march as a well-oiled cohesive unit. They would be knighted as Marines. They'd paid the price to earn the title.

A sea of green carpeted the parade ground. Six hundred men stood erect and proud. The graduating platoons stood in disciplined ranks. Their flags and guide arms fluttering in the soft breeze. A warm sun cast its rays over these warriors in forest green. As the Marine Hymn thundered across the base a loud voice bellowed, "Detail tension!!" Forward March! At shoulder arms the platoons stepped off simultaneously. The crash of marching feet echoing throughout the area with family members and friends gaped in awe at this awesome disciplined event unfolding before them. Some wept but all cheered as old glory and the Marine Corps flag led the way. As they passed the reviewing stand, the command, "eyes right!" brought these new young marines into focus. They were now part of the Marine Brotherhood and would be till they died.

At parade rest the novice marines stood erect and tall. They watched as the commanding general strode to the podium. General Adam Samuel's gazed out at the green contingent. He noted the youthful faces. He could feel their energy. Sense their pride and knew their discipline. Scanning the spectator stands, his stars gleaming in the sun, his adorned medaled chest exposed for all to see. He stood erect and still as a respectful silence embraced those in attendance.

He voice resonated echoing across the expansive parade ground, "Marines, Ladies and Gentlemen! Today you have participated and witnessed a Marine Corps tradition, the recruit's graduation. It is the spearhead which propels these fine young men into the Marine Corps family. I am always thrilled to be able to gaze upon a sea of green clad Marines. You have earned that title! You've suffered indignities, pain, and much hardship. But I assure you it was all necessary. You have sworn to protect your country. You may be called to give your all in honoring that oath. Here on this island we have strove to instill discipline and pride the very foundation for marines. You have succeeded in the endeavor. Those to weak were plucked from your ranks. The uniform you now wear radiates legend and pride which was paid for in blood by those who went before you. Don it with pride, walk erect and display the forest green with loyalty and honor. Embrace your corps and join the ranks of those who serve with courage throughout the world. I would hesitate to disgrace or soil this uniform. For the ghosts of those who made the supreme sacrifice will torment your soul. The corps is a unit of legend, tradition, honor, and discipline. You now fill the uniform and bear the title Marine! Wear it well, good Luck and Semper-Fi!"

Broken Rose, LaPore, LeSage and LeBron stood mute in the shadows observing quietly while their fellow platoon brother's mingled with family and friends. The ceremony completed the novice marines had been granted four hours to celebrate and visit with family members, blessed with the opportunity to take leave of the rock. Marines and family scrambled to waiting vehicles and they would share dinners in Beauford. Time was vital for at 1800 hours they were to board buses which would transport them to Camp Lejeune.

The four buds starred at the dust the scampering vehicles left behind. As the thick vapor disappeared the tall lean figure of Sergeant Baker, like an apparition appeared through the thick haze. "Oh shit!

Exclaimed LeBron, the devil himself is coming right at us. Mother fucker, I thought he'd gone back to Hell City." In a moment Baker was on them. With a smirk he uttered, "Well my little monkeys, what's this? Even your families think your shit stains, how come no show?" The four rookies, smiled sheepishly. "Don't know sir, they just didn't make it." "Well, fuck it, come on." He herded the four to his old 52 ford. "Get in he ordered. Tonto, tonight you sit in front with me," barked Baker. Broken Rose silent climbed in to the front passenger seat. He'd been designated with the name Tonto months ago as a green civilian. It fit him due to his heritage and his learned skills.

Baker pulled into the lot of a fast food restaurant. All ordered burgers and fries with vanilla frappes; even Broken Rose had found that white eyes fare was not bad. At first the young pups felt discomfort. They'd experienced Baker's wrath for sixteen weeks. Baker sensed this and with a smile put them at ease. "Look guys just call me Sarge. You handled everything we threw at you. You never whined or bent. You earned that uniform. One day you may find that what we drilled into you may save your ugly butts. Just remember keep your mouths shut and your heads down."

They participated in small talk for several hours. Finally, Baker glancing at his watch, whistled. "Okay jar-heads time's a wasting. Got to get your asses back to the Rock for those buses won't wait and you'll be fucked." As they pulled into the lot where six gray buses idled. All five exited the vehicle. Baker ordered them to line up then he proceeded to shake their hands and said "Good luck Marines. Do yourselves proud. Remember; where ever you go you represent America and the Corps" With a smile he about faced and entered his vehicle and in a plum of dust was gone. All four stood transfixed. LeBron broke the silence, "man that mother fucker ain't so bad after all." Broken Rose hissed in a whisper, "He's a warrior. Let's go, the bus is waiting."

Entering the barracks, they retrieved their duffel bags and weapons. Yes their rifle would be their bride. It would accompany them always as they journeyed through the corps. As they reached the hatch, all four turned as one and gazing on the squad bay, which was home for sixteen weeks, they stood quiet each with their reflections and memories. Their sweat, blood and tears were etched in the bulkheads and deck. Discipline and determination the giant steps which propelled them from boyhood to warrior.

Loaded with their cargo, the six buses lumbered through the gates of Hell. Their exhaust creating a grayish haze as they depart the Island.

At first the loud crescendo of voices resonated throughout the bus. They'd exited Hell and those young marines were excited with their adrenaline pumping. All were nervous anticipating what awaited them in the forests of Lejeune. Darkness descended on the caravan quickly and eventually voices tapered off and here and there a whisper still broke the silence. Bodies tired succumbed to sleep. Lejeune was hours away and it would be a gruel some ride. Broken Rose, LeSage, LaPore and LeBron had managed to stay together. They had long ago vowed their brotherhood would beg, borrow and steal to remain together. As Broken Rose stated "their spirits would act as one, as the wolf pack."

Broken Rose gazed out the window. Lights from passing homes and farm houses flickered as they cruised by them. He knew only one step and it had been taken as a green warrior. But it was a great step, he smiled. Hell he'd leapfrog the rest of the way. He was confident, cocky and had found PI to his liking. He'd graduated top in his platoon and admired the PFC stripes on his shoulders for this was his reward for excelling. Eyes growing heavy, he whispered softly, "Two Wolves, I will not fail. I shall make the ancients smile with pride. I will dance to the warrior's song as my spirit clings to you. It harbors your strength and wisdom. Make me strong and wise. Let me carry the way of our people so that I may guide my sleeping brothers that they may one day return to the lodge of their people."

At 00:30 hours the large lumbering buses halted at the gates of Camp Lejeune. They loomed before them emitting an aura of desolation. Forlorn in appearance, the large scarlet and gold sign bore the inscription United States Marine Base, Camp Lejeune. The inhabitants on the buses gazed into the darkness, watching as NCO's boarded the buses and instructed the drivers to their destination within the confines of the huge camp. The caravan continued its travels and in twenty minutes the buses slowed and came to a stop in front of a large tin structure. Lights flared from the oversize quonset hut. The buck sergeant who'd entered their bus ordered the men out and to enter the hut in single file. Then and only then did the men realize they were in a mess hall. Bright lighting revealed rows of tables stacked with sandwiches. The men tore into the display of food dining on horse cock and black hot coffee. Their meager meal complete, they were ordered to fall in outside by platoons. Six hundred nervous souls stood at attention in the semi darkness. A burly figure emerged from the shadows and in a crisp authoritative voice he bellowed, "I am Gunnery Sergeant Murphy! You marine impostors will be marched to your assigned quarters! You will have the weekend off to get squared away and acclimate yourself! Training commences on Monday 0430 hours! Your sergeants will guide you and instruct on how things are done here! You will learn the S.C.P. Your battalion commander is Lt. Colonel Wes Brown! You will meet your meet platoon and company commanders tomorrow at 1300 hours! Don't worry about your non cons, they've seek you out! Okay, cannon fodder! Right face! Forward, March!"

The troops were marched to an area flanked on one side by dark forest and the other a swamp carpeted by a grayish mist. Lines of quonset huts, separated by walkways, faced each other. The command "dismissed" given the confused troops scrambled into the huts which housed fourteen bodies each. Broken Rose, LeSage, LaPore and LeBron all took refuge together. duffel bags and weapons were laid to rest at the foot of the racks. Bodies exhausted fell out. Their cots, equipment and weapons would have to be squared at reveille.

The strains of a bugle resonated throughout the camp roused them promptly at 0530. As sleepy eyed men left the security of their cots, the door to their quarters sprung open. A tall lanky red haired corporal entered with his eyes scanning the interior. "Alright gyrenes, I'm Corporal Henderson! I'm your squad leader assigned to baby sit you rookies for the duration of your ATR training! The NCO's hooch is located in the first hut on the left! You'll meet your sergeants shortly! Now don your utilities for we march to chow in five minutes! Fall in outside! We march in company formation!"

Morning chow consisted of toast, eggs, S.O.S., coffee or milk were the liquid options, other than water. Shit, shower and shave commenced at the completion of chow. Corporal Henderson instructed them to stow their gear and stack weapons. The day was theirs too explore and reconnoiter the area. Noon chow was at 1200 hours.

At 1100 hours, the squads were formed into platoons. Given parade rest, the platoons meshed into a cohesive company. It was at this time that platoon sergeants and the top soldier, 1st Sergeant Mayer were paraded before the company. 1st Sergeant Mayer or Top as he preferred to be addressed, welcomed them to ATR. Speaking with a command voice, he explained that now they would train and perfect their thinking in the art of warfare. He was adamant in that PI was just a foundation builder and that now training would heat up and that stage two was about to commence in their march to be combat trained marines. The 1st Sergeant whirled about and was gone. The company was dismissed and the trainees sauntered off to their individual hoochs.

The week end passed in somewhat leisurely fashion. The troops busy squaring away their gear, cleaning weapons and time reading and writing letters. They marched to chow. The mess approximately three blocks from their area. NCO's sauntered in an out of the quonset huts checking on those assigned to their command and taking the opportunity to know their people. At 0430 hours on Monday, the buglers piped the notes to reveille. Young marines formed ranks in front of their huts. NCO s led them in P.I. and a three mile run. Then it was time to shit, shower and shave and that completed, they marched to morning chow. At 0600 the foundation for the day was laid with weapons and gear inspection by the platoon Commander Lieutenant R.J. Kelly and his NCO s They then marched to the cattle trucks where they were driven into the boondocks. Their lessons began with the fundamentals of infantry tactics of how to lay an ambush and the importance of fire control. They were instructed in map reading and learned how to decipher coordinates and how to use the buddy system in the night. Instructors were seasoned combat veterans and spent hours filtering their experience and knowledge to those fledglings' marines. Day after day they trudged through the boondocks in route step digesting the methods of booby traps, trip wires and green troops were at intervals abused by instructors both day and night whether at work or rest. Their intent was to make them always aware for a marine never slacks.

In the still of the night smoke bombs would be unleashed at camp sites and blank rounds fired from all directions. The novice marines would scurry about seeking cover. Moans and groans of intense stress penetrated the area. NCO's yelling hoarsely rattled them, teaching the discipline of defending their perimeter. That fire discipline had to be implemented quickly. Gradually these green young troops began to absorb and learning the value of self-discipline and reacting to the issue at hand. Several times the troops weathered the tension of the infiltration course both day and night time engagements with machine guns firing, apparently just three feet above them, as they snaked their way through barbed wire and numerous obstacles which lined the way. Night infiltration was the worse for one could see the line of tracers firing overhead. They suffered through the anguish of water discipline which involved hours without h2O in sweltering heat. They were led through bush and swamps at double time. Mechanical targets would leap from the woods. One had a second to fire or pass depending if the silhouettes were friends or foes. When out on numerous maneuvers, their commander would often have live artillery fire over them reasoning that they would soon learn the sound of outgoing and incoming. He mused to himself they'd learn the screech of incoming in a most bitter way.

For weeks the rookies ate dust and dirt and lived and forged in the boon docks. They washed and shaved out of helmets dined on c-rations. NCO's snarled and badgered them constantly as well as instructing in judo in the silent kill of the knife as it pierced and twisted one's unprotected kidney and the use of wire to garnet and decapitate an adversary. How one's hands and elbows even fingers were weapons. Slowly these young marines were learning the ins and outs of combat conditions. However, there was no test, no score kept. One would know if he graduated successfully if he survived the world of real combat.

Weeks went by quickly. LeBron, LeSage, LaPore, and Broken Rose, stayed loose always in eye contact. They covered and protected each other. The NCO s were impressed for on a rainy day, Broken Rose slithered into the woods where he surprised and captured an instructor who was lying in a bush. Broken Rose displayed his skill at rendering various signs in the boon docks and soon was designated the point man for his unit. Surprise ambushes ceased and the Rose uncovered adversaries' attempts long before they could be implemented. The Rose's reputation had been laid. Soon his name spread throughout ATR.

Theirs was repetitive training with the bayonet along with many hours of night firing, judo, hand to hand, grenade instruction which was hammered into them. They could uncoil in a moment from sleep. These men in green were trained for one reason, combat! To kill before you were killed. They'd been trained and indoctrinated with this one thought for weeks. Now their initial combat training was over. They would be assigned to various units throughout the corps and one thing was certain no matter where assigned whether an air wing, embassy duty, navy yards, cooks or bakers, they would always be infantry men first and foremost.

Staff Sergeant Brandon Schupp stood tall and erect, facing the troops. He was a large man who reeked of strength. He was a master of close combat and he was renowned that he preferred to live in the boon docks rather than the barracks. Sergeant Schupp coughed clearing his throat. "Alright girls, listen up and listen good! One day you'll find yourself in the bush and if you're not prepared will come face to face with Hell. The bush can be your ally as well as your enemy. It can conceal the enemy but also can cloth you with protection. Learn its secrets. How the grass lays and what belongs and what doesn't. Listen to the birds. The jungle animal's quiet is a strong message that a warning that something is amiss. You are being trained to inhale the jungles mysteries. It can be the difference not only to you but your unit whether you survive or parish. You will learn this week the fundamentals of walking the point, how to advance on the skirmish line, how to flank your enemy, how to read a map and compass. You will be drilled into hastening the importance of calling in coordinates for the artillery boys but, most importantly how to lay down fields of fire. He who commands the field with superior fire power brings home the trophy and if it's the enemy that trophy will be your head. Ladies you're not here for a recess break from life. You're not preparing for a high school prom. You're marines now and your profession is to kill to close with your adversary and cut his balls off before he defaces you!"

Broken Rose sat listening attentively. He appreciated the Staff Sergeant's knowledge of the bush. He starred long and hard into the instructors eyes and saw the soul of a warrior. On a short break, he spoke softly to his three buds, LaPore, LeSage and LeBron, "listened respectfully; you know that sergeant's spirit is one with that of the forest. He walks with the animal spirits and feels their fear, hunger and anger. Listen well for he's of the forest and the soil."

Sergeant Schupp was relentless. He continuously observed the platoons as they went about their training, grabbing those who were sloppy and handing out extra training and harsh words, until the individuals showed signs of digesting what they practiced. He forced them to read maps and ingest the importance of coordinates, to use the sun and stars to effect movements. He taught them the importance of the swift, quiet attack. They absorbed the importance of interlocking fire. They digested the reading of hand signals until it was like a second language. The troops marveled at the various methods of camouflage that he showed them and how to melt as one into the bowels of the forest. Upon completion of this point in training, Sergeant Schupp stared long and hard at the young excited faces laid out before him. "You marines have spent the past week learning the arts that just might save your ass one day. Instructors can teach, but you won't know the true horrors of combat until you yourselves experience the hot flare of Dante's Inferno. You have now ingested this segment of training and you will soon learn to perform in combat as a team with heavy armor. A word to the wise, be attentive, here we play games but someday the game will be serious and your reward will be either life or death. Good luck, you fighting marines and Semper-Fi!" With a salute, the large powerful Sergeant Schupp wheeled about and was gone. A small puff of dust trailed him into the forest.

The four best friends took a bus into Wilmington. It was their first liberty and the need for reprieve from the vigorous training was a beacon for relaxation. Upon entering the town they exited the bus, cognizant to the glances to the forest green uniforms that adorned them. LaPore purchased beer in a convince store and LeSage hamburgers at a local eatery. The four found a recluse area by a pond surrounded by trees and bushes. It concealed them from prying eyes. They'd elected to chill in this fashion as LeBron could not drink or eat in the local eateries. LaPore in a soft whisper broke their revere. "It's just wrong; man can wear the uniform of his country but because he's black isn't allowed to mingle with the white folks. Land of the free what hypocrisy!" "Aw, Lance, fuck the mother fuckers, piped up LeBron. There be bigoted white's everywhere. At least down here they announce it. Up north they do it behind your back. And they look you in the eye and smile. Then when you disappear in a puff, they call you nigger. I'm use to this shit. Broken Rose emitted a small chuckle. "What man!" rasped LeBron "What's funny about that shit?" Broken Rose's dark eyes bore into LeBron, "nothing funny old shoe, yes the black man suffers but the red men, and my people were all but destroyed. Look my soul brother; be wise, there are evil men of all colors and creeds. But on a whole there are many decent folks in this world. It will be decades, but one day all will be free. Men of good will shall prevail and men such as we will persevere and the Great One will set things right. There are many men with infections of the mind and there are no antibodies. But good will out do evil in the end. Those who have gone before us pave the road to triumph. Remember dreams are the connector between the dead and the living. Live with straight eyes and clean spirit and follow your dream in time we shall all smoke the pipe of peace."

The young marines retreated into their own solitude, lost in thought, reflecting on the past and future sipping their beers. They nurtured what dreams they experienced in silence. They were relaxed and comfortable with each other. The hoot of an owl startled them. It was only then they realized the sun was shedding its last peek over the horizon. Night was laying its dark tarp. In unison they jumped to their feet affecting a steady jog. Arriving at the bus terminal a large green and white bus loomed forlornly before them. "Aw," uttered Broken Rose, "the monster iron horse, our ride back to the swampy lagoon."

Their first liberty had gone without incident or fanfare and 0430 revelry dawned quickly on them that brisk Monday morning. A chilling wind bit into their flesh at roll call. Today would descend on them with a grueling forced twenty five mile hike with full packs. LeBron as usual started his day with his usual observation of the military world. "Man fuck this shit! What the fuck! Why we gotta make these silly asses walks? We suppose to shoot and kill these mother-fuckers crazy!" Broken Rose, stared at LeBron, "Hey my man, it gets you prepared. No way you can face an enemy and not be in mental and physical readiness. These are trained warriors showing us the way. They've been there and done that. So hush yourself. Sometimes you bore me. You're in the corps not some street gang. One day you may need to cover my ass best you're ready and able."

The company stepped out smartly with their packs laden with 80 lbs. leaned into the wind with the sergeants yelling and cursing as they climbed hills, and forged streams. The morning chill had dissipated and was replaced by a flaming North Carolina sun. Sweat ran in rivets down their faces, cursing through their bodies. Moans and grunts and obscenities marked their path. The young marine's bodies had grown lean and hard and yet muscles still howled with displeasure. Marches of this nature were intended to discipline the body to push one's self to the limit. Always the admonition of the platoon sergeant echoed in their subconscious. There are no limits in combat only agony and death. Mercifully the command "take ten" echoed through the ranks. Weary jar-heads fell where they stood. Cigarette's flared up and down the line and the metallic click of canteens creating a musical chorus in the lush vegetation which had embraced this young warrior breed.

The four buds had seated themselves alongside and under a majestic pine. The sweet smell filled their nostrils and each sat still lost in their own silent world. They were exhausted but it was a good feeling knowing they had been able to maintain the pace. Comfortable with their surroundings, gazing upward they sat in awe as the pine reached high in the sky. The soft chirps of birds lolling them into a peaceful stupor as they sat transfixed as a mother raccoon sauntered through the under brush with her four young scampering behind her. They watched fascinated as worker bees labored timelessly flitting from flower to flower. All about nature was at work for this is a reminder that one's destiny was mapped in the book of life.

Broken Rose broke their reserve, seated in the squat position, he uttered "this is good; warriors need to be quick and cunning and must learn to adapt the ways of mother earth. Wrapped in her arms one embraces the foundation to life's structure, love, honor, integrity, accountability, laughter, tears, joy and grief. Always be mindful one day she will welcome your spirit as life ebbs and you rejoin your ancestors." LeBron, LaPore, and LeSage listened with interest always impressed with their friend's take on life.

They rose as one as the command "saddle up, move out!" thundered through the brush. As one a line of green clad warriors took up the march. Dust enveloped the column. Birds hawking their annoyance frittered from trees and foliage. Leading the way as their numbers blotted the sun and colored the sky with their brown and grayish hue. Under a blazing sun and merciless sky, they pushed on in route step. Back packs bit into their shoulders. Webb belts embossing raw welts about their stomachs and waist. The marine's bodies screamed in silent anguish to no avail. NCO's prodded, taunted them to press on. Compassion was not present for these boys were now being tormented and cajoled relentlessly for this was the warrior's way. To a man, they knew they were being groomed for one thing and one thing only. A marine's calling, combat. Their bodies settled into an automatic mold. One foot forward was their quest. Caked in sweat their utilities grew sour and stiff. Helmets 5lbs of them, weighed a ton. They were allowed only sips of water, as water discipline was practiced and enforced. The company column pushed on.

Soon the sun sat low in the sky and its red glow sinking behind the tall trees which engulfed them. Night birds shrilled their calls. Then the infantry man's constant enemy suddenly was among them. Mosquito's the size of flies sought their prey feasting on fresh young blood. The constant slapping and swatting along the column echoed throughout the boon docks. Curses and obscenities ruled as dusk settled about them. The command "column halt!" brought relief and smiles on two hundred red grimy faces. The marines had reached their destination. Their looming before them was the infiltration course. They would bivouac for the night commencing at 0530 reveille to enter and complete this physical and physiological grueling exercise. Engrossed in setting up pup tents and preparing hot c rations for evening chow they were prepped by NCO s who informed them they would run the infiltration course by day and then repeat the process in the dark. Platoon NCOs filtered through the ranks checking gear and feet admonishing those who failed to heed corps men advice in how to limit foot blisters, an infantry man's nightmare.

The night was bright with campfires. Wood smoke permeated through the brush. Embers from the fires danced in the twilight as worn, exhausted marines wolfed down c ration of beans or burgers in a can. The smoking lamp was lit as young men lost in thought, sought refuge and comfort beneath a small canvas tent and with their mattress that of mother earth. Broken Rose, LaPore, LeBron and LeSage sat by a small fire which controlled the night chill from over taking them. All but Broken Rose fired up a Lucky. The grayish smoke drifted up and away looking eerie in the light of their fire. LeBron gazing into the fire broke the silence. "Shit man! That fucking recruiter in Brooklyn never said shit about this crap. All he did was point at a picture of some pretty boy in dress blues saying, "Dude think how good those duds will look on you. Why, broads will be going crazy! You'll get all kinds of pussy." "Mother fucker, I believed that prick." His three buds laughed softly. "Jake you're under a rock," whispered LeSage. "Anyone knows ain't no blues available for a black dude," again laughter. "Aw fuck you LeSage, you know what mother, see here its dark and I got me natural camouflage. You whiteys got to put black paint or mud to hide your ugly ivory skin. Shit you gonna die." "Hey, Jake," uttered Broken Rose, "I'm red, I'll look like the sun, got no worries." They were startled by the voice of Sergeant Hemming, "hey shit heads, knock it off. Lights out and get some sack time. Like now! 0530 comes quick and you girls will start whining. Hit the fart sack won't say it again, understood?" "Yeah, okay Sarge," whispered LaPore, "No problem, Semper Fi." "Don't be a smart ass, LaPore! Get your ass under that canvas, and no playing with each other!" The four rolled into their tents while the fire slowly calmed and glowed small embers. Soon only the light of glowing stars twinkled through the tree tops which stood as sentinels about them and the soft light casting a soft shadow on the forest floor. In the darkness, young men twisted in discomfort as muscles seldom used groaned in rebellion for it was impossible for one to get comfortable. As the night dragged on, exhaustion and fatigue won out and young boys in men's utilities sought comfort and refuge in the blackness lost in thoughts of home and loved ones.

In the black abyss, a lone figure squatting in front of his miniature tent with his hands resting on his thighs. He sat perfectly still and his eyes scanning the dark tarpaulin which engulfed him. He listened attentively to the musical chorus of hundreds of crickets calling to each other. He smiled inwardly knowing that male and females were involved in the sequence of life. He remained still fine tuning his senses as grandfather had taught him. In the stillness of the night only an occasional cough or snoring cascaded from the numerous pup tents. Shielded in the cloak of darkness, closing his eyes, he allowed his sense of hearing to hone in on different sounds of the night, the soft whir of a mosquito, the slight movement of grass as brother snake slithered past. His keen senses were like radar, as he heard the first yip-yip of cousin coyote off in the distance. There to his right the silent flap of a night owl caught his attention. With years of practiced discipline, he honed on the death gnarl of sister's owl's prey." These green warriors are good, ´ he thought, "but they fail to develop the bodies' senses for tobacco and spirits deluding them," he uttered softly whispering in prayer to his ancestors imploring them to guide him as he fulfilled his warrior's quest. Broken Rose then raised his right hand in blessing first to the north, then to the south, continuing west and the east. Like his brother lion, he returned silently to his small alcove of refuge.

A soft breeze caressed the foliage that stood as sentinels ever watchful over the sleeping forms of two hundred and fifty future warriors. Most tossed in fitful sleep their muscles screaming their displeasure. The night ebbed slowly but eventually the sun began its, in slow ascent, played hide and seek with Camp Lejeune's tree tops. Small rays filtered through casting a soft light that danced along the ground their tentacles reaching towards the tents that housed weary sleeping forms. Suddenly the solitude of the forest exploded with the guttural commands of NCO's prodding the wary souls from their slumber. "Up and at em, drop your socks and grab your cock s the corps doesn't pay you for sleeping! You clowns think you're on a camping trip with mommy and daddy. Get out of them sacks! Move your girlie asses! It's time to serve your Uncle Sam. Get shaved, heat up some chow! You got 30 minutes of spoiled time! Move! Move! Move! God Damn it you're as slow as a cluster of pregnant broads! Thirty minutes people! Then company formation and roll call!"

Bleary eyed troops staggered from their tents. Oaths and cursing echoed through the forest. Bodies raked with pain inhibited movement, but these boy men were marines and discipline prevailed. The ranks set about their task cooking fires ignited. The small bluish heat bars casting a bluish haze in the semi-light of dawn. The mixture of grayish mist and blue smoke cast eerie shadows on the men's faces. Helmets filled with lukewarm water served as utensils for sponge baths and a shave. Packets of coffee made with water brought from lister bags brought minimum comfort and contentment. Cigarette smoke whiffed upwards and outwards beating a quick retreat into the thick forest vegetation. Birds chirped loudly announcing their annoyance with this invasion of their habitat.

"Good morning and Semper-Fucking Fi," blurted LeBron as he joined Broken Rose, LaPore and LeSage for a quick breakfast of beans and hot dogs a la carte in C ration issue. "Mother fuckers gonna kill us by starvation! Ain't no doubt! How come no hot chow? Ate this same camel shit last night! Mother Fucker should have joined the Air Force. Them mothers, eat good. Sleep on clean sheets, shower, and got all those perks. What we got? Pains in our ass and bugs and cruds and who the fuck knows what else!" LaPore chuckling "Jake, you know God damn well the judge gave you a choice, jail or the corps and here you are having a gourmet breakfast with your buds." "Fuck should of chose jail. Three squares a day and a bed. This shit is for snakes and critters. Not fit for a man. God damn it! LaPore, I haven't had a woody since I got here." "Really," piped in LeSage, "thought I heard you pounding the drum last night." "Aw, fuck you guys; man can't have an intelligent conversation at all." LeBron gazed at Broken Rose, "so Tonto, why you not shaving?" Broken Rose smiled, "no need my charcoal friend. No Beard. The Great Spirit blessed Indians with smooth clean skin, unlike you darkies and pale faces. "Aw, horse shit," spat LeBron. "Custer fucked up, should have offed all you savages." Broken Rose spooning some beans into his mouth, laughed softly. "You know what's interesting, ever notice when the blue soldiers won a battle it was a great victory, but when the red men won, it was a massacre." "Who gives a fuck," retorted LeBron. "Blue coats, Indians, shit it make for great movies." "Hey," LeBron whispered, "LeSage how's that rock your under, shit man you guys bad for 'ol Jake. Always fucking with my head." "Alright assholes saddle up and police the area! Company formation in five minutes! Grab ass hour is over!" Men assembled to scramble to and fro under the intimidating glace of Sergeant Hemming. His reputation as a tough non-com proceeded where ever he went and the bearer of the Navy Cross tolerated no shit from the troops.

The company slung arms and stepped off in route step. The blistering sun bathed them in intense heat. Marines up and down the line vented their displeasure with plenty of oaths and curses. NCO's prodded them on shouting commands and orders with corps precision. At last the command halt thundered through the ranks. There standing before the heat weary grunts lay an expanse of open land surrounded by thick vegetation and trees. They gazed curiously at strands of barbed wire that stretched for yards across the open field. Several shacks adorned the perimeter and a plat form which rose 50 feet into the sky. Several lister bags containing tepid water ringed the area. There was a military ambulance bearing a large red cross and several jeeps and a helicopter parked haphazardly abutting the field before them. To the recruits right stood the battalion training officer surrounded by an entourage of officers and high ranking enlisted nom coms.

Sergeant Hemming stood to their front, "alright ladies unshoulder your weapons and take 10. The smoking lamp is lit. Broken Rose, LeBron, LaPore and LeSage sat in a half semi-circle studying the lay out before them. LeBron speaking in an excited voice pointed toward the end of the field, "Man those machine guns, what the Fuck! God Damn! What's going down?" Broken Rose chuckled, "those are fixed mounted guns Jake." Set to fire approximately three to four feet over these barbed wire strands." "Jesus Jake, snorted LaPore. This is the infiltration course. What you expect those midnight specials you carried in Brooklyn?" "Aw, fuck LaPore, you fucked up real bad." "Alright knock it off." A burly three stripper stood lean and tall in front of the company. "My name is Sergeant Manuel Sanchez, Sergeant, to you night crawlers. As you can see behind me is a stretch of barbed wire and further on are three 30 caliber machine guns. They are armed with live ammo. Every third round is a tracer." "Hey Sarge, piped up a young freckled face from the rear, seems to me some one fucked up. That wire's only about 4 inches off the ground." Sanchez glared at the young marine. A smirk lit his face. Boy you gonna see real soon how your mom-ma's boy little ass gonna skittle under that wire. Now you impostors for marines listen and listen tight. Your weapons are what will get you through the course. You'll crawl on your backs digging and pushing off with your boots and elbows to wriggle under that wire. You'll utilize your weapons by pushing the barbed wire up and away from you. Now be advised those guns will be firing directly over you so keep your asses to the ground and don't get a hard on else a 30 caliber round will de-ball you. Alright first 10 move out on your backs and commence the run. The rest of you turds line up to my left and as the first of your girlfriends get ten feet inside the wire the next ten move in. Remember, on your backs. Keep your weapons on your chest and push up. GO! GO! GO!" Ten marines slid under the wire, squirming and pushing. The wire bit into hands, fingers, scraped the stocks of their weapons. Machine gun fire laid a hail of lead above them along with explosive devices detonating all about them which ripped utility jackets. Torn bleeding hands and fingers ruled the moment. Barbed wire resisted their attempts to push along, but slowly and painfully the green clad figures snaked their way through under agonizing conditions.

Broken Rose, LaPore, LeBron and LeSage were in the next to last group. Almost all who entered struggled frantically to escape this nightmare. Several noncoms observing the drill watched in awe as Broken Rose slithered through the tangle of wire like a snake slithering in the grass. His motion slowed only because of the marine in front of him battled furiously to escape the clutches of barbed wire and psychological fear which enveloped him. Sergeant Sanchez turned to Sergeant Hemming, "who's the dark marine right there? Shit he's going through that iron garden like he's on a Sunday walk." Hemming smiled, marveled, "that's our Indian. His name is John Broken Rose, He's one of a kind and I'll tell you he's going to be one hell of a marine."

Sergeant Sanchez stood facing the ragged ranks before him. His surveillance honed in on numerous grunts whose bodies displayed cuts and numerous gashes to arms, hands and faces. Blood oozed generously. He chuckled softly noting torn and frayed uniforms. The grunts stood at rigid attention. Their eyes locked on the smirk which outlined the instructor's features. "All right girls, stand at ease. This segment of the exercise is terminated. That's the good news and now ready for the bad?" His laugh was a howl giggling he was able to squeak out, you fodder softies, YOU GET TO DO IT AGAIN! Commencing at 2100 hours! Be brave and grateful the dark will hide your little girl tears! All right shit heads, fall out and form on your noncoms. Oh, I'm looking forward to spending an exciting evening together." Laughing he about faced and sauntered off humming, "What Makes Little Girl's Cry?"

Sergeant Hemming faced his command that stood at parade rest. "All right listen up, its 1600 hours and you have till 20:30 hours to lighten up, smoke sleep and treat your little boy cuts. Do whatever the fuck suits you for the next four and a half hours. But at 20:30 hours your asses are mine. Then he pointed at a large blue spruce. No stragglers, any late comers will run that gauntlet twice. COMPANY ATTENTION!!! Alright fall out and make sure you hydrate. That means filling your asses with God's water and plenty of it." He turned and headed off in the direction of training company's officers and

NCO's who were eyeballing them and gesturing to each other. The weary grunts exploded in frenzy. Heading every which way to their midget tents and water ready to digest and enjoy a few hours reprieve.

The four buds sat in a semi-circle all but Broken Rose sucking on Luckies. "Man that shit is for the fucking monkeys," uttered LeBron. The other three smiled. They were used to LeBron's bitching it bemused them. For his admonitions caused laughter and a semblance of inner peace. "Mother fucker, I'm telling you, these lifer's is crazy! I'll bet they recruit them from the funny houses and Ryker's Island. God damn, What the fuck chuck. Ain't no enemy gonna spoon dirt on us. It's gonna be these fuckers. You see their eyes, fuck the devil ain't in Hell, he's here with his legion of disciples. That Sanchez, I'll bet two to one he fucks little animals. That mother's demented and his brain cooked and he spent too much time in this fucking forest green nut house. Shit look at my hands. All fucked up and my ass feels like it's been fucked by a camel." Soft laughter emitted from their small campsite. All up and down the line clusters of grunts were bitching and failing in attempts to find a comfort zone.

LeBron continued his epilates, "who the fuck the enemy, out in the world or are they these crazy men?" Broken Rose raised his hand. "Jake you're okay; you bring laughter that's good for one's soul. But remember these instructors and noncoms and most of the officers have gone in harm's way. They have walked Hell's byways and now their preparing us for what might come. What we're experiencing ain't shit and you know it. When the, if and when shit hits the fan, at least, we're be professionally prepared. It's up to the individual as to his mental state." "Yeah Tonto, okay you be right but shit a guy could get killed in this outfit." "Right again Jake, Many souls marched before us sadly, many more will route step the same trail rut I'll tell you. We're all going to die sometime, but I'd rather die now for something rather than nothing later." "Hey guys, let's get some rest. Let's police up our c's and take twenty winks" "Right on my bro, right on, Jake straighten out on the ground. Gazing into a blue lit sky, sighing he whispered, "God I love these guys, hope we stay together."

The sun dipped low in the sky it glowed red and angry as though disgusted what lay below. Noncom's frittered up and down the line badgering the grunts to saddle up for the night exercise. Weary men stretched and yawned reaching deep for energy and mustering all their strength for the rigors that lay with amused patience for its victims. True to the North Carolina weather, the descending darkness while spreading its tarp brought uninvited guest. A cold wind huffed and puffed and bodies stiff with sweat and grime groaned in frustration and then it began a cold rain pelted the anguished grunts. A chorus of curses pierced the once quiet solitude. Birds screeched in anger as they fled their perches. Soon the ground was a quagmire of mud and silt. LeBron standing with his buds stated, "Hey man maybe they'll cancel." His wish died in his throat as the guttural voice of Staff Sergeant Kelly screamed "saddle up assholes! Fall in and sling arms!" "Fuck," uttered LeBron another demon. God Damn, I died and I'm in Hell." "Aw Jake, shut the fuck up," blurted LaPore. "What did you expect here, a camping trip?" The formation was given the command right face and stepped of smartly, en route to the demon's nest.

They were halted yards from the course. Once again, they were greeted by Sergeant Sanchez. His face lit up with a demonic grin. "Well, ladies just what the doctor ordered a nice shower. It'll wash the stink from your cruddy bodies. All right you know the drill. First ten hit it and keep your asses down low. Men on their backs entered the wire. Darkness had now enveloped them. They twisted and turned slinking slowly forward. Once again the wire bit into flesh. Yelps of pain could be heard emitting from under the wire. Now the grunts were faced with additional dilemmas. They scurried in globs of mud and vision was nil. They could only get bearings when an explosive device lit up the night. Cold rain pelted them. It came in sheets forcing one to shut his eyes to avoid the stinging pain. Here and there men became entangled with each other. Now and then the guy in front kicked his mate behind him. It made for bad bed partners. To make matters even worse NCO's would lob rocks into the wire. A hit was marked by the sudden grunt when a target was struck.

As the men wiggled and pushed their bodies through the mud, they were tormented by the red streak of tracers like tentacles streaking by two feet above them. The cold and rain continued to punish them, but there was no mercy until the last man scrambled from under the wire thus terminating the exercise. Slowly they formed ranks. Then their nemesis from Hell stood grinning at them. Tucked under a poncho, Sergeant Sanchez roared, "Well, all you assholes survived! My congratulations! Now you've an idea of live fire!" With a show of humanity, he leaned forward and in a soft voice, "remember this was training those weapons were fixed. In the real world of combat those rounds and tracers will be aimed at your asses. Okay, tomorrow at 0800, you will be introduced to the practical course. You may find that more to your liking. You'll get the word and S.O.P. on arrival. For now fall in on your noncoms, oh leave your birdies alone tonight." He turned and disappeared into the night.

Staff Sergeant Kelly surveyed the mud caked zombies facing him. "Okay, listen up! We're marching to our bivouac area. You'll unload your weapons and march to a pond where you can wash off that elephant shit and try to regain some semblance of marines. No sack time till you clean your weapons and you best make formation in clean utilities. All right, right face, sling arms, Forward March!" They stepped out en route step. LeBron turned to Broken Rose, "Tonto, I'm telling you, these people are demons and they're insane. We gonna bath ice water, fuck this shit. They should have showers installed out here." Broken Rose smiled, "Jake you think you're a guest of the Hotel Ritz. Lighten up Jake; you're in the marines and not in a boy scout troop, besides your black and no one will see you in the dark or your goose bumps. Stay with the program. Jake, these men are proven warriors. Look, listen and be silent. They've been where it's at. Their teachings may just save our asses one day."

The grunts chilled as the wind rose in volume. Rain continued to saturate them. In the pressed quarters of their pup tents, the men labored furiously to clean weapons. They knew a weapons inspection loomed bright right after morning chow. The men shared pup tents on the buddy system. Each man carried two stakes and half of a shelter, thus two men would quarter together. LaPore and LeSage lay back in their small den, their body heat minimizing the cold damp air that hovered like a thick cloud over the bivouac area. As the wind howled, its fury men struggle to seek comfort in their small refuge. Soon all was quiet and weary bodies had succumbed to the abyss of sleep.

LeSage lit up a Lucky offered one to LaPore who accepted quickly as he'd run out of smokes. An occasional cough somewhere down the line a reminder that there, in the dark, buds were all about them. "Hey," LeSage whispered, "LaPore you're from Oakland, right?" "Right on Lee and I never left till I joined the corps." "What's your family feel about it? You know being a jar-head and all?" "Ain't got a family Lee and I was adopted when I was 6 weeks old and had twelve nice years, and then my adopted parents were killed in a car accident. I had no relatives, so I was placed in an orphanage." "Shit! How was that Lance?" "Aw, you know regimented. We ate our meals every day at the same time lights out early and early reveille, supervised sports and an occasional flick. But mostly studies. We slept in large wards with no privacy to speak of. But you got three squares and a warm bed and a roof over your head. Hey look, they did their best. They cared for some fucked up kids you know. Poor bastards, there were lots of psych problems including yours truly. Took me forever to get over my folks deaths and I still haven't really." "Jesus, Lance I'm sorry." "Hey, no sweat Lee, it is what it is. This is my family now, you, Tonto and Jake." "Yeah, I know what you mean bro. Hope we stay together. What about you Lee, What you got back in the world?

What's cooking there?" "Shit nothing Lance. Went to a prep school and won a baseball scholarship. Blew that, had a girl but dear John-ed me at P.I. My folks aren't thrilled I joined the corps. You know mom and pops want only the best for their kids. But I had to get away. Had to find myself." "Why, the Corp's Lee?" "You'll laugh or think I'm full of shit. But I wanted the toughest because I wanted to see if I got game and could I measure up and tough it out, so far, so good. Just don't know the ending." "Yeah, know what you mean. Well old shoe, time to get some shut eye. You warm enough? Keeping dry?" "Yeah, fine Lance. Glad we met up." "Right on, so am I. Tonto and Jake, good people." "Yeah, we'll be a okay watching each others backs. There was no response. LaPore was fast asleep. Smiling in the dark, LeSage lay back. His pack as a pillow lulled him into a quick sleep. An owl hooted softly and creatures scurried in the brush. The rain drops beating a soft tattoo along the line of tents. Only silence of young men that tossed and turned in their small sanctuary each with his hopes and dreams. Above them the majestic trees of Camp Lejeune peering down at them like sentinels. They stood guard and in a small way offered protection to the sleeping forms below.

In the adjoining tent, Broken Rose and LeBron lay quiet listening as rain pelted the canvas roof like a soft cadence. LeBron glanced at Broken Rose, "Tonto you really believe these dudes is sane? Come on, man, on the rock they treated us like animals but here they forever hassling us. Shit, ain't necessary, man, we's human. Treat us like men." Broken Rose stirred then bolted upright. "Look Jake you can't walk softly. This is the Marines Corps. Their history dates back to your revolution." "Wasn't my revolution." "Yes it was and is. Look we're both on the fringes of the white man's world, but one day society will right itself. Shit Jake, check it out. In our armed forces we've got blacks, Indians, Puerto Ricans, Mexicans, Germans, French, Italians, Russians, Japanese, Chinese, and Koreans. We've got 'em all and all serve the colors. All march to the same beat of the drum and all bleed red. There isn't another country in the world that has such a diversified military. America is a stew of all races and creeds." "Yeah, there are discrepancies, bigotry, hate, greed, yet through it all we carry on and the price of our freedoms comes high. Freedom isn't free. These are the times that try men's souls. Tyranny like Hell is not easily conquered. From north to south, east to west, the white crosses of dead Americans stand proud and erect in just about every country on mother earth. Be proud Jake, we, the corps, army, air force, navy coast guard are the stirring pot that will light up a better world and safeguard our country. For future generations, in the meantime, live life fully while you may and not reckon the cost. Life is a head slap of reality. Make each day count. Oh well I, Broken Rose will now take rest and dream of my ancestors. Good Night my friend." Jake lying transfixed whispered, "Good night, Tonto." He lay there digesting Broken Rose's words. He felt a shiver up his spine. Beautiful words the Indian speaks the truth and sleeps with straight eyes as he closed his eyes. The yip-yip of a lone coyote lulled him into a peaceful sleep.

Lonely men without women spent a restless night with their muscles screaming in anguish and fits of sleep invaded by bouts of pain and loneliness. Slowly the night passed and soon a gray haze shrouded the tree line. Men roused from their humble refuge were greeted by a thick heavy mist and a chilling drizzle with the ground, a swamp of mud and water running in rivulets, coursing in an around the bivouac perimeter. Bars of blue heat ignited to heat water for packet coffee and shaves, cast eerie tongues of bluish flame which filtered into the thick grayish moisture creating a surreal effect. Grunts appeared as gray ghosts like the dead had risen from the grave.

The troops breakfasted on beans and other government delicacies. Two cigarettes flare flaming as beacons it the hovering mist. Here and there men entered the private world of shit trenches in performance of their morning constitution. Coughs and curses ruled the moment, with their morning chow complete. Now shaved and sporting fresh utilities, plucked from packs. The company stood erect in formation. The command port arms thundered in the ranks. Rifles were snapped in crisp precision. Captain Mulcahy, the company commander, along with 1st Sergeant R LaJoy in close pursuit conducting an intense and thorough weapon's inspection for he was side stepping through the ranks individuals were admonished for a speck of lint in a chamber or a spot of rust on the trigger housing. "Too much oil marine!" snapped Mulcahy. "Wipe it Clean!" "Yes, Sir, responded an embarrassed grunt Whoa! What the fuck is this! Cried Mulcahy, as he peered down a rifle barrel, my God rat's found their way! You've got a nest and a whole fucking family in here! Get out of ranks! Depart from my presence and clean this weapon! You've fifteen minutes, best it be spotless or your ass will belong to the 1st Sergeant!" "Yes Sir! Marine Private Reynolds caught his weapon, as Mulcahy moved along the line, heaving the weapon at the frightened grunt. 1st Sergeant LaJoy stifled a smile. Mulcahy was a good officer and had earned his spurs in Korea an excellent training officer. Cognoscente, that these troops were being trained and prepared for regular assignments around the globe.

Weapons and gear inspection complete, the men remained in ranks at parade rest. Sergeant Hemming approached and exchanged salutes with his company commander. "All yours Sarge!" barked Mulcahy. "The inspection sucked! Your NCO's need to get on these troops! You've been there! God Damn it! Get them willing and able when we get back to quarters! I'll want weapons and gear inspections frequently and unannounced, understood?!" "Yes, Sir! Look Sarge, they're coming along, but they're green, they have got to get the word that their weapons and gear are there lifeline. You know it and I know it." "Carry on, Mulcahy and his1st Sergeant turned and marched briskly towards the C. P."

Staff Sergeant Welch along with Sergeant Hemming studied their company with contempt. Welch broke the silence, speaking softly and menacingly. You maggots think your marines. Bull shit, I feel like I'm back in the boy scouts. No, belay that, the girl scouts. You pissed off the captain. You've made me the 1ˢᵗ shirt. The gunny and all the NCO's look like beaver shit. Well, get the word, when we get back to quarters your asses will drag till you tickle us and make us smile again. The captain felt he was conducting a fucking Chinese fire drill. Well, camel shit there won't be a repeat performance. It was Private Reynolds who in a high pitched voice startled the ranks. "But Sarge it rained all night and still is. How are we supposed to keep these weapons dry?" Welch exploded. Little girl, you shove it up your ass that'll work! God Damn, you people! Listen tight, that weapon is what counts, not you! It kills that prick that's out to kill you! That weapon is an extension of you! You were taught that at P.I! Best you fuckers get serious and you coddle that weapon! Protect it safe guard it! Treat it like you would a nice soft pussy! That pussy won't save your ass but that weapon will! There'ii be no more questions or bitching this isn't a democracy here! It's not your way but the marine way! One day you may hit a beach and make God Damn sure your weapon is in the ready, not only your ass depends on its readiness, but that of your buddies! One thing to let your-self down it's unacceptable to fail your comrades or unit!"

"Okay, enough for now. I'm turning you over to Sergeant Hemming." "Listen up and pay attention. Be alert Get in the zone. You're going to enter the practical range. It's the closet we've got to the real thing. Bear in mind it's not. Eat, drink, sleep shit, and fuck with one thought. One day you may be in the shit. What you learn here, see here, hear here, smell here may one day get you home for if you fuck up and grab ass you may come home in a body bag."

The men marched to a thick row of hedges and called to a halt by Sergeant Hemming. The command rest bellowed by Sergeant Hemming caused a stir in the ranks, men shifting and bobbing expending nervous energy. Before them stood a burly gunnery sergeant and close by a group of officers and non-cons. "Alright you sad sacks I'm Gunnery Sergeant MacDonald. Behind these hedges is a thick populace of pines and brush. It's an inviting sight but within its borders lying in ambush is the course you will run today. You will observe instructors along the route. They will be monitoring the exercise to my rear are two corporals as you can see. The table next to them contains boxes of 30 caliber live ammo. You will each be issued three eight round clips on entering you will insert one clip in your weapons and lock and load. You will traverse the trail marked in red in single file. Now listen tight at intermittent intervals metal targets will leap at you from behind well-chosen locations. On sight you will fire and a loud ping will alert you as to a hit. Three misses and an instructor will snare your ass off the course and you'll run it again and again to our satisfaction. You'll step out slowly and keep three yard intervals between your sorry asses. Oh also various explosive devices will detonate during the process. Okay in single file retrieve your ammo. Be alert and good luck.

The file of green snaked into the thick vegetation. Heads swiveled side to side anticipating a metal enemy surprising them along the route. An occasional instructor was observed and up ahead sporadic rifle fire echoed through the underbrush. Birds fled the area in an angry frenzy. Men hit the dirt as explosive devices detonated. There was enough kick to them that grunts were showered with dirt and debris. Due to the rain the ground was as quicksand. Boots sucked into the wet marshy soil creating a slurping sucking sound. The entire morning spent bobbing and weaving. Here a target over there another. It could be one at time or several. The ping of hits registered far and wide. Finally as the sun shone high in the sky, the grunts exited into a large field. The smell of hot chow alerted their senses. They'd been on the run for a week without let up and the aroma carried by a slight breeze ultimately propelled them forward at double time. Called to formation they stood tall and tight in the ranks. Sergeant Hemming and Sanchez stood to their front. "Good show girls you all came through with flying colors. Your reward is to our rear, hot chow and java, when dismissed stack your weapons and you've a two hour break. Then we march back to the bivouac area. There your get the S.O.P. on when we return to regular quarters. Okay, Dismissed!"

Grunts stacked their weapons and double timed to the chow line. Hot stew and coffee with biscuits were devoured. Men sat and satisfied their appetites. Sanchez turned to Hemming, "hot chow always rings well with hungry grunts, right Mike?" Hemming smiled, "yeah makes me happy."

Sanchez fired up a camel. "Mike that Indian kid, what's his name, Rose? I forget." "John Broken Rose," answered Hemming. "Yeah well that kid ran that course in under 18 minutes and hit every damn target on the run. I've never seen that. What gives?" Hemming turned and facing Sanchez spoke in a whisper, "Manuel, I don't know. All I can tell you he's Indian with senses I've never witnessed. That kid I swear heard the whir of those targets as they sprang. He's out shot; out ran, out done everyone in the company by far. I told you before; he's going to be a hell of a marine."

Broken Rose had taken leave of his buds and entered the woods. His pace was quick and steady. Finally he halted surveying his surroundings. Satisfied, he'd gone deep enough safe from prying eyes, he stood erect raising his right hand in supplication. First to the north, then south, east and west and he began to pray. Oh Great Spirit, bless the wind that brings forth great things. Bless the water which sustains life. Bless the sun that warms mother earth. Bless the moon and stars which gives light in the dark. He then squatted by a lone pine, content to be in the forest. He'd vowed never to distance himself from mother earth. Her soul brought forth the beauty of life and the wild creatures that excelled in survival depending on stealth and cunning. He listened quietly and smiled for he could hear and sense and smell the creatures that hid in caution. Sitting alone and erect he sensed a whisper on the wind as a soft breeze shifted. The words of his grandfather came to him as a leaf spiraling in the currents. "Always look, listen, and be silent. You will honor your ancestors and you will bring pride to the ancient warriors. Blessed are you. Go my son for you are among the green and know that the Great One and your senses will be your strength and guide."

After evening chow, the men were critiqued by senior noncoms as to their success or failure in running the practical action course. The company grew extra attentive as Sergeant Major Klobar stood before them. He was old school and tolerated little if any grab ass. In a loud authoritative voice he bellowed, "You people listen up and listen tight! In a couple of weeks your ATR training will be completed! You will then receive orders and be assigned duty stations around the globe! Hopefully you'll have digested what we trained you for! It might just save your ass! There is talk that air power will be the savior of the good guys!! I wish! Planes and whirly birds are sexy as hell, but they don't win anything on their own! Never have, never will! Boots on the ground is what wins things! The future belongs to the infantry and that my lad is you! All marines are basically infantry no matter their MO! In the scheme of things it's that grunt with a sharp eye and a good instinct and cold steel that takes and secures an objective! History shows that tons of bombs were dumped on Europe and in the pacific operative, but it took infantry to storm Normandy and Iwo Jimi and the entire Pacific Island! Okay you'll march back to your bivouac area! Fall in on your noncoms! Once there, you'll police up the area, break down your shelter halves and prepare for a night march back to mainland glancing at the company noncoms! He scowled, take charge of your platoons and carry on!"

Brow beaten and harassed by their NCO's, the company had the area secured by 1500 hours. Bearing full packs the company stood in tight formation. Sergeant Hemming stood to their front. "Okay girls, time to hit the dirt! Right Face! Forward, March!" The crunch, crunch of boots echoed through the woods. Sighs and whispers emitted from the ranks. "Knock it off!" Blared Hemming, "you're not sailors your fucking marines, act it!" In a loud musical chant he began to call cadence, "Hup, two, three, four! You're left! You're left! You're left, right, left!" Under the midday sun, the company snaked across the green woodland, approaching a dirt road which would lead them home.

The grunts trudged through the woodlands in route step. They'd resigned themselves that this was a 25 mile hike in reverse. A night march tests the senses with different smells and the sounds of critters moving to and fro. The lay of the land takes on a different appearance. One must depend on moon light and the stars and his own senses to negotiate obstacles that lie in ambush along the march. LeBron spoke out in a hoarse whisper, "buds I'm telling you these mothers are fucking insane. They've zero brain power and they need to get laid or jack off. God Damn, this is fucking nuts. I should have joined the navy shit better still the air force, even fucking better, I should have stayed home with mom-ma." LaPore choked, "then you'd be on Ryker's Island numb nuts getting butt fucked. Those within hearing chuckled softly. "Shit man, I'm being fucked here and it don't feel so good at all." The column moved on in silence only the rustle of canteens striking hips and loose packs. The crunching of boots and an occasional cough broke the stillness. The sun had long bid them good night. Dark quickly embraced the column in its black curtain. Five miles on the march, the lead elements found the dirt highway leading to the mainland. The column split in two. Columns now route stepping on each side of hell's highway. Then they heard them.

What is the twenty century signature sound? You could debate about it. Some might say the slow drone of an aero engine. Maybe a lone fighter crawling across an azure sky or the scream of a fast jet passing low overhead was shaking the ground, or the whop, whop, whop, of a helicopter. It could be the roar of a laden 747 lifting off, or the crump of bombs falling on a city. All would qualify them as all uniquely twentieth century noises. They were never heard before, in all of history. No, the twentieth century's signature sound is the squeal and clatter of tanks in the night. It's a brutal sound and it's the sound of fear. It speaks of a massive overwhelming advantage in power and it speaks of remote impersonal indifference. Tank threads squeal and clatter and the very noise they make tell you they can't be stopped. It tells you you're weak and powerless against the machine. Then one track stops and the other keeps on going and the monster wheels turned and lurches straight towards you. Roaring and squealing that's the real twentieth century sound. The noise came at the column through a sudden night fog. They heard the grind of the drive gear and felt fast pattering bass shudders through the soles of their feet as each new thread plate came off the cogs and thumped down into position. They heard grit and stove crushed under their weight. Then they saw them. The lead tank loomed through the mist. Moving fast, pitching a little and then staying flat, with its engine roaring, behind it another and another. All in line like an armada from Hell. The lead tank rolled past them. Its engine bellowed and its weight shook the ground. Its tracks squealed and clattered and slid on the gravel. The second tank rolled by, then a third and a fourth and a fifth. The noise was deafening. The huge bulk of exotic metal buffeted the air. Gun barrels dipped and swayed and bounced. Exhaust fumes swirled all around. All together twenty tanks in the formation covered the grunts in thick clouds of dust. The foot marines cursed and two hundred fifty middle fingers reached into the misty night. But the iron monsters roared on and soon their noise and vibration faded into the night mist and were swallowed in the night. And just as they came they were gone.

The column enmeshed in thick balls of dust. They appeared as gray colored tchotchkes, as NCO's flitted up and down the line checking bodies and yelling, "take 10!, take 10!" Rattled troops sprawled on each side of the road. The sound of canteen covers unscrewed creating a metallic musical symphony along the column. Cigarettes flares cast an eerie glow up and down the line. Major John Dawson stood with 1st Sergeant Jim Miller, "you know Top, and this armored convoy was a surprise but I think it did these grunts good. Now they know the sound of heavy armor in the night and it's an experience they will never forget." "Yes Sir. Fortunately no one got crushed." "No Top, wouldn't want that on our watch." Top looked around they're all just kids. We toughen em up but is it enough? Soon they'll be assigned duty stations around the globe. They're training is hard as it should be, and why? Someday, somewhere, they'll be heading in harm's way." "You're right Major. Just months ago these kids were frolicking at high school proms and copping a feel in movie theaters. We cause confusion and harassed them and we kick ass and instilled pride and discipline in their psyches. That's what the corps is all about. The end result, they'll do what they've been trained to do. Marines prepare for one thing and one thing only combat."

Major Dawson smiled softly emitting an audible sigh. "Yeah Top, it's all about Semper Fi. Have the noncoms get them on their feet. Let's saddle up and move out."

Wearily the company trudged on. Fatigue their constant companion. The green warrior had a grueling two weeks of training session and practical exercises. Hours of bayonet drills. Realistic type house to house combat in a small prefab town constructed in the middle of bum fuck for extensive training. LeBron as usual broke the ice. Taking the edge off the solemn solitude that had infested the company. "Man, the mother fucking tanks. God Damn! They'd be scary shit! Fuck the ground was shivering and groaning, like it was in pain. I swear trees were crashing back there. Lord have mercy, wouldn't want one of them mothers coming at me. No Way! Shit my balls are still wedged in my asshole." LeSage chuckled, "goes to show you Jake, Imagine how those poor bastards felt in the Bulge." "Yeah, man, must have been one hell of a glimpse into Hell."

It began to rain creating added misery to the column of wretched troops. They could feel the grime coursing down their faces. Already soaked in sweat, rain water and dust created a mixture of a white cake like substance covering their utilities. It added to their torment in as it thickened making each step a laborious effort. Now boots sluiced and slurped in mud. The rain beat a tattoo on helmets. Men resigned themselves to the age old adage of the infantryman, one foot up and one foot down. The column continued slowly snaking across the countryside toward dry racks in metal structures.

The company stood at rest in front of their quarters with their weapons at order arms. "All right my little scout troop!" bellowed Sergeant Hemming. "You sad sacks made it, as they say in the British marines, good show old boy. Now I've some bad news and some good news for you little ladies." His eyes scanned the company. "Okay, here it is weapons and equipment inspection at 0900 hours." A groan rose through the ranks. Dawn was just peaking over the horizon and still the drizzle hammered them. "Now hold on ladies, continued Hemming, those passing inspection catch a ninety six hour pass. Now you can bitch and moan or hop to. That's all she wrote, COMPANY ATTENTION!" Two hundred fifty pairs of and caked boots crashed in thunderous unison. "COMPANY DISMISSED!!"

As one the grunts sprinted to their assigned quarters and quickly shedding their filthy utilities down to their skivvies. Quickly they commenced field stripping weapons. Tooth brushes, q-tips, cotton rags, their momentary weapons of choice. They attacked rust, lint, and mud, grime, working feverishly and timelessly. Their exhaustion forgotten with the lure of four days of R&R overcame whatever fatigued possessed them. Broken Rose, LaPore, LeBron and LeSage sat in a far corner laboring on their equipment. There could be no oversight here. A piece of lint, a speck of rust would confine them to the base. Weapons and equipment inspections were a marine's nightmare. Officers and senior noncoms zeroed in on any flaw no matter how trivial.

LeBron puffing on a Lucky, suddenly sat upright, "God damn, mother fuckers, the devils gonna have our asses." "Why?" questioned

LeSage. Because shit for brains, How we gonna get this Webb gear dry in time and those satanic fiends knows it."

Broken Rose sat quiet, and then slowly rose from his squat position. "Not to worry my black brother." That said, he sprinted out the hatchway, at a run, his travels took him to the mess hall where he quickly found Gunnery Sergeant Lucca in his kitchen. "Hey Tonto what brings the red man to my play pen?" "Gunny we need your help. Will you, can you?" "Shoot savage one. What's the skinny?" "Gunny we've just returned from the boondocks and our gear is as wet as the river runs wild." "Weapons and equipment inspection at 09:00 hours prompt." The gear will never dry. "Hmm, the Gunny finger to his mouth, thought long and hard. "No problem my savage friend, we'll bake em." "What? What'd you mean gunny?" "Simple, we'll dry that shit in my ovens." "Damn gunny, may the Great Spirit bless you." "Whoa, whoa, my Indian friend, it'll cost each man two packs of Luckies." Broken Rose smiled, "no sweat Gunny this is one time, Indian grateful for the cavalry."

The word spread through the company area soon designated runners from each quonset hut leader with Webb gear were double timing to the mess. Standing in the shadows, Lieutenant Sisco, the company XO along with 1st Sergeant Miller observed with amusement. Sisco chuckled out loud, "Well Top they're learning. They're becoming marines." "Yes sir, your right, but all in all it's a bitter price they pay to die for their country."

0900 sharp the company stood at ram rod straight attention with perfect alignment. They were in impressive formations. Boots shined and glistening in the early morning sun. Fresh pressed utilities along with faces pink and clean shaven. One would never guess they'd arrived only hours before from Hells playpen in the field. 1st Lieutenant Sisco with 1st Sergeant Miller conducted the inspection. Weapons crisply snapped back and forth were checked thoroughly. Webb belts and canteen covers and cups, invaded by prying eyes and quick hands, even leggings were checked for mud smears or minuscule pieces of debris. 1st Sergeant Miller even checked ears for cleanliness. Nothing was skipped or missed. Finally after nearly two hours Lieutenant Sisco and his top soldier moved and took position to the front of the company. Sisco eyed his company made eye contact with Broken Rose, "P.F.C. Broken Rose front and center." Broken Rose took two steps back wheeled about and sprinted to the front and halting one pace short and now eyeball to eyeball with his XO. The lieutenant peered over Broken Rose. "Men the inspection I'm pleased to say went well. I want you to know the past two weeks have been tough I know you did well, real well. Before you're dismissed, it is my honor to promote PFC Broken Rose to the rank of Corporal. He merits this promotion because he has demonstrated leadership abilities and has outshone everyone in this command." Leaning in close to Broken Rose, He whispered, "That was smart blowing on your Webb gear to get it dry." With a soft smile the lieutenant offered his hand congratulations. I'm sure it doesn't end here. Oh here are two packs of Luckies for Gunny Lucca.

Broken Rose displayed no emotion, but his respect for Lieutenant Sisco went up several decimals. The son of a bitch knew. Sisco turned to the Top, "Alright first Sergeant, dismiss the troops and let em roll." 1st Sergeant Mill/er in a deep authoritative voice thundered, "ATTENTION—YOU MEN PICK UP YOUR LIBERTY CARDS IN MY OFFICE! HAVE A GOOD TIME! COMPANY DISMISSED!" The company took two steps rearward and with a thunderous cry rose from the ranks. "Urara! Urara! Urara!" In seconds the street was deserted. Liberty hungry young marines poured into quarters exchanging field utilities for class A's. Happy whoops and back slapping ruled the moment. RR is a marine's perpetual dream and they were on their way. Broken Rose, LeBron, LeSage had gathered round their footlockers. LeBron and LaPore had quickly donned their forest green uniforms and were busy making adjustments in the mirror. "Hey bro's, barked LeBron, how come you two ain't prettying your selves up?" His question was directed at LeSage and the Rose. "Aw we're too tired and don't feel like moving is all, was LeSage response. We're just gonna hang here and catch up on some sack time."

"Shit that's bull shit," shrilled LeBron. Man there's living out there. Damn you've got to separate yourself from this shit. Otherwise your section eight outta here. Come on you refobates there's poo-tang out there. I can smell it. Got to get some otherwise your get blue balls and your dick shit the bed. Naw, you guys go ahead and have some fun. Me and Tonto here, be fine." LeBron twirled in front of the mirror. "God Damn, I look good. Them broads gonna wet themselves. Minute they set eyes on old Jake." "Knock' em dead." "Aw well fuck sit here and play with yourselves. Hey, LaPore is you ready?" "Yeah, Jake I'm good to go. Let's shake, rattle, and roll outta here." Broken Rose blocked their path, "where my brothers going?" "Oh hell, we're just hitching a ride to Fayetteville. Just a stone's throw from here. Check the dump out see what's cooking and hooking. Ha, Ha, Ha, I'm a poet and I don't even know it."

Broken Rose stood quiet as LaPore and LeBron disappeared through the hatchway. He remained standing staring at the hatchway door swaying in a gentle breeze. He returned to his bunk. LeSage sat on his foot locker engrossed in writing a letter. "That to your girl, Lee?" "Naw, John ain't got one. Dear John-ed me on the rock." "Oh, yeah sorry didn't mean to ignite bad memories." "Oh shit John it's nothing wasn't anything just two kids groping at life. I don't blame her. "Hey, let her enjoy her high school events. It's only once in a life time. She's there I'm here. What can you do? Say John what'll we gonna do? We staying here or are we going to skedaddle?" "Lee, I was thinking on going to the woods, you know, rest easy with the critters. Enjoy the night breeze and the starlight. Get close to my kin. Do my Indian thing. Get my drift?" "Yeah John I do. Hey, let me come. Let me share and learn some of your Indian ways. Come on

John. You can show me the wonders of the pastel forest. Me being a city boy. There are lots I could learn. Come on bro, say yes." Broken Rose sat quiet with a smile on his face. "Fine Lee, come along. We bring only knives, salt, water and smokes for you. We live off the land. If you're hesitant then best you remain here." "No, no, John, I really would like to join you." "Fine, line up your gear and let's slither out of here."

Broken Rose and LeSage headed west into the heart of camp Lejeune woodlands. Soon they were deep in the forest where the sweet smell of pine and flowers welcomed them. Various birds sang and chatted. Crows squawked their warnings regarding their presence. They walked in silence. Broken Rose deep in thought. His spirit was not of this moment and he had retreated back to another time, another place. LeSage remained close but silent. He'd come to understand the Rose's moods and solemn ways. He was startled as Broken Rose spoke. "Always watch the stars they guide you. Remember moss clings on the north side of the tree. Listen for the sound of birds. If all is quiet something is wrong. Follow the lay of the land. One blade of grass out of place tells you something. Listen to the forest, it conceals many secrets and reveals little. You must learn to adopt and accept its ways. The shifting winds. The sighs of the bushes and trees. Study the animals; they can lead you to water and shelter. Learn to mask your shadow, it may save you one day. Listen to the call of the critters and gauge if they are distant or close. Never take the forest for granted. Move slowly and stealthy, for she is a master at camouflage and concealment. Embrace her. Respect her. Protect her. For she will provide food, shelter, and refuge from the elements and maybe someday cover from an enemy warrior. Learn where it is wise to bed safe to eat. Learn to use the forest as a blanket, a tarp to shield yourself from preying eyes and black hearts. Learn to respect the creatures that inhabit this design of great beauty. Know that no man should starve in the woods, or thirst. The forest provides for the critters and one may have to adopt the critters ways to survive, but in doing he will survive. Long to go my ancestors found that the Great Spirit dances and exist where the heart of the forest beats. For many, many moons, my people have searched for this great heart only to embrace failure and great disappointment were their reward. But as you Christians search for your God's hiding place, it is as one to us Indians search for the heart of the Great Spirit.

They stumbled on a gurgling stream bed surrounded by brush and lilies and numerous other flowers. Dark had silently arrived and night frogs began their serenade. They both built crude lean twos and ignited a fire between the two. Hungry they dined on berries and some beef jerky they'd brought along. Broken Rose had also picked mushrooms and had uncovered a fistful of wild onions. The taste of these morsels fried was fulfilling. LeSage lay back inhaling the sounds of the forest listening to the yip-yip of coyotes off in the distance along with the mixed musical calls of night birds that filled the night. The hoot, hoot, of an owl, who gilded by silently through the quiet night was an amazing sight. This was a sight that Broken Rose was familiar with, but it made LeSage stare in pure awe.

LeSage relaxing against his make shift bed of leaves and pine needles while his mind in over drive with thoughts of home and family. He missed the comforting presence of his parents with their warmth and laughter. They provided a safe and secure environment enhanced with each others love. His thoughts brought him to remember his first love Chris and how life was treating her. He felt a sudden nostalgia for he shared a young pure love with this girl. But fate and life had other plans and each had traveled their own byway. He was startled by sudden movement and sat up right and then relaxed. Broken Rose was adding wood to their dying fire. The wood crackled and snapped with tongues of flames that danced in the night. The warmth felt comforting as he gazed in awe as he saw Broken Rose wearing just a loin cloth and had painted himself with berry juice. Standing up right his arms rose to the heavens. LeSage listened to the musical chanting of his friend. He knew he had crossed to the other side and was calling to his ancestors. LeSage smiled in his small refuge. He loved this man and felt safe and secure in his presence. The sigh of the wind and soft guttural sing song of Broken Rose lulled him to sleep. He felt contented and knew he'd forged a bond with this man warrior forever.

LaPore and LeBron had hitched a ride with a Jay Hedges, a soul brother in another company, He and LeBron had hit it off once they'd discovered they both were from Brooklyn. LaPore sat in the rear listening to their excited nervous chatter. LaPore was unsure of the vehicle for it was an old beat up Chevy. The floor boards all but gone and the upholstery chewed to pieces by who knows what. The two rear tires were as bald as a babies' shining new born ass. The rear passenger operated the windshield wipers by yanking on strings. Firing up a Lucky, he joined in the on the conversation. "So say gyrenes, where we headed?" LeBron turned in his seat with his white teeth flashing a huge smile. "Where we going, LaPore, whiteys can't come. We gonna drop you at the edge of town. Whiteys don't like us darkies contaminating their world. So we pick you up about 2300 hours tonight. Be where we drop you. Got that?" "Man! Fuck, I don't think I want to be alone. What the fuck chuck? Don't know no one here or the town. What the Christ I'm gonna do?" "Look Lance we gonna get us some pussy but its dark pussy. Honky's ain't welcome, so sorry, that's how it is. You'll be fine. Just smile and bat those blue eyes of yours. You'll be a okay."

Hedges pulled over to the shoulder. LaPore stepped out on the grassy shoulder. "Okay, my man, the towns that away. He pointed west, about a mile down this road. Have fun and we'll catch you at 23:30 hours, Semper-Fi." The old Chevy groaned as it lurched forward. Both tail lights were out. "Fuck thought LaPore these good ole boy cops gonna get their asses." LaPore at a quick step took off down the old broken down road. Debris lined the shoulders. Burn out tracks zigzagged endlessly. Oil blotches gave the road a nasty forlorn personality. He trudged on. Several pickups passed, but sailed by. "Fuck em," he thought. "fucken red neck farmers, anyway." H came to a small dented sign covered in bush. Welcome to Fayetteville, population who knows. He found himself standing at a cross roads. Ahead lie what appeared to be a business district. So he headed in that direction. Quickening his gait, he was soon within the business districts perimeter. He passed a general store. A small convenience store and an old one pump dilapidated gas station. Wrecked vehicles lay in various positions all about the premises. Two workers gaped at his uniform. His wave was ignored. He saw a neon sign about a block ahead and honed on it. As he grew closer, he could see it was a White Castle Restaurant. "Fucking a," he thought a chow stop and I'm hungry. He entered through a squeaky glass door. Once inside he stopped. Surveying the interior, the walls were dirty gray and were screaming for paint. The tiled floor was chipped and stained showing its wear for years of service. Three ceiling fans hummed in unison, straining to distribute cool air. Only one customer sat at the far end. He could hear soft music wafting low from the kitchen. He took a seat at the counter and reaching for a small cardboard menu. "Hey. Hey you." It was the old man calling to him. He swiveled on his chair and was staring at the old man. The old man was stooped over his meal and you could see bits of crumbs in his beard. His clothes were pock marked with numerous unidentifiable stains. His ears were large and he had a bulbous nose criss crossed with bluish veins. His boots were torn and muddy. When he spoke his voice was raspy. "Hey, you a fucking soldier boy?" "No sir, I'm a marine." "Marine, soldier boy, what the fucks the difference? You all end up cannon fodder." He began to laugh, which brought on a wheezing and coughing spell with phylum dripping from his nose on his soil jacket. LaPore sat bemused, "this was one poor fucking civilian."

He was startled by a soft feminine voice. She had slipped up quietly. "Don't let him rattle you. He's our town bum. We feed him out of pity. He's got nobody or nothing. Nothing at all and he's a loser." LaPore swiveled around and was looking into the face of an angel. She had brownish hair with big oval gray eyes that sparkled and danced. Her smile was captivating. "Well, sir, how can I help you?" LaPore was tongue tied. She smiled, "Come on marine, I know you're hungry. What'll you have?" "What do you have," he stammered. "Well we've got home made stew, choice burgers, fixed as you likes' em. We've got a large assortment of sandwiches and homemade corn chowder. What's your pleasure?" "Yeah right. Okay, give me a bowl of the chowder and a burger with raw onion and ketchup, well done, please." "Sure and to drink?" "Oh how about a Dr. Pepper?" "Oh no, down here it's Mister Pips, same thing though, that be alright?" "Fine, that'll be great." "Okay, General, be back in a jiff. Oh want a coffee while you wait?" "Yeah, great. Make it light with two sugars." "Got it." He watched as she flitted away, she had a nice posterior, no question. She had a dancer's leg full and muscular. Her waist was thin and though she tried could not conceal ample breasts.

LaPore lit up a Lucky and began to hum. The waitress laughed as she set his coffee before him. "That song you're humming, that played its course long ago." "Yeah but I always liked it." "What's it called?" "Oh, "I'm Coming Home." "Oh yeah, where is home?" She made no effort to leave. "Oh I'm from Oakland." "Wow California!" "Yeah that right." "Gosh, you're a long way. Got a girl?" "No, no I don't?" "Well, you must miss your family." "Nope, don't have one of them either." Her smile faded the sparkle in her eyes dimmed. "Come on, you'd got to have a family." "Oh, I do, I do." "You said you didn't." "Well, you see my mom and dad were killed in an auto accident when I was 12. I'm an orphan and the Marines Corps is now my family." "Oh God, I'm so sorry. I always ask the wrong questions." "No, no that's okay. How 'bout you? Boyfriend, husband, what's your gig?" "No boyfriends and no husband either, I'm not ready to play house." LaPore sipped his coffee. "Don't take offense. But what's your name?" "Oh it's Jean. Jean Simmond, What's yours?" "Lance,

Lance LaPore." "Well, Lance LaPore from Oakland, it's nice meeting you. Oh, here's your lunch."

A large burly man had appeared with the meal. "Oh, Lance this is my dad and we work the restaurant and have an apartment in the rear. It works out well for us." Lance extended his hand. "My name is Lance." The older man wiped his hand on his apron and then griped LaPore in a vice like grip. "Nice to meet you. Just passing through?" "No sir, I've got a four day pass and I'm new to this area of the country and I am curious to see what makes it tick. You know see the sights. Meet people get a feeling and a heartbeat of the community." "Are your staying here all four days?" LaPore looked at Jean. "I'd like to, but I'm a target and know no one." Jean jumped in, "There's a nice motel two doors down. Very reasonable rates, I think you'll like it. There's a pond in the rear and the rooms are clean and neat."

Jean's father had moved back into the kitchen to continue his cooking duties. "Look Jean, I don't mean to be presumptuous, but I'm lonely, and I've only a short stay and I've never spent time with a girl, never had the chance. Could you, me, maybe spend some time together? Maybe a show, or a dance, or just a walk is it possible?" Her eyes twinkled, "Sure Lance, why not. Name your desire." "Well, your work is just about done here. How about I take you to supper tonight?" She mulled it over in her mind, "that would be awesome." "Okay, where?" "There's a nice restaurant, the cabin in the sky. It's up on that mountain, good food and they have a three piece band." "Yeah, Jean, how do we get to it?" She laughed softly, "look you get checked in at the motel, rest and refresh yourself and I'll pick you up at 7:00 o'clock, if that is agreeable." "Hell yeah, I'm beat. I can cop six hours of sack time." "My poor tired marine, go sack out and I'll see you at 7:00." She whirled and was off to another customer.

LaPore lay on his bed, his mind whirling in excitement. His stomach did leaps and bounds with butterflies. He was both nervous and excited at the same time. He fired up a Lucky and stared out the window where a family of ducks scrambled in the pond. Clutches of fatigue took hold of him and stuffing out his cigarette in a chipped ashtray, his thoughts of a gray eyed girl lulled him into a contented sleep.

After dumping LaPore, LeBron and Hedges cruised deep into the heart of the colored section of town. They were appalled at the conditions that confronted them. Rickety shanty shacks lined the streets. Some had wooded roofs that showed the beginning of decay. Most of the wood showed evidence of dry rot and the roofs warped and ready to collapse. The lucky ones possessed tin roofs but had rust and the brutality of weather. They showed signs of wear and tear. Residents sat in front of the dwellings, most with the thousand yard stare seeing nothing. Children playing in mud covered walks, some half naked and some in clothes that reeked of filth and poverty. Malnourished dogs skittered through and fro barking at them as they drove slowly pass. "God damn Hedges, this place makes Brooklyn look like the lords paradise. These poor brothers is fucked up. What the fuck, look at the young sister over there. Can't weigh 80 lbs., shit let's get outta here. This is bad shit. Hell critters live better than this." "Yeah Jake heard about this shit, didn't believe it. Man, this is just wrong, ain't human, red neck whiteys responsible. Shit why we in this uniform? Fuck white mother fuckers use us for camel fodder." "Oh come on, there's good honkeys. Hey, LaPore, LeSage, there's good and bad everywhere my brother, you knows that." ""Hey! Screamed Jake, slow down! Yeah, hook a right here." "Why mother?" "Because, look at the pretty dude over yonder by that rib wagon." "Where"? "Damn, are you blind or stupid, that mother fucker standing over there with the yellow pants, purple jacket, and with the white hat." "Yeah, what about the dude, boy that there is Mr. Pimp and he gonna supply us with some good young pussy. Pull up on him. He sees us coming and he's creaming in his pants knows business is in town."

Hedges pulled alongside the wagon. The older man stood stock still. "What you soldier boys want?" LeBron stepped out and walked briskly around the front of the Chevy. He halted two feet from his query. "Look brother, don't go dumb nigger on me. You know what we wants. Something young and clean like. And don't fuck with us, because I'll cut your balls off and feed em to those skinny dogs we passed!" "Whoa boy, don't get pissy on old Doc Buzz in here. Got just what you want, two brown girls, big tits, and ass. Give you both a ride in the sunshine." "Old man, where and what's the price?" "See that white shanty thereabouts?" "Yeah, pop I see it." "They be there two nice beds. Gonna cost you cash, $15 dollars up front. No Bartering. You takes it or leaves it." Jake laughed, "grandfather, here's $30 bucks. Best they've be clean, ready and good. Oh Jake needs to be happy. As I said, don't fuck with us." "No problem boys, we don't fuck with soldier boys."

Hedges spat out the car window. Dumb mother fucker, we's marines, shit for brains, Oh so scary marines, the best." They were ushered into the shack LeBron went to his right Hedges to his left. The interior was poorly lighted. Two candles burning supplied a hazy soft glow. As their eyes adjusted, they revealed two young girls naked lying on straw beds waiting to ply their trade. Both Hedges and LeBron stripped naked. Their hunger displayed by swollen hardened testicles and penises. There was little fan fair or foreplay. They mounded the young flesh beneath and began pumping like pistons. Grunts and groins emitted loudly from the shack. Finally the two brothers exploded almost simultaneously. They pulled themselves upright and dressed quickly. LeBron stared at the girls. He elbowed Hedges, "God damn bro, them bitches be only 13 and 14." "Aw fuck it Jake. Pussy, is pussy and they be happy they gonna eat tonight."

LeBron was angry, wasn't his appetite to fuck a child, as they exited the shack. They saw Dr. Buzzard, the pimp, standing by a small fire. He was alone and as LeBron surveyed the area, he realized no one was about. He nudged Hedges and raised his fingers to his lips, "shh, shh, shh." Then in a flash was on the pimp. A chop to the back of the neck and the Buzzard collapsed in a heap. LeBron searched quickly and his hands groping, finally he found what he wanted. He pulled a wallet from a vest pocket and snatched a wad of green backs. He estimated maybe $300 dollars in contents. Hedges stood silent, then, Jake your crazy man. This mother fucker probably got strong arms nearby. "Fuck em. We ain't staying." He ran toward the shack. "Jake, what's you doing?" Running up to the girls he flipped two fifty dollar bills on the floor. "That's for you girls and you never saw us." Then he and Hedges jumped into the old Chevy and in a flume of dust were gone.

Dr. Buzzard awoke an hour later wondering what the fuck had hit him. He suspected but his profession negated him from going to the police. "God damn bitches, never find em. Them's being 30 thousand swinging dicks in that camp. Fuck, maybe they'll get the fucken clap."

Hedges had the pedal to the metal. The old Chevy quivered and rattled aborning all but the old engine could only reach 60 mph. Hedges kept his eye to the rear view mirror. "Jake you're a damn fool. They catches you and you're a dead man." Jake chuckled loudly, "Well you know bro, I'm a black man born, I'm a black man bred, and when I die, I'll be a black man dead. Drive on James, they never gonna catch us. Mother can't call the cops and sure as Hell's fire he ain't coming to Lejeune to fuck with thirty thousand marines. We good boys, we be good." "Jake, where to now?" "Aw, let's drive down to Raleigh and see some sights." "Yeah, what about LaPore?" "What about him? He'll be okay; some bitch probably got his balls on fire. Go ordered Jake, drive numb nuts for the further we get from here the better." "Right on bro." The old Chevy sputtering and coughing sped into the night.

They rode about 10 miles in silence a soft wind waltzed through the tree tops. Then rain drops began to pelt the windshield. LeBron grabbed the string and worked the windshield. Its motor had died long ago. Hedges turned and looked at his friend. "Jake why'd you fuck up that dude back there?" Jack reminisced silently then exhaled a loud sigh, "because that mother fucker sold us children. Lord, my soul is as black as my ass. I fucked a child, Hedges, a fucking child. That's wrong as all hell." Hedges stared into the night. "Damn Jake, why'd you do it then?" "Because a dick has no conscious and man that pussy looked good. Now I'm fucked up in the head." "Aw Jake, come on it is what it is. That's the way it is down here." "That's bullshit Hedges. That's the way it is everywhere. Young black girls being exploited not only by that shit head we left behind, but in every city and town in the good old U.S.A." Brothers abuse young black girls along with whites. Mother fucker, we just did. Just drive Hedges. Get us to Raleigh. A dude told me about a swinging soul bar. I needs to get drunk, cleanse myself. Shit, I'm training to protect kids like that." "How we gonna do that, Jake? Society and whites and our own kind won't let us." LeBron tilted his head back on the head rest ingesting Hedges words. He fell into a fitful sleep and he had no answer to his question.

He woke suddenly from a deep sleep. LaPore rubbed his eyes and at first he was disorientated grasping at where he was. He lay still gazing at the white ceiling and his eyes scanning the light green walls slowly. He realized he was in a motel. He rose from the bed and headed for the head where he splashed cold water on his face and relieved himself. He walked to the picture window and gazed at the pond located only yards from his room. He pulled on his trousers and exited the rear door and headed to the pond where a family of ducks swam slowly and contentedly close to shore. He inhaled the comforting scent of flowers which grew in clusters by the water's edge. A small bench beckoned to him, so he sat. Fumbled for his cigarettes and fired up a Lucky and inhaled deeply. LaPore sat quietly enjoying the calm solitude of the moment. His mind wandered and soon he traveled back through the hands of time, which placed him in the presence of his adopted parents years ago. He remembered the happy times, the love, the laughter, the bond of family. He felt a chill of sorrow deep within his chest. The sad call of a morning dove, calling to his lost mate added to the melancholy that had seized his conscious. Stubbing out his smoke, he whispered enough of this. He stood his mind snapping a photograph of this lovely quiet place. "Hey gyrene, you've got a date?" He turned and strolled briskly back to his room.

He enjoyed a hot shower basking in its warmth, remaining still for half an hour relishing the sting of the warm water cleansing his body and soothing aching muscles and refurbishing his spirit. Stepping from the shower, he shaved and rinsed his mouth with a small bottle of mouthwash supplied by the motel. He patted various parts of his anatomy with a pleasing after shave. His toilet completed, he dressed quickly donning his forest green uniform. He gazed at himself in a full size mirror attached to the inner side of the bathroom door. "Ur-rah," he growled satisfied with the mirror image peering back at him. He sat in a high back chair with the cushion hard, but comfortable. He lit up a cigarette and gazed at a small wall clock which read 6:30. His heart skipped a beat. Jean was to pick him up at 19:00 hours. His heart stuck in his throat. Would she show? He sat quiet and watched as the North Carolina sun began its slow descent beyond the pond and in the semi darkness waited.

He was dreaming someone was knocking on his door. He stood opening his cobwebbed eyes. He'd dozed off. There it was again a knock on his door. He sprung from the chair and in two steps he was opening the door. He drew in a breath. There she stood with a wide smile displaying perfect teeth. She had on a rose colored dress which hung just above the knee and black leather boots with pearl earrings dangled from small ears. Her gray eyes twinkled with mischief. "Well marine, ready to roll?" "Oh yeah Jean, all set. Gee you look good." He felt heat at the neck and knew he was blushing. Why I thank you. You look quite the hunk yourself uniform fits you well. Well come on I got my motor running and I made reservations at the restaurant for 8:00 o'clock so we've got to fly." Slamming the door, he took hold of her hand. They walked the short corridor to the main entrance and stepped into the night. "Over there, the yellow duster." "Damn, that's cool Jean, yours?" "Hell yeah, she's my baby." She looked up at him. "Hey you gotta a license want to drive?" Naw, you drive, I don't know where the hell we're going, but you do. You know the lay of the land. I'll just ride shotgun and enjoy the scenery." "Okay, big boy, buckle up. I like's too let my baby run free." "Say what?" "You'll see," as she positioned herself behind the wheel and hit the accelerator. The car lurched forward with a powerful thrust and exploded in a cloud of dust onto the highway. LaPore sat tight. This girl was under a rock. In no time the meter read 80 mph. "Damn girl what's your rush?" "Lance oh boy, I'm hungry, why the big marine scared?" Lance chuckled then turning, "Yeah, shit there's only a thin rail and I'm seeing the shoulder and we/re climbing a mountain." "Good show there jar-head, we're going to the cabin in the sky, remember? And that's where the crib sets. Where the sky kisses the mountain, not to sweat I'll get you there in one piece. After all you're buying so stop crying."

He laughed aloud; this girl was an okay, chick and no prude or nerd. She was a hellion and he looked forward to a jovial evening. Jean had the pedal to the metal and road signs and brush were a blur as they roared through the night. Lance sat staring straight ahead. He was cognoscente of the deep gorge just feet from where he sat. He was jolted upwards when Jean shifted down suddenly and made a hard right into a large parking lot. The lot was surrounded by tall pines and maples. She cruised slowly and found a parking place close to the entrance and killed the engine.

"Ok handsome we're here. Hey buy a lady a dinner?" He smiled, "that's what we're here for, I thought." He caught a glimpse of an ample thigh as she slid from the wheel. His mouth dry, he'd never been alone with a girl in his life. He feared she could hear his heart beating. His adrenaline flowing through his veins had him wired. "Damn need to gear down and get control." They approached the entrance where the maître de stood posed with a beaming friendly smile. "Hi Jean, got you a table over in the north corner where you can view the valley, if that is okay?" "Oh wonderful Paul, thank you." "Follow me." He led them through a large dining area where dozens of eyes honed in on them. He stopped at an oval table close to a large glass picture window which spanned halt the room. "Here you are love birds, enjoy." He held the chair out for Jean. Lance sat himself. "Enjoy you meal and the view." He bowed slightly and sauntered off. Lance surveyed the room. High chandlers casted a soft light from the ceilings and the rug was a reddish hue and had to be three inches thick. The walls were mahogany and adorned with expensive paintings. In the south corner was a stage where a three piece band was setting up. Waiters and bus boys were going from table to table and applying their trade. "Yup, a 5 star restaurant," he thought. He gazed out the window and was looking into a lush valley. The moon light added a surreal setting. He could see tall pines and maples. Maybe even a cluster of oaks. He could tell the brush would contain gardens of flowers, hidden by the tarp of night. He turned and faced Jean, she was studying him. Her lips compressed in a slight smile. "Beautiful don't you think?" "Yeah Jean it sure is. Hey, that Paul guy, you know him?" She emitted a soft chuckle, "Yeah he comes to my dad's restaurant every now and then." "Oh, think he's interested?" "Yeah, I do but it's a dead end for him. No spark there you know. I don't lead him on or anything. He just comes. He's a nice enough guy but he's not in my horoscope." "I see." "Lance you don't see, how can you? You don't know us or what the hell we think, do or practice." "Guess you're right, Hey Jean, don't get sour, I meant no offense. I was curious, is all." "Yeah, you're right. Hey, let's check the menus, I am starved." "Good idea, so am I."

"Oh hey Jean, what's the big white cross across the valley there, you know with the florescent lights?" She turned in the direction he was looking. "Oh Lance that's the Lord's Valley and that cross was placed there and paid for by area residents in honor of our war dead. "Oh wow, that's awesome; people here must be pretty patriotic and dedicated. Her gray eyes bore into his, "they are lance. You're getting looks of admiration from everyone in this restaurant. We appreciate our service men, especially our marines. Don't be embarrassed Lance. Around here we know that uniform stands for protection and security and we respect it."

He whispered a soft, "Thank you," and spread the menu on the table before him. He did a double take and his heart skipped a beat when the embossed entrees and prices jumped at him. He remained quiet and still in his seat. "Oh Jean would you excuse me, I need to go to the head. I mean men's room." She smiled and nodded busy studying the menu. He walked briskly to the men's room. Fortunately it was unoccupied. He yanked his wallet out of his rear pocket, opened it and began counting his fortune or misfortune. He would know in a minute. He leafed through a wad of greenbacks and breathed a sigh of relief. His back duties pay totaling $425.00. He was good to go. He checked himself in the small oval mirror directly over the sink. Okay, asshole you're with a pretty, classy girl. Cover your flanks and don't blow it.

Returning to his seat, he found her busy with the waiter, ordering for them both. "What. What'd you order for me?" She gave a throaty laugh, "You'll love it, steak, and stuffed shrimp, baked potato, salad and a cold beer. How's that for your big gullet, big boy?" "That sounds great Jean, thank you." The waiter came and stood by Lance. "I've got to ask you know about the beer and all? How old are you?" A deep menacing voice responded from an adjoining table. A large farmer type male sat with his wife staring at the waiter. "He's wearing that uniform, he's old enough. The waiter snapped his book shut, "Yeah guess he's right," and quickly marched off.

They ate slowly each wanting the moment to last with the flame of a burning candle casting a golden hue on their faces. Music wafted through the restaurant and both rose from the table. He led her to the dance floor where they meshed in each others arms. The dancing of soft strings of, "In the Still of The Night" played throughout the restaurant," at their request the band continued with this melody repeatedly. It was as if they were alone embracing and dancing on a cloud. Patrons watched in silence and they were mesmerized by the music and movements of such an attractive couple. Soon the lights dimmed and the hour was at hand. It was time lights dimmed and it was time to leave. They drove to the motel in silence. Their mood somber each experiencing feelings they'd never known. The red neon light of the motel acted as a beacon and Jean slid the duster smoothly stopping in front of the entrance. LaPore took her hand. "It was a nice evening Jean. I've three days left. Might I see you again?" She smiled in the darkness, "sure Lance, I'll call." He exited the vehicle never looked back and strolled through the entrance continuing through the lobby and he exited the rear door heading to the beach. He sat heavily firing up a Lucky. He gazed at the pond which illuminated by a full moon with a symphony of frog calling to each other, his only company. He needed to think reflect. Feelings never known to him coursed through his being. He felt contented but fearful, afraid that Jean wouldn't call. He watched quietly and intently as a family of raccoon's approached, ignoring him, they proceeded to quench their thirst with their soft lapping of water relaxing him. He was confused for newly minted marines fresh from basic training find civilian life contemptibly lax, one marine friend had commented. This place makes no sense, people slouch, doors close in front of old women, people are too fat. I hate the rudeness the chaos, field stripping his butt. He headed to his room. He felt suddenly alone and the scent of Jean still strong in his nostrils with his stomach in cartwheels. "God," he realized he liked this girl. He never hit the light switch upon entering his room and stripping in the dark, he climbed into the bed. Lighting up a Lucky, he stared in the dark at nothing. Her face kept reappearing and sleep would not come.

He had dozed off but was jolted from his fitful slumber by a soft tapping on his door. LaPore listened intently, yes there it was again. Tap, tap, tap, he bolted from the bed pulling on his trousers in the dark. He stepped quietly to the door. His body coiled and he was in alert mode and was in the defensive posture. He could not imagine who could be at the door. Then he relaxed when he heard Jean with a soft voice say "Lance it's me Jean. Please open the door. Still in an adrenaline rush, he flung open the door. She stood looking up at him with a beautiful smile on her face. He could see in the dark hallway lights she had changed, shedding her rose dress. For red shorts and a tee shirt. She looked beautiful with her legs a golden tan and her hair flowing to her shoulders. "Hi, can I come in?" And she pushed by him and he closed the door shut and switched on a small table lamp. The soft light illuminated their shadows dancing on the wall as she moved towards him and fell into his arms. Their mouths found each other and their lips entwined in a lingering kiss. Arms reached out and pulled each other hard and close. Emotions and desires exploded. Soon they were tearing off clothing and she stood naked in the soft light. He marveled at her beauty admiring the fullness of her breast and the silk triangle that cloaked her secret place. With frenzy, he lifted her off the floor and spurted to the bed where he laid her gently on her back. He crawled beside her and immediately their hands began probing, exploring each others bodies. His loins were on fire. He tenderly sucked on her breast greedily and she moaned and threshed on the bed in a sexual frenzy. His tongue lapped at her with an inhibited hunger. His fingers found her honey pot and he began to probe deeply enjoying the warmth and wetness.

She screamed with passion and pulled him to her. She could not believe how LaPore made her feel at that moment, for all she knew she must have him and not a moment to wait. He entered her gently at first but then his cock hungry for release began to pump her harder and deeper. She wrapped her legs around him attempting to pull him further and further within her. Their breath came in spasms and they were experiencing a pleasure never known to them. The moon light cast a glow on their bodies which sheened with body sweat and fluids from their torrid love making. With loud gasps of pleasure they exploded together, sharing the ecstasy of human love and giving. He collapsed on top of her. Their hearts beating as one, slowly their labored breathing subsided and they nestled in each others arms. They lay quiet as she stroked his head tenderly. Both enjoying and savoring the afterglow. He lit a Lucky and offered her one, she declined. He gazed into her grayish eyes trying to read her true feelings. She smiled and cooed soft loving words to him. He stroked her flanks and he felt safe, warm, and content. In his young life he'd never experienced such a wondrous fulfillment.

She looked small and vulnerable in the large bed and in that moment he knew he wanted to be with her and safe guard her. He raised himself on his elbow devouring her nakedness with his eyes thankful and delighted with her young ripe beauty. They embraced and curled up close making small talk in the quiet solitude of their small refuge. She told him how she lived and worked with her dad and had tried to take care of him and fill the deep void that afflicted him with the loss of his wife to cancer ten years before. "I was nine at the time," she told him. "I thought it was the end of my world." He could relate for his mind drifted back to the death of his adopted parents. How he'd been placed in an orphanage and how he'd searched for his biological mother, to no avail. It was futile. She'd disappeared from his life. He felt wetness on his chest. Tears coursed down Jean's face as she recollected the loss of her mom. Lance pulled her tight to him. "You know honey life is completely weird. A person lives 60 years and does all kinds of things, sees all kinds of things and knows all kinds of things. Then in a heartbeat it's over. Just like that. He reached over and snapped off the light. Moonlight flooded the room in a hazy glow. They snuggled close and she pecked his cheek. "Hey, big boy I'm off tomorrow." "Hot damn, that's great Jean, we'll spend it together." "Doing what?" She asked with a chuckle. He pulled her to him and, "a lot more of this."

The wind rattled the window pane. Rain began to beat a tat-tat on the roof and some where an owl hooted. There was the mournful wail of a train in the distance and in the semi darkness young love planted its seed. With the morning sunrise would bloom and grow.

Time has a way of never standing still and their treasured moments together were carried by the wind. Their time together was spent making love and having simple meals. Jean had brought him to her home where he got to spend time with her dad. They'd had a pleasant meal and evening together. Their last night they spent by the pond giggling at the musical chorus of frogs and staring in awe at shooting stars as they swept through the heavens. They held each other tight content in each other's arms. Near midnight they returned to their lover's sanctuary and under a starlet sky whispered words of endearment. Nothing in this world compares to a new found love and karma had directed their fate and they'd fallen in love. At the bus terminal they embraced long and hard. Reluctant to separate, "Jean honey I'll come every liberty. We're not so far apart and you know I love you." She smiled her gray eyes boring into his. "I love you, Lance. I'll be here and I don't want to let you go from my arms," as he started to board the bus. They're eyes locked and he disappeared into the dark interior. She watched as the bus roared into the dawn mist. A rope of exhaust followed and she stood transfixed honing on the behemoths taillights. They grew smaller and smaller as they twinkled in the semi-darkness as they disappeared swallowed in the distance.

Slowly green clad figures filtered through the main gate. Their ninety six over, most had solemn forlorn looks on their faces resigned that they were returning to a world of regimentation and discipline. LeBron had hooked up with LaPore, "that's what sucks about liberty, LaPore, You've got to come back to this world of insane shit." LaPore chuckled, "so Jake how was your parole time?" "Aw, it was okay, what the fuck man? Ain't much for a colored guy to do down here, signs everywhere whites only. Colored sit in the back and even have separate water fountains. That's just wrong! Fucken brothers die and bleed red same as whites." "I know Jake, maybe one day some righteous honest God fearing dude will right all this. This is why we're here in a way. Hope springs eternal old shoe. Guy's after us all trying and giving to end such bigoted injustice." "Yeah too many hateful mother fuckers, hey, there's LeSage and Broken Rose." "Yeah, squatting in front of our hut, shit they look like fucking Stewart's Rangers." The four scrambled inside anxious to share their experiences of the past four days.

Changing into field utilities, the quonset huts babbled with excited cat calls and boasts of outrageous female conquests. Sergeant Hemming had peeked in and bellowed, "Formation at 0800! Move you girly asses!" LeBron gazed at LeSage, "See, Satan never goes away, the fucker always by your side." "Jake looked at LeSage hard, "so what'd you two jungle monkeys do?" "Huh, eat snake, possum crow, all that good shit." "God damn, I think you two fuckers are under a rock. We do this shit week after week and you get a ninety six liberty and you stay in the woods. God you need to the call the man. You know the one with the little book, call em shrinks. You know why they call' em that?" "No Jake, why?" LeSage took the bait. "Because they got no balls and little tiny dicks, that's why." Broken Rose coughed lightly; he was learning the white man's ways. "Jake, you're fucked up, Lee here and I ran into a Girl Scout camp. Made it with two scout leaders for all four days." "Say what, mother fucker, you an Indian, you tell no lies?" "No Jake, I speak with forked tongue. We fished, hunted and study the ways and means of the woods and its critters. Something all of you should know." He'd raised his voice so that others preparing for formation would hear, and hear they did. The quarters went quiet. "One day my brothers, he continued, you and me are gonna be in the shit. Best you know the ways and the heart of the forest. Feel its pulse, because you better believe that other guy will." With that he stomped out of the hut. His comrades followed.

As the company fell in formation, Sergeant Hemming called the company to attention. Lieutenant Sisco took over. "Okay, your NCO'S will march you to morning chow. When you secure from that you will mount full marching packs. We're going on a little stroll and work off all that civilian shit you piled on. Now don't look harried, we're only doing 15 miles today. Why, because I feel sympathetic towards you sad sacks. Besides I've got a date with something nice. At 19:30 hours, oh, that means there'd be a lot of double time. I'm not gonna be late for this one. Take charge Sarge." "Yes Sir!" Hemming saluted and turned to the company, "Right face, forward march!"

Morning chow finished the company was double timed back to their area, where they donned full field packs. NCO's filtered through the ranks checking packs and weapons. The company was brought to attention and given the command, "Right face, forward march!" Lieutenant Sisco headed the column and set a brisk pace. The company snaked its way down the asphalt roadway and soon found themselves raising dust on entering the boondocks. As luck would have it, it began to rain and at first soft and quiet almost refreshing. Then an angry sky bellowed and rain fell like a deluge cascaded on the column. Moans and groans, and curses permeated the dismayed grunts as ponchos were broken out and weapons slung upside down. There was no reprieve as Lieutenant Sisco roared, "Double time march!" Leg muscles grew taut and stretched yelping their displeasure. Back pack straps dug into shoulders and the thump, thump of entrenching shovels tattooed their backsides. Boots were sucked into mud doubling the effect. The grunts were found to expel in order to continue on. LeBron caught Broken Rose's ear. "These fuckers are marines. I'm telling you they got their brains from pickle jars. We gonna catch that chest shit. What you call it, pneumonia. God Damn, Tonto, these feather merchants in the rear gonna get sucked under all this camel shit. How we know there's no quick sand? That fucking Lieutenant Sisco, he ain't even huffing or puffin. My balls hurt, my ass hurts, that greasy ass shit they gave us for chow stirring around my innards. Talking all kinds of shit. Fuck it! I up chuck, I up chuck." Broken Rose remained silent. He enjoyed the run. Lifted his face to the cool rain, smiling as he continued to tolerant LeBron's ranting; he knew he was good for morale and that a bitching marine is a happy marine. LeBron looked back at LaPore and LeSage trailing right behind him. "Scuttle butt has it that we going to double time up old baldy. That's that big ass mother fucker hill that tanks can't climb." "That's not its real name, Jake," uttered LaPore. "Who gives a fuck it gonna be a bitch. These critter's from Hell gonna make us all crazy. Shit, I had an uncle was in the corps in Korea. Poor fucker was insane. Used to drool and play with himself hours on end. Now I know why. These fuckers made him crazy. The run continued, with hearts pounded, lungs taxed, but the grunts persevered.

Training was proving its method and success. Their bodies were adjusting and adapting to the corps adage. What is a marine? A lean mean killing machine, Sisco finally gave the command, "route step, march!" The company continued the march at a snail's pace. Boots sucked into the mud taxing the grunts stamina. Finally, they approached old Baldy. The men called on their reserved strength and strained and groaned their way to the summit. Then reversed direction and clamored downward. The march to their area proceeded uneventful, but to the satisfaction of NCO's and officers there were no stragglers. They were dismissed to quarters and ordered to clean weapons and equipment for they were informed that after evening chow there would be a weapons and equipment inspection.

Exhausted grunts sat on foot lockers cleaning weapons and fine tuning equipment anxious for chow, for stomachs were growling and gurgling with hunger. As usual LeBron began his tirade. "Mother fuckers, but was cut short when Broken Rose approached. His amber eyes were menacing. He placed the palm of his right hand on LeBron's chest. "Jake you a good man and I believe you'll be a hell of a marine, but that word it's offensive, degrading and I don't like it." "What word Tonto?" "What word? Mother fuckers. Don't you respect your mother?" "Hell yes, Tonto. "Then why use such an ugly insulting work in your vocabulary?" "I never knew my mother, but I can revere the word for the Great Spirit breath's new life in a mother's womb. You or anyone else has no right to tarnish or degrade the word mother. My mother's spirit is a beacon in the heavens for she guides me. Her light tells me that she is ever watchful like all mothers who have gone to their reward. Honor the title, protect it, treasure it, you still have your mother. You should love her, cherish her, and keep her close to your heart. For one day she also will be a beacon in the heavens." The hut had grown silent and not a sound, not even a pin drop could be heard. LeBron open mouth stared at his friend. "John I'm sorry. You're right it's a filthy word. I picked up in the streets. Trust and believe I'll not use it again. I'll just say fuckers from now on. There was quiet laughter from the squad. Broken Rose at that moment stood tall. He patted LeBron's shoulder. "Okay brother that I can live with."

Weapons and equipment squared away, they were marched to evening chow, dining on hash, beans, some kind of meat, milk and coffee. They were then double timed back to their area where a rifle and equipment inspection was held under the command of Lieutenant Sisco. Inspection completed Sisco took his place in front of the company. "Okay, inspection wasn't bad you drag anchors are getting the word and shaping up. That is good. Now we're going to take on a little overnight get away. Now don't look so dejected. You'll have rations for two days and secure full packs and be ready to march in one hour. Oh, here's some more good news. Some marines from the regular 2nd marine division feel they've carried the right to have fun and fuck with us. So they're going to infiltrate our night defense perimeter just to show how weak and unprepared you ladies are. Okay, dismissed and formation in one hour!"

The grunts headed to their respective huts. Broken Rose, LeSage, LaPore and LeBron, headed to their rack s and began assembling full field packs. LeBron turned to LeSage, "See no sleep, no rest we go back to the shit. God damn those fuckers, spend all their free time thinking and planning how to fuck us." "No, Jake chimed in LaPore; they just want to see how much we've observed and see where we need fine tuning. You know in three weeks most of us will be posted to the F.M.F. Fleet Marines Forces. These instructors and officers and NCO's don't want egg on their faces. Well times a wasting. Hey where's Broken Rose?" "Don't know he slipped out the rear door." "Yeah, but his pack and weapons went with him. He uttered, LeSage you know Tonto. He slithers and slides while his buds debated." Broken Rose had high tailed it to their supply hut. There he approached Gunnery Sergeant Ed Cahill. "Hey Gunny, need your help real quick like." Cahill stared at Broken Rose, "Yeah what you need, Tonto?" "My sergeant sent me to get rope, 40 feet should do." "What the fuck, he's gonna repel Mt. Everest?" "Naw Gunny, some exercise he wants to demonstrate. Who's this for Sergeant Hemming?" "Yeah, right Gunny, said you'd understand." "Aw fuck him, yeah come on in back, I'll give you the rope. Don't hang yourself, ha, ha, ha."

Broken Rose doubled timed to the area just in time for formation. Sergeant Hemming eyed him curiously but said nothing. "Company attention, Right face! Sling arms! Forward march!" The company in route step march made good time and soon had entered deep into the boon docks. Night was laying its dark cloak. Crickets began their serenade. Fire fly's darted and twinkled about the ranks. The crunch, crunch of marching boots echoed in the forest. Vision was nil as the tarp of darkness now enveloped them. Still the march continued.

They came to a small stream and skirted it and found themselves climbing up a small knoll.

On reaching the summit they were greeted by a large campfire with a large Staff Sergeant standing alongside feeding logs as he watched the column approach. As they came closer he growled, "spread out and drop on your butts in a semicircle around me. DO IT NOW!" The grunts sat thankfully relieving themselves of the heavy packs. To be able to shed them for 5 minutes was paradise. "All right cannon fodder, round the sergeant, the smoking light is lit. My name is Staff Sergeant Haunchmaker. I'm here to advise on the do's and don'ts in the brush. You listen and God damn listen tight. What I tell you might just save your cherry asses. Those butts your smoking, a flame of a cigarette can be see for three miles. The smoke of a cigarette on a mountain down slope can be detected a half mile away. If you wash with soap or use after shave, a good adversary will hone in on your clean little asses and kill you dead. You wash with luke warm water if you can. The most important parts of your anatomy that you need to pay attention to are the crotch and your arm pits and feet. That's where the jungle rot will strike the hardest. Carry extra socks at all times and if you draw new footwear make God damn sure they're broken in before you replace the old. If you don't your feet will blister and you won't be worth shit. Make God damn sure your weapon is clean and ready for instant reaction. If your lax with your weapon your be wax in a box. That's of course if your ass is recovered. Now you've been told this shit over and over. Best you don't forget. Forget and your dead and maybe your buddy's too. Once more thing if your ever in a combat area and have poggie bait or gum don't discard those wrappers or feel you can bury them and be safe, that's bull shit! Somewhere out in the wild world some gung-ho highly trained adversary will track it and your company will be no more, UNDERSTAND?! Use your brains and common sense. We advise and train but it's up to you dumb-dumbs to grasp and secure this knowledge. Okay, this area is your home for the night.

Your officers and NCO's will take charge. See that you set up a decent defensive night perimeter. As you know unwelcome guests are on the march as we speak."

A soft breeze rustled through the forest and a full moon bathed the bivouac area in a golden glow. Lieutenant Sisco had posted pickets surrounding their perimeter. He'd also had his troops set up crude warning devices yards away from the perimeter. They consisted of empty c rations cans and trip flares which he hoped would give his newly minted marines ample time to repel their attackers. He was worried for he knew they were up against force recon from the 8th marines. He scanned the bivouac area. These kids are fresh from P.I. Shit there's no way we're a match."

Broken Rose lay in his pup tent. He had not closed his eyes. He listened to the deep breathing of his tent mate. LeSage had fallen into a deep sleep. He smiled they had lucked out and had been passed over for picket duty. Broken Rose sat up and removed his boots and he reached under his field pack which served as his pillow and retrieved the rope he'd requisition from supply, while his comrades enjoyed evening chow. He'd left their presence for twenty minutes and that was enough time to cut the rugged tine into five foot lengths. He removed his shirt and dog tags, strapped his k-bar to his left hip. Rising quietly he rapped the sections of rope around his waist. Lifting the rear flap of the tent, he slithered out and away into the darkness. Entering the brush, he surveyed the camp. It was a good defensive position but his Lieutenant had made a white man's mistake. A big one at that it was erected in a manner that the moon light cast shadows of the tents on the forest landscape. He studied intently and knew there would be infiltrations from the rear of their perimeter and would minimize their own exposure to moonlight. He crawled slowly, deliberately, calling to sister snake to guide and bless his movement. He crawled into a hole in the center of a small knoll. He'd blackened his face and torso with mud and leaves and only his amber eyes were left unshielded. He unsheathed his knife and coiled widths of rope in his left shoulder and waited.

The night drifted slowly into the wee hours of morning. "Ah, they come." He'd heard a faint boot step and felt the change in the air drifts to his right. He saw movement a solitary figure advancing in a crouch. Closer and closer. He sprang cupping his right hand over the infiltrators mouth. He placed his knife to his throat. "One sound even a sigh and I'll cut your throat." The figure dropped his weapon, relaxed and followed Broken Rose's instructions to kneel quietly, and hands behind his back. He was quickly secured to a tree tied and gagged. For the next two hours, Broken Rose slithered and slid, repeating his exploits, six more times. His Oscar, catch the commander of the recon infiltrators. An embarrassed 1st Lieutenant. He climbed a tree and saw silhouettes. The bulk of the attackers, crawling towards his company's perimeter. He'd begun lobbing flares and smoke grenades, he'd borrowed. His exploits lit up the night, housing his comrades and alerting the pickets. The infiltrators were lit up and completely exposed. Lieutenant Sisco and two platoons surrounded them and they were forced to surrender.

Two days later, the Force Recon Commanding Officer one Captain Dane Douglas stood at parade rest in front of Lieutenant Colonel Bill Hawley, the commander of the ATR regiment. "Well Captain, you requested this hearing. Speak up loud and clear." "Sir, our exercise against that ATR Company was just that, yet one of your raw marines threatened bodily harm with a weapon, not only to grunts but their CO. If that wasn't enough, he tied the officer to a tree just in his skives. I don't believe that kind of action was warranted and shouldn't be tolerated." Colonel Hawley sat silent, then stood with a smirk on his face. "That's your bitch Captain? Well sir, you see, I mean, no Captain, I don't see, we're all marines, trained for one purpose to win a fight at any cost. You lead a company of elite combat troops but were outfoxed and foiled by a grunt that obviously is a natural and skilled in the ways of the forest. This is the first time I personally can remember; a raw training company repulsed our heroic Force Recon." "But sir." "No buts Captain if you're looking for discipline to that individual marine, it's not going to happen. This is what we're about, out smarting, and out maneuvering and kicking the enemy's ass. Now Captain, I dare say maybe your troop's need a refresher in tactics and Captain take this with you. Only the dead have seen the end of war. You got a surprise. Pray it never happens when the game is for real. You're dismissed!"

Lieutenant Sisco was elated. He led his troops back to the mainland on easy route step, and allowed then the luxury of several breaks where the smoking lamp was lit. All of the troops were excited and had found a sense of new found pride pounding in their hearts. Scuttlebutt had run its course and the word filtered through all of Lejeune how a solitary marine had ambushed and secured six recon marines and their platoon commander to trees. Marines of all ranks and grades gossiped over beers in the slop shoots and giduncks Force recon members were greeted by regular marines holding pieces of rope. It was an embarrassing time for recon and uplift for regular marines. But the respect and admiration for force recon never wavered. It showed that marines were being trained and trained well.

Lieutenant Sisco stood at attention in front of Lieutenant Colonel Hawley. "At ease Lieutenant, good job the other night, now tell me about this Broken Rose." "Sir, he's just a natural in every manner of speaking. Damn sir, he enters the woods and it's like he isn't there. He's mystical, I swear. He talks to the animals and they listen. He's one in a million, sir. I've been in the corps for eight years, saw combat in Korea, Have served with the best and this guy scares me. I'm glad U.S.M.C. is stamped on his uniform." "I see, he's that good?" "Sir, he's better than good, there are no words to describe his skills. "What rank is he?" "Sir, he made P.F.C. out of the rock." "Fine, now lieutenant, you're the acting company commander, when you return to your area, promote him to Corporal, that's all, dismissed." "Ah, one minute Lieutenant Sisco, who was about to exit and effected an about face. "Yes sir we both know what that kid did. He took out their advance scouts and then lit up the entire infiltrator platoon with a fireworks display. Outstanding! Out fucking standing! Carry on Lieutenant. Cultivate this kid." "I think your right. No, I know your right. We've got a Hell of a warrior in our midst.

Broken Rose sat with his three buds, LaPore, LeBron and LeSage. They were sharing a stew ingredients unknown prepared by the Rose. They ate heartily reminiscing about their successful encounter of the previous night. They were interrupted by the sudden entry of Sergeant Hemming. "Tonto the lieutenant wants to see you and I mean now. Let's move!" Broken Rose entered his CO's office. "Sir P.F.C. Broken Rose reporting as ordered." "At ease, marine, Lieutenant Sisco rose from behind his desk, smiling, he held out his hand, clasping Broken Rose's in a firm handshake. "As of right now you're Corporal Broken Rose. You've raised a lot of eyebrows and impressed your instructors and the ATR CO. You display all that a marine could and should be. Very few leave training regiments with two stripes. You're a credit to the uniform. Now you inherit responsibilities. Good luck and you're dismissed."

Broken Rose had remained silent. His eyes locked on his lieutenant. "Yes sir, thank you, sir." He made an about face, and departed quickly for he was lost in thought and headed to his comfort zone. His steps led him into the forest as the sun sank low in the west. He walked slowly and then began a steady jog, which brought him to a gurgling stream. He sat quietly the sound of cricket's music to his native ears. He gathered broken twigs and branches which lay in abundance on the forest floor. Adopting the methods of his forefathers, he prepared a small fire by rubbing sticks together and igniting dry moss and brush. Then adding twigs and larger branches, soon a comfortable fire offered warmth from the evening chill. He knelt before the fire and with his arms raised in supplication reaching towards the heavens. "Eyiee, Eyiee, grandfather it is I, Broken Rose. I call to your spirit. Let your voice come to me in the wind. Let me see the vision which will guide me in the footsteps of my ancestors. Let the howl of the wolf steel my heart for that which is to be. Let the host of the owl fuel my spirit with its wisdom. Let the stars of the heavens show me the way. Let the Great Spirit cloak me in his breath so that I may walk in the footsteps of those who have entered the Great Lodge. I, Broken Rose, Grandson of Two Wolves, seek the great ones strength and the blessings of our ancestor's so that I may be the true warrior. A crack of thunder and bolt of lightning like a pointed finger leaped at him from the dark heavens. The wind began to screech and the trees nearby swayed and danced with a whoosh. A vapor like force rose from the stream bed. A guttural voice rasped in the night. Faint at first, but it rose in a high pitch, then thundered. Its echo resounding through the forest, "my son, listen to the wind. It carries the voice of your ancestors. It brings their blessings and guidance. The spirits of our Lodge are always with you." The voice grew fainter and fainter, as he stood in wonder. The vaporized form burst into puffs of dust and as a small cloud rose into the night sky, Broken Rose fell forward into a deep sleep. He was awakened by the howl of a distant coyote. All was quiet the fire now only dwindling embers. He felt exhausted but at peace. He rose and kicking dirt on the dying fire. Satisfied all was right, he strolled from his secret refuge in the dark. The hoot- hoot of an owl brought a smile to his flushed face. He knew the breath of ancestral warriors had nourished his spirit.

The hut was quiet and dark on his return his squad deep in slumber. He'd entered as a shadow unheard and unseen. He walked as a feather and climbed silently into his rack. Broken Rose lay in the dark with the guttural voice of his grandfather fresh in his mind. He listened to the mournful wind as it shook the quonset hut. The sounds of men sleeping, tossing, turning, moaning an occasional cough or an emitted sigh brought comfort to him. He was in the company of fellow warriors. He felt content. His course had been charted moons before and he was determined to bring pride and honor to the Lodge of his ancestors. He fell into a fitful sleep and had a vision of a young pretty girl which he thought he heard cries in the night. He woke to the pounding of the wind and knew the vision was a dream of his long dead mother he'd never seen. His mind drifted back to another time when he'd questioned his grandfather about dreams involving loved ones. As a young buck he'd stated to Two Wolves that they're only dreams, right?" His heart thumped hard in his chest as he remembered Grandfather's dark eyes boring into his and in a hoarse whisper answered, "Are they?" It is the only way the spirits of our loved ones reach us from the other side. He rolled on his side, tears welled in his eyes, and he'd at last seen his mother and fell into a deep sleep.

It was an off day and his buds and the rest of the squad crowded around him. Back slaps and congratulations offered. Broken Rose smiled sheepishly, as LeBron fell to his knees, waving his arms, we bow to El Hafi. "Yeah, now you be the boss, Tonto. The squad roared with laughter and then then one by one sauntered off. Liberty was the word and all donned their forest green uniforms anticipating moments of freedom and recreation.

LeBron had borrowed his soul brothers vehicle and the four compadras headed for Fayetteville. The old rusted chariot chugged and puffed the exhaust coughing black smoke. Laughter and teasing resounded in the vehicle. They pulled in front of Jean's diner and piled out. The diner was doing a brisk lunch hour but they were able to find an empty booth in a far corner. Jean spotted LaPore and sauntered to their table. A radiant smile on her face, LaPore stood and they embraced to the hoots catcalls of the diners. Jean I want you to meet my buddies and proceeded to make introductions. Another waitress brought a coffee pot, excused herself and sashayed off to a nearby booth harboring a hungry construction crew. The four studied the menu. Broken Rose had taking a liking to the white eyes food and ordered a burger with onions, ditto for his buds. Their meal completed the Rose, LeBron and LeSage shook Jean's hand and that of her father and left LaPore with smiles and high fives. They clamored from the diner and climbed into their rust bucket. LaPore watched with amusement as they roared from the lot in a cloud of dust and black smoke. LaPore sipped his coffee, sitting along watching as Jean went about her duties. He felt content for he had this day and the next as liberty. Butterflies somersaulted in his stomach for the anticipation time alone with his girl.

The three headed down the road in silence starring at the countryside flashing by. "Lots of farmland down here," uttered LeSage. "Yeah, hell of a lot cleaner then Brooklyn, sighed LeBron. Hey dudes, LaPore is set what we gonna do, any ideas Tonto?" asked LeBron. And please let's not play in the woods today. We get enough of that shit!" Broken Rose laughed, "Not to worry, let's find us some friendlies and just chill." "Sounds good John," coughed LeSage. "Hey Lance got himself a nice looking lady, don't you think? Broken Rose emitted a soft sigh, "yes my friend, he's found his life's flower. They grew quiet. The old Chevy continued to shake, rattle and roll as they cruised to where they did not know.

The Rose, LeSage and LeBron had returned early. They sat in the predawn darkness waiting for LaPore. A steady rain beat a drum beat on the tin roof of the quonset hut. No one spoke, each lost in their own soul searching reflections of their lives. Yes, they were marines, lean and mean. But, they were also young men who shared in the American Dream, the love of a woman, a home and the laughter of children. They realized they'd chosen a rugged road in the spring of life and though strong and confident, they also experienced fear. Fear of the unknown, far from home and loved ones. They looked to each other they'd built a brotherhood on a stairway of blood, sweat and tears and they looked to each other for comfort and encouragement. It was a bond not understood by civilians. It was nourished and strengthened by the dependence of survival in where fate would lead them.

tears and they looked to each other for comfort and encouragement. It was a bond not understood by civilians. It was nourished and strengthened by the dependence of survival in where fate would lead them.

The final weeks of ATR were spent in repetitious training. Hour after hour on the rifle range and the use of the bayonet and rifle butt, Judo and the secrets of hand to hand combat. They trained with armored units by day and night, soon they realizied that each offered protection for the other. The green warriors trained with mortars and machine guns. It was continuous process so that these green young warriors would react instinctively. NCO's sweated and swore indoctrinating them in the art and skill of combat. A staff sergeant called a break one day lit the smoking lamp and as they sat stony face and attentive, he told them, in combat you don't fight for flag or country. You become as an animal and fight for each other and survival. He grew silent allowing his words to be absorbed turned and marched off.

It was over. Advanced training had ended. They stood in ranks awaiting their orders to various assignments. 1st Sergeant Bevans called their names loud and clear. "Murphy!" "Here 1st Sergeant!" "Embassy duty, Moscow!" "Yes 1st Sergeant!" "Klober!" "Yes 1st Sergeant!" "Brooklyn Navy Yard!" "Down!" "Yes 1st Sergeant!" "Norfolk Navy Yard" The list was endless. Broken Rose, Yes 1st Sergeant, "8th Marines, 2nd division!" "LeSage!" "Yes 1st Sergeant!" "8th Marines 2nd division!" ""LeBron and LaPore were also assigned to the same unit." The four smiled and embraced happy they'd remained together for no matter what they would come up against they would at least be able to be there for one another.

The troops stood at parade rest while issued orders had been presented. "Alright!" bellowed the top kick, "you now have your assignments. You'll pick up your travel orders and leave papers in my office. Be advised pack all your gear in your duffel bags. They travel with you. You've awarded fifteen day leaves. Enjoy and good luck in your assignments, Semper-Fi!"

Young men, who'd experienced the Hell of P.I. and the sweat of ATR, embraced and shook hands. Bonds of camaraderie had been well established and now each was being dispatched in harm's way throughout the globe. There were smiles and yes, tear rimmed eyes. The words "Semper-Fi" echoed in the breeze that cooled them. Then a line resembling a serpent formed at the Top soldier's office. Men retrieved their orders and in small groups sauntered off. Soon only the soft hum of the wind whistled throughout and about the area. For the moment it would remain quiet as a grave thought 1st Sergeant Bevans for soon a new batch of raw fresh recruits from P.I. would arrive and the process would repeat itself once again. It would continue over and over till the world entrenched itself in peace.

The four buds chatted as they packed their duffel bags. LeSage looked at LaPore, "bet I know where you're spending your 15 day leave." "Oh, wow be a gambler snarled LeBron. You know damn well he's gonna be off to the diner." LaPore smiled, "look my bro's, I need a favor, the three stood quiet waiting, "Well!" yelped the Rose, "what is it?" "Look, I want to get engaged. I've seen a nice ring at the PX, but I'm a little short. Could you each loan me $50 bucks. The sale's woman is holding it for me, but only so long. Jeanne is picking me up at the main gate in an hour. I'd like to give it to her then." "Hey man, no sweat," uttered Broken Rose. The three dug into their wallets and each handed over their share and then hugged and shook LaPore's hand. "Good show Lance! Yelped LeBron, Good show!" "Thanks guys'. I'll see you in fifteen days with the good ol' eighth. He then sprinted out the door and with a wave double timed to the PX.

LaPore looked at the Rose and LeBron, "Well, I guess it's time to skedaddle. Hey John, Where are you off to?" Broken Rose had grown silent and distant. "Oh, I've really nowhere to go. I'll probably hang around the base." LeBron chortled, "Yeah sure. You mean play Indian in the woods!" LeSage placed his hands on Broken Rose's shoulder. "No John, you're coming home with me. I've already talked to my folks. They'd really love for you to spend your leave with us. Don't forget my mom is half Indian and might very well puff the peace pipe with you. "Oh, Lee I don't know." "Yeah, you do. It's already written in stone. You're coming. No argument, right Jake. "Tonto, he's right. His old lady will feed you right. Might even make you possum stew." They all laughed. Broken Rose looked at LeSage. "You sure Lee? I don't want to be a burden, you know impose. You should have time alone with your people. "Yeah, you're right John and you're one of those people. So let's finish up and hit the road. Time's a wasting." LeBron lit a Lucky and exhaled blue smoke. Listen my brother with the Chevy; he's got some slut a few towns from here. He's gonna shack with her. He dangled a set of keys; he gave me the keys, so we got our transportation at least to Brooklyn. Then you guys can hop a train at Grand Central to Hartford. Oh, and share in the gas." "Sounds okay." LeSage laughed. "You think that bucket of shit will survive the trip?" "Hey as far as Brooklyn, my man. If it dies there, shit the streets are littered with fucked up junks every which way. "Okay Jake, you've got two passengers. Well, are we finished?" "Yeah," whispered the Rose. They took deep breaths and looked long and hard at what had been their home for weeks. Then arms around each other, "we made it," Sighed LeSage. They hoisted their duffel bags and headed out the main gate. Home ward bound, where the sweet stew of family, love, laughter and home cooking awaited them.

They threw their duffel bags in the rusted trunk and piled into the tired old Chevy. LeBron and LeSage up front. The Rose preferred the rear seat where he could curl up and cop some ZZZ's. The atmosphere in the vehicle was fairly quiet. All three anticipating their leave both happy and excited at the same time. They knew they looked sharp in their forest greens and displayed an air of confidence and yes a little cockiness. Like LeBron blurted, "God Damn we sure as hell bled, sweated and cried to wear em." Broken Rose had dozed off. LeBron and LeSage chirping away with small chatter. "Hey," LeSage barked LeBron, "What'd you think of that asshole Nolan? You know the dude that the civic cops busted for raping that white bitch. Where was it? Oh yeah, the Roadside Cafe. Lousy bitch claims he raped her in the parking lot. Shit that place crawling with all kinds of assholes coming and going. Nobody heard shit. She swears she was screaming". LeSage staring out the window. "Well Jake, you know the old saying, there's her story, his story and then there's the truth." "Yeah, well fuck that, he's still in a four by eight cell and blew his leave and the corps gonna fry his ass if the civics don't. It sucks man. How's he gonna prove his innocence. "Yeah, know what you're saying Jake, I guess the only safe measure is keep it in your pants." "Fuck that Lee, I likes brown sugar even white sugar pussy's it's a gift from God. Gonna get me all I can before they plant my ass down under. God Damn right much as that poo-tang as ol Jake's dick can handle."

LeSage nudged LeBron, "Hey there's a diner up ahead. Let's get some chow. I'm hungry as a pregnant elephant." "Yeah another greasy spoon gonna fuck up all our training. LeBron, shit right on, good ol burger will sit well bout now. Wake up Tonto, Fucker hasn't said a word, sometimes I think he's in another world." "He is Jake. He's out there with the stars and the forest and his beloved critters. He's special Jake; he's like, well like a well-oiled machine. He's leaps and bounds ahead of the rest of us. He was chosen and nursed to be what he is and we ain't seen anything yet."

LeBron turned into the lot and a red neon sign winked on and off. Lou's Tasty Vittles. LeBron laughed softly, "Yeah sure as shit, hope the slop ain't fresh road kills." "Yeah," laughed LeSage. He turned, John wake up, it's chow time. The Rose stirred, sat up, rubbing his eyes. "What's up?" "LeBron come on Tonto, time to dine in this all American cuisine." Broken Rose peered out the window. "Eeha,

Eeha," his war whoops startled several passerby's. "God Damn, Indian! You scared the shit out of those whiteys. Think you're gonna scalp em. Or some shit. Look at them ghost like faces, cut the shit savage. We still are in the south. They'll call them "Good Ole Boy Cops" and they likely to blow us away." "Okay, okay, you're right, let's wolf down some grease and make our stomachs happy."

They sat awhile enjoying coffee. LeBron and LeSage fired up the smoking lamp by sucking Luckies. Broken Rose spoke softly, "You know that's shit your sucking into your lungs, I can smell a smoker from way off and someday, hopefully not, somewhere, sometime a professional enemy gonna have your asses." "Nah, that won't happen, broke in LeBron, not as long as we have our war chief around." The Rose smiled. "Maybe yes, maybe no, but I'll tell you if we ever get in some shit, The Rose slithers into the forest and mist likely will fight it out on my terms, smoke, alcohol, bad food will announce your presence in the forest, trust and believe." LeSage had been quiet, "You know John your right and we know it. You've proved it not so long ago. We'll do our best, but guys like you will show us the way."

They paid their checks as they exited the diner. The wind began to howl and rain had burst from the heavens and at double time headed for the old Chevy. LeBron laughed, "Well Tonto you get the strings." Broken Rose laughed softly, "Yeah, Indian always gets forked. Sit in the back and work the wipers and you know I'm a good guy, See I'm a corporal and you two are future meat for some mean eyed sharpshooter. I could pull rank, but as you all say fuck it, some other time." LeBron spun around. "Tonto did you say the F word?" Broken Rose smiled, "come on; let's go before my war paint runs." All three laughed and fell into the vehicle as a monsoon type rain began pelting the parking lot.

The three shared small chatter helping the miles slip by. The wind screeched and moaned. Rain and fog hampered visibility. LeBron drove slowly the Jersey Turnpike was immersed in fog. "God Damn, I can't see fucking shit," shouted LeBron. "Maybe two feet ahead is all." LeSage turned to Broken Rose, John you need a break from working the wiper's?" "Nah, I'm fine. It's good for the arms. Besides helps keep my butt awake." "Okay John, you need relief sing out." "Better believe son, better believe," smiled the Rose.

As rain battered them a sudden horrific explosion illuminated the dark sky about 200 yards ahead of them. The concussion rocked the old Chevy. She screeched and tilted and LeBron gripped the wheel hard battling to keep the vehicle level with the road. Then another explosion roared ahead. Flames flashed into the night sky. The smell of gasoline and burning rubber and plastic filled their nostrils. LeSage yelled, "Pull to the right Jake." The gasoline truck is engulfed in flames. Several vehicles were embedded in the rear and side of the behemoth truck. Screams of terror and agony echoed all about them. "Jake you're on the shoulder. Kill the engine. This place is lit up like Times Square on coming vehicles will see the carnage and hopefully stop. Come on people need help and fast!"

Three marines sworn to protect and serve leaped from the vehicle and proceeded with caution. Debris littered the highway. Tires and glass even luggage was strewn. It was as an obstacle course, but this was real, a body loomed before them blackened and its arms raised in grotesque supplication to the sky. Instinct and training took hold. They could see life had been stolen. Heat from several fires limited oxygen and inhibited movement. A white Pontiac blackened by soot and fire lay on its side. They could see a woman clawing at the rear window and heard her screams of terror and pleas for help. Fires were licking at the roadway. They moved stealthy cognoscente that tentacles of fire were reaching for the Pontiac. LeSage stumbled on a large piece of iron. It was the remnants of an axle. Grabbing one end, he screamed, "Come on! No time to lose!" They ran to the Pontiac yelling to the woman, "to move back from the window!" They could see the look of terror on her face. But she acknowledged and retreated further into the vehicle as far as she could. LeSage raised the metal arm and smashed out the window. The woman was crying hysterically as she handed out an infant to LeBron. It was crying and squirming. LeBron at first experienced difficulty in getting a solid grip but quickly pulled the small body to his chest. LeSage dropped his make shift ram and he and Broken Rose reached into the interior pulling the woman through the shattered window. She screamed in agony and they saw bone protruding from just below her right knee. Also the right side of her face contained a very severe cut that was bleeding profusely. The carried her to a safe area. She was babbling, my husband, my husband, pointing to the Pontiac. LeBron held on to the infant as LeSage and the Rose sprinted to the Pontiac with flames now only feet away. They peered into the vehicle gasped in horror. It was a scene from Hell. A body was enmeshed in the steering wheel. The head lolling back and forth on the floor severed from the torso. They retreated knowing it was futile. He was beyond help. Victims were crawling from cars staggering around in a daze. Disoriented, they assisted several to the area where LeBron cradled the infant and attempted to sooth its mother with soft reassuring words. In the distance the wail of sirens pierced the night growing louder and intimidating as they drew near.

There were bodies lying in the roadway. LeSage and the Rose sprinted back and forth checking for life. Looking for pulses Two were carried to their make shift refuge. Four were beyond help. Spotlight flooded the area as state police arrived in numbers activating their spot lights. Fire apparatus were also arriving in strength as were ambulances. Traffic was at a standstill in both directions of the highway. Fire brought all weight to bear and flames were quickly being extinguished. As the fog lifted a scene from Dante's Inferno was unveiled. The gasoline truck was a hulk of blackened steel and at least 10 vehicles shared in its fate. Bodies and injured were quickly being placed in ambulances and as each received its cargo roared off into the night with sirens wailing.

Emergency personnel had removed the mother and infant and other injured from their makeshift triage. LeBron, LeSage, and the Rose, stood quietly. Their uniforms soaked and their faces blackened by soot. Human waste and blood covered their hands and clung to uniforms. They remained mute for no words could escape them. They'd witnessed a scene never to be forgotten. They were shocked and emotionally drained as they stood in silence. A State Police Sergeant approached. "Hey guys, Semper-Fi was in- in 52. You okay?" They stared at the trooper. Finally LeSage spoke, "yeah Sarge we're okay. "Well listen lots of folks witnessed what you gyrenes did. Is this your vehicle over here? He pointed at the old Chevy. "Yeah, it's okay". "Holy shit what the Hell's holding it together? Marine spit!" They smiled, "you might say that Sarge." "Well anyway, where you guys headed?" "We just finished ATR and got us a fifteen day leave and we're on our way home, LeBron spoke up. I'm headed for Brooklyn and these two are headed for Connecticut." "Damn Hell of a way to begin a leave. Okay my name is Sergeant McDermott, N.J. State Police and you guys pile in that bucket of shit and follow me. We're going to my barracks where you can shower. We'll get your uniforms dry cleaned and get you a square meal. "Damn!' Spoke up LeBron, A good guy cop." The trooper smiled "Yeah you guys from Brooklyn think we're all nasty types. Come on lets go. My guys are on it. There's a lot to do here.

The three scanned the area and obtained a life time picture photographed in their young minds. The trooper roared up in his cruiser. "Follow me!" They got in the Chevy. As usual it coughed and sputtered. Finally the engine roared to life and they fell in behind the police vehicle. Sergeant McDermott headed right to his watch commanders office. He had the three marines in tow. He introduced them to his lieutenant and deliberately and thoroughly indoctrinated him of their actions at the scene. They were ushered into a large shower room. Clothing was scrounged and laid out on a bench for them. They reveled in the hot shower and quickly donned dungarees and New Jersey State Police sweatshirts. Their uniforms had been dispatched by State Police cruiser with a post haste request to near bye cleaners. They were treated to a splendid meal of steak, mashed potatoes, salad and warm Italian bread. Coffee was in abundance and they shared small talk with in again out again state troopers.

Finished with their meal, Sergeant McDermott approached. "Hey jarheads, follow me." They followed him down a long corridor. The walls were light blue and the tiled floor was spotless. He smiled and pointed into an office, he'd halted in front of. We go hence. They entered a midsize office room. It contained photos of troopers killed in line of duty. The American and State Flag and a large desk were positioned in the corner. Seated behind it was another trooper. His lapels displayed silver oak leaves and embossed in large black lettering on a name plate in the center of the desk were the words Lieutenant Colonel James Philips. He rose with a smile as he extended a large meaty hand. He stood approximately 6'3 in stocking feet. He possessed the shoulders of a New York Giant's lineman. "So the Marines have landed. I'm Lieutenant Colonel James Philips and the Sargent here and many of my troopers and citizens have raved about your heroic exploits. I want to thank you. The Marine Corps always come through and you three certainly displayed its code of honor, integrity and faith fullness to the fullest this day. I have your names and rest assured those who need to know will be so informed by this agency. In the meanwhile if you men need anything sing out. You saved quite a few lives today at your own peril. It's comforting and reassuring to those of us in the civilian world that the Marines are ever on guard both at home and abroad." He threw them a salute. "Good luck guys and hope you enjoy your leave. You won't forget this incident but don't dwell on it. Enjoy your leave. You know how the military world revolves you don't know when there's a next one, thanks again and Semper-Fi."

He strolled from his office, turned left and was gone. Sergeant McDermott smiled. "The colonel meant what he said. He's a good one for he was on Iwo in WW II. LeBron spoke softly. "He was a Marine too?" "Hell yeah, won the silver star on Iwo. You can believe your superiors will get the word. Look your uniforms are back and they are laid out in our living quarters. I've got to run for I need to return to the scene. "Hey Sarge, asked the Rose, do you know what the casualty list was?" Ah corporal it's not good. Quite a few D.O.A. and many injured. We don't know, no official count yet, so many were brought to several area hospitals. Well, once again thanks and Semper-Fi. If you're ever this way again, stop by and say hello. We'll shoot the shit and good luck to you all." "Hey Sarge," he stopped and turn. Broken Rose threw him a salute, "thank you for what you did for us. We know you guys hold the corps in high esteem. But know this, where would we be if it weren't for the men and women in blue?" McDermott smiled and throwing a half salute headed out into the morning mist.

It was time for a quick exit. The police barracks was now a beehive of activity. Concerned relatives were in abundance. The news media, area politicians flowed through the door. The Rose spotted a side exit, "this way, let's beet feet." They scrambled into the old Chevy. It groaned in dismay coughed and spat black exhaust, then sputtered to life. LeBron made a quick turn onto the highway and the Chevy trialing pungent exhaust came to response to the command and roared away from the nightmare from Hell. Few words were exchanged each lost in their own thoughts. As the hellish carnage lingered in their thoughts, the look of terror and anguish of victims etched deep in their hearts and minds. They felt relief when the miles were distancing them from Hell's tentacles. The Rose roused them from infectious depression. "Look bro's it is what it is. Life's a gamble and every day you play the odds of survival. We happened into this thing and we helped save lives. The Great One acts in His own way. True sometimes we think maybe strangely, even cruelly, but he is the power of the universe. It's not for us to delve into his reasoning or secrets. Let this horror seep from your mind. Wipe away the images. This leave is our R&R and we earned and need it. Oh sure we'll always experience bad memories. But we can't allow them to wrap chains on our souls, Okay?!!"

LeBron and LeSage exchanged glances. "Your right John, you're dead right on." The Rose leaned forward, his chin resting on the passenger's front seat. "You know Indians have visions and this was a real life vision. Perhaps it's a prelude to us of what might be or maybe somewhere in time."

R&R it seems too ends quickly. LeBron, LeSage and Broken Rose, somehow reached Lejeune safely and with time to spare. The old Chevy had coughed and sputtered and breathed it's last as the main gate came into vision. Men in twos and threes sauntered through the entry lonely and already home sick. It would take days for the backlash depression to fade away. The three headed to the 8th Marines area where they checked in at the duty hut. They were directed to their billets by a lean blond hair corporal who greeted them with a warm handshake and broad smile. "Hi, I'm Corporal Hendricks, The company clerk, you three are assigned to B Company, 1st platoon. It's now 0430 revelry is in an hour and company formation is at 0600. So you've just time to get squared away and get in your utilities. You just head right when you leave here. Your hut is the sixth one on the right. All new guys, oh by the way Corporal Rose, I've a note here from your platoon commander. Says you're the 1st squad leader. LeBron and LeSage slapped his back. LeBron, stating "Yeah boss, you be Mr. Chief right now. Yes Sir!" Rose looked at the corporal, "whose our platoon leader?" "Hold on, oh yeah, Lieutenant Sisco. He came over from an ATR outfit." All three yipped and yelped. "Hot damn, what a gift from the gods. Platoon couldn't have done better."

They walked briskly to their assigned quarters. It was like a raided whore house with excitement. The squad was minted with several veterans but mostly fresh meat from ATR. LaPore sprang from his foot locker to great his buds. He'd arrive just fifteen minute before. They talked excitably and loudly happy to be together. Rose excused himself and stepped to the front of the hut scanned the interior satisfied his entire squad was present. He got there attention by barking. "All right listen up! For those who don't know me. I'm Corporal Broken Rose, your squad leader. We're all Marines here. I ask that you be squared away. Mind your p's and q's and I'll do my best to see to your needs. We're in an infantry company so we all know what that means. I'm no hard ass but I'm no lamb either. We're all in this together. Brother's in green. We do things right. It's easier on us. You got gripes see me in private. Here we live in close quarters and I want us to be a family. The scuttle butt is that this is one hell of a battalion. The guide arm weighted with battle streamers. Like you, I'm new to this outfit. Like you we'll get the word. Okay enough Rah, Rah, formation is at 0600. That's in 45 minutes from now. Stow your gear and get in utilities.

The men approached individually shaking his hand and returned to their small area's preparing for the life of a grunt. LeBron, LeSage and LaPore chose racks towards the rear of the quonset hut. All three would nest close together. The only downside was that Broken Rose as squad leader would stow his gear up front in the lead rack. LeBron looked at LaPore. "Well did you do it?" "Do what?" asked LaPore. "You know, get yourself engaged." "Yeah bro, we did, no date set or anything. We thought we'd wait a bit to see how this world of shit we're in revolves." LeSage spoke up, "good thinking Lance, she's a great kid. She'll wait." "Yeah, she is. You know, it's been lonely for me. But now I've something to live and reach for." LeSage and LeBron shook his hand. "Yeah Lance, just be cool."

Broken Rose stood by the hatch in full utilities and shouted, "All right 1st squad, outside in company formation!" "Well, well, well, look what the fuck the demon sent us. I'm Gunnery Sergeant Pat Mazzone and it's you poor slobs misfortune to land me as your platoon sergeant. The ugly fuck to my left is Sergeant Killian. I've been in God's Corps for sixteen years and never witnessed such a disgusting apparition of assholes that I'm facing now! You look like remnants of a fucking Chinese fire drill. I've spent more time squatting over slit trenches then you have sucking your mother's tits. Jesus, Mary, and Joseph, and the poor fucking donkey, what am I supposed to do with you piles of camel shit? You land here thinking your Marines, Bull shit. You haven't shed your training bras. Your faces remind me of a baby's pink little ass. Well! Listen up and Listen tight! You'll earn your emblems in this outfit. We don't tolerate shirkers, masturbators or piss ant whiners. You've been assigned to the greatest fraternity in the world Bravo Company 8th Marines, 2nd Marine Division. Our battle streamers flap with pride earned with blood, sweat and tears. The company commander is Captain Guth Heinz. The Battalion CO is Lieutenant Colonel Striker. Real soon you'll be meeting the devil's disciples your NCOs. If you haven't we'll assign you to squads and your billets where you can play with your little baby dicks. Oh, you fuck up and my ugly ass will be all over you. Turning to Sergeant Killian, he barked, take over!" He spat on the ground and in a puff of dust marched off.

Sergeant Hemming faced his platoon. Okay, you'll march to the company area where you will assemble and proceed to morning chow. You will assemble after chow and return to the company area where you will meet the company commander and top Nom Coms. You'll receive what scuttle butt is a need to know and order's at that time, Broken Rose!" "Yes Sergeant." "March the platoon to our company area." "Yes Sergeant!"

Broken Rose facing the platoon for the first time barked, "Right Face, Forward March!" The platoon marched to the Marine sing song cadence of Broken Rose. The clash of boots on pavement loud and clear echoed in the crisp morning air. Reaching the assembly area, the platoon stepped smartly joining the other three platoons, Able, Charlie, and Helo. The company stood at rest in an impressive array under the early morning sun while wisps of vapor danced in the morning haze. A tall burly staff sergeant loomed before them. LeBron hissed between his teeth, "God Damn, that fucker's, built man, like a condom full of walnuts." "Bravo Company listen up! I'm Staff Sergeant Ranee Laurent, 1st platoon's platoon sergeant. Ten-shun! Right face! Forward march!" Womp, womp, womp the cascade of two hundred and fifty pairs of boots thundered through and around the assembly area. Bravo Company marched with precision to morning chow.

Lieutenant Colonel Striker, 8th Marine CO sat at his desk. He'd arrived early poured himself coffee, black and leafed through several service records of personnel under his command. He perused several and finally placing the stack aside when he found what he wanted. The name Broken Rose, Corporal USMC 1620097, embossed on the manila folder, drew his interest. He'd heard of his exploits at ATR. He scanned the personnel information before him. The list was limited as this was a newly minted marine but he had been given a heads up by the ART regimented commander and it peeked his interest. Striker was a damn good officer. A rising star with the Navy Cross gleamed on his left breast which sat at the top of his bedecked rows of ribbons earned in Korea at the "Frozen Chosin" He returned the file to the mountain of folders before him as a knock at the door interrupted his concentration. "Come!" He bellowed. He smiled as the battalion exec entered. Major Frank Pezzone strolled briskly into the room. "Good morning Colonel, another day in the corps, to serve God and country." "Morning Frank fresh coffees in the pot fill up and have a seat. I want to go over some of our training agenda. Oh and I want the battalion assembled at 1400 hours. I want them to see our ugly asses." "Yes sir." "Also at 1600 hours, I want all the company commanders here in my office. Some know me, others don't. I want them to understand from the one yard line where I'm coming form. What I demand and expect. Also reach out to the Sergeant Major. I want him in attendance also." "Okay Eric, I'll get the ship afloat. Now sir, what's on the agenda?" "They'll have it easy today, Frank, but tomorrow we start. I want a cohesive well-oiled machine. You know that. I want reveille at 04:30. We start the process at 05:30 with a 20 mile hike, no packs. But make sure the lister bags are full. I want to see who the workers and shirkers are. Frank we're a combat trained infantry unit. We've got hot spots worldwide. Let's get them ready for what we're paid for." "Yes sir, anything else?" "Yes, have my clerk reach out to Colonel Pearson, the 105's CO. I need to confer with him a.s.a.p. Do it on your way out and oh Frank you're on the hike also." "Yeah skipper, I know that. Look boss, I'm damn thrilled and proud to be hooked up with you. I know the kind of outfit you'll mold." Striker laughed softly, "Well combat isn't play time and if and when this outfit will be ready." "Aye, Aye, Sir." Pezzone rose and exited closing the door softly.

Striker reclined back in his chair. An early bird, he loved his moments of solitude in the wee hours of the morning. He found that he was able to plan his moves and decisions best in semi-darkness. In class A's, he fingered his ribbons reflecting on good men who'd given their all in the wastes of Korea. He'd vowed long ago as a gold brick lieutenant that someday when he held command status. Men under his command would be well trained and fit. He was a no nonsense officer. He felt there was no room for levity in a combat unit. Readiness and instant responses to a hot spot was a constant reminder that his was an awesome responsibility that was his and he alone sat in the chair. Yes, he knew how to smile but he disciplined his mind and body so that he would lead by example thus ensuring the loyalty and courage of his troops.

He lit a Lucky—bemusing himself in creating smoke rings that floated up and away in the tarp of semi-darkness. His adrenaline coursed through his veins for he lived for the corps and loved its traditions and camaraderie. He loved to look out his window and observe troops on the move and the sound of a bugle in the distance. He loved the flap of the colors as she swayed in the wind as well as the image of the eagle, globe and anchor which personified loyalty, honor, and integrity and yes guts. But Striker had fear that his leadership would fall short and that subordinate officers could or would not measure to his level of expectation. For that was the reason his reputation of a task master proceeded him. He would train, train, train, his troops pushing them beyond maximum effort. Every day he vowed to the ghosts of deceased warriors that his battalion, his Marines, would be ready to endure whatever an adversary's method and means would confront them. Physical training and mental conditioning in the end saved lives. There could be no lapses or failures. They resulted in tragedy and confusion. Weak officers and NCO's would be kneaded out of his unit. As a commander, he knew full well that noncoms were the backbone to the corps. He was always on the hunt digging into files looking for exceptional talent as well as courage and leadership. This was his forte, he knew when, how, and where to find them. He was on a mission, a goal; scuttle butt at Division had it that a full battalion would be dispatched to South America for enhanced and rigorous jungle training. It was his obsession that the battalion would be his. "Yes God Damn it," he said aloud. "I want it, it's ours. It belongs to the 8th Marines, and son of a bitch, through blood, sweat, tears and courage it will be!"

Finished with chow, the company marched back to their area where individual platoons branched off and in cadence marched to their quarters. Staff Sergeant Laurent stood broad and tall before his platoon. "All right rest! Listen up! It's now 08:15; at 14:00 the entire battalion will assemble to meet its commander. You will have till then to get squared away. Get comfortable in your quarters. You NCO's make damn sure weapons and equipment received top priority. We'll assemble in class A's. For the record you won't don them again for some time. The battalion skipper is knee high in training physically, mentally, and a hell of a lot of spent energy on our part. So get yourselves psyched and mentally prepared. This is no free ride or Boy Scout Enterprise. You're Marines in a combat ready unit. Best you adapt and condition your mental state to this fact. Oh and get this and take it to the bank! I do not tolerate slackers, whackers, or whiners. Take a look to the guy standing beside you. Take a good look. One day you're gonna depend on him and he's gonna depend on you, Dismissed!!"

The battalion stood at rest in an impressive array of green. Color guard at its front with the colors and Marine flags sighed softy in the light breeze. The North Carolina sun brought warmth and its rays basked the landscaped in a brilliant hue. Company commanders stood in front with senior Noncoms. The sky a brilliant blue played host to ivory cumulus clouds in the distance the hum of a lonely plane with its controls trailing behind added a surreal effect. Suddenly an authoritative voice thundered to their front battalion, "ATTEN---TION!!!" Like thunder the crock of heels clashing at 45 degrees resounded echoing and bouncing beneath the brilliant sky. It was an impression sight and sound to see the rows of class A's come to attention in perfect unison with such discipline inscribed on their faces.

Lieutenant Colonel Striker with the erect Major Pezzone in close step and the battalion Sergeant Major Thomas Whitaker hove into view. Reaching the center of the battalion's formation they halted in front of the color guard and negotiated a crisp left face and stood at parade rest. Lieutenant Colonel Striker took two steps forward, his voice deep and authoritative barked, "BATTALION REST!" He was an imposing figure being 6'2" lean and muscular. Troops marveled. They were impressed by the rows of ribbons adorning his chest for they knew he had faced many obstacles to obtain them.

Striker scanned his battalion noting the youthful faces here and there as well as older veterans that pock mocked the ranks. With his eyes locked on the colors he began to speak. "We are the 8th Marines 2nd Marine Division. We exist to serve God, Country, Flag and each other. In the world many of you experienced and witnessed prejudice and bigotry. That's all behind now. Here the only color we recognize is green. You have Chosin and been trained to be Marines. Make no mistake you will be molded into the finest fighting machine in the world. We are from different walks or life with different creeds and religions, but all Americans, who will honor the commitment to honor, integrity, fidelity. If we fail, ghosts of those who wore the green before you with blood, guts and pride will rise and brand your souls with dishonor. Across the globe the bones of brave and honorable Marines lie at rest beneath white crosses that bleach in the sun. They will breathe courage and strength into your spirits. Reach to them. Embrace their courage and pride. You will be trained to the point of exhaustion. But I promise you, I'll be there with you. On your left breast are stamped U.S.M.C. you've already paid a down payment with blood, sweat and tears to warrant those letters. The price comes high and why? Because one day you may be called upon to serve your country and perhaps to lay down your lives but it's my job to minimize that loss. I expect you as Marines to perform with zeal, dedication and most importantly with honor. Remember who and what you are and what your primary function may be. Have confidence in your officers and NCO's. I tell you now if they don't measure to the corps standards, they will be drummed out of this outfit post haste. Marines, I am honored and privileged to lead and serve with you. Be ever mindful to the words Semper-Fi for they are now embossed on your souls till the day you die." He turned and with the Exec and Sergeant Major marched quickly off and soon was lost in the glare of the sun.

The battalion was marched off under the heat of a late afternoon sun each company and platoon stepping off into their respective quarters. There the troops were given the word about the next day's hike. They commenced squaring away gear, writing letters, reading or napping. Evening chow wasn't till 1700 hours. Free time was precious and they relished the chance to chill.

Lieutenant Colonel Striker sat erect behind his desk. Seated in a semicircle facing him were his company commanders. Striker cleared his throat. "Gentlemen the smoking lamp is lit please rest easy." Chairs scuffled as the officers fished for their smokes and struggled for comfort in the hard wooden chairs. A window fan offered little relief from the mounting heat caused by bodies in a confined space. "All right, began Striker you are the company commanders of this outfit. It is my intention that when you leave this office it is with the full understanding that I expect you to command by example and common sense leadership and I will hold each of you accountable to lead in the highest tradition and standards of our Corps. Each of you commands rifle companies we all know what that entails. I do not wish to be surrounded by yes men. Nor do I expect all decisions by the book. I insist on my commanders to function and confront adversity and problems as they arise. Initiative and adaptation to situations is paramount for officers under my command. Now training will commence tomorrow at 05:30 hours with a 20 mile forced march. I strongly recommend that you officers as we train in stages see that your companies are in top physical and mental condition. I demand you conduct physical training exercise and that weapons and equipment are maintained in readiness. The Marine Corps has tradition, discipline and in my opinion the best basic training regimen in the world. It also has rules and regulations that have proven their mettle over time spent with the two B's, battle and blood. I also have rules, you officers must depend and regulate to your junior officers and Non Coms. Remember in a fire fight your Non Coms are indispensable. Pick your Non Coms carefully. Select those who are competent and loyal. Weed out the malcontents and inept. I hold you and you alone responsible.

We as you realize are a combat ready unit, but I am not satisfied where we're at. I push for the maximum effort and beyond. It means sacrifice, hardship and discipline, your infantry officers you're supposed to be good or you wouldn't be here. All well and good, I sure as Hell will find out. Lean on your platoon commanders. The here and now is where you decide who's capable and who is not. Best you make the correct decisions if your wrong, not only your ass but those of Marines you lead will also be on the line. Also be cognoscente of your corpsmen. They are the life line of your company. See to their needs and well-being as well as the grunts. Okay, I won't belabor our set to. You men know what I expect. Remember your biggest asset as an officer is capable leadership only then will you earn and retain the respect of your troops." He rose, "thank you, gentlemen." The officers sprang to attention as their commander exited the room. As he strolled out the door he turned and bellowed, "CARRY ON!!"

At 05:30 the battalion stood at rest. A hazy mist shrouded the area in a thick fog. Lieutenant Colonel Striker stood to the front. "Company commanders report." "Sir, A Company all present and accounted for, Sir. B Company all present and accounted for." C and H companies rang in as well. Striker whirled and took position to the extreme right of his battalion. His voice resonated through the early morning haze. "Battalion Company Commanders echoed the command, "Right face!" The crash of boots rattled the early morning quiet. "Forward march!" The battalion marched off boots beating a drum beat tattooing the asphalt. It snaked across the expanse of the parade ground and quickly marched into the boondocks swallowed by the thick foliage. Striker displayed freely that a quick pace was in the making. The battalion disappeared under the canopy of the forest. Birds chirped and a soft breeze hummed though the tree tops. An odor of a mixture of wood rot and mildewed vegetation and waste of creatures filled their nostrils. Sweat poured down faces and coursed down dripping arm pits. Skivvies clung to their groins as perspiration proved offensive to genitals. Striker was relentless. Approaching a hill he quickened the pace. Feather merchants in the rear of the platoons double timed to keep pace. Officers and Non Coms moved up and down the line, encouraging their troops on. Discipline and pride a motivator to the grunts, they were lean and hard. Months of training had steeled their bodies. Muscles still ached but had grown accustomed to the rigors and labor placed on them. The battalion flowed forward one foot up and one foot down.

Three hours into the march all companies were intact. There were no stragglers. No one fell to the side. Approaching a small stream Striker called a halt. The grunts quickly finding comfort in the soft beds that paralleled the stream, the smoking lamp was lit and as the men relaxed, they heard the roar of trucks with their throttles, crashing through the boon docks. Suddenly six deuce and a halves appeared on their right flank. A dirt road had been camouflaged by vegetation. Officers shouted to their companies and platoons, "that hot chow and beverage trucked up," The men formed lines that went for a mile down the beaten path. KP Marines served steaming coffee and a stew like substance, which the grunts devoured with relish.

LeBron, LeSage, and LaPore, sat together by the stream bed, LeBron standing, inhaled his lucky, wisps of smoke drifted from his nostrils. "Fuck, all I ever see now is fucking woods and critters and all kinds of fucked up bugs. Shit, I'm a city boy, this kind of shit never would survive in Brooklyn." "Yeah," uttered LeSage, "the fucking smog fumes would kill it all." LeBron looked at LeSage, "Yeah you be right Lee. You know there is a beauty out here. Nature is one hell of a creature. It controls life no matter where you look. The forest

feeds and provides a refuge to all manner of creatures, even man
if he chooses. Damn I feel sorry for my kin. They've never seen or
experienced this green world."

"On your feet! On your feet!" NCO's ran up and down the line.
"Let's go we're moving out!" Again the sound of boots meshing
leaves and twigs resulted in a musical tattoo through the forest.
The grunts bemused as birds flew in different directions as they
approached. Now and then the sun peeked through the curtains of
tree tops. The column continued and climbed several hills and knolls
splashed through streams and bogs. Their boots wet and caked with
mud. Their uniforms stained with sweat. One foot up, one foot down,
the miles clicked by. The sun now high in the sky, Striker continued
his pace, one hour, two hours, three hours; they'd been on the march
for nearly 7 hours. "Take 10," came the cry from commanders.
Grunts approaching exhaustion, dropped where they were. Lay on
Gods green grass and soft earth. Cigarette smoke curled upward
towards the forest canopy. Canteen covers, their metallic clicks
echoed through the boon docks. Men sighed and groaned vowed to
continue, the finish line was within their grasp.

Colonel Striker stood on a small knoll surrounded by company
commanders. "God Damn it this is fantastic. Not one dropout. Out
fucking standing! You officers are to be commended. The physical
training you levied is paying off. Okay, five miles to go. Get em
up and saddled. We'll beat the dark and grab evening chow. Oh
listen up! Battalion rifle and equipment inspection is on the agenda
for 0900 tomorrow. It's Friday and inform the troops, if okay,
liberty commences at 12:00 hours. Okay gentlemen return to your
companies."

The battalion had limped into their area. By 1700 hours,
twenty up twenty back. They'd covered forty miles in 10 hours, an
outstanding exhibit of physical prowess, after stowing gear. They

were marched to chow neglecting to shower or don fresh utilities. After chow they were marched to their respective quarters where the evening hours spent cleaning weapons and web gear. Utilities scrubbed and hung to dry. Then hot showers, the men luxuriating in the warm water soothing offended muscles and washing grit and grime from exhausted bodies. At 0900 lights out, the sound of taps echoed throughout Lejeune. Men without women tossed and turned in their racks and each with his own thoughts and dreams. Maybe of home, a girl, nights were the demon to these young grunts. That's when loneliness tore at ones soul.

Broken Rose satisfied that his squad was squared away and bedded down, in his quiet way moved to the end of the quonset hut. He sat squatting on the deck in front of his three buds racks. "How are you doing guys?" "Hey Tonto, How is you, boss man?" uttered LeBron. They spoke in hushed tones so as not to disturb sleeping buddies. "Quite a walk today," whispered LeSage. "Yeah," blurted LeBron. "That Striker, God Damn, he be something else. Led the way and never wavered." Broken Rose spoke softly, "No one did. He's molding one hell of a battalion. Scuttle butt has it he won "The Cross in the Chosin." "Yeah, saw it on his class A's sighed LaPore. "You know these lifers are top notch, know their shit." "Yeah retorted LeSage, they've been there, been to Hell and back." "Okay guys," hissed Broken Rose, "get your sack time, big inspection tomorrow by the man himself. Hey, one more thing. Where you guys going on liberty?" LaPore creaked; I'm going to see Jean. What about you bro's? Want to come?" Broken Rose speaking softly, "thanks but no, me I'm going to the woods, any takers?" LeBron's voice quivering shit Tonto we just came from that fucking place. Not me, I'm going with LaPore to that diner. "Okay serves me even through I'm black, how about you LeSage?" Hesitating LeSage said you know town sounds nice, but I'm gonna go with the Indian." "Shit, you fuck's crazy man," snarled LeBron. "Christ himself told me so, said they be under a rock, crazy fuckers. They all laughed softly, "Okay bro's get your sack time," and was gone as quietly as he came.

Inspection went smoothly and the battalion a formidable sight in full combat gear. Colonel Striker filtered through the ranks stopping at random to inspect an individual Marine's rifle or webb gear. He would ask others what their first or fourth general order was. He would chat with squad leaders. Seeking answers as to their responsibilities. He would question fire team leaders by questioning them on their knowledge of interlocking fire and the procedure for laying down superior fire power. He would interrogate B.A.R. men as to the nomenclature of their weapons. He even had a heavy weapons team disassemble and reassemble a 50 caliber machine gun.

Inspection complete to his satisfaction he had the battalion fix bayonets and sling, gave a right face. His exec paraded them before him for one hour with the bayonets gleaming in the bright sunlight. Yes, Striker thought as he watched in admiration. This is what I love. What a magnificent sight. A combat battalion on full parade it makes the blood boil and sends goose bumps up and down the spine. Nearby other companies and officers and NCO's stood still as they watched. General Green peering out his window turned to his exec. "Look at that, that Striker he's a rising star. That bastard has created and developed one hell of a combat ready outfit."

"Inspection over, the men once dismissed, sprinted to their quarters quickly donning class A's. Liberty call had been sounded. They lined up at company and platoon offices to draw liberty cards. In a heart beat the battalion area lay quiet and deserted.

Broken Rose and LeSage packed rations for two days and in utilities and sporting only their knives and canteens. They sauntered into the woods. Summer was ending and the cool air of fall breathed new life into the forest. They camped by a babbling stream. The

Rose tutored LeSage, in the life and means of the forest. The lessons started with how to look for grass that men or creature disturbed and how to gauge the wind. How if one mastered the earth he could hear the tell-tale signs of movement. The land in its own way would telegraph sound and how to listen for frogs in the night. They were a source of food. Other teachings in how to look and search for the nests of birds for their eggs are another source of food. How to make snares to entrap small creatures that could strive off starvation rabbits, squirrels, and possums could offset danger and delay slow death. How to find grubs that if needed could be mashed and boiled. They were source of high protein. How to make a spear that could be used as a weapon of defense and assist in the hunt for game. How to make a basin to catch rain water another way to have drinking water.

Sitting by a warm fire that first night the Rose took LeSage in his confidence. "Lee if we ever get into the shit. The Rose will most likely act alone and in the night where the tarp of darkness conceals movement, when an enemy is most likely to rest and his thought process taxed. Why alone John? Broken Rose was slow in answering. "I mean no offense, but the white man reeks of tobacco, alcohol and spirits inhibit his thinking. The spices that he consumes can emit odors that could or would set off a sharp enemy's mental radar. The Corps trains us well but they cannot flush all those telltale warnings from the white man's body. No Lee the Rose will lead, but in most cases, hurt his enemy alone and in the dark." "But alone, John that is crazy" "No, the Rose will not be alone; the spirits of my ancestors will slither and walk beside me." He threw wood on the fire. "Lee, get some rest" and stalked into the night. LeSage lay in their lean two and listened attentively. Eyiee, Eyiee, he smiled to himself. "Yup there it is He's calling to his ancestors."

Time marches on and the battalion's skipper ordered intensive training. Hours and hours spent on the firing range. Striker insisted his grunts trained in the use and nomenclature of an infantry men's arsenal. It wasn't enough to be familiar with an M-1 Garand it was imperative they be adroit with the B.A.R., the 30 caliber machine gun, the 60 milliliter mortar. They received and shown the awesome efforts of the simulation mortar. He pushed them to the limit. Bayonet and hand to hand combat under a blazing sun was continuously endured. Staff Sergeant Laurent called a break. "Okay, the smoking lamp is lit. Listen up and listen tight. Someday you may be in the shit. You're out of ammo and the enemy is all over you. Now you've seen war movies. FORGET THAT HOLLYWOOD SHIT! In combat you're embarked in a world of savagery. Hate and fear rules the day. Your buddies are buzzard meat. Mass confusion and chaos rule supreme. Your officers and NCO's are struggling to survive or perhaps maybe dead or to fucked up to lead. What then? Marines are trained to win no matter how dirty or unfair. There's always a rock there's your helmet, your entrenching tool, your hands and feet, elbows, even your teeth. Hey if it comes to survival, bite his balls off. Or rip out his juggler vein. Teeth are a weapon. You are a weapon. You've been shown and taught how to kill. Retain it. Don't pooh, pooh this shit. One day what you learn here just may save your asses. There's no room for sympathy or compassion with a son of a bitch who's trying to cut out your heart. What morals and religion ingrained in you, forget it. If you want to avoid a body bag then steel your heart. That goody, goody shit works at a church bazaar not where you damn well may be headed. Hey look, I'm no atheist, I pray to Jesus Christ, Allah, and Buddha. I've got to be right somewhere. Whatever your beliefs, know this, in combat none of the above will appear. You'll be on your own. Some of you were altar boys, boy scouts and you even helped that old lady across the street. That's nice. But in the shit an old lady may just feed you a grenade."

After hours under a hot blistering sun, the troops marched to their quarters. Hot showers, chow and then a chance to relax, but only after weapons and equipment were squared away. NCO's constantly badgered their subordinates that weapons and equipment came first. It was paramount that an infantry unit could be activated and dispatched to hot spots at any given moment.

Broken Rose satisfied his men had seen to the care of weapons and equipment, strolled to the end of the hut. His friendship with his three bro's eternal but his duties as squad leader limited time together and he was always paranoid and fearful of displaying weakness and favoritism. "Well guys, what's up?" The three startled by his usual quiet approach, shuffled around and gazed at their corporal. Smiles lit their faces. "Hey Tonto," cried LeBron, "How be the boss man?" "Hey Tonto," he continued, "You our squad leader, right?" "Yeah, you know that." "So you check our weapons and gear, right?" The Rose Laughed, "Jake what's your point?" "Well that Staff Sergeant said today we're a weapon correct?" "Yeah, he did and you're a weapon." "Well listen if I'm a weapon you should inspect me and I've got some kind of an evil rash on my dick. Think it needs inspection." The Rose eyed LeBron. You know it's one of two things, you either don't bath or you planted that weeny in the wrong hole." LeSage and LaPore giggled like school boys. "Ain't so, Tonto," "He chokes it too much that's the problem" "Oh fuck you guys," uttered LeBron. "Hey Tonto, that Laurent knows his shit." "Eh, yeah I'd say that. He won the Big C in Korea." "How?" "Don't know. Scuttle butt has it something he did at Seoul. Maybe one day I'll ask the Top. "Well shit-birds get some shut eye. Another hike tomorrow, 0430 comes quick." LeBron calling the Rose back, "That fucker Striker gonna walk us to China one day." The Rose turned slightly, "that may be Jake, but I'll say this, thanks to his training and leadership, we'd do it. Semper-Fi and good-night."

The soft melody of taps wafted and echoed within the huge base. Broken Rose lay quietly an occasional snore or one of the troops stirring the only eruption to his solitude. His thoughts drifted back in time. His mind presence brought him to the comfort and security of the forest. The image of his grandfather, two wolves, clear and strong in his mind. He could hear the laughter they shared. He remembered looking into his dark eyes and how they could penetrate one's soul. He drifted off and pictured the mother he'd never seen. He called to the Great Spirit to protect his creatures that inhabited and roamed his precious forest. For he was concerned how they were faring in their wild beautiful wilderness. Sleep had its grip as he drifted off. He'd felt content, proud, and secure in the knowledge he was following in the footsteps of his ancestor's. He had answered their summons, that of a warrior.

LaPore tossed and turned for thoughts of Jean raced through his mind. He could feel her softness and smell her scent. His heart pounded. His soul nourished in that at last he'd found love. Someone to dream and plan with, to walk hand and hand through the byways of life. He thought of his dead adopted parents while tears welled in his eyes as he remembered the day they came and told him the dreaded news. His parents were no more. He groaned and sighed, for his dream world suddenly became a nightmare. He remembered the orphanage. A life of regimentation and loveless atmosphere. He dug deep and through, is my biological mother still of this world? Does she know of me? He rolled over and wiped away his silent tears. He listened to the life sounds of his buddies. He smiled, yes this is my family and now I have my Jean.

LeBron sat up right in his rack peering into darkness. He thought of his dark past. The numerous brushes with the law and the strong armed robberies, the muggings and stolen cars. How his juvenile youth was one of violence. He could smell the poverty and despair that filled the rat infested apartment. LeBron replayed the images of an alcoholic father ranting and raving, discouraged and ashamed that his life was in free fall with no hope. He remembered finally the judge's words, "Marine Corp or jail." He chuckled, "Yeah I'm a Marine and son of a bitch I won't admit it but damn proud. There are my brothers. He laughed inwardly as he reminisced how the brothers and sisters stared at him in his forest greens and felt proud. "Yes I needed this. My life has been turned around. These good men have shown me the way." He fell back in a second, fast asleep.

LeSage lay back. A perennial Lucky held in his fingers. The occasional glow as he puffed lit up the small area in reddish hue. His thoughts brought him back to prep school where he'd earned a baseball scholarship. How in his junior and senior years, he'd been selected to the All-State Team. How colleges and pro scouts were honing in on his successful exploits. He agonized over his short coming. How he'd question a priest instructor on a religious issue and his disagreement was the response. How when admonished by administrators, he couldn't or wouldn't recant. His integrity and pride had been his demise and he sank from high to the low. His parents were distraught and heartbroken. The world lay at his feet and he kicked it away. Inwardly he struggled and his soul in turmoil. His youthful heart discouraged and in dismay. He ebbed further and further into depression. He had to find himself and see what he was made of. See if he could reverse his despair and so one day alone and lonely, he joined the Marines. His father exclaimed, "why the Marines? They're cannon fodder." "Dad I wanted the toughest, need to see and find myself. Maybe the Marines are the antidote." LeSage smiled to himself. "Good choice. I've got buds and I think I'm measuring up with the best." He whispered softly, "Good night world."

PFC Charles Murphy reread the letter under the glow of a pen light. Tears coursed down his checks. His stomach in knots, nausea and searing tightness churned his stomach. The sour taste of bile and a burning sensation in his chest created labored breathing. He sprang from his rack. Pulled on his utility trousers and with unlaced boots sprinted to the head. Private Andrew DiLonsa woke. His bladder sending signals that he needed relief and fast. He tip toed through the hut unwilling to disturb his squad from their restless slumber. Yawning he pushed open the hatch and entered the head. He gasped, took one step back and raised his right hand to his mouth. He muffled a scream. There sitting against the bulkhead, his eyes open but unseeing was the person of PFC Murphy. Blood oozed down his shirt. A large puddle lay on the floor. The sweet sickening smell of congealing blood breathed in by DiLonsa. The offensive odor and horrific picture brought on retching and then vomit. DiLonsa rattled executed a quick about face and double timed to his hut. Crashing through the hatch he yelled, "Corporal Broken Rose! Corporal Broken Rose!" Shaking the racks, men stirred with some cursing, "What the fuck! Shut the fuck up, Asshole!" Broken Rose awoke with a start. "What DiLonsa? What's your problem?" "Corporal, The head! Come to the head! It's Murphy! I think he's dead! Come on, please!" The Rose was instantly alert in a flash. He was in utilities and on the move. He and DiLonsa double timing to the head. Squad members were puzzled. "What the fucks happening," yelled LeBron. "Who the fuck knows?" yelled Private Sullivan. We'll know soon enough. Some of the squad curious and concerned headed to the head.

Broken Rose followed by DiLonsa crashed through the hatch. One look told the Rose it was bad. Blood seeped down the walls and Murphy's head looped to the side. He'd cut his throat severing arteries. His bayonet still gripped in his right hand, lay by his side. "DiLonsa, get to the duty hut. Have the duty clerk notify the O.D. and Sergeant of the guard. And for Christ sake wake up Doc Little. Get him here yesterday! Move! And tell those trench rat's out there to stay the hell out! Go! God Damn! Go!"

Lieutenant Sisco and Sergeant Hemming O.D. and Sergeant of the guard roared up in their jeep spraying dust and debris in all directions. They were met by Corporal Broken Rose and entered the bloody scene. Lieutenant Sisco turned to the Rose, "has the company commander been notified?" "Yes Captain Klober is on the way and so is the skipper, Colonel Striker. Yes sir, also the liaison officer for

N.C.I.S. has been informed." Corporal, very good, keep the men away. He'd taken note that the small walkway leading to the head had congregated with curious Marines. They stood about in groups in front of their quonset huts. Sisco again addressed Broken Rose, "Has the scene been contaminated?" "I don't think so sir. The doc was here and pronounced him dead." "Where is he?" "Right over there sir," Sisco looked over his shoulder. "Doc, over here," the corpsmen sprinted to his Lieutenant. "Yes sir." "You're declaring him D.O.A?" "Yes Sir, been gone about an hour, maybe more, hard to say." "Okay Doc, hang loose. The skipper may want to talk to you."

The commander excused the squad from that day's hike. N.C.I.S. investigators swarmed into the area. They questioned Broken Rose at length. "Was there any reasons or telltale signs?" "No, they questioned squad members to a man and they confirmed he was a good Marine. Sharp, disciplined, never complained and did his duty and conformed to orders." N.C.I.S. investigators are sharp and through. They began combing his personal effects with a fine tooth comb. It netted results. On the floor by his rack, concealed by his utility jacket, they found a letter. The contents proved to be his undoing. Six months before his mother had passed. The letter found he'd received just that day at mail call. It revealed that his fiance two months pregnant had been tragically killed in a horrific car accident. Further investigation revealed there was no one else in his life. His father was a drunk and one day disappeared, gone in the night never heard from again. Colonel Striker when hearing this ordered PFC Murphy's body be laid to rest near his last residence, Camp Lejeune. He was buried with military honors. His squad handled the revered ceremony. Funds for the funeral home and grave site provided by his battalion commander, Lieutenant Colonel Striker had tried to keep anonymous, but good deeds like beautiful flowers sprout and bloom and so his troops knew but respected his privacy.

1st Squad, 1st Platoon Company B was lolling about the hut relishing a rare down time on a rainy Thursday afternoon. Small chatter filtered wall to wall with the men exaggerating conquests of women and also who could chug a lug a pitcher of beer. Who was the best shot in the platoon? Gossiping about noncoms and officers for Marines love to bitch and this was a bull's eye bitch session. The hatch flung open and Gunnery Sergeant Mazzone entered as usual snarling, "Afternoon ladies! Bradley's has a sale on bra's get your asses over there quick before the squids do a run and buy em all, Tonto!!" "Yes Gunny." "You and the two blind mice, LeBron and LeSage get your girly asses over to battalion H.Q. The boss wants to see you. Class A's you've got 20 minutes. Don't be late or your asses will be mine and I'll roast em on a spit." "Okay, Gunny, why are we being summoned?" "How the fuck do I know. I'm not the skipper's private secretary. I'm only a gunny, ain't privy to everything. Just put on your silk panties and double time your asses over there. He did a half face and glared at the squad. "Nosey fuckers Marines, Marines my ass, you remind me of a chicken coop, all feathers and no eggs." He stormed out the door. LeBron couldn't resist BAC, bac, bac, chic ca chic ca mimicking a chicken. The gunny like a bull in heat roared through the door. "You fucks you wouldn't make a pimple on a Chinese Marines ass. He retreated out the hatch and still muttering, headed to the platoon office. Laughter filled the hut. It finally finished and the squad returned to their bitching session.

The three Marines entered the battalion H.Q. The staff sergeant stood. "Well girls who do I have the pleasure of greeting?" The Rose spoke up. "Staff Sergeant we were notified to report to the Colonel." "Is that so? Is that right? Well who the fuck are you?" "I am Corporal Rose, and this is Privates LeSage and LeBron." "Damn, I'm sorry guys, the bands left for the day. But you can hum me the Marine Hymn. Well I'm waiting." Rose looked at his three buds. In unison they began to hum. "Oh shut the fuck up, I'm just fucking with you. Stay loose I'll let the skipper know you're here." They stood in silence with nerves on edge beating their brains wondering if and where they may have fucked up.

The commander's hatch opened and the Staff Sergeant beckoned them forward. "The Colonel will see you now." The three entered and stood at attention. Corporal Rose barked, "Sir Corporal Rose and Privates LeSage and LeBron reporting as ordered." Lieutenant Colonel Striker sat erect and proud. A smile formed at the corners of his mouth. "At ease Marines, I have an impressive letter here from headquarters Marine Corps signed off by the commandant himself. Seems you three were involved in an accident on the New Jersey Turnpike a short time ago. Seems your actions saved lives at your own pearl. Seems the courage and brotherhood you displayed impressed the New Jersey State Police and civvies involved." He stood and strolled around his desk. You personified the meaning "Espirits de Corps." You did that uniform proud. It is indeed my pleasure to inform you all, that you are the recipients to the Marine Corps Meritorious Medal. Furthermore Privates LeSage and LeBron are promoted to Private First Class. Corporal Rose, you've just made Corporal out of ATR. No promotion here just yet. But be advised a notation of your action is entered in your service file. That goes for you other two as well. I am damn proud to have you under my command and fully expect your pride and dedication to that uniform will continue to excel. He hoisted a small black box from his desk top and commenced to pin the ribbons denoting their awards on their chest. Marines, thank you and congratulations. Semper Fi. They snapped to attention and knew they'd been politely dismissed executed an about face and marched out the hatch. The Staff Sergeant was waiting. "Hey guys good going, just another star that announces what the corps is about." "Thanks Sarge and they exited the battalion H.Q. and at a brisk pace, returned to their squad's area. As they approached the hut, they were hailed by the raspy voice of Gunny Mazzone. They halted and Mazzone snarling and got in their faces. "Did you purchase your bra? Are they white, Pink or black? I say pink you remind me of fairies. Then a broad grin lit up his face. Look the words out Semper-Fi. You Jar heads are A-Okay. Those ribbons look good. Keep it up, next liberty, the beers on me." He turned stepped off smartly and then looking over his shoulder, "you can take those silk panties off now." He marched off still laughing.

Colonel Rappert Van Meer sat slightly slouched behind his desk and the eagles on his collar twinkling brightly due to the overhead light falling at just the right pitch. Lieutenant Colonel Eric Striker and Lieutenant Colonel Stan Simpson sat quietly across from him in silence. They had been summoned with a call from their regimented commander to a private meeting. Now at his side and waiting patiently in anticipation as to why the summons at such short notice. Van Meer spoke softly and both light birds leaned forward so as to hear better as to what was being said. "Gentlemen, you've been summoned here because we are about to commence our annual war games. General Greene, the Division Commander has approved this exercise and feels strongly we should commence forth with. Thus you, Colonel Striker, Eighth Marines skipper and you Colonel Simpson, CO of the Sixth Marines will lead off and jump start operations. Greenleaf slated for this weekend. You Colonel Striker will command red group and Simpson the blues. Your battalions will square off and attempt to out maneuver each other commencing at 0400 this Friday. Division has been notified and neutral referees will be on site to determine victor and loser. That's it. Return to your battalions. You are at liberty to move your battalions at your discretion. Good luck." Both Striker and Simpson rose simultaneously, "Yes sir, thank you, sir."

Striker chose a night march for his battalion on Thursday. Maneuvering in the dark minimized prying eyes and the troops were ordered to keep noise to a minimum. Striker set a quick pace. His motive was understandable. He wanted to have his battalion positioned on a midsize knoll before sun up. He had several squads moving on the flanks and up front hoping to avoid surprise from

Simpson's blues. The knoll offered an advantage of the view of the area where the reds and blues would skirmish. They had begun their march at 0200. Striker had notified no one. By 0600 they were entrenched on the knoll. His troops dug in deep and his flankers set up position three hundred yards from a body of water. This body of water was a midsize pond that sat approximately three quarters of a mile from the knoll. The troops waited in quiet snacking on cold rations. The smoking lamp was out. Verbatim till further notice. Striker had positioned Broken Rose's squad to his front with orders to warn of the blues approach and direction.

At noon, Corporal Rose hissed into his radio. "Robin three to Red Robin." Striker took the hand piece from his operator. "Robin one go ahead robin three." "Sir, the blues have been sighted looks like they're setting up a perimeter on the other side of the pond. No flankers or skirmishers in sight." Striker grunted, "okay, robin three out." Odd he thought, "you'd think he'd have eyes out. He has no idea we're on him." He summoned his runner. PFC James Little moved quickly in a half crouch. "Little get to my company CO's. Tell them to keep the troops quiet and in their holes. No talking, no movement, no smoking. If they have to relieve themselves their hole is their heads. Now move and stay low." Striker was amused. Simpson had no idea he'd already exposed his position and still he'd ordered no patrol activity. They wore on slowly. A hot sun baked the troops in a hot sweat but movement and noise was minimal. Striker's drilling and method of discipline were now paying dividends.

As darkness approached Striker crawled to Broken Rose's position. A voice hissed "who goes there?" Striker came the reply from him. "What's the password?" Striker smiled, "Broken," the voice confirmed with the proper response "Rose". He slithered in Rose's hole. "Good evening sir." "Evening Corporal, any new developments over there?" "No sir. Lots of movement, they're not very quiet. They're even lit some fires." Striker stared across the pond. "Jesus Christ, your right. What the fuck is Simpson thinking? Shit, leave it to the pogey bait 6th, Corporal." "Yes sir." The Rose sat erect staring into his colonel's eyes. "You got any ideas?" "Yes sir I do." "Well share it, speak freely." "Well sir, let me take my squad. I'll use half for a diversion and the other half will assist me in destroying their CP and taking their commander." "You mean their colonel?" "Yes sir, I do." "You think you can just march in and take him?" Striker chortled, "come on, this isn't ATR." "No sir, it's not, but look at them. It'll be a piece of cake. Look sir, the worst that can happen we're captured. But we're only a squad. Those amateurs over there have no idea that we're even here." "I don't know Rose." "Well sir, you asked. I believe it'll be a walk in the sun." Striker stared into his young corporals eyes and saw the confidence and determination. Okay Corporal do it whenever you're ready. But leave two men here as an LP for our main body." "Aye, aye, sir." Striker smiled and crawled back to his command post.

Darkness had landed its black tarp. The Rose and nine men minus boots, dog tags, and webb gear crawled flat on their stomachs to the pond. LeBron with three men broke to the left. Rose with four men broke to the right. They carried just knives and each man had strapped three smoke grenades to their chests. "Okay," Rose whispered, "let's go." He and his mates slipped into the pond to minimize sound they elected to swim mostly under water. They'd wrapped and rewound tape over their grenades. After a five minute swim, they reached the bank. Weeds and pussy willows offered camouflage. They lay still, watching, listening; only laughter and chatter came from the camp. They watched as two officers exited a tent by a large pine. Approximately twenty five yards from the pond. A squatted man with silver oak leaves laughed heartedly at something one of the officers had said as they departed. Broken Rose nudged LeSage. "Shit that's the CP, the Great One smiles on us. This is too easy."

They lay immersed in mud in water. The camp still as men tired from the march bedded down. All was quiet. The four crawled forward inch by inch. There finally a sentry pacing slowly back and forth. Just feet from them. Broken Rose sprang up life a tiger and grabbed the sentry from behind. His hand over his mouth and dragged him to the water's edge where LeSage, LaPore and two others pounded on him. Tying and gagging him. He was subdued through threat and physical pressure rolled and left by the edge of the water concealed by darkness. Broken Rose and his cohorts made their way to the tent. Slowly painfully it came into view. Only the flicker of a quarter moon blinked in the night. Broken Rose unsheathed his knife and working quickly cut a hole in the side of the tent. They entered. The interior lay in darkness. Only the shallow breathing of the colonel on his cot could be heard. But it was enough. It was a beacon and the Rose struck. Planting a hand over the sleeping form. Simpson felt pressure unable to breath. Strong hands had him in a vice like grip. He was quickly wrapped tight with rope and gagged pulled from his cot and dragged along the ground. LeSage and LaPore hung smoke grenades on the tents flaps with the pins half out. Strings from the pins pinned to the flaps. The colonel was pulled into the water. His face kept up right and like a log floated across the pond.

Broken Rose let out his "Eyiee" call as they approached once they were on the opposite bank and safe. It was LeBron's signal to create their planned diversion. He and his comrades began yelling and screaming, taunting the 6th Marines with insults. They then began tossing their smoke bombs. Red, green and yellow smoke lit up the dark. It was like a rainbow in the blackness. Their actions created chaos in the blue's camp. Troops roused from their sleep. Officers and noncoms running amok shouting orders that went unheard in the confusion. The four carried the colonel at double time towards the knoll. Striker had been notified by the LP of their safe arrival and that a package was about to be delivered. Simpson's Exec along with two Company Commanders quick stepped to their Commander's tent thinking they were under full attack by the reds. They looked to their CO for orders and direction. Receiving no response to their calls, they pulled on the tents flaps. Womp—womp—womp---womp four smoke grenades blossomed beneath the night sky. The blue area lit up as Times Square on New Year's Eve. The officers looked at each other in dismay and knew they'd been had.

Colonel Striker ordered Colonel Simpson brought to his C.P, a form encased in rope and tape squirming and gurgling all the way. When released an enraged Simpson stomped and raged as spittle flowed from his mouth. His skives wet and blackened by mud added to this embarrassment and dismay. Colonel Stan Simpson sat in disgust in Strikers C.P. "your fucking trench rats pulled a bushers stunt. They showed no courtesy to a high ranking officer. I demand they be disciplined. Shot even! What the fuck kind of shit is this? Come on Eric, you certainly can't condone their actions." Striker sat silent and said nothing. The tent flap flew open and the Division Commander Major General Greene entered followed by his aide Major Ralston. Both men sprang to attention. "At ease, as you were," General Greene took in the scene and scanned the tents interior. His eyes locked with Strikers for only a moment. He then gazed at Simpson. "Jesus Christ Stan you look like you spent the night in a cheap whore house and exited a rear window fleeing from a pimp. Simpson red faced squeaked General it ain't right. I was shown no respect or courtesy by Striker's men. I implore the General that an investigation be initiated and those men disciplined. Maybe even Colonel Klink here. The General glared at Simpson. "No! No! No! Colonel that's what these war games are all about initiative and adaption to a given situation. You and your command were caught with your pants down around your ankles. If the moment were real you'd be dead and your command destroyed. This incident displays a lack of discipline and combat sense within your command. I highly recommend you return to your battalion investigate what the hell your sentries were doing and by God find out who the fuck was responsible and fumbled on the one yard line. Jesus H. Christ Stan, you would have lost an entire battalion. Go back and lick your wounds and when you return to your HQ you best kick some ass. You're embarrassed and pissed off. Good! That means no instant replay. When we return to quarters, contact my aide here, Major Ralston. He'll set up an appointment." "Begging you pardon General, Chimed in Colonel Simpson, an appointment with who?" The General stared at the floor. "The closest thing to God, with me, looks like I need to kick ass!"

Greene stared at Striker, Colonel please get Colonel Simpson here some utilities. I can't bear the thought of him prancing through your area in skivvies. Good day gentlemen." He crashed through the tent opening slamming the flap. In a moment later a jeep's engine coughed and the General and his aide roared off in a trail of grayish dust.

After Simpson had donned fresh utilities and was about to take leave, he turned to Striker, you didn't play fair Eric, you're a prick. Striker rose from his steel seat. He roared Stan, where is it fair in combat. I've heard enough of your bullshit. Get the fuck out of here before I go through you like shit through a goose." "Yeah, you're a bad ass Striker, Semper-Fucking-Fi!" He angrily pulled open the tent flap and looking straight ahead quickly departed the 8th Marines sector. Major Pezzone had waited for Colonel Simpson to vacate his CO's tent. He entered gingerly. "Well Eric what do you think?" "Simpson is gone Frank. The General wears the big medal earned on Iwo. The Cross and Silver Star from Korea for he's an infantry man Frank. He can't and won't forgive Simpson's weakness." "Which is what skipper?" "He's no infantry commander. It's simple as that. He's gone". "Where, Colonel?" "Who knows who gives a shit, logistics, and motor pool? Back to the world, whatever it is it's a safe bet he's gone."

Colonel Simpson sat quietly in the outer chamber of General Greene's office. His mood somber shunned by fellow officers, he'd isolated himself in his office separated from his peers and battalion. There was no surprise when he was summoned to Division. The General's door swung open. Major Ralston, the Generals Aide beckoned, "Sir the General will see you now." Having said that the Major strutted away and made his exit through a side door. Simpson reluctantly entered, snapped to attention, "Sir, Lieutenant Colonel Simpson reporting as ordered." The General Sullen shuffled papers lay out on his desk. He swiveled his chair and gazed out his window which offered a view of the expansive parade grounds. "Sit, Colonel." He swung around facing Simpson. Eyes locked on him. "Colonel I won't snowball this issue. I'm relieving you of command of the sixth battalion. They deserve better. There is a history of pride, honor and impeccable courage. Your recent actions or lack of same in last week's exercise borders on criminal neglect. If in combat your command and good men would have perished. Fifteen years in the Corps and your record is lean and no out of country duty. You were a paper tiger in the pentagon and other duty stations." "Sir" "Hold on Colonel, I'm not finished. Somewhere down the line you hooked a rabbi and he or she decided an infantry assignment would enhance your career movement with a rising star up the ladder. Unfortunately for you this choice back fired a blessing in disguise for the Corps. You will report to the B.O.Q. to await further orders and instructions that will be all Colonel Dismissed." Simpson rose and came to attention. "Yes sir." Executed an about face eyes straight ahead. He walked briskly form the office with his future in doubt.

The eighth Marines were on the march. Striker continued to drive them. Determined to mold his battalion into a cohesive fighting machine. He knew full well the rigors and devastation of combat and had every intention of exposing his troops as much as possible to the sounds and conditions of battle. The troops were in top physical condition this he had brow beat and striven for. But he was concerned with their lack of exposure to effects that rattled even seasoned combat veterans. Striker in the lead maintained a vigorous pace. The men laden with full combat packs bent into the wind with one foot up, one foot down. The battalion wound its way through woodlands crossing small streams climbing hills and knolls. They slipped and sloshed through wetlands, bogs and where an unwary grunt suddenly disappeared in unknown sink holes and was pulled quickly upright by fellow Marines. Their utilities caked with mud and sweat weighed heavy. Helmets abused their scalps, pack straps bit into shoulders. Pride and fear of ridicule drove them ever forward. In private cadence they would whisper one foot up one foot down.

Striker gazed off into the horizon. He'd labored tediously to ensure surprises to his troops along the line of march. As they approached an open field, high grass swayed in the soft wind. Birds screeched their annoyance disturbed by the sudden appearance and disruption caused by a thousand troops chomp chomping through their habitat. As the column pushed through the open field, the whoosh, whoosh of artillery resonated somewhere off in the distance. A deafening whir, whir, whir could be heard over head. It sounded like the high pitched sound of a locomotive or diesel trucks gearing down. The clash of thunder meshed as one. It caused goose bumps up and down the spine. Explosives initiated maybe three quarters of a mile to the front and left flanks. Still the column snaked forward. Thunder like sound overhead and explosions continued it seemed for an eternity, in fact, the outgoing artillery barrage swept over them for all of fifteen minutes. Senior NCO's cajoled their grunts. "Now you know the sound of outgoing, incoming a whole new ball game. You bet your asses you'll quickly learn the differences.

Striker quickened the pace. Time was golden he'd arranged additional treats for his troops. Winding a bend they could make out the dark shape of old baldy. A haze like ring circled its summit. As the column approached, a high pitched roar exploded to its rear. The troops turned in unison. Apprehension and excitement creased their faces. Adrenaline pumped as they stared in fascination as four specks appeared in the sky looming larger and larger on their approach. They stared in amazement as the specks became fighter planes coming in low and quick. The thunderous roar as the planes swept in causing ringing sensations to the ear. The ground shock and rolled trees bent swaying crazily in the after blast. The grunts gasped in disbelief for they could see the pilot's helmets and visors as they screeched over at tree top level. The fighters conducted several fly overs. Then in tight formation soared upward a trail of exhaust contrails pointed their way of departure as far as the eye could see.

Leg muscles groaned their displeasure as the struggle to climb old baldy took hold. Packs weighed heavily and rivulets of sweat coursed from their bodies. Utilities soaked liked they'd stood in a hard rain. Men gasped gulping in air in labored breaths. There was no break. The pace was stepped up. Water a no- no, water discipline ruled the moment. One step up, one step down, finally they reached the summit and their trek downward a challenge. One had to lean back call on reserve strengths so as not to run over the grunt ahead. Eyes watered red rimmed from constant sweat, NCO's displaying top conditioning and leadership sprinted up and down the column, cajoling, yelling, and encouraging their troops to move — move.

Reaching the bottom the column in route step and still tight clambered into a small clearing. Suddenly the woods exploded the intimidating roar of diesel engines echoed throughout the forest. Loud crashes as trees lurched and twisted fell to the ground. The surreal sound of tank, thrashing, mashing and grinding, screeching and bellowing, shuddering, resonated across the clearing. It was intimidating to the grunts. Long snouts poked through the vegetation weapons of fear and carnage crashed through the underbrush. A squad of tanks confronted the grunts revving up their gears, clanging and clunking coming right at them. Nozzles of their cannon pointed at their faces. Dust and grime created a cloud of grit and dark haze. The ground shook as an earthquake was upon them. The roar of the huge behemoths deafened the ears as they thundered by on the flanks of the column. Tank commanders, their heads peering from turrets gave thumbs up as they roared away with their threads spraying bits of earth and rocks into the wind. As quick as they appeared in a cloud of dust and flying brush they were gone.

Striker ordered a halt. He ordered his company commanders to have their units relax in a semi-circle, smoking lamp lit. A thick haze of blue smoke curled up and away into the hazy sky. Men drank greedily from canteens, admonished by NCO's to Drink slowly and conserve. Striker stood tall facing his command. In a loud voice he addressed his battalion. "Today you were introduced to the sound of outgoing artillery, experienced the roar of fighters flying low and menacing and felt the intimidation of armor. Remember this, these were our guys, in the shit, armor is hell and so is artillery and air power. As infantry you are and will be confronted and deal with all three as well as your counter parts, their infantry. This is why here in this command; you are driven past the maximum effort. Both physical and mental conditioning's are paramount to your survival. There is no room for weakness or the soft in combat. This is a combat command. You and I must keep in a state of readiness. The summons could come like a thief in the night and usually does. We can train, teach, advise, gentlemen absorb, digest, ingest, retain. Discipline your bodies and minds. Retain a firm resolve and remember this is combat. You're surrounded by enemy and buddies but you fight alone and die alone." He strode off followed by his Exec Major Pezzone who in a loud clear voice bellowed, "Company commanders, assemble by the big pine located north of our position. There will be a meeting of officers in 20 minutes!" Pezzone halted, returned and faced the troops. "Remember this, somewhere in the world some fuck is also training. You must be better, stronger, and quicker, smarter. It's that simple, Semper-Fi!" He turned and double timing caught up with his commander.

1ˢᵗ squad was entrenched in cleaning weapons and gear. Small chatter bounded off the walls. LeBron spoke softly, "this country is fucked up." LeSage queried, "how so Jake?" "You didn't get the scuttle butt? Two brothers from Able Company got their asses kicked. Seems they tried to gain admittance to the all night cafe and some fat ass big red neck took to beating them with a black jack. They're now in sick bay suffered all kinds of broken bones. Bigoted cops did nothing. Rumor has it they stood by and watched." Broken Rose was attentive and quiet but listening. "Come on Jake," retorted LeSage. "You've got to be shitting." "No way, my man, it went down America the Beautiful. Only down here if you're black, you do the dance or get your ass kicked. Whitey has free reign."

The Rose said nothing. The squad was perplexed. For three weeks Broken Rose took liberty, preferring to go alone. The Rose stood in the shadows. His amber eyes took in the bright lights. The large neon sign winking red on and off, "Girls, Entertainment fun for all, the all night cafe welcomes you, beckoning potential patrons. He stood perfectly still. His eyes scanned the parking lot. Several vehicles parked sat silent. Most of the patrons had long departed. An owl hooted while the moon took refuge behind a passing cloud. A figure emerged from the rear door. "Eyiee," whispered the Rose. He comes, dressed in black for he meshed with the night. He moved quickly stealthy like brother wolf. The big man approached his truck. The Rose sprung. Right hand grasped the big man around the mouth. His left hand drove deep into the kidney. A soft moan escaped from the big man. The Rose spun him around a knee to the groin and a chop to the throat. A palm blow to the nose and an elbow to the solar plexus. The big man crumbled and fell to the ground. The Rose kicked him in the face and blood spurted in a geyser. Then the Rose placed the big man's hands on the ground and with his booted feet mashed them into the ground. The big man squealed and passed out. His hands were crushed and broken. Broken Rose stood over his prey. "Eyiee, Eyiee, he chanted in a whisper. Do not fuck with the green warriors.

Raising his hands to the air, "Great One, justice served." He flipped an eagle globe and anchor on the chest of the unconscious form and stole into the night.

The battalion assembled on line. To their rear a small stage had been erected housing the visiting dignitaries, senators and congressmen in attendance to observe the awesome fire power and capabilities of a Marine Combat Battalion. The sun peaked low, low, on the horizon. Night was spreading its dark quilt. Stars began to twinkle and night birds flitted about and their calls echoing in the descending darkness.

Lieutenant Colonel Striker stood with the spectators. There to answer questions and to officer insight if queries were asked. He watched as Gunny Sargent Mazzone walked the line he could hear his crisp commands as he exalted the troops. "Interlock fire! Interlock Fire, lock and load!" The troops had been issued live tracer ammo. Their targets loomed in the semi darkness. The hulk of an old burned out tank, the remnants of an old rusted deuce and a half a rotted and dilapidated wooden structure. Striker informed the observers that the line would soon explode in a crescendo of riffle fire. They complied by stuffing cotton in their ears and several donned ear plugs, waiting in anticipation as excitement as electricity fingered the air.

Gunnery Sergeant Mazzone stood tall and erect to the rear. Checking his watch, he bellowed, "Fire!" The night exploded in a thunderous explosion as the Marines fired with disciplined precision. Red streaks pierced the night. Rounds bouncing on targets split the air. The night howled with booming. One could hear the B.A.Rs 30 caliber and 50 caliber machine guns roaring in unison. The dignitaries were startled by the womp, womp of 60 millimeter and 81 millimeter detonations. Huge geysers erupted on and around the targets. The onslaught continued for fifteen minutes. Then Mazzone screamed into the night, "CEASE FIRE!! CEASE FIRE!! CLEAN YOUR

WEAPONS AND PICK UP EMPTY CARTRIGES! NCO'S MAKE
DAMN SURE WEAPONS ARE CLEAN AND ASSEMBLE YOUR
SQUADS AND PLATOONS!"

The smell of cordite hung heavy in the air. Smoke bellowed in
the night sky creating a ghost like haze that hovered in about the
dignitaries. They watched in awe as the battalion formed and marched
off into the night with boots thundering in unison. Striker stood
quiet erect and proud. A voice called to him as the moon brightened
the stage in a golden hue. "Colonel don't you think our military is
in overkill with its training?" Lieutenant Colonel Striker faced his
questioner, "sir, whom do I have the pleasure of addressing?" "Oh,
I'm Senator Collins from Ohio." Striker cleared his throat, shifted his
legs. Remained silent and gazed into the night. Then spoke slowly
with a slight menace in his voice. "Well sir, I'll say this. If you were to
summon the ghosts of good men who gave their all on Omaha, Anzio,
the Bulge, Africa, Iwo Jima, The Canal, Okinawa, Sai Pan, Korea,
Midway, their answer would thunder through American Cemeteries
which ring the world. Their crosses gleaming white in the sun. The
colors reigning supreme as she flips in the wind. Their answer would
be train, train, train. Our airmen, soldiers, sailors, Marines, must be
smarter, stronger, and superior to our enemies. No sir, there is no
overkill." The senator smiled sheepishly, "touché Colonel, touché."

Striker was pleased and felt his battalion had performed
magnificently. Displaying skill and discipline in that nights fire
display for the countries leaders. Satisfied his troops were bedded
down for the night, he returned to the B.O.O. His quarters were
comfortable, but sparse like most billets in the military. He entered
a dark living room and switched on the wall light and sat in an old
stuffed recliner that had seen better times. It was his favorite and had
seen many commands with him along the way. He couldn't part with
his old trusted friend. He reclined in his old standby and took sight on
his walls adorned with photos and numerous citations. There at the

top in an old twisted frame, his award for the Navy Cross. Below and to the right the citation as a recipient of the Purple Heart. He sprang from the chair and headed into his small kitchen and opened the fridge and retrieved two beers and returned to the living room. Tired he spanned on his old scarred couch. It too had been though the test of travel. He gulped one beer then sipped at the second. He closed his eyes. Mental fatigue dulling his senses. He sought sleep but his brain was in overdrive. Semi-conscious his mind wandered traveled back in time to another time, another place. The sounds of battle raged and he felt the quakes of explosions. The smell of cordite. The screams of men in agony. The gurgle of dying men. The blare of Chinese bugles in the night as they swept over his platoon's MLR and how he'd cajoled his men. Rallied them to counter attack and hurl the hordes of enemy back. He thought of fire power and how discipline had turned the tide and saved the moment. He dwelled on his response to the Senator and knew he was correct. He'd witnessed and been involved in the death of Marines in Korea and determined to train, train, train, his battalion. He vowed that the ghosts of his young troops could or would not haunt him if he failed in lack of leadership or training. He'd attended Annapolis suffered the indignity and rigors of the academy. He conditioned his mind and body pushing him beyond the maximum. His goal and dream to one day command a combat detachment. He'd succeeded in that quest, but hadn't reached the summit yet. No, he had to continue to push his troops, to motivate his officers and NCO's. He'd experienced the sting and horror of combat. It was his job no, his responsibility to motivate his command, to steel them, and discipline them for what could or might be. His was a combat command and by God he exclaimed in the dark, through blood, sweat, tears and discipline they're be ready. The faces of dead comrades loomed in the night. Voices raised in a crescendo. Let no man's ghost say if only your training had prepared us. Falling into slumber he sighed, train, train, train. Push them beyond endurance. Get them prepared for the face of hell and its demon fury.

The battalion rewarded with a 96 hour liberty bashed in the thought of four days away from the rigors of training. Men shaved and shared showers and donned their forest greens and braved the line for liberty cards. LeBron, LaPore and LeSage hammered at Broken Rose to join them in loose fun. LaPore would have preferred to see Jean, but she was out of state for a relatives wedding. The Rose finally gave in. He would accompany his buddies and gaze at white eyes method of entertainment. The four piled into the borrowed old Chevy. It sputtered and gasped black oily smoke bellowing into the air. With a cough and spasm the tired engine exploded into life and they were off cruising into the night.

Their travels brought them to the All Night Café. They entered through the front door. Smoke and the dark odor of human sweat offended their nostrils while the glow of red lights creating a surreal and sexy atmosphere. Girls half-clad swayed and twisted on a make shift stage. The interior stunk of aged beer and ripe bodies. The four buds found an empty table in the rear of the salon and ordered four beers and whiskeys. Waitresses in skim costumes fritted among the patrons. Spending and laboring to satisfy paying customers. Broken Rose downed a whiskey, his first ever. He choked and gagged. "Shit, this is fire water!" His three buds laughed heartily. "No sweat Tonto, you'll soon feel good and won't give a shit." The music blared off beat sounds that rattled throughout the café with the crush of human body's souls attempting to discard and forget troubles. The lights were on couples dancing, laughing, bullshiting. All seemed to be enjoying the evening. The door burst open and in strode a menacing group of bikers. They were clothed in black leather. The words happy dicks embossed on the rear of their jackets. They pushed and shoved their way through the revelers. Their leader, a big man, with a huge belly muscled his way to the bar. He leaned on the bar and reached over and grabbed the barman pulling him close. "Listen fuck nuts, the happy dicks are here. Fuck these Marines. You make us your priority. We're at the head of the class, got that worm lips?" The bartender shook and quivered, "Err, I think so." "No thinking asshole, just do it!"

PFC Richard Parkinson sitting at the bar overheard the exchange. He looked at the big fat biker. "Sir," beers ahead and bleary eyed he gaped at the biker, "hey fuck head what puts you ahead of the line?" The biker, an amused smile lighting his face, glanced at his inquisitor. "Why you little fuck, strength and power, we'll kick your jar-head asses from here to Lejeune, is that good enough?" Parkinson gazed off into the smokey haze. "Listen lets you and I have a drink? Then we'll see who talks the talk and walks the walk outside." The big biker snorted, "you gotta be shitting. Okay, little man, order up. The drinks came. Parkinson raised his glass in a toast. The fat biker raised his glass to his lips. Parkinson struck like a cobra, smashing the big man's drink into his mouth with the palm of his hand. Blood and teeth spewed into the air. Parkinson tore into him like an enraged panther, with a blow to the throat, a knee to the balls and a kick to the jaw. The fat biker collapsed to the floor. But Marine Parkinson continued his onslaught stomping and kicking his fat adversary into oblivion. Fellow bikers rushed to his aid but were cut short by a sea of forest green. The bar erupted in chaos bodies were slammed against walls. Grunts and groans as fists and elbows and feet found contact with soft flesh. Neutral patrons fled from the bar and dancing girls screaming in dismay descending the stage. Broken Rose laughing, feeling no pain from ingested spirits grabbed a biker by the neck and spun him around and chopped him in the throat with a geyser of blood spewing into the air. LeBron seized the moment, donning an unconscious bikers jacket and helmet he sprinted to the bar. He hefted the cash register and fled through the rear door bellowing "Buds, buds, this way!" Broken Rose, LaPore, and LeSage heard their prearranged call and fled out the door in pursuit of LeBron.

They reached safety in a triangle of shrubs. "God damn," exclaimed LeSage. "What the fuck did you do?" LeBron laughed sheepishly, Hell got us four hundred fifty bucks. Boy, lots of smokes and poo tang. LaPore shaking his head, "LeBron you're under a fucking rock." "Maybe so Lance but they're think one of them asshole bikers took it as he shed the leather jacket and helmet. Look buds not to worry old Brooklyn got it covered." When the cops arrived they found happy dick bikers laid out in various contorted positions and not a Marine was in sight and witnesses swore the bikers turned on each other.

Doc Little had the weekend medical duty. Dispensing whatever treatment weary Marines warranted. Happy held down the duty this weekend as most of Bravo Company enjoyed liberty. He kept himself busy checking supplies and folding linen, stocking small poles in neat concise piles then placing them in proper bins. Sitting, he reviewed medical records of Marines who sought treatment in the past week and determined who warranted follow up treatment and jotting down names and platoons of those who needed further attention. He smiled most of these troopers suffered with pulled muscles, abrasions, some severer than others within the structure of an infantry unit the rigorous of training inevitably led to injury. Oh sure there were slackers and whackers, but they were easily weeded out and sent scurrying back to their outfits. He laughed quietly thinking how grunts would sheepishly seek his help. "Hey Doc I've got the itches." "Naw, you fuck, you got the crabs," as he dispensed a can of powder. "Another gee Doc, it hurts when I piss." "You fuck you put it in a dirty hole and got the clap. Hop up on that table and drop your drawers," as he whacked him with a bayonet type needle. "Keep an eye on it and double time back if it doesn't improve." His portable radio set low hummed soft music alone he leaned back in his chair turning back a page in his mind. He was back on the streets of Baltimore. Hailed from a poverty stricken neighborhood, had grown depressed and dismayed at his surroundings. The poverty, apathy and lack of respect for life, found him in a downward spiral with no relief or future. He'd also found interest in the medical field and devoured books and articles that revealed its secrets and mystic. Witnessing the suffering that plagued his surroundings piqued his interest in that field. It was his dream to help those in need, rather than hide his head in the sand like an ostrich. His father was an unknown and he tired of new uncles who paraded in an out of the wretched tenement called home.

On a rainy day, he bused into the heart of the city, exiting he began walking it didn't matter where. A light rain began falling. He watched as pedestrians fled for cover. Doc Little entered a coffee shop and ordered a light with sugar and continued his stroll with his head bent to ward off water droplets. He ducked under an overhang for cover sipping his coffee. His eyes riveted on a large neon sign winking on an off over a small glass enclosed structure. The words U.S. Navy recruiter beckoned to him. Crossing the street, he pushed opened the door. The Navy recruiter sat at a gun whale colored desk. "Hi, can I help you?" Within the hour he'd enlisted. It was an escape from his hell whose tentacles were sucking him deeper and deeper into life's sewer.

He'd had basic in the Great Lakes and scored high in various exams and test's. His high standing opted him a choice and he was ecstatic when accepted to be a corpsmen. How fortunate he thought the door is ajar and I can pursue my dream and climb the ladder medically. The Navy trained him and encouraged him. He felt wholesome, productive and excelled by throwing himself without hesitation in assembling and mastering that which proved the way to being a Corpsman.

He graduated at the top of his class and was given a choice of duty assignments. He weighed his decision carefully and chose Fleet Marines Force Recon and he quartered here. I am in Camp Lejeune N.C. with a bunch of jarheads and I love these crazy bastards. Nowhere is a Corpsman shown more respect or gratitude. He picked up a medical book and reading carefully ingesting its contents. Study,

study, study, he vowed, he'd never cease till the title Dr. prefixed his name.

Captain Andrew Klober Bravo Company Commander sat in his office and spread before him; on his military issued desk were the personal files of personnel under his command. The hour was late. Night had fallen and a soft wind rattled the window pain. There was a threat of rain but had held off so far. Klober was known to burn the midnight oil. The Eighth Marine's entire Company Commanders familiar with their battalion skipper Colonel Striker knew this was Gospel expected of them. Klober studied the files, occasionally writing notations and fingering the goods and the bad, the dos and the don'ts concerning individual highs and lows. All of his top NCO's experienced and were mostly combat vets of Korea. His 1st sergeant a top soldier second to none and his gunnery sergeant a legend and top platoon sergeant were the "Big C". His finger traced downwards resting on the list of corporals, his squad leaders. All were young and inexperienced. He sat back. Lit a camel and blew smoke into the air, watched as it curled into the semi-darkness. He felt concern, with unanswered questions nagging at his conscious. "What do they know? What do these kids know?" He called to his top kick, 1st Sergeant, "Yes sir," the reply came. "1st sergeant Robert Gates had flown into the office. "Top, have the company clerk reach out to all the companies squad leaders. Have those corporals assembled here by 2000 hours." "Yes sir."

The Junior NCO's were ushered into the empty office of the company commander. A few lucky ones sat in straight backed chairs, but most stood and leaned against walls of file cabinets. 1st Sergeant Gates entered, "Ten-sion!" The men stood and boomed off the walls with a crisp attention and eyes straight ahead. "At ease, at ease!" bellowed Klober. The men shifted standing at parade rest. "Men rest easy stand comfortably. Okay, I've assembled you my squad leaders because you lead fire teams. They are the arms and strength of a rifle company." He sat, lit a camel. "Now my question, do all your men know the workings of the B.A.R?" Some of the young NCO's squirmed uncomfortably. "Well gentlemen I asked a question. I expect answers. Okay, one on one then." He repeated his question. Half his corporals replied in the affirmative and the other half negative. "Shit!" he barked. "Men what if your B.A. R. man and his assistant are taken out? We need that fire power. You can't teach in combat. Okay, here's the scoop. Tomorrow, an off day, I'll expect you squad leaders and your squads here in formation at 0800 hours. Understood? Very good," with a wave of his hand, he barked "Dismissed!" The grunts came to attention and filed from the room.

Klober watched them depart. He then grabbed his land line and rang the firing officer in charge of the range, his friend, Major Frank Tinker. "Major Tinker here." "Frank, Klober here. I need a favor." Tinker laughed "no you can't have my old lady." "That's too bad Frank. Here's my problem." Finishing his summation Tinker chuckled, "Yeah have your boys here 0830 sharp." "Thanks Frank, owe you one." "You mean another one." "Right Andy," Klober laughed and rang off.

The next morning the entire company marched to the range. Every man was indoctrinated thoroughly not only in the functions of the B.A.R. but its bigger sisters the 30 caliber and the 50 caliber machine guns. The extra training commenced at 0830 and to Klober's satisfaction terminated at 12:30 hours. Addressing his company, "every man now is familiarized with our heavy infantry weapons at a given notice. I expect my Nom Coms to stay on their people as to fields of fire, weaponry, etc. etc.; we're not in school here. There's no report card. If you don't retain here then you'll die there. It is imperative that Marines possess a keen edge and able to field strip and reassemble the infantry men's repertoire. I expect it and will stay on it. Dismissed!!"

The squad had drawn weekend liberty and lonely men embraced freedom. Long lines of green clad figures streamed out the gates to points unknown. Bent on good times, Broken Rose elected to spend liberty alone. Grabbing his knife and self-made life pouch, he sprinted through the huge base allowing his run to extol him ever on ward. As he passed rolling hills and lush foliage he marveled at the vast expanse of Lejeune. His legs propelled him forward ever forward. He inhaled the fresh air. He loved the scent of the forest. The sweet aroma of giant pines along with the fragrance only a forest offered a mixture of rotted wood and flowers. The music chirps of birds the various species orchestrating their humble talent to the world with the yip-yip of coyote's and the gobble-gobble of wild turkeys and the bass melody of frogs in the night. The bite of the winds as bats wings zinged in the dark. His heart felt young, vibrant as he jogged into the green world he loved. He marveled at the majesty of the hawk soaring high and free. As he ran the power of the Great Spirit was all about him. The sun, the moon, the stars, the crescendo of nature's opera filtered his hearing. He felt free, strong as his spirit sought refuge and solitude with his brothers and sisters those who roamed and inhabited this green world. He respected the mystic and secrets only the Great One had hidden in this sphere of life.

He never tired, His legs churned up and down. Small beads of sweat coursed down his body yet his spirit pushed him onward and onward. Now and then he would halt and face the four winds and chant "Eyiee, Eyiee." The spirit of the ancient ones, join me. My spirit runs free and true never alone. The Great One and ancestors walk, run hunt, beside me ever beside me. I Broken Rose have fulfilled the oath and am now warrior. Now I must trust my spirit to look to my heart to be brave and my spirit to be clean and my eyes to see straight. The wonders of life spread before me. I must be like the eagle, free of hate, bad habits and laziness. I must think like the wolf ever mind full of danger and error. I must be as sleuth as the snake and slither by enemies. Smart as the fox and out think those who would pierce my heart. I must be strong as the ox and wise as the owl so that I Broken Rose will lead men in battle pure of mind and courageous in spirit. Eyiee, Eyiee, Eyiee, two wolves whose blood flows in my veins and whose spirit gave life. Whose wisdom guides me grant me life's vision and strength that I shall one day earn the right to sit and smoke the pipe of peace with the Great One. Also that I shall dance within the warriors circle that of triumph and peace. That my spirit one day joins that of my mother and ancestors that my ears shall hear the chant of the old ones and that my eyes shall gaze upon the Great One and bask in his glory. By the riverbed Broken Rose collapsed and slept. Dreams of ancient ones blanketed him with peace in the forest he loved surrounded by images of ancient ones. He slept the deep sleep. A soft breeze eclipsed his still form with the breath of the Great One displaying pleasure and granting his blessings.

The sun settled beyond the horizon. He set to make a small fire and roasted corn he had foraged that morning. He chewed on beef jerky but found it was no comparison to his dried venison for the meat was too salty for his tastes. Happy and content alone in his comfort zone, he found peace and tranquility surrounded by pines and lush foliage. The croak of frogs leap frogging in the stream filled him with a deep nostalgia. He needed this time alone to refresh his spirit to expel impurities from his lungs. To control blood flow, listen, watch, and learn, the wise words of Two Wolves ever in his mind. The others needed to spend leisure hours in the towns and bars but not him. He could talk to creatures in the forest. He understood them. They killed out of necessity and there was no idle gossip. They didn't rape. "Ah," he sighed. Here we train to kill. Man is the true animal. He wondered and marveled at the constellation of the stars and watched the happy glow to the moon. He crawled into his make shift lean to for he was refreshed spiritually and physically. Yes Two Wolves was right, remain free of tobacco, spirits, and discipline yourself to the weakness of flesh. Return to the forests for strengthening and refreshing to spirit. Be mindful to the temptations and weakness

187

of men. Run free feel the wind on your back. Breath deep of the untainted air and drink of the pure springs Listen, watch, learn, and remain silent. Night birds entertained him with their musical chorus. Safe and at home in the forest he slept the peace of the well-tuned warrior.

Colonel Striker sat behind his desk. His company commanders sitting erect and respectfully in a semi-circle. Smoke curled and floated about the room. The men indulging in the intake of cigarette tobacco. "Gentlemen, I've assembled you here for one reason. Force Recon is seeking Marines of high standards for that elite unit. Your company commanders know your people better than I. I'm looking for input as to nominees. Bear in mind that this is a volunteer assignment. Only those with impeccable records are to be considered. You should know that it is my intention to filter a recon platoon into this battalion. So I hold you responsible and accountable as to those in your commands you so choose. You've had ample time to access those you command. It is imperative that you submit those who measure to the highest standards of the Corps both physically and mentally. There's no room for guess work here. You all know full well my intolerance to the inept and incompetent. It is paramount that you officers are right on in your assessments. You are the backbone to this battalion and that is why you sit before me. You've displayed loyalty and unparalleled leadership. You know my intent which is to mold a cohesive combat unit. Submit your choices to the 1st sergeant and gentlemen choose your best. I'll accept nothing less. You gentlemen are dismissed." Chairs scraped the floor as company commanders sprang to attention. "Aye, aye sir," and filed from the office.

Gunnery Sergeant Mazzone roared into the quonset hut. "Bellowing "Broken Rose, LeSage, LaPore, LeBron, get your asses up to the company commander's office, I mean on the double!" The men busy squaring away gear, gazed at the Gunny. "Good morning Gunny, nice morning." "What the fuck, you assholes weathermen?

Nice morning my ass. Every time I look at you, I think of Dr. Spock and how the Corps is going to shit. Problem is you dick heads play with yourselves too much." He turned to leave, "well, why aren't you four girl scouts gone yet?" The Rose and his three cohorts fled out the door under the fierce glare and growls of their gunny.

Broken Rose spoke for the four as they entered the company office and stood before the 1ˢᵗ Sergeant. "Top, we were ordered to report to the company commander." Top Soldier, Robert Gates shuffling paperwork, gazed up at the four young Marines standing before him. "Oh, I'm sure the CO is thrilled beyond words and is just looking forward to meeting with four cherries. Yeah, go on in. He's expecting you. Get out of my face. You make me nauseous and I feel like vomiting. Shit Marines, Marines my ass, fairies is more like it. Go! He bellowed, Go!"

A knock on their skipper's door brought the salutation, "Come!" All four entered through the hatch and came to a ram rod attention. "Sir, Corporal Rose and PFC's LeSage, LaPore and LeBron reporting as ordered." "At ease gentlemen," Captain Klober walked around his desk and took a seat on the edge close to his four Marines. He wanted the ability to look into individual eyes when he made his presentation. "Men the Battalion CO is seeking new blood for Force Recon. I've selected you four based on your performances here and at ATR. I think you have the fortitude and stamina to earn your jump wings. It's your choice. Strictly voluntary. No need for an answer this minute. When dismissed you have till 1300 for your decision. Thank you for your time and give it plenty of thought. Dismissed."

They filed out the door past the 1ˢᵗ Sergeant heading for the hatch. They were halted by the horse command of their 1ˢᵗ Sergeant, "whoa girls do I smell perfume? Jesus H Christ, if I had you drop your drawers I'll bet your wearing sweet colored silk panties. I'd bet money you shave your legs. God damn the emblem sheds tears in shame get out of here and get back to your whore house!" He turned muttering to himself, "Marines, Jesus Christ, couldn't and wouldn't stand for em, and we must be recruiting coeds, time to refine. Fucking perfume, now the skipper will think it's me the office stinks." They scrambled out of the company office enroute to their quarters. Broken Rose gazed sideways at LeBron, "Damn Jake why did you have to bath in the girlie juice. Now the Top's pissed off." "Damn Tonto, a man got to be able to stomach himself. Shit those bitches in the world ain't gonna bed a dude that stinks like jungle rot and critter piss. I've been saying right along these fuckers are insane and have gone south. Their brains is cooked. Probably because of WWII or Korea. Somewhere back there they lost' em and ain't even found em. Look Tonto, if we even get in the shitter. I'll shit myself, piss myself and rub critter shit and piss all over my black ass. If that'll save it. Damn straight. Ole Jake will stink like a French whore hiding crotch rot, but that's then and sure as hell ain't now. Crazy fuckers, you think the Top's or Gunny's old lady's put up with boon dock shit. Ain't no way. No way at all." The Rose, LeSage and LaPore chuckled softly. "Hey uttered the Rose, Let's head over to the slop shoot. Our gear is squared away and the afternoon is ours. We can discuss the skippers offer. Wolf down a burger. What'd you think?" LeBron ain't no discussing, No way this black ass gonna leap out of a healthy plain. This boy ain't playing bird man. If the big man wanted me to fly, I'd been born a crow cause I'm black. This boy hugging good old mother earth. "Jake," interrupted the Rose; "it means fifty bucks a month more from the paymaster." LeBron stood shock still, "Say what? The Fuckers gonna fork over fifty certino's extra to play superman?" "That be right, Jake, extra booze and poo tang."

They pushed open the hatch door and entered the slop chute. Hazy smoke cast a thick cloud rising to the ceiling. The hour was early and only a handful of Marines sat drinking pitchers of beer and chomping on burgers or hot dogs. LaPore had gone straight to the bar returning with a pitcher of 3...5 beers. Four glasses and one containing tonic water for Broken Rose. A soft sad melody blared from the jukebox box. The four sat quietly listening. Thoughts of home flashed in their minds. "No, no, no," blurted the Rose. "Let's not go there. I'm gonna take the captains offer. What about you guys?" LeSage spoke almost in a whisper. "I don't know John, Recon's tough, Shit they run everywhere they go." LeBron laughed aloud, shit what the fucks the difference, Strikers got us training for the world marathon. Shit running ain't no hassle." "So Jake you're interested?" quizzed LaPore. "Yeah, could use those extra greenbacks plus we escape the Top and Gunny for a while. LeSage Retorted, "You know Jake, we've got to train with the frogmen too." "What, what the fuck for?" barked LeBron slamming the table. Jake interrupted the Rose. It is what it is. You got to be able to do all kinds of shit. God Damn, Tonto. Now you want my black ass in the deep. Shit there be those big ass fish with teeth. What's you calling them?" "Sharks, Jake, Sharks." "Yeah that's right, only with my luck one of them fuckers hone in on my black ass. May love chocolate; think I'm a Hersey bar. Come on Jake you saw and lived worse in Brooklyn. We swore we'd stay together and bond leads to Recon. Are we agreed? All shook their heads in the affirmative. LeSage whispered, "We'll give it our best shot. It's no cakewalk. Hear a lot of guys don't hack it. Tonto stared at his buds. "Hey, we're Striker's boys. We'll make it." LeBron glared at the Rose. "Well you inform the Top you're the Corporal. I'm not going near that fucker. That man's Satan for sure."

Eighty Marines handpicked from Strikers and sister battalions stood at rest under a blazing sun. They stood in combat regalia. A large figure of a man appeared to their front. He had a barrel chest and arms and legs like tree trunks and scanned the ranks that stood uneasy melting under his glare. I'm Gunnery Sergeant Joseph Burke and I've been told that you flower girls have been chosen to be Recon Marines. Jesus Christ, I must have pissed off Christ and all the Saints in heaven to inherit such shit. I see standing before me. I thought at first you were a Boy Scout troop who lost their way.

Ok girls you volunteered. I warn you, you're gonna think P.I., ATR and Lejeune were cupcake duty. As the saying goes you ain't seen nothing yet. Now we're gonna board those deuce and a halves behind you. What do you think Uncle Sam was gonna send you first class? We've rations and will chow somewhere along the way. I want no grab assing with civilians. I catch one of you horned up bastards eyeballing some bitch, I'll nail your ass to a tree like a rusty nail. Now we're going to Fort Benning. That's doggy country. You best be sharp and able to take whatever they cook up for you. They're be in charge but you bet your sweet asses, you fuck up you'll answer to me. That's a big kennel down there and those instructors know their shit. Best you look good and God help the fuck who whines. You're Marines and you best act the part or I guarantee I'll smash you like a bug. Hit those trucks, sit tight, we've got a ride ahead. The smoking lamp is lit but make sure you field strip them butts. Remember no grab assing with the civvies." He turned and entered the passenger side of the lend truck. The engines coughed loudly and in a plume of smoke, the five truck convoy departed Camp Lejeune to destination Fort Benning, Georgia home of the paratroopers and doggy land.

The troops felt confined in the enclosed truck bed. Those in the rear were able to enjoy the scenic countryside and wave freely at motorists, mostly those of female persuasion. A constant shuttle of men moving rearward and forward as they exchanged seats so all could enjoy the view. They passed numerous farms and occasionally a convenience store gas station. They whiled away the time with idle talk and the number one priority women. Then they gossiped about officers and noncoms, who was fair, who were the hard charges. LeBron said his piece, "this Gunny Burke, man he looks like a grizzly. Man is scary as shit." Another Marine sitting toward the front shouted "they call him Bear. But not to his face. He's the Gunny of the 6th Marines Recon. What's he doing with us?" "He's our nurse maid. Scuttle butt is these dog soldiers won't fuck with him. Seems he tangled with three staff sergeants at Benning and split their heads like melons with those huge paws of his. His rep precedes him. He's the game warden. We can't fuck with them and they won't fuck with us. Gunny Burke was sent as a defense mechanism. Colonel Van Meer is sharp and knows we'll be kept in line. Well shouted LeBron I sure as Hell won't fuck with em." "No, no one will," came the reply.

The convoy had pulled to the side and parked by a small pond that housed a family of ducks, honk, honking away in contentment. LeBron approached Gunny Sergeant Burke cautiously, standing alone gazing out at the horizon. Gunny, "can I talk to you a moment?" The rest of the contingent all ears waiting for the Gunny's explosive response. Burke turned slowly eyes boring into LeBron. "What?! What the fuck you want low life? "Gunny, me, err and the guys just wondering these sky soldiers any good?" Burke shifted his weight. His bulk would intimidate an enraged bull. "Well ass wipe, think about it. Any man jumps out of a plane gotta be crazy and that sure as hell makes for one hell of a fighting man. God Damn right, they're good and you wanna be's had better measure to their standards otherwise be advised I will vaporize your sad little asses. Get back to your chow and leave the thinking to me. Go home; go you've interrupted my privacy time with Jesus."

Burke strolled over to the trucks where the grunts stood or sat smoking cigarettes or spooning c rations into their mouths. "You shit stains listen up and get this! Benning is a training haven for the elite military institutions of this country even for foreign military. They host rangers, pathfinders, their own paratrooper's recruits plus shit heads like you. The 82nd airborne calls Fort Bragg its home. The 101st hangs its hat in Fort Campbell. These are proud elite units on a par with the corps. Discipline and pride is their forte, just like us. Be ready and able they're instructors are the crème de la crème. You talk the talk now you'll walk the walk."

The grunts set in their trucks which offered minimum space for stretching and relief to muscles that barked in displeasure. If one passed gas, he was ostracized and herded to the rear of the truck to expel his offensive discharge. The sky had turned gray and forlorn. Soon rain tattooed its dance on the canvas roof. "Shit," exclaimed LeBron. "Fucking rain again! I tell you all the Saints in heaven, laughing. Love to fuck with an infantryman."

Broken Rose sitting quiet spoke loud and clear. "Rain is good! It cleanses and nourishes Mother Earth. Rain are the tears of those who have gone to the Great Lodge crying for us because we are weak and impure. We embrace the weapons of entrapment. The evil one lays before us, tobacco, evil spirits, lust for the flesh, gossip, our ancestors attempt to wash away these inequities with their tears!" The truck grew silent, each thinking, remembering loved ones long gone. Then the chatter grew excitable. Young men in green displaying peer courage, apprehensive excitement and fear regarding their designated training.

The miles whooshed by the atmosphere in the crawling trucks, somber. Smoke curled upwards and exited through the truck beds rear. These warriors in green were lean and well trained and they displayed an air of confidence and yes a young man's cockiness. Now they were faced with a new challenge. They have to reach deep down to garner further courage. LeBron broke the somber mood. "Man we be crazy! Jumping out of a plane, crazy man, crazy, but Marines are crazy anyway, part of our forte and so brothers "Semper-Fi" and as those troopers say "All the Way."

The convoy turned off the highway headed down a worn asphalt road that was lined by pines and maples that stood as sentinels gaping at them. Ahead was a gate with a guard shack in place and painted with typical military decor. As the convoy halted, in a swirl of exhaust the engines idling creating a deafening roar. The sentry in crisp army fatigues left shoulder displaying a black arm band with large white lettering MP, approached the lead truck, leaned in slightly through the passenger window. "Welcome to Benning. May I see your travel orders?" Gunny Burke handed over a manila envelope containing orders and reservations allowing them entry and access to the expansive military installation that lay open before them. The sentry studied the paper work. Satisfied he handed them back to Burke. The gate rose before them. "Okay Gunny, pass on through. At the fork in the road you'll take a right. that'll bring you to training command. There you'll receive your itinerary. Good luck and welcome to Fort Benning." "Thank you, soldier and Semper-Fi mack." The sentry smiled gave a half salute, "you bet Gunny Semper-Fi and oh Gunny, All the way." Burke chortled, "These girls of mine better go all the way or their ass is grass." The sentry took a step back, waved them on through and the grunts entered another chamber of hell!

The convoy screeched to a halt in front of the receiving officer. Gunny Burke exited from the truck bellowing, "You dick heads sit tight, no grab assing army eyes are on you. Fuck up and your history!!" Burke entered the office. A corporal rose from his desk eyeing the chevrons on Burke's lapels, asked "may I help you Gunny?" Burke handed over his orders. The clerk clutched them in his hands and did a fast retreat to his desk perusing the paperwork. He reached for his land line. After a short pause, he barked into the headset. 1st Sergeant the Marines have landed. A tall lanky 1st Sergeant appeared from a rear office. His left breast donned in four rows of ribbons. Above his awards sat the winds of a jump master. "Morning Gunny, how's the Marines this rainy morning?" "Morning Top, we're reporting as ordered." "Well welcome aboard." "Thanks Top, an honor to be here." "Okay Gunny, your unit is assigned to quarters in H section. You'll take your next right. You can't miss your quarters a huge H is mounted in front. It's two story barracks and there's plenty of room for your troops. There are three master jump Staff Sergeants assigned to your group. Get squared away in your quarters. The mess is located one block down on your left. Chow call is at 17:30 hours and reveille is at 0530 tomorrow. Any questions feel free to field them with me names 1st Sergeant Welch." "Okay Top, thank you." "No problem Gunny and Gunny tell your troops for me, all the way." "Thanks top, Semper-Fi." The 1st Sergeant enroute to his office stopped short, "Semper Fi Gunny, Semper-Fi."

The trucks screeched to a halt in front of their assigned quarters. They fielded into the barracks scrabbling as to who would inhabit the upper tiers or lower bunks. They stashed their gear all the while kibitzing as to their quarters. Gunny Sergeant Burke stormed into the barracks. "God damn it maggots you sound like an old ladies sewing circle. Get Squared away and knock off the bullshit. Chow's in a half hour. Now you pukes pay attention. We're gonna march sharp and proud to the mess. Doggy eyes are scoping us out and we better display Marine discipline and pride. After chow clean your weapons and gear, lights out at 2100 hours, reveille at 0530. Army jump masters will rouse you from your pussy assed slumber. Best you don't get caught choking your chicken. Remember at all times you represent the Corps and all that you do will be witnessed and stored away. Be Marines. Remember what's been drilled into you. You fuck up here and I'll have your wanna be asses in body bags. The ghosts of former Marines are ever watchful. These dog faces are good but your steps better. Best you prove it and do it. These sky soldiers will own your asses for the next three weeks, but Just remember you come back to me. Colonel Striker has full faith in your abilities and dedication. Whoa, to the fucker who lets him down! Now set to and get squared away and relax. Hell begins tomorrow and oh remember I'll be watching, Semper-Fi and good night." Gunny Burke turned and stormed from the squad bay.

Broken Rose watched as his squad labored at cleaning weapons and storing their gear so they would display neatness in pride and in appearance. He encouraged and pointed out flaws to subordinates. LeSage, with his rifle dismantled gazed up at Broken Rose as he passed. "So John what do you think?" The Rose halted, scanning his squad, "listen my brothers, listen to the voices in the wind. These sky soldiers, they will teach us to strike prey, as the hawk, the eagle, and the falcon, surprising enemies from the sky. Listen, learn, and be silent. These are good men. Proven themselves on D-day and Korea, ingest, digest what they teach. Respect their knowledge and courage. Their battle streamers are of courage, blood and sacrifice. Honor them respect them, inherent their knowledge, for then and only then will you be the complete warrior." He turned and headed out the hatch. LeSage whispered, "he seeks his ancestor's blessings and approval."

The men lay in their racks. The soft waves of taps echoing throughout the base filled them with an apprehensive nostalgia. Sun rise would bring new challenges, another step in harm's way. Men tossed and turned apprehensive, nervous, excited as to what lay before them. One by one they drifted off to sleep each with his own fears, dreams and hopes.

"Get out of the racks!" Bright light blinding them, struggling from their soft warm cocoons, they observed a burly Staff Sergeant in army fatigues standing erect and authoritative in the center of the squad bay. "Well, good morning Marines. It's my honor and privilege to play host to uncle Sam's elite. Now listen up. Your asses belong to Uncle Sam's Army for the next three weeks. You will breathe, eat, shit, everything you learn here. I am not intimidated by U.S.M.C. Uncle Sam's misguided children. I will be your mother, your father, your priest, minister, whatever the fuck for your duration here. If you need to know my name is Staff Sergeant Simmons and I've pissed and stood in latrine lines longer than you've taken breaths. I'll tolerate no grab assing. Airborne is too vital and hairy to fuck with. You will deal with competent dedicated jump instructors. Pay attention and you'll do just fine. Fuck up and daydream and we'll send you back to Lejeune in a bucket. That's right a bucket. You goof off and fuck up hear, there's no body bags. We scoop your ass with a blotter. Okay, outside in 1-10 form up. We'll march to chow and then the fun begins any questions?" LeBron couldn't resist, "Staff Sergeant" "Yes Marine." "Would that be dry blotter or wet?" Simmons took three paces forward. Now within inches of LeBron's face. "You listen maggot brains! Don't fuck with me! Don't kid with me! Don't smile at me! I've eaten kittens like you for breakfast! You bet your sweet ass I'll be watching your dark ass!" Now turning to all of them, "the Army is generously gonna feed you gourmet chow." He turned and stormed from the squad bay.

Gunny Sergeant Burke unnoticed had been observing in the shadows. He pounced like a tiger and grabbed LeBron by his stack and swizzle. "You little puke! You pull one more stunt like this and your ass will be on a one way trip to Hell! You brainless maggots listen up and get this! Don't fuck with these people! They've been there, done that! You've yet to prove your merit! You're here for good reason to be Para Marines! No more jokes, funny questions, giggling or wiggling! I hear one more asshole get out of line and I'll rip out his spleen and have it for lunch! Now as the Staff Sergeant ordered, turn too!"

The men were marched to chow and treated to shit on a shingle, potatoes and what looked like eggs and toast. The coffee was strong but did its job and woke up their slackers. The march back to quarters short lived. They're quarters two blocks from the mess. The grunts were impressed on the march they passed platoon's of Pathfinders, Rangers, Special Forces, and contingents of the 82nd and 101st airborne. LaPore nudged LeSage, "Damn Lee, Uncle Sam's crème de le crème is all about." "Yeah Lance quite a show and an eye opener and kind of thrilling and humbling. Best we measure up." "Yeah or Burke will march us back in body bags."

Reaching their quarters, Simmons called a halt and ordered right face. "Okay people, you've 20 minutes to shit, shower and shave! Formation is at 0730! Uniform is boots trousers, tee shirts and your covers! 0730 sharp! No Johnny come lately, shirkers or whackers! All you men volunteered for this training! Your road to kill begins today! Listen, we're here to train, to instill knowledge that was earned with blood, sweat, tears and yes even many deaths! We're not hard asses! You either have the heart and want it or you don't! If anyone has had a change of heart, step out of ranks! No one will think any less of you!" "Bullshit! Staff Sergeant the Bear will! Simmons smiled, "you mean Gunny Burke?" "Yes Sir, just what I mean I'll rather free fall then piss him off." "Okay Marines, we all serve the same flag, share love and pride in our country. Yes, we ride you, push you, gore you all in the name of motivation. It takes special men, maybe crazy ones to leap into the sky. But you know what? When you're standing tall and the man pins on your jump wings, a feeling of pride you've never experienced will send shivers up your spine. Okay, dismissed and oh by the way if any of you are wondering, don't. I and all instructors will measure up and be there with you. Remember airborne, all the way!" The grunts responded as one with their voices resonating through the base. "All the Way!!"

0730 sharp the grunts stood in tight precise formation. Gunny Burke had handed the guidon to Broken Rose. "Look sharp you represent the Corps. The ghosts of those long gone are ever watchful. You piss ants volunteered for this chapter in your military careers. I want no drop outs. There's no room for failure. If you come up short here, then you'll come up short in life. You're here because you were chosen. A select few to train with the elite. Success here lays a cement foundation to your future. Good luck and Semper-Fi. For the next three weeks your paratrooper meat. Be proud! Be strong! Be Marines!"

Staff Sergeant Simmons had suddenly appeared. "Thank you Bunny Burke for a short duration. They belong to me and the army." He faced the grunts, "Detail, ten-shun, right face, forward march! One, two, three, four. Hup, two, three, four!" Now training would commence in earnest. At the double time march. The grunts shifted into double time. Under an early morning sun rise they double timed through the base. Legs moving like pistons. Boots tattooing a drum beat on the pavement passing other contingents. They would shout "Airborne, All the way!" Their run continued one mile, two miles three miles, onward they ran. They felt exhilarated, confident, and proud. Simmons kept pace finally calling a halt in an open field. But there was no reprieve. Calisthenics, put in motion immediately, push-ups, leg raises, sit ups, side straddle hops. The exercises continued for two hours. Then they reversed their run back to quarters. Time for noon chow and the troops were marched to a large mess hall. Where they dined on beans, spam, mashed potatoes and thick slices of white bread. Milk was plentiful and in demand. Chow completed, they were granted a 20 minute rest period and the smoking lamp was lit. They sat in the shade kibitzing, and sharing in idle chatter. The troops stared at elite sister contingents as they swooped by with the sing song call of cadence ringing loud and clear throughout this hallowed base where brave and dedicated men had aspired with success and courage to be sky soldiers.

At 13:30 hours, Simmons regrouped them and off they went another run. Simmons sang out "I don't know but I've been told. Pussy is still good when its old and cold" The men in unison echoed his chant. Simmons continued. "I don't know but I've been told my old lady's ass is as good as gold." The men responded in unison. Their run led to hills and knolls and through a stream. They negotiated a trail through woodlands. Now leg muscles began to howl. Sweat poured down faces as a hot sun baked them mercilessly. Their engines now pushed them forward on vapor alone. They were nearly out of petrol. The sun settled low and they breathed a sighs of relief as barracks roof tops hove into sight. "Okay, Marines good job. Chow is at 17:30 hours. You've an hour to unwind and relax, shit, shower, whatever. Formation at 17:30, Airborne, all the way!" Dismissed!"

The men marched to evening chow. The clang of mess trays and coffee mugs mixed with the chatter of hundreds of troops resonating, bouncing off walls throughout the mess. Broken Rose, LeSage, LeBron and LaPore shared a table with several Special Forces soldiers. They exchanged stories of training experiences, gossiped about their noncoms and officers, shared laughter over corny jokes sharing camaraderie that only those who experience deprivation, degradation, fear, tears, sweat and blood truly understand. LeBron nudged the Rose. There's Gunny Burke sitting with a bunch of airborne instructors. "Where?" uttered the Rose. "Right over there, see em, table by the far wall." "Yeah, I do, quite a site." "Warriors, all." "Yeah," whispered LeBron, your right Tonto. Tough but good men. Countries damn lucky and fortunate. They serve its flag." LeSage Jumped in "What? What's this Jake, a moment of weakness? You're actually showing some nostalgia." "Yeah well, you know. I know I'm an asshole sometimes, but these guys are the real thing. Been there done that, all that shit. Hard to argue. No way can you dispute courage and dedication. When they reek of it. Not only their ribbons are a road map of what they've done or where they've been, it's their bearing, their pride, their discipline. That speaks volumes." Broken Rose smiled softly. His amber eyes scanned the table. "Yes Jake you're right on. We are training to be warriors. They already are."

Evening chow completed, the men stomachs happy and full marched back to their quarters. Simmons called a halt and stood to their front. "Okay Marines, the rest of the evening is yours. Be advised reveille is at 0530. Only tomorrow don your helmets and your weapons and be prepared for another track to the woodlands. Be furthers advised that this time we're going to lengthen our line of march. Soon we begin the intricate points of the parachute jump. Muscles stamina and confidence is paramount to your success or failure. It's my job and that of brother instructors to ensure that you're physically and emotionally prepared for the rigors of the jump. So far you've displayed excellent physical conditioning. That's no surprise. Leave it to the Marines. Emotionally only you as individuals know what burns in your souls. Okay, dismissed. Oh remember 0530 reveille. A word to the wise, I'd make certain your weapons and gear are ship shape. Your Gunny is lurking and ever watchful. Dismissed! And all the way!"

The men stormed into their quarters. LeBron stood in the hatch. "God damn, another run. I'd thought we'd left the devil at Lejeune. Shit, he's got disciples in every God damn base. Be it Marines, Army, balls I'll bet he's on every ship and Air Force Plane." Broken Rose smiled, "no Jake, he's only shadowing your ass." "Why me Tonto?" "Because somewhere, somehow, sometime, you pissed him off."

0530 reveille jolted the grunts from their snug small cots. Another active day, after morning chow, they marched to an open field. Standing in the middle, as huge sentinels, was six deuce and a halves parked on a line in military precision in front of the rear tailgates stood Sergeant instructors. A burly Master Sergeant greeted them. "Morning Marines, sit yours selves on God's earth facing the trucks. Smoking lamp is lit. My name is Master Sergeant Tinkler. Today you are going to learn and practice the PLF, parachute landing fall. The Sergeants facing you will demonstrate and drill you in this all important technique. It may at first seem silly and boring to you but it is paramount you get the PLF right from the get go. Tilting his head sideways, he barked over his shoulder. "Sergeant Riley; give these men a demonstration so they'll understand what I'm talking about." Sound off with the proper steps. Riley jumped on the center trucks tailgate. "Okay this is a plane and you're in the hatch and the command, go, go, go, explodes in your ear. You're leaning forward, head down, once airborne, facing the horizon with bent knees, both hands on the reserve chute. Feet pointed towards the ground. When you hit you roll on the ground. The wind will dictate right or left but roll and land on the front of your feet." He leaned forward and threw himself from the tailgate. Hitting the ground he rolled quickly to his right. Tinkler studied the Marines. Okay looks easy, right?" Line up in front of the trucks. Let the fun begin. But be advised what you learned here today and master saves broken bones or worse."

At first the grunts enjoyed what appeared to be child's play. But the sergeant instructors extolled, harangued, cursed, and pointed out deficiencies. Four hours and repetitions of PLF exercise the grunts felt fatigue. Landing feet first and rolling had become tedious and leg muscles cramped. The instructors called a halt satisfied that they had retained the art of the PLF. The sun sat low in the sky as the grunts were marched back to quarters. Sergeant Simmons halted in front of their barracks. "Detail left face, at ease. Okay, chow call at 1800 hours. Lights out at 21:30 hours. Big day tomorrow, reveille at 0530." "Hey Sarge," came a voice from the rear rank. "What's up tomorrow?" Simmons smiled, "you'll see. Tomorrow you'll go in the harness." "Harnesses, what for?" "Like I said, wait and see, formation for chow at 17:50 dismissed."

0530 found the grunts in tight formation. A Sergeant 1st class stood facing them. "Okay Marines, my name is Sergeant 1st Class Nathaniel Davis. You'll be in my charge the rest of the way. Training to jump will get real interesting beginning at 0900 hours. Detail ten- shun right face. Hope you enjoy the chow, forward march." They dined on strict military fare, eggs, shit on a shingle, toast and strong coffee. Milk was plentiful. Assembled outside the mess and marched back to quarters where the three S details were performed, shit, shower, and shave. Weapons checked and clean. The squad bay squared away in case of an unexpected inspection.

They stood in ranks precisely at 08:30 and army paratrooper Sergeant 1st Class Davis greeted them. "We have a half an hour till we begin the next chapter of your training. Ten-shun left face. Hup two three four, Hup two, three, four." They marched in discipline array. Their boots a drum beat on the pavement. Other units passed some marching, some double timing. The base resonated with the cadence of NCO's leading their details guiding them to another horizon in their quest to succeed as sky soldiers.

A fifteen minute march brought them to a square structure. Davis halted them allowing them to observe. A wonder tower loomed before them. Soldiers were mingling about gaping at them. Davis addressed his charges. "This tower is thirty four feet from top to bottom. Here you begin the bulk of your training. Here is where you go for broke. You will ascend up the ladder to the platform above. You can see the opening from here. Instructors await your arrival. You'll notice the large mound of dirt located just below the opening. You men will be connected to a harness and then descend down a cable to that earth mound. However, when you are propelled outward and downward in that harness you will be experiencing the parachute shock. This exercise is a simulation of what you'll experience when jumping into God's sky. All right first rank hit the ladder. No more games. Now we get real." The men scrambled up the ladder and were greeted by two corporals who connected the individual Marines one by one to a harness. Adjusting straps, the men peered below. It looked far more intimidating. Heart beats quicken. Thumping in their chests. Adrenaline causing anxiety. "Okay Marines, you see we've one of your buddies ready to go. Be advised make damn sure you adjust your family jewels so those crotch straps don't mash your balls to jelly. Wherever and whenever you jump protect your manhood or you may fuck no more."

The exercise commenced. Men were shot off in the harness and within four to five feet experienced the shock of the pull force on their bodies. It was an unexpected shock. Your torso pulls and tightened the grip between your crotches. You were in suspended agony for seconds and then continued down the cable landing on the mound of dirt. Disconnected and returned to the top of the tower and did it again. On and on it seemed like an eternity. Pain in the shoulders, chest, groin that one's body needed to adjust to. The brain and muscles howled in anguish. But instructors knew this new agony would subside that the body would adjust and steel itself to this invasive abuse.

Five hours later and numerous trips down in the harness. Davis called a halt to the training session. Tired, sore, weary Marines stood disciplined in ranks. Sergeant Davis scanned their faces. "Okay Marines, rest. Smoking lamp is lit. Today you experienced new pain and hardship. Remember no pain, no gain. I want to tell you this. It's not my job to harass, badger, curse, or ridicule but to instruct. Stamped on your breast are the letters. U.S.M.C. you've already paid heavy dues. Everyone knows and respects the corps your discipline and past training will be the catalyst which will motivate and propel you ever forward. As Marines you've experienced and paid a heavy price to wear that uniform. Now you have to ante up to earn your jump wings. The cost isn't cheap. Once again payment is forthcoming in blood and sweat. There are the times that try men's souls. Once you complete this training, you will be compete infantry warrior. All of us share in this challenging quest and why? My answer is to safeguard and protect our country from tyranny. When you hit those racks tonight, fatigued in pain and thinking why the hell I volunteered for this shit. Here's my answer. Tyranny like Hell is not easily conquered. Okay detail, ten-shun, we'll head back for chow. Tomorrow we do it all over again, right face, forward march."

After evening chow, the men sat around the squad bay kibitzing and gossiping about anything and everything mostly about the day's events. LeBron exiting the head screamed startling the entire squad bay. "Fuck! I think I lost half my dick in that harness. One of my nuts is in my left arm pit and the others in my asshole. God Damn that was one world of shit. I'm afraid to get a hard on. Shit, it even hurts to piss!" The troops laughed. "Aw come on," yelled PFC Lacrosse "wasn't all that bad." "Shit you say. Look at the welts on your fucking ivory shoulders. God damn you white boys bruise easily." Broken Rose gazed at LaPore. "Ole Jake keeps us loose." "Yeah, probably become a comedian when he returns to the world." LeSage lay on his rack staring at nothing. Broken Rose sauntered over and sat on the foot locker. "Hey Lee, you okay?" "Yeah just hurting a little in several places." "Yeah we all are. But we've been there before. We'll get through this. "I know John, as they say here in Benning, All the Way." LeBron staring out the window shouted "Oh shit! The devil's here." The men scrambled to their feet. "Who Jake?" It's Burke, Gunny Burke. He's headed this way. Oh shit!" Men scurried about dashing towels and other articles in their lockers. Kicking other debris under their racks. Suddenly the bulk of Gunny Burke slammed through the hatch. "Well good evening girls. Thought I'd drop by and check on my ladies. Oh, brought you some muscle rub for your beau beau's. He dropped three tubes of Ben Gay on a nearby rack. Heard you pussies did okay today. Tsk, tsk, must say I'm surprised thought for sure you would be calling for your mommies by now. Everyone still got their nuts? He laughed heartily. Thought I'd drop by. Knew you'd be missing the old Gunny by now. Oh by the way, take some good advice. Don't stroke it for the next week or so. It'll hurt like hell." Laughing he strolled out the hatch into the night.

LeBron jumped off his locker. "That man be Satin's full cousin. I'm telling you. He's got feathers in the brain. Besides how he knows it hurts if we stroke it? You know how? Because he must of done it. That fucker stroked it and probably still does." "Hey Jake, yelled PFC Lamont, why don't you tell that to the Gunny?" "You a fool Lamont ol Jake here ain't that mad to say shit to that demon, no way." "Hey Jake, shouted Private Whitaker "Yeah mole, they called him mole cause he always slink-ed around the squad bay. "What's you think of that doggy, Sergeant Davis?" LeBron was silent for a moment. Well you see he's a brother, been where's it at. Come up hard and poor. You see he treats us as men. Knows about being a man for he learned hard and quick. "Hey Jake," Broken Rose called, "he's good no question. But remember Burke, all of em, all men, all warriors, everything they say or do is four our survival. Remember that." "You know Tonto, you're right. But Burke, I don't know. He got some of the devil in him." "Yeah Jake could be your right. He's been to hell and back."

The bugler blew reveille precisely at 0530. The grunts scurried into formation and marched to chow and back to their squad bay. There they indulge in the three S rituals, and they scrambled outside deployed in unit formation. Sergeant 1st Class Davis had been waiting. Ram rod straight, he called his charges to attention. Gave a left face and the command double time march. The sun peeked its smiling face over the horizon as the grunts completed a five mile run. Then calisthenics for an hour. Davis marched them another two miles calling a halt in front of several large warehouses which appeared vacant. Loading doors protruded from the docks where a rehearsal of three hours commenced performing the PLF under the intense scrutiny of Davis. The men jumped hit the ground and rolled. Grunts and groans resonated along the line, but there was no reprieve. As the sun rose, heat enveloped the harried troops and perspiration coursed down their faces and armpits stained with soggy sweat. Two hours later Davis ordered a halt terminating the exercise. The men formed up in front of the docks. Rest barked Davis, smoking lamp is lit. You've got ten, and then we return to the harness tower.

Noon day chow consisted of spam sandwiches and hot coffee and then a return to the harness tower where the grunts commenced the repetition training from the day before. Down the cable, experience the shock of the simulated parachute pull, hit the ground, disconnect and back up again. On and on it went. Instructors critical in their observations. Encouraging, pointing out flaws here and there. But now the grunts were gaining confidence having been driven hard and long. They'd grown accustomed to the abusive suspended agony and shock of the parachute pull. The exercise terminated at 16:00 hours. Davis stood before them. "Okay you guys have done well. I appreciate there were no shirkers or lurkers, no whining, no crying, didn't expect any, not from Marines. You wouldn't be here if your superiors hadn't recommended you. Tomorrow we hit the two hundred and fifty foot tower. There you'll get a real feel as to the parachute jump any questions?" LeBron could not resist. "Yeah, Hey Sarge any chance of landing on soft pillows?" Davis smiled, "you-re sitting on it. Detail ten-shun left face." They were marched to quarters, grimy, sweaty, fatigued, and full of anticipation for the next day's events. "Detail chow call at 17:30 hours, dismissed."

The four buds sat quietly towards the end of the squad bay. A soft wind rattled the window panes and rain tattooing the roof with a drum like beat. The squad bay laid in semidarkness and most of their comrades asleep only an occasional cough or the wheeze of snoring cut through the silent night. They spoke softly and listened attentively as LaPore spoke of his adopted parent's death. How an out of control truck with defective brakes had slammed into their station wagon, pinning them and killing them instantly. How when the strangers came for him and informed him of this horrific tragedy and how his guts had churned and he soiled himself. He told his friends how he got through the funeral numb with grief and pain. How the fear of an unknown future loomed on his horizon. He spoke of his arrival at the orphanage in the company of strangers and when entering the concrete structure and greeted by a cold unloving interior. How his life now became one of regimentation. Lights out at a certain hour, meals on cold trays never a choice. How some of the staff tried to be kind and show compassion. But most were enforcers of the institutions rules and regulations. Tears welled in his eyes as he continued it was not a child's life. His buds looked away granting him a private moment. You'd look out windows and see other kids frolicking with their parents, laughing, playing; you envied the love, the sharing, for you were without. Your soul was bare and though others were around you, you felt alone, isolated from a world that embraced you with love and warmth. Broken Rose, LeSage and LeBron placed their arms around his shoulders, whispering their condolences ensuring him that now they were his family. They were brothers and whatever fate or karma had in store. They would live and die as brothers. Broken Rose placed his hands on LaPore's cheeks and felt the wet tears in the dark. "Lance my brother," he whispered, "as the moons pass eventually we lose everyone and everything we love. All go to the Great Lodge. In my world as the grieving mounts it is called The Mountain of Tears."

05:30 reveille, the men scurried about dressing quickly. Utilities, laced boots, clean skivvies, move, move, and move. Always that word, the motivator to a Marine. LeBron sang out, "Shit it's fucking raining. Hey Tonto you don't think we're gonna do that tower thing today?" Broken Rose laughed, "Jake you're not joining the ladies auxiliary here. Hell, yeah, Davis will have us there." "Fuck LeBron carried on. We'll get wet asses and mud and shit up to our dicks!" Private Parkinson pointed at LeBron, "then Jake you can take your bayonet and scrape it off and remove all those critters you've accumulated on it all these years." The troops bellowed with laughter. "Aw fuck, you pogey Brit assholes won't be laughing when that devil Gunny Burke show's up tonight pulling one of his demon inspections. Yeah won't be so funny. The squad bay quieted down and knew LeBron could be right. Gunny Burke loved to come storming into the squad bay when they'd trained in inclement weather. He'd cruise in with that smirk of his. Ranting and raving. LeBron, lighting a lucky, "best have clean assholes he may white glove those too."

Chow complete, the grunts were marched to a gray green structure and filed into a gray drab classroom. A large black board covered the west wall and several benches facing its direction. Photos of troops in parachute away adorned the walls. Old glory stood honorably in the right corner and the battle streamers of the 82nd Airborne and 101st displayed with pride on the left. Those of other airborne units from various military organizations, both domestic and foreign were there as well. They were ordered to sit. Sergeant Davis stood to their front, "okay today we continue on your quest to be airborne warriors. Here to my left is Staff Sergeant McClosky. He will instruct you as to the various obstacles which could confront you when screaming Geronimo and exiting a very good plain in your hurdle to earth. Listen up and ingest all that he tells you."

"Morning Marines, okay this afternoon you will experience what it feels like to drift to earth from the 250 feet tower. Believe me when I tell you that's a piece of cake. The real challenge calls on Monday four days hence. Now in the plane and by the way your taxi, carrying you will be a C119. Over the years, experience has proven that a good combat jump is made from fourteen hundred to eighteen hundred feet. That's the safest and quickest way to descend. In flight at the jump point you will be ordered to stand, hook up and shuffle to the door perusing your buddies gear in front of you. The jump master will then order you to go, go, and go. There can be no hesitation when exiting the plane. You are to jump with both hands on your reserve chute, head down, and you will count 1000 one, 1000 two, 1000 three, if your chute fails to activate. You damn well better engage the reserve. He pointed to a photo behind him. You'll see that little handle located on the right of your reserve chute, pull it and pull it fast. Now you can steer yourself somewhat by either pulling on the left visor to go left or the right visor to drift right." "Sarge what's the visor? A Marine called out from the rear. "Eh, sorry you're right. When your main chute deploys you grab the visors. You'll know you've already experienced the jump shock at the 34' tower." "Thanks Sarge." "All the way, marine, okay you see you're headed for a water landing, at tree top level. You perform the quick release that will free you from the harness and canopy otherwise its weight will pull you under. Now the other scenario, if you approach electrical wires. You place your right hand under the left and put the left under your right armpit. After once again performing the quick release, of course, you've already been instructed during descent to watch the horizon and as you prepare to hit bend the knees feet pointed to the ground and then of course the PLF. Roll to the right or left whichever the wind dictates. If you land in treetops, I won't lie it can be tough. That's why you have sheathed knives. You may be compelled to whittle yourself free and pray no enemy is about. Okay I'm going to return you to the clutches of Sergeant Davis. Memorize what you've been instructed. Take it to bed with you. It's your asses nobody else."

They assembled quickly alongside the structure. Sergeant Davis called a left face and gave the command forward march. The detail marched maybe a mile when a soft drizzle and mist enveloped them. Hup two, three, four, Hup two, three four, through the grayish haze a mammoth structure suddenly appeared. The men gaped in awe. It stood straight and pointed endlessly into the sky. Mist like a Helo engulfed into its top. As the men drew closer, hearts pounded. Adeline pulsed through their bodies. Nerves frayed for there just ahead beckoning stood the 250 foot tower.

They stood at its base. It was Goliath compared to the 34 foot tower. LeBron shrilled, "God Damn! That the devil's dick. Shit! Man gotta be soft in the head do this shit!" LeSage nudged LeBron, "Hey we're Marines of course. We're loony." "Yeah, but that fuckers up there man." "Yeah, sure is Jake, but you know these troops know their shit. Been there done that. We'll be fine and your broads will love those wings." LeBron smiled, his white teeth glowing in the mist. "Yeah bro, more poo tang."

The men marked time to the cadence of Sergeant Davis. NCO's and a scattering of officers mingled and conversed softly at the base of the tower. To their rear the grunts observed a large white canopy attached to a hoist at ground level. Davis called them to a halt. "Okay, there it is. Today you'll experience free fall in a parachute. We'll have just enough time so that each of you can participate at least once during this exercise. Remember as you descend to enact everything you've been told and shown. This is only a prelude to the real thing. So get it right. You fuck up at 1400 or 1800 feet your viscera for the critters. All right, they're ready when you are first man go, all the way, Men, All the way!" Hearts pounding apprehensive about the unknown, instructors assisted each individual securing them in the harness attached to the white canopy. Then up they went hoisted two hundred and fifty feet above mother earth. On reaching the top, they were quickly released and floated to earth. All experienced an adrenaline rush. A high only experienced by those who leap into the sky with the wind snapping at your face and limbs as the intake of air and the earth seen from above along with the shock of pressure from the canopy and the jolt of hitting the ground and rolling right or left. True the real jump would be much more profound but this was one hell of a peep show. Davis and other instructors observed intently and scrutinizing their every movement men who had dared nature pointing out flaws and jumping hard and quick to carry them. Now was the time. Later would be too late.

They were given a thirty minute beak for noon chow. The fare beans and shit on a shingle. The men ate slowly. Those who had completed the maneuvers relating what they'd experienced to those yet to experience the exercise. LeBron, Broken Rose spoke softly, this is good for you get an understanding of the magnificence and power of the eagle, the hawks, and hunters from the sky. They truly are God's sky warriors. I don't know about you, my good friends, but I felt the power of the Great One imagine how much stronger and defined it will be when we leap into God's mythical highway and descend to our mother earth and to be able to view off in the distance. The Great One's power as his hand blessed the earth. LeSage, in a whisper, "Yeah John, sometimes we doubt some and don't believe. But when you smell clean air or the scent of a rose, or the cries of a baby, or the protective embrace of a mother, there is no doubt. I believe as you that out there in the infinity of space the Great One watches. He may get angry, frustrated, annoyed with his earthly creatures, yet he continues to provide heat from the sun and stars in the night to guide us in the dark. LeBron laughed softly "God damn Lee, you got to stop spending so much time with Tonto. You're beginning to sound like him." LeSage stared into Broken Rose's amber eyes, "yeah you're right Jake." LeSage shrugged his shoulders, "not a bad thing huh Jake." "No I guess not." LeBron smiled and walked off firing up a Lucky.

Those who'd completed the exercise lounged on the ground observing their comrades. LeBron snorted, "Oh shit." The huge hulk of Gunny Burke loomed before them. "What the fuck is this you shit heads think you're on a sabbatical? You look like a bunch of pussy's frolicking in the sun. Working on tans? Get on your fucking feet! God damn it! These doggies are watching and here you are lying about like you're in a Boy Scout Camp, on your lazy ass feet!" "But Gunny came the voice of PFC Golden, We did our jump we're just waiting for the detail to be complete." "Shut the fuck up!" bellowed Gunny Burke. Get in formation!" The men scurried to comply. "All right, right face, double time march. Burke ran them several miles. Then led them through push-ups, side straddle hoops, knee bends, sweat poured off their torsos. You fuck's, how dare you embarrass my corps? You'll earn those wings but you God Damn better know you rate' em. I catch you homos on the ground again, and I'll have your asses in a douche bag! These are paratroopers! God damn it they don't understand nor should they! Broken Rose next time I see these girls doping off it'll be your ass you're a Corporal, son of a bitch act like one!" In the shadows Sergeant 1st class Davis smiled. "Yes, the Gunny's right! Stay on their asses! This isn't Coney Island! It's training for the real thing! It only gets tougher! There's no quitters in combat, none!!"

Training concluded at 17:15 hours. The grunts were marched to evening chow and upon completion reverse their route returning to their quarters. Sergeant Davis dismissed them after informing the grunts that training would continue the next day at 0530 hours. As the grunts filed into their squad bay, they were startled by the bulk of Gunny Sergeant Burke leering at them as he stood in the center of the barracks. Footlockers were turned upside down. Their contents strewn about the deck and racks were overturned and bedding was scattered along the bulkheads. Burke red faced, bellowed, "you pieces of shit. This squad bay looks and smells like a Chinese outhouse! You people have pissed me off! Best you hop to and field day this fucking shit trench you call home. Now, get this, ladies! The way you're headed Chinese rejects will kick your ass. I, the Corps, will not tolerate this bullshit. Turn too, and best this rest home gleam in an hour. Bunch of sad sack fuckers para marines, shit you wouldn't, couldn't make a pimple on a real para marine's ass. Square this shit hole away and I mean like yesterday!" He stormed from the barracks.

Broken Rose took charge. "Okay, stop your bitching and turn too. Let's square this place away pronto!" "Aw shit," whined LeBron. "The man's gone crazy! This place was as clean as a virgin's pussy! Shit!" "Enough LeBron!" barked the Rose. "The Gunny's pissed off, no doubt. Here we are Marines, guests of the Army. He comes to observe as to how we're doing and what's he sees is half of us lying about like F Troop. Fucking off, that's what really upset him as we were right there under the ever watchful eyes of doggies. The Gunny's a lifer, a professional. How did you think he was going to act? You can believe he's going to be on our asses for quite a spell. Let's get it done. LaPore, LeSage and Parkinson, you've got the head detail. The rest of you set to in field daying this squad bay and quickly. He will be back."

The be labored grunts worked feverishly, scrubbing, swabbing everything in their sight. The squad bay glowed spotless. It smelled of soap and fresh air. They labored till taps. Gunny Burke was a no show. The grunts turned to and hit the racks. In the dark men, thought of home, girlfriends, wives, the comfort and security of a life filled with love and compassion. Here it was all about improvising, adapting, overcoming obstacles and endless challenges. It tried one's soul, played havoc with nerves. Forced them to dig deep and hoist themselves above and beyond the endless exhausting discipline and challenges of infantry men.

0530 reveille roused them from restless slumber. They marched to morning chow and then formed up in ranks to a sing song cadence of Sergeant Davis and marched to another day with the 250 foot tower. The sun descended along the dirt road, its rays bouncing through tree tops causing vegetation to glow some orange others red. Surreal white clouds drifted in the distance like cotton balls in a glass. The men gazed at the sky as the drone of planes pulsed overhead. Suddenly the white canopies of parachutes appeared descending like white mushrooms. They could see the parachutists with their legs and arms as they swayed in the air. The C119's moving off disappearing in the distance having expelled their loads of sky warriors. Hearts thumped from an excited fear that soon, very soon they too would plunge into the sky and drift to earth. Each running through his own mind what they'd been trained to do. Most relaxed for they'd been pushed hard and instructed over and over again on the principles of the jump. It was becoming a second nature, an extension of their minds and bodies.

In step the detail approached the tower. Their boots cascading through the area as heels meshed gravel and sand kicking up small puffs of dust as they drew closer. They saw Gunny Burke standing with a cluster of Army NCO's. He eyed them approvingly. A smirk on his face, Sergeant Davis halted the detail and gave a left face. Gunny Burke approached, "morning Sergeant Davis, how they hanging?" Davis smiled, "morning Gunny, high and tight." Burke laughed, "See you got my Girl Scout Troop here all spit and polish and looking cute." He turned faced his Marines. "All right, All right, pull up your little girl panties and stand easy. Sergeant Davis here informs me that you girls are performing well. That's good. Makes the Corps happy, makes me happy. You've three more days with the tower and then Monday the big show. The sergeant here has talked me into granting you liberty this weekend. Go if you want but my advice is rest easy on base, up to you. Oh, I know you think I forgot about our date last night, belay that. I checked your rat's nest while you were at chow, not bad. You're getting there. Oh, I found a cricket in the head. I've made him an honorary corporal. Don't hurt him. He's airborne. I expect you to provide and care for him. Make him a barracks so he can live in privacy. Make sure he's warm and fed. Best you believe I'll be checking. Okay Sarge they're all yours. Make sure your bras are snug." He shuffled off laughing rejoining the other NCO's there to observe.

The rest of the week flew and the men repeating their training at the mammoth tower. Reenacting what they'd been trained to do and preparing for the final test being the zenith to a sky warrior. To be able to jump from the confines of a C119 and experience the flow through space and to share and grasp what eagles and other great birds have known and enjoyed since the beginning of time, freedom of the heavens to be able to observe the great beauty of God's earth from above.

Friday came and went as the sun settled low in the sky. Sergeant Davis marched the grunts to their quarters. "Gentlemen", he began, "you have displayed pride, courage and the willingness to learn. Your training is now complete. On Monday at 10:00 ours you will disembark from a C119. At 1400 feet, I know nerves are on edge. It's the unknown. Look we all always hope and pray that the chute deploys. Be advised the packers are experts in their field. Remember, the rules of the jump and you'll be a okay. It was a pleasure to have you in my charge. It's now 16:00 hours. You have the weekend off. Enjoy the R and R. We march to the field at 0900 on Monday, where you will be harnessed in your chutes by choice instructors prior to embarking into the C119. Okay, enough for now. Have a good weekend dismissed. Oh and All the Way." The troops responded as one "All the Way."

The men filed into their squad bay each drifting to their small space of privacy and each with their own thoughts and apprehensions. It was Broken Rose who sauntered to the center of the barracks. "Listen up guys. I don't know what each of you is planning for this liberty call, but I think Gunny Burke is correct. We should stay on base. Rest easy and like a prize fighter psych ourselves for Monday. We're not familiar with the area and moneys tight and they've got a nice enlisted man's slop shoot on base. Anyway you're free to make your own choice. Those remaining on base give me a show of hands." It was a landslide. All chose to band tight together.

LeBron exited the head. "That Gunny's gone completely south. That cricket he spoke of it's the size of a fucking mouse. Looks like Burke. Hopping all over like he's got the itches. Shit now we gotta baby sit a fucking bug. Fuck I was crazy before now I'm stark raving mad. That man making us all brain dead." "No," spoke out LaPore, "He's doing his job. Preparing for who knows what and who knows where or when. So we honor the bug for a week. So What? Find a match box or a c-ration box. Give it a home and keep Burke happy." "Shit!" responded LeBron only thing that makes Burke happy is the smell of cordite and watching our asses sweat with pain." "Jake," admonished the Rose, "stow it. We've come a long ways. Soon we'll earn our wings. Be the ultimate warrior. It's what the Corps is about. Think of it to soar with the great creatures of the sky, awesome. But we're never equal the eagle, his senses are leaps and bounds ahead of us." Suddenly the hulk of Burke filled the hatchway. "Well!" he roared. "How's Corporal Cricket? Have you introduced yourselves to him?" LeBron rolled his eyes. The men stared at the floor. "I take that as a negative!" snorted Burke. "Now you pansies line up and in single file march to the head and personally introduce yourselves to Corporal Cricket. Do it now!! He thundered, "and be military and polite." The men did as ordered and slowly returned to their bunk areas. "Thank you ladies," chortled Burke. He turned and beckoned to three troopers in army fatigues who carried a case of beer. "Set them down here guys and thanks." The Gunny ran his eyes over his troops. "Okay men, a little treat. Enjoy, I know you're nervous. Don't be. You're Marines. Well Trained and disciplined. You'll be fine and be damn proud when you pin those wings. Have a good liberty and don't fuck with the doggies. We're their guests," as he strode out the hatch. He turned slightly "Semper-Fi" and in a whirl was gone.

The men leaped to the golden treasure. LeSage nudged LeBron, "Well Jake, kind of put a needle in your balloon don't it? All the hot air hissed away." "Yeah," whispered Jake, "I get it now. It's like P.I. all over again. He wanted to test us to see who would break. But we all stood tall and tight. If anyone were going to drop out, they would have done it by now. Well fuck, lets guzzle this brew and damn it's cold. Ol Gunny knows his shit and way of getting around." The men indulged in loose excited talk. Broken Rose a smile on his face, took a brain photo of this moment a picture that all vets take somewhere in time that lasts forever.

The grunts attacked the beer and in a short time the golden brew was consumed. Buds exited the barracks in two's and three's seeking the comfort and added spirits from the base slop shoot. LeBron was giddy staggering about the squad bay. Broken Rose, the nondrinker produced a fifth of Jack Daniels as though by magic. LaPore and LeSage and Parkinson encouraged LeBron to indulge in consuming the fiery liquid. LeBron sucked it down shot after shot toasting the devil, Gunny Burke, his DI's, his mother, his battalion, on and on until finally he waved to and fro bouncing off the bulk heads stumbling and crashing into footlockers. LaPore and LeSage guided him to his rack giggling. LeBron stripped to his shorts bellowing I'm going to crash for twenty four hours. Collapsed on his rack and immediately passed out. Broken Rose, LaPore, LeSage and other conspirators sprang into action.

Two buckets containing heat bars used for cooking were placed at each side of LeBron's rack, loaded with paper and wood chips scrounged from a nearby pile in the rear of the barracks. One each placed at the head and foot of the bed. Broken Rose had crept silently from the barracks during LeBron's bout with the booze. He returned quickly and quietly and under each arm was a duck their beaks taped closed. PFC Axe had retrieved a step ladder from a nearby tool shed. He stealthy placed the ladder by LeBron's rack, climbed the ladder. Broken Rose handed him the ducks, now secured fastenings made from torn bed sheets. He taped and tacked the fastenings to the bulk head directly over LeBron's rack. The ducks now suspended four feet from LeBron's prone figure taped to their heads large cardboard ears fashioned by the conspirators. Three grass snakes were placed on LeBron's stomach held in place by clear tape.

LeBron snored away peacefully. The conspirator's taking great pains in ensuring he was indeed in a passed out condition. Three cans of shaving cream were gently applied to LeBron's body. His feet were secured to the foot of the bed by parachute chords. LeBron snored away oblivious to his fate. Broken Rose went to the hatch and beckoned PFC Parkinson who entered escorted by an Army band member in possession of cymbals. Again the Rose signaled. Lights were extinguished. The buckets torched flames licked up as tongues reaching level with LeBron's bed. The tape was removed from the ducks beaks. Broken Rose, his face painted red, yellow and black, knelt at the foot of the bed only his eyes were visible. He began chanting. The army band soldier clashed his cymbals. The sound exploding in the confines of the squad bay along with the ducks cawed and screeched defecating on the sleeping form beneath them. The noise was intensive and horrific. LeBron bolted upright, his eyes white and large as saucers. Rubbing his red rimmed eyes, he felt wet gooey matter filter into them. His eyes focused on two horrendous creatures swaying and emitting awful sounds above him. "Mother Fucker!!" he exclaimed. 'They've horns.' The cymbals continued to clang, their noise deafening. It was pitch black except then LeBron screeched, except yes, fire. I'm on fire. Mother of God his thrashing loosened the snakes. They slithered along his torso, up and across his face. He howled in agony. A voice from the dark roared at him.

PFC Jake LeBron, you are in the fires of Hell condemned by Gunny Burke. You are now one of the devil's disciples. LeBron thrashed and pulled unable to free himself. His feet were anchored. He could not free himself sitting up he saw ten apparitions from hell. The painted face of Broken Rose gaped at him from the dark. Guttural sounds emitted all about him. All he could see was the fire. The grotesque face and the squawking, squealing devils swaying above him, "Lord have mercy!" he cried. "Momma I've died and am in Hell." The voice continued to bellow, "PFC LeBron you will now ante up for past sins. Your soul belongs to the devil." LeBron was hysterical. Tears rolled down his cheeks and what was this shit on his body? Could it be so? Had he died and gone to hell? Then he heard the sound of hysterical laughter. The lights switched on. Broken Rose stood at the foot of the bed. His painted face in laughter reaching downward he cut LeBron's feet free. LeBron blinked forcing his vision to recover and saw he was covered in shaving cream and duck shit. He sat on the edge of the rack harassed by the laughter of his mates. His brain full of cobwebs, he managed to stumble into the head and threw himself into the shower allowing the soothing hot water to cleanse him. His heart pounding, he returned to the squad bay. The grunts lolling about, all smiling, LeBron head aching, stared at them. "Yeah mothers, good show. You made your point. But remember ol Jake here will even the score long after you forget." The ducks were gone buckets removed. He was bemused to discover his rack had been cleaned and fresh linen lay in a pile at the center. He'd sobered quickly and then then began to laugh. Turning to his brother's, he uttered "Semper-Fi" winked and chortled, "sleep well my brothers, sleep well." With a knowing smile he rolled on his side and soon fell into an exhausted sleep.

The sun rose high in the sky greeting a new day and spreading it's comforting warmth to its adopted child mother earth. It was Sunday and some of the men had roused themselves early and exited the barracks. Each seeking peace in the various religious citadels that pock mocked the huge base. It made no never mind what denomination be it Catholic, Baptist,

Methodist, Lutheran, all sought some comfort and a sense of security for their soul. Most lolled about the barracks soft murmurs wafted through the squad bay. Tomorrow was the big day. The ultimate test to what they'd pushed and trained for. Apprehension cut through the barracks. Like a gleaming knife, these were boys existing in a tough man's world. Most youths of their age were in the comforts of their homes, battling acne, going on dates and church dances and copping a feel in the rear of a dark theater or the back seat of a fifty five Ford. These boy men had long exited that world. They'd grown hard both mentally and physically. Now members of an elite military institution and would expound by earning their jump wings. The price was high, fear, sweat, blood and self-denial the ingredients that mixed the stew of courage. These Marines spent the day writing letters, cleaning weapons, or just chilling out on their racks.

As the sun sank low in the western sky, Gunny Burke and Sergeant 1st Class Davis stormed through the hatch way each clutching four large pizza boxes. "Okay girls," snorted Burke, "Party time." The two top NCO's laid their fare on an end rack. Slowly the men sauntered to the waiting treat basking in the delightful taste other than the usual military cuisine. Gunny Burke spoke softly, "men gather round." The grunts formed a semi-circle facing the two top noncoms. Burke ran his eyes over his grunts. "Tomorrow is the event you have worked and sacrificed so much to reach; I know your nervous, belay that, you're ready. Five jumps are required to qualify and earn your wings. I've rode you hard, but I know you'll do me proud. When you return to Lejeune you'll be sporting jump wings. Your here because you were handpicked from many. Rest up and relax. You've been through a hell of a lot worse. Sergeant Davis, You have anything to add?" "Yes, formation at 0830 and you'll march to chow at 0530. Corporal Broken Rose will be in charge of the detail. As Gunny Burke stated, you're ready, more than ready. Just remember to practice the principles of the jump and you'll be just fine. Good Luck and I'll see you at 0830. All the Way, Marines, All the Way!" The grunts responded in a loud thunderous chorus, "All the Way!"

Monday reveille, the bugle call roused the grunts from their racks. Most had spent a restless night in their racks due to the apprehension of the following day. Broken Rose marched them to morning chow where there was a military setting of eggs and shit on a shingle, strong hot coffee and burnt toast. The grunts marched back to their barracks having Army personnel gaping as their boots thundered across their route of march. The sing song Marine Cadence drawing interest. From their brothers in Army fatigues. The squad bay was quiet. A somber mood permeated as the men shit, showered and shaved. This was their day of reckoning. This was the day they'd trained for. The aches, the pain, each man displaying a false bravado. No one individual wishing to display his inner fears. Say or think as you will, but any sky soldier experiences that inner small doubt. What if the chute fails to deploy. Emotions run high and hearts pounded, adrenaline coursed through ones being like an out of control locomotive. Sweat forms under the armpits and crotch while mouths go dry. Yes fear, fear of the unknown.

They formed in ranks with weapons slung over their right shoulder. Sergeant Davis called them to attention and ordered a left face and gave the command forward march. They marched several miles and soon a large field loomed before the. Two C119's were parked waiting, their engines idling low. Instructors assisted the grunts into their parachute rigging double checking their labors. Once satisfied all was well the men stood waiting in ranks. There was a slight murmur in the ranks when the hulk of Gunny Burke appeared to their front in full parachute regalia. "Yes girls, I thought you'd enjoy my company. You've been well trained now ante up. Mount the planes!"

The men shuffled under heavy weight to the waiting big birds. They clamored inside thirteen to each bullhead. The hatch was closed. The engines thundered and the big planes taxied down the air strip. Engines roaring, the planes picked up speed and in a heartbeat lifted into the sky. The jump master was an army staff sergeant. Two lights were adorned to the bulkhead behind him, one blinking red. Over the dense noise of the aircraft, he commanded, "stand up! Hook up! Shuffle to the door!" The hatch was opened and the jump master peering intently at the little beacon of light. Red flashed off and the green light glowed ominously. "Go! Go! Go!" He ordered bodies flew into the air and screaming, "Geronimo!" 1,000-one, 1,000-two, 1,000-three, with a violent tug the chutes deployed. Now they felt the exhilaration of descent in God's sky highway. It is an experience only one who jumps can relate to. Calling on all they had been trained for, the men put their efforts into the proper parachute drop and landing. They hit hard rolled and kissed the earth. The week flew by. They'd completed all five jumps without mishap.

On Friday afternoon, at 1500 hours, they stood in ranks in their dress greens. This was the moment of glory, of honor. They would receive their badge of courage, jump wings. Gunny Burke bellowed, "Tenshun!" The men both surprised and thrilled when they observed their battalion commander, Lt. Colonel Striker crossing the parade ground in the company of the training facility, Commander Army Colonel Rom Mueller. The officers approached smartly. Gunny Burke stood at rigged attention and threw a crisp salute, "Sir, Platoon Seventy Five all present and accounted for." A staff sergeant followed to the rear of the officers. In his hands a large box. Colonel Mueller addressed the troops. "Congratulations on the successful completion of your intense training. Welcome to the sky soldiers fraternity. Your commanding officer will pin on your wings. Colonel Striker followed by the staff sergeant flowed through the ranks slowly pining jump wings on the individual Marine, congratulating each one and rendering a firm sincere hand shake.

The ceremony complete, Colonel Striker stood facing his Marines and gave the command "at ease." The men snapped to parade rest with their newly pinned wings glistening in the warm sunlight. "Marines!!!" bellowed Striker; "you have now entered the sacred realm of the ultimate warrior. Now you can attack from both the air and the ground. You have expounded on your combat abilities to safeguard our great nation. Wear those wings proudly. You've earned them. The Corps thanks our army brothers and most certainly they have our profound respect. We will be returning to Lejeune momentarily. However, this time your travels will be in somewhat more comfortable fashion. You'll return in those green buses located to my rear. I am granting you people a ninety six hour liberty, starting at 0800 tomorrow. You'll return to duty on Wednesday at 0800 hours, again, congratulations and Semper-Fi." As he marched off, the men were drawn to the jump wings which adorned his chest above the cluster of ribbons. They had looked at them with admiration and respect and knew the hardship it took to obtain them.

Gunny Burke turned and faced his troops. "Okay, we depart shortly and will mount those buses in twenty minutes. But first we have someone to thank and wish good adieu. Detail ten-shun! Right Face!" He marched them briskly to their squad bay to retrieve gear and personal effects. Sergeant Davis was waiting and had a huge smile on his face. He felt satisfaction and pride in that he'd had input into the creation of well-trained sky soldiers.

The Marine grunts surrounded Sergeant Davis. Gunny Burke strode through the ranks carrying a midsize package wrapped in red and gold paper. "Sergeant Davis on behalf of the Marine Corps, I respectfully and gratefully present this gift as a token of our gratitude. We salute you." Gunny Burke placed the gleaming package into the out stretched hands of Davis snapped to attention and whisked off a smart salute. Davis somewhat embarrassed returned same, unwrapped the package tearing the paper gingerly. A wooden box soon laid exposed embossed with an eagle, globe and anchor. Davis lifted the cover and removed a pewter replica of the Iwo Jima monument. A note affixed read from platoon 75 U.S.M.C., all our respect and gratitude to the airborne and Sergeant 1st Class Davis. Davis visibly moved, stood still and quiet for some moments. He then gained his composure and faced the Marines and in a crisp voice. "I thank you. This icon will always rest in a place of honor. We may wear different uniforms but we all serve the same flag. Have the same goals and mission to protect this land we love. I was proud to be your lead instructor and will always carry fond memories of this unit and your beloved Corps. Thank you, Semper-Fi and All the Way." Throwing a salute, He quickly marched out the hatchway into the military world of the unknown and unbroken.

Sergeant Nathaniel Davis, US Army
Paratrooper prepared for a mass drop in 1958
Ft. Brag, North Carolina

The bus ride to Lejeune was text book in excitement. The confines of the behemoth carriers filled with cocky, confident young Marines who had successfully passed the rigors of parachute training and earned coveted wings. All thrilled to the upcoming ninety six hour liberty. Young men were laughing, singing, the cream of youth looking forward to a semblance of freedom and carousing. Some planned to go home, while others desiring to embrace the challenges of unknown towns and cities and what they could or would provide in entertainment.

Broken Rose sat in the rear with his three buds. As usual he elected to go to the forest. LeBron loudly exclaiming his decision to head home to Brooklyn, "get me some soul meat. They see these wings; pussy will flow like fine wine to ol Jake." LeSage and LaPore had agreed to Fayetteville to be with Jean who had invited LeSage as she had a girlfriend in tow who wanted to meet him. The men consumed box lunches provided by the Army mess. The miles clicked away. Soon the mammoth gate of Camp Lejeune stood as a beacon welcoming them home. The men were exhausted and at 0200 hours threw themselves into the warmth and security of their racks filled with thoughts of liberty and R & R. In the darkness, young warriors all forged their plans for their upcoming ninety six. They were content in the knowledge that their skipper had rewarded their success. Each drifted into a deep slumber.

0800 Saturday morning as the bugler blew reveille. The troops sprung from their racks. The squad bay a bee hive of activity as men, showered shaved and donned their greens and in minutes the barracks lay empty and forlorn. The grunts dispersed each going their separate ways to be with loved ones or to seek thrills that all men seek in order to relieve stress and mental fatigue. A few remained electing to rest easy on base. Broken Rose headed off into his beloved forest. LeBron with a bro from Alpha Company headed north to Brooklyn. LeSage and LaPore hitched a ride with Corporal Donald Ash from

Charlie Company. He had relatives in Fayetteville and would spend his ninety six with them.

Conversation in the old Ford was minimal. LeSage commented on the vast farmlands. Ash was by habit and personality quiet, responding with short yes's and no's. The aging vehicle chugged along but they made good time and soon pulled up in front of the diner. Ash drove off after they'd agreed to meet at the eatery Tuesday night at 2300 hours leaving them ample time to return to base. LaPore and LeSage entered the diner. Business was brisk as it was lunch hour. Jean spotted them and sprinted to the door hugging LaPore. She planted a kiss on LeSage's cheek. "Over here," she uttered. "I've saved a booth by the rear window." Satisfied they were seated and comfortable, she took their orders. LaPore ordering fish and chips and LeSage, a hamburger steak well done and mashed potatoes' with salad and buttermilk biscuits. Both requested cold milk. Jean laughed "I'll bring a pitcher." As she sauntered off, with the voice of her father yelling, "Jean table five's order is ready. "Come on girl move, you're falling behind!" He waved at the two Marines smiling, "hello boys, she'll be off and free shortly."

Slowly the diner emptied patrons paid their fares and exited quickly. Only a few diners remained. The jukebox emitted a soft romantic melody. Cooking odors filled the interior and all in all it was a warm comfortable setting. The sun was shining, birds were chirping and life was indeed worth living. LeSage and LaPore both fired up Luckies. Sipping hot fresh coffee and their meal had left them refreshed and content their stomachs full with good southern cooking. Both men commenting on photo's that adorned the walls neither had noticed the petite brunette that strolled through the door greeted by Jean with her arm around her friend who wore a big grin. "Lee, Lance I want you to meet my good friend Elisa Blare. Both men smiled shaking her extended small hand. All were quiet. Elisa smiling at Lee stood all of 5'3 with short black hair with piercing blue eyes. She was dressed in slacks and a red turtle neck. She was an attractive sight with a full figure and a smile that could melt butter. Jean left and returned shortly carrying a tray with coffee and all the fixings, cream sugar and sweet rolls. For the next hour the four were content to relax and conversed about anything and everything. Jean sat close to Lance. Elisa sat by LeSage. Their eyes locked several times. LeSage felt an inner nervousness. He'd not been in the company of a female in months and this girl was somewhat older but oh so nice. Her voice soft and husky and her eyes danced when she smiled. He could feel her body heat and smell the soft scent of her body. He felt a stirring of an emotion he'd never known before. But surely he thought it's only because I've been lonely.

The four lay plans to go to the cabin in the sky that evening. LeSage and LaPore drove to Jeans house in her old jalopy and Jean and Elisa went for a quick shopping spree. Lee and Lance spent the next two hours with Jeans dad. They relived the older man's past. He'd come up hard and had served in the Big Red One during WWII. How he'd scraped and saved to purchase the diner. How the loss of his wife to cancer left him devastated. But he and Jean had bit the bullet and went on with life with the old man stating "yes there's death but life must go on."

The slamming of the door startled them as the girls sashayed into the living room. Both had purchased and wore new attire, Jean in a light blue dress, and Elsa in a red dress with a modest neckline. Jean giggled time to go boys. We girls want to be wined and dined. Bending, she planted a kiss on her father's forehead. "See you later dad and get some rest." Her father smiled, "you kids be careful and have a good time. He watched from his window as the foursome entered Elisa's Pontiac. His eyes welled, and a soft smile played on his face. "Oh to be young again, youth is so fleeting.

The four acquired a booth with a good view of the stage and dance floor. They ordered their drinks of choice and began their night of relaxation and entertainment. The four danced and conversed the hours away. Laughing and exchanging jokes and reveling in stories from their youthful past. But the hour grew late and Jean and LaPore were anxious to be alone. It was an awkward moment. It was Elisa who saved the day and came to their rescue. You two skedaddle don't worry about Lee here I'll take care of him. Lance and Jean beamed "Thanks Eliza. See you guys later." They waltzed out of the nightclub to Jean's jalopy which she had parked earlier. The two sat quiet watching as Lance and Jean exited the club. Lee ordered two rum and cokes and they conversed softly for the next hour. LeSage finally stating it's late, I guess you can take me to that motel in the center or hope you will. Elisa gave a throaty laugh. "Motel Hell! You're coming to my place. Don't look shocked. I won't bite. Come on, I've an extra room and you'll save some bucks. Hey, you're a Marine, a mean lean fighting machine what you afraid of? She stood laughing, pulling him out of the booth.

The moon glowed brightly. Stars danced and twinkled in the night sky as they drove slowly through the back roads. Finally Elisa pulled into a dirt roadway. The headlights revealing a quaint ranch house with tall pines standing as sentinels and an old barn. It's antiquated wood stood in the rear. It had seen better days. Killing the engine, she took his hand and led him into the house. Lights filled the living room as he hit the light switch. A homey setting greeted him. An old comfort couch along the far wall and a wooden rocker and recliner sat facing it. A thick rug lay before the fireplace and a small TV rested on a table in the north corner. He turned as she spoke, "excuse me, I've got to use the ladies room." "Sure Lisa, take your time." He had taken to calling her Lisa. "There's beer in the fridge," she called out as she left the room. He walked to the mantel and studied a photo of a soldier in an eight by ten frame. The eyes stared out at him with a hint of a smile along the mouth. Her voice startled him. She'd come up softly behind him. "My husband Lance killed in Korea, in 1951. He was with the Eighth Army in the assault north. He was twenty one. "Yeah makes me twenty four. I was eighteen when he was killed, haven't been with anyone since, except for tonight. Her eyes fixed on his. They stood close. He could hear and felt his heart pulsating. He'd never known a woman. He felt guilt yet desire overwhelmed him. She came closer reached out and gently moved them off and away from the mantel. Her lips were opened slightly. Her eyes glazed with emotion. She wrapped her arms around him. He moved in close pulling her to him. Their lips met in fiery passion. Her hands moved up and down his back. "Oh Lee, I've been alone so long. I need and want you. Please, please, love me, just for tonight. Let this evening be our lifetime together." They sprinted to the bed room caressing, exploring, soft tender sounds emitted in the semi-darkness. For Lee it was like finding and entering paradise. An experience he'd never had before and as this was his first time would probably never have again.

Spent they lay back experiencing the satisfied fulfillment of giving to each other in sharing life's greatest gift. Where two souls entwine and the world stands still. After a while he rose and set too preparing a fire in the stone fireplace. She shrilled with happiness. "Oh, I've haven't shared a warm fire in years. They stood naked, neither ashamed taken by the magnetic pull that drew their bodies and filled their souls with ecstasy that only a man and woman in the throes of lovemaking experience the young and healthy sharing a loneliness. Two people found shelter in each others arms. They slept in bed way past dawn.

He woke first and eased his arm from under her and checked his watch, almost eleven, he had slept nine hours and had the finest sleep of his life. Elisa was asleep beside him. She was on her front and had thrown the sheets off during the night. Her back was bare all the way down to her waist. He could see the swell of her breast under her. Her hair spilled over her shoulder and one knee was pulled up resting on his thigh. Elisa's head was bent forward on the pillow curving in following the direction of her knee. It gave her a compact athletic look. He kissed her neck, she stirred, "Morning Elisa," he said. She opened her eyes. Then closed them and opened them again. She smiled a warm morning smile. "I was afraid I dreamed it," she said. "I used to once." He kissed her again tenderly on the cheek, then with passion on her lips. Her arms came around behind him and he rolled over with her. They made love again and again. As time flew by they showered together. His first time ever and what pleasure he had experienced. Breakfast was next on the agenda. They ate like they were starving. Time it seems when you're with loved ones and having a good time never stands still. The hours and days clicked away for Elisa and Lee spending and cherishing the hours in each others arms. They went for drives, walks, ate at the diner, once meeting up with Jean and Lance. Try as they may, they couldn't stop the clock. Tuesday night they held hands in front of the diner exchanged promises to keep in touch with the future unknown to them, they hugged hard. Lee entered the vehicle and in a puff of black smoke was gone.

Broken Rose walked slowly inhaling the scent of the forest. He was content exploring and experiencing the wonders of a world he loved. He chose a campsite by a small pond and began busying himself constructing a modest lean too. Then dug a pit and placing rocks around its perimeter made a fire that he may cook on and for it to provide warmth. The fragrance of pines filled him with nostalgia. Thoughts of his homeland danced in his brain. He took stock of his provisions. He'd purchased beef jerky and berries at a local mom and pop store in town. He'd asked and was granted permission from a local farmer and gathered several ears of corn. He sat mesmerized by the sun's rays dancing and frolicking off the ponds surface. A family of ducks swam by and the mother honking encouraging her young trailing behind to keep pace. Lost in thought he heard whimpering from deep brush located to his rear. Knife in hand, he stalked the area. The small cries grew louder demanding as if imploring for help. He brushed aside twigs and branches and came face to face with a wolf pup. It was just lying there eyes sad and pleading. He scoped the area and there some feet away lay the pup's mother. She lay still and ridged. He knelt and examined the still form. Determined the creature was dead apparently from a random shooter. With his knife he dug a three foot grave and wrapped the cold furry body in an old utility jacket and gently buried her. He prayed over the grave calling on the Great Spirit to guide and reward this brave hunter and mother.

He returned to the pup and after examining him and ignoring his whimpers of pain, Broken rose discovered its right front foot was broken. How or why he couldn't determine. Checking the perimeter, he was satisfied no other pups were abandoned. He gently lifted the injured pup and carried him to his campsite where he tenderly fastened a splint from solid branches and torn pieces of cloth from an extra t-shirt. He laid the pup inside the lean too by the warm fire. Digging into his life's pouch, he extolled the little creature to share his beef jerky. The pup ate ravenously with his eyes pleading for more. The Rose obliged. Then filled his canteen cup with water from the pond and placed it by the pup's nozzle that began lapping and drinking immediately. The Rose added wood to the fire and dined on berries and corn for his meager supply of jerky depleted by the hunger of his wounded pup. The sun sank low and soon the tarp of darkness would envelope them. He covered the pup with his poncho and lay beside him shielding its small body from the nights chill. He could feel the loneliness the pup was going through since Broken Rose had lost his mother at such a young age.

The chirping of birds roused him from his sleep. His small friend stirred beside him. He rebuilt the fire and shared the last of his berries with the pup. Kicked out the fire dumping water and making certain there were no hot embers. He'd made his decision and he'd fashioned a carry all out of the remnants of his old utility jacket, applied straps from his webb belt and carried the wounded pup on his back. Jogging threw the forest back to base. Marines gaped as he flew past curious as to the luggage on his back. He jogged to company headquarters and entered quietly in his stealthy way. Gunny Burke was alone at the small gray iron desk. "God damn it Tonto. You got to quit sneaking up on people, Jesus, your scary as shit." "Sorry Gunny it's just my way." "Yeah, I know might pay dividends one day. What you got there?" "A wounded wolf pup, mother was dead, some prick shot her and left her there." "Well what the fuck you going to do with the pup?" Broken Rose smiled sheepishly, "Gunny let me nurse him back, won't be able to domesticate him anyway. He's a hunter, a soul of the wild. Let me keep him in the squad bay till his leg heals." "Aw, shit Tonto, your bringing me a headache you know that. I'll have to clear it with Sisco and Klober." "Come on Gunny, Alpha has a pet cat. Charlie company has a pet raccoon. He'll only be a quest till he heals then his instinct and the call of the wild will beckon and He'll saunter off. But he's vulnerable now and defenseless." Burke rose from the desk reached out and nuzzled the pups head. "Ah, what the hell? Go ahead I'll clear it with the top and company officers. Have the doc check him out and get him some chow." "Thanks Gunny." "Oh fuck! Get out of here! Crazy fucken Indian!"

The Rose ecstatic, raced to sick bay where the doc replaced the crude splint with a proper cast. Broken Rose forged and located a large wooden box that once hosted grenades. He had placed several blankets within and gingerly put his new friend in same. Positioning the box alongside his rack. Gunny Burke entered with the first sergeant. The squad bay empty of its occupants still off on liberty. The Top spoke, "Got a name yet?" "Haven't thought about it Top" "Well, I have. If you want to play nursemaid, that's fine, but his name has been added to our rolls." "What name Top?" "Leatherneck," Gunny Burke uttered, "Ur-rah, Ur-rah." The two senior noncoms exited the squad. When the grunts returned from liberty they were delighted in their new squad member. All taking turns feeding, watering and cleaning. Leatherneck received love, respect and tenderness. The Marines loved him. But Broken Rose's prophecy held true. One day, Leatherneck rubbed against each of his adopted family. He'd grown large strong and healthy. Then one night he simply romped away into the forest. For years it was said that Leatherneck would stand by the base's perimeter and howl his love and thanks. It became legend. Broken Rose would often sit quiet. His spirit with Two Wolves. Was it he who guided the pup to him? No one knows or ever will. But it makes one wonder. Fills one's spirit with the thought the spirit world lives.

Lt. Colonel Striker sat rigid facing his Regimental Commander Colonel Von Meer. "Rest easy Eric relax and smoke if you like." Von Meer was a burly man and stood 6' in stocking feet. He'd been in the Corps twenty years and saw action in the Pacific and Korea. He reclined back in his chair. His desk adorned with family photos and some action shots from the past with old units and buds. Behind him standing tall and proud in their standards the Color's and Marine flag. "Eric you've been pushing your boys hard and it shows, well-disciplined and good physical shape, a ready-made combat unit. I commend you on your hard work and ingenuity. Where's your battalion now? What's on the agenda lately?" "Well sir, they're out at the motor range today. I know we have a heavy weapons platoon but I want all my boys familiar with our arsenal of weaponry. It's imperative that each and every one of them could step up and know the nomenclatures and workings should the need arise." Von Meer smiled, "yes you're right Eric. Wish all my battalion commanders had that foresight and initiative. Damn excuse me Eric, there's hot fresh coffee, help yourself." "No thank you sir, give me the hibby gibbys." "Okay, Eric not a problem. Here's the scoop. Scuttle butt has it that the division commander who's been summoned to Washington, as we speak, favors dispatching a battalion to South America for intense jungle training. You know the boss. He's got vibes concerning the orient smells trouble. Like a cat seeking his litter box. You and I know there are a lot of hot spots in that part of the world. He wants a well-trained elite force should the keg explode. So, how would you like to take your boys down there?" Striker stared at his commander, Colonel I know you're not asking but telling. Hell yes,

yes sir. They're the best sir, more than ready and they'll past that test."
Again Von Meer smiled, "I know that Eric that's why when the general
reached out to me for a recommendation there was no hesitation on
a choice. I immediately recommended your battalion and the general
whole heartily agreed."

Striker squirmed in his seat. "Sir, where, what country will we
be going to?" Von Meer raised his hand. "There's no need to know.
You'll be going incognito. The host nation knows but Washington
wants no international nit picking. They're not interested in rousing
suspicious and giving cause to international politics." "When sir?"
"I like that Lt. Colonel you're right to the point, no patience. Okay,
today's Thursday, give your boys a three day pass. Have them saddled
up and ready to debark Monday at 0800 hours. Your unit will be
trucked to Fort Benning where four globe masters are reserved as
your air taxis. You'll land on an isolated field in the host country.
Be met by military personnel who will act as guides. It's imperative
this operation is kept hush, hush. Your troops need not know at
this time. You may inform your company commanders but in strict
confidentiality. I want no leaks. You will be allotted five days' worth
of supplies, provisions, etc. However you'll be stomping in the boon
docks for ten days, which means, I'm sure you know that you'll
have to forge and live off the land for the other five. That's what
this operation is all about. Learning to live off the land should the
need confront us. Any question?" "Yes sir, do we lock and load and
carry live ammo?" "Yes but your restricted on that matter. You can
neither hurt nor fire at anyone unless of course your command is
attacked. But that won't happen. Where you're going there are native
inhabitants but you're a large force and I doubt you'll be harassed.
Should you be accosted let the local militia who will be escorting you
handle the situation, unless they're overrun, use extreme discretion.
You've been chosen to lead this foray because you've displayed to us
a well-honed disciplined battalion." "Sir, will we carry radios?" "Yes,
but I don't know how effective they'll be. It's pretty dense where

you're headed. Here again, it will be a good test on how equipment measures up. Okay, Eric that's it. I'm leaving for Washington myself this afternoon. So I won't see you off. Won't be returning till next Wednesday, good luck and make damn sure you touch basis with those Globe Master pilots. You need to synchronize with them as to a time and pick up point on completing the mission." "Yes sir." Striker rose stood at attention and performed a crisp about face and quickly strode from the regimental commander's office.

Striker headed directly to his battalion headquarters. On entering his clerk stood to attention. "At ease Dawson, Reach out to Sergeant Major Whitaker and 1st Sergeant Gates. Have them report here forthwith, hot Coffee?" "Yes sir, just put on a fresh pot." "Very good, please bring me one, black, no frills." "Yes sir." "Dawson also, contact Doc Little. I want him here ASAP." "Yes sir, on it sir." "Very well, carry on." Striker hurried into his office. There was a lot to do and prepare for and little time to get it done.

Sergeant Major Whitaker and 1st Sergeant Gates reported within ten minutes. Entering their commander's office, they stood at rigid attention. "Oh fuck!" uttered Striker, "at ease gentlemen, at ease." Both senior NCO's came to a relaxed parade rest. Striker pointed to two chairs facing his desk. "Sit, please sit and relax." Both noncoms nodded and took seats positioning themselves as comfortable as possible in the hard straight back chairs. Striker lit up a Lucky. "Relax guys smoking lamp is lit." Both senior NCO's fired up. Striker appraised his NCO's then spoke softly. "Sergeant Major, I want you to reach out to my company commanders. I want them here in this office at 1700 hours. Also I want the logistics Officer Lieutenant Morgan in attendance. Do this quietly and softly. I don't want a lot of fanfare and buzzing from junior officers and the troops is that understood?" "Yes sir," uttered his two top soldiers. "Okay, get it done. And I want you two in attendance and also Gunny Sergeant Burke and Doc Little, dismissed."

The 8th Marine Officers sat in a semi-circle facing their Commander's desk. He had yet to arrive. Sergeant Major Whitaker and 1t Sergeant Gates along with Gunny Sergeant Burke stood by the hatch ever watchful for their skipper. The logistics officer Lieutenant Morgan and Doc Little leaned against a far wall. "Tension!" barked Gunny Burke. The assembled officers jumped to attention. "At ease, gentlemen, as you were," ordered Colonel Striker as he strolled through the hatchway and headed directly to his desk. The officers returned to their seats and waited in suspense. "Okay gentlemen, here's the scoop. This battalion is going on a training excursion to South America on Monday coming. I want you, company commanders, to get on your platoon and squad leaders to make damn sure the troops gear is in complete readiness, Doc?" "Yes sir," responded Doc Little. "Make damn sure that your Corp's men request and receive ample supplies of salt tables, water purification pills, salves ointments, expellant, and penicillin. When I said ample that's just what I mean. You're the Doctor you know damn well what you and your team require. Get it done and set up overseas shots for the troops tomorrow, understood?" "Yes sir." "We'll get it done, very good. Lieutenant Morgan." "Yes sir." "Your logistics, you'll requisition five days' worth of provisions and live ammo. Make sure we have wire and rope. Also latch on to some Springfield 03's with scopes, at least one for each platoon, understood?" "Yes sir." "Now listen up and listen tight this trip of ours is confidential. What's said in this office stays in this office. There be no gossiping or grab assing over this issue. His scanned his officers, understood?" All responded "Yes sir." "Okay any questions?" Bravo Company's commander spoke up. "Colonel where are we going, that we'll need to be in possession of live ammo?" Striker smiled, "Captain we're Marines, a combat unit, we don't travel with blanks and if you're wondering it's not a combat mission but an intense jungle training foray. As to our destination we're incognito. No need to know that's all I can tell you." Colonel Von Meer had authorized a three day pass for the battalion commencing on Friday. I'll go along with base liberty. We embark in a convoy early Monday morning. I want no stragglers or Johnny come lately. Base liberty only, First Sergeant you got that?" "Yes sir Skipper, no sweat." "Okay get cracking and ride your noncoms. It's imperative that the troop's equipment is carte blanch. Okay, make sure extra socks and skivvies are in their packs, anything else, any further questions? No, you all understand. Now get it done. Dismissed"

As the officers began to file from the office, they halted and listened as Doc Little asked, Colonel the troops are gonna be curious about all those shots. How can we cover that and explain?" Striker chortled softly, good show doc, you're right. So all listen up simply inform them we're getting ready for a med cruise. Everyone got that?" "Yes sir." The officers and senior noncoms walked briskly out into the night. Major Pezzone, Striker's exec, stormed into the office. Eric Morgan states he's to draw five days' worth of provisions. Thought we were going for ten. Striker laughed we are Frank. They're getting the word when we land in East Bum Fuck, sewer city or out house country. Where they learn the meaning of improvise, adapt, and overcome." Pezzone smiled, "Okay, Colonel you're the boss."

The next morning, after morning chow, the troops were marched by companies to the main medical dispensary for a flurry of overseas inoculations, typhoid, malaria and other such various diseases. LeBron strode up to Doc Little, "Hey bro." "That's Petty Officer 1st Class, to you maggot." "Oh come on Doc, can that shit, what these shots for man? God damn, you people sticking us like we voodoo dolls." Doc Little smirked, "PFC LeBron, they're to rid your sorry black as of all those critters swimming and frolicking inside your ass." "Well if my black ass got creatures, what about your black ass?" Little laughed, because you low lives from Brooklyn stick your baby dicks in all kinds of shit. Whereas an upgrade like me pork's only choice pussy. Crème de la Crème. You wouldn't know or understand that Jake. Now move out down the line, your holding up the works."

"Shit," muttered LeBron them needles and all gone to your head, you be fucked up." "Move LeBron! Go or I'll stick you with this." He brandished a large syringe with an eight inch needle. LeBron eyes widened and double timed away from his nemesis.

The troops were dismissed and dispatched to their individual quarters, where in the platoon sergeants and squad leaders descended and began inspection of weapons, webb gear, boots, helmets knives, individual Marines were chosen and issued machetes and instructed to keep them in top condition. Honed and coated with light oil. The men were curious and inquisitive but told little or nothing, in fact, in most cases admonished by their NCO's and told to shut up and get prepared. Their NCO's were forgiven when informed they had base liberty for the next three days. "Shit!" screamed LeBron sleep time and dove into his rack. Broken Rose smiled, walked over to LaPore and LeSage, "what you guys planning?" LeSage pointed at the already sleeping figure of LeBron, "just what he's doing gonna catch up on lost shut-eye. What about you? The woods again?" "Naw, think I'm going to band here with you white eyes. Rest sounds good, real good."

The grunts spent the weekend lolling about grateful and basking in the leisure time allotted them. From time to time, some in small groups, would saunter off to the slope chute reveling in cold 3.5 beer and uncooked burgers. Weapons were cleaned and checked then the process redone applying light oil to gleaming metal to make sure weapons well cleaned. Cotton swabs rammed down the barrels with a touch of linseed oil. Then webb gear was examined with the hunt for fraying and tears. Grunts checked their equipment like it lay under a fined tuned microscope. Sunday evening was busy stuffing packs with vital essentials like soap, shaving cream, razors, extra socks and skivvies and yes utilities. LaPore glanced at LeSage busy packing. "Hey Lee, he asked, How come you always carry that small jar of Vicks?" LeSage smiled, "well Lance I love this shit. Reminds me when I was a kid, you know, mom used to rub your chest with it when you had a cold. I love its fragrance. Love sniffing it. It's a touch of home. I always carry with me. It's my security blanket. Lance, what can I say?" LaPore smiled, inwardly he thought, a touch of home. Don't have that. He looked around him scanning the squad bay. "Yeah, this is home. This is my family someday I'll carry these memories as a touch of home."

The 8th Marines battalion command center was quiet. A typical Sunday morning, Corporal Dawson busy processing paper work and alone in the office. He sat back day dreaming of home life when the incessant ringing of the phone severed him from his nostalgia. Reaching for the receiver, he spoke concise and professionally. "8th Marine's, Corporal Dawson here." "Corporal, this Colonel Von Meer." "Yes sir." "I want you to contact Colonel Striker right away. Have him land line me at this number." Dawson scribbled the number on a yellow notepad. "Yes sir right away." Dawson pulled a small index box, sorted through names and found strikers number. He dialed and waited on the third ring the gruff voice of Colonel Striker came on the line. "Lieutenant, Colonel Striker here." "Sir, this is Corporal Dawson. You are to call Colonel Von Meer immediately." Reciting the number he waited for the Colonel to respond. "Thank you Corporal the line went dead." Striker dialed the number. It took five rings before Colonel Von Meer answered. "Sir this is Striker, what's your pleasure." "Ah Eric looks like Washington wants you to arrive at Benning in the dark. So your mode of travel is pushed ahead to 1400 hours on Monday. The powers that be want to minimize prying eyes. So set that in motion with your outfit, understood?" "Yes sir, roger that, okay." "Good luck, see you on your return," and disconnected. Striker then contacted Sergeant Gates. Filled him in on the change of orders and instructing him to contract the Sergeant Major and Company Commanders. Satisfied that his orders were understood and passed along he hung up. Sat back in his recliner and mind in overdrive settled back lost in thought.

Monday 1400 the battalion in full battle array stood in ranks. Noncoms shuffling back and forth checking their squads and platoons, inspecting weapons, ensuring they'd packed personal essentials. Up and down, eyes always on the alert scanning their ranks for flaws and soiled worn gear. Company Commanders signaled his peers that the battalion commander with his small entourage was making his way enroute down the line. Eight hundred and fifty pairs of boots clashed as thunder. The battalion made a formidable sight. Striker marched briskly scanning his battalion and took pride in their appearance. The battalion Sergeant Major marched a little behind and to his right and his exec Major Pezzone to his left. He halted in the center of the formation and took note of the guidon flapping in the breeze. He truly loved these moments when he came face to face with his battalion of warriors, young, fresh viral. "Ah, what a picture," he thought. "I love it." To his rear a convoy of troop carriers. Eighty strong idled waiting patiently. Their diesels coughing and belching small clouds of black smoke throughout the base passing Marines paused to gape at their brother's in green. A Marine combat battalion in full battle regalia leaves one's heart pounding and staring in awe and pride.

The company commanders sounded off. "Sir Alpha Company all present and accounted for." Down the line those words were echoed. "Bravo all present and accounted for." "Charlie Company all present and accounted for." The words echoed carried by the wind. The officers snapping off brisk salutes to their commanders who returned each and every one with a crisp military bearing, Striker paused then bellowed "8th Marines dismissed! Mount up in the trucks!" The Marines scrambled boarding the huge vehicles. As the last man mounted and the trucks coughed to life and headed to the main gate. The Marines grumbled under the canvas enclosures. "Where the Hell are we going?" Whispers of a hot spot in the orient, no maybe the Middle East could it be Cuba or Taiwan?" Broken Rose sat quiet. Learn, listen be ever watchful. These words branded in his mind, so it begins he thought. "A warriors adventure, somewhere, someday, sometime the Marines will land and shed blood, guts, sweat and tears. This is the warrior's way."

The trucks roared through the base gate. MP's holding traffic at bay. The long line of green military vehicles raced down the highway. The sky had grown ominous. Dark clouds laying its gloomy tarp and it began to drizzle lightly. The road glistened with small beads of water. Here and there tires striking these small pools spraying water in all directions. Civilians waiting in traffic stared in excited amazement and the Marines waving and smiling as they passed. The youthful cream of America, confident and proud, they possessed in their souls and that feeling of immortality that all youth holds dear. The miles clicked by as they drove into the Blue Ridge Mountains. Their peaks like fingers poking into the heavens attempting to suck the clouds downward. Men smoked and joked like fishermen each bragging of home and personal exploits. Ah yes, the treasure of youth only then these young warriors had no way of knowing it is fleeting.

Army Captain Jon Wilson strolled slowly and headed to Benning's Main Mess Hall. As he drew close, he was happy to observe that the mess was a beehive of activity. Lots of people to feed, he thought, what with our own troops, trainees from other military institutions, both domestic and foreign. He entered the hall and headed to the kitchen area. He caught sight of Master Sergeant O'Malley and walked briskly up to him. "Might I have a word with you?" "Sure, yes sir. What's up Captain?" "Look I just got off the phone with the base commander. There's a battalion of Marines headed this way. They should arrive at our location around 2200 hours. They're outward bound. The Colonel wants box lunches supplied to them as they'll be departing almost right away. Four sandwiches and a container of potato salad should satisfy their palates temporarily." "Jesus Captain, that's a tall order. You're talking thirty four hundred sandwiches. It's already 1600 hours. I've got evening chow that we're preparing. I'd have to call in the morning crew." "Well Master Sergeant that's just what you'll have to do. But Captain, Christ it's just about impossible." The Captain looked off startled by the crash and clanging of pots and the sorting and clearing of dinner utensils. "Master Sergeant this is a training haven for airborne troops. We confront impossible tasks on every front but overcome. I don't give a rat's ass how you do it but get it done. The Colonel isn't interested in your concerns. So pull up your big boys pants and get it done. It's not a request it's an order. We're airborne; we rise to the occasion and overcome. Understood?" "Yes sir, we'll get it done. Where the fuck are they going?" The Captain smiled, "Sergeant, I'm not privy to the Colonel's confidence. China, Russia, who the fuck knows. And for the moment I personally don't give a shit. Have those provisions ready at 2200 hours. Make sure some of your mess people are here to provision them, anymore lame questions?" "No sir." "Thank you Master Sergeant, know its short notice. But you're wearing those stripes for a reason. Ride herd on your guys. Those jarheads are gonna be hungry and there's no MacDonald's wherever they're going. Good night Sergeant" "Good night Captain." Wilson turned slightly as he walked off and called over his shoulder, "thank you Master Sergeant, air-borne all the way."

The convoy sped ever onward. Rain pelted the canvass tops beating a arithmetic tattoo that combined with the hum of the huge tires lulling many into fitful sleep. The low murmur of conversations as these boy warriors swapped stories of a youth now sacrificed and forsaken to serve the colors. Darkness descended on the convoy. Headlights burned bright and their glare giving the appearance of rain drops dancing and glistening in the darkness. Quiet enveloped the interior of the large trucks. Each man full of anxiety as to what fate waited. The unknown is always difficult for the human mind to digest. Many had left the warm comfort of home life. Some had exited a world of loneliness and hardship or lack of love, little or poor nourishment. Some etched out a difficult life on city streets and all had dreams and hopes but a cloud had a grip on their souls where were they headed and why? These were young Marines in the summer of life. Disciplined physically tuned a well-oiled machine. They'd made their choice the Corps was their father and the colors their mother. There was no turning back. The dye was cast when they swore allegiance to their country. Now they were left to the hands of fate and karma.

The huge trucks rumbled through the gates of Benning. They were waved on by a white helmeted sentry. Their engines whirred and coughed as they plowed through base roads. Their sudden appearance was not new to this base. Troops were coming and going at all hours day and night. The behemoth carriers halted on line in front of the huge mess hall. The grunts ordered to enter single file where men in army fatigues dished out box lunches as they shuffled along. The line of troops snaked through the mess hall returning quickly to the idling trucks. Again the carriers roared to life and in the dark the grunts journey pushed ever forward. Shortly the headlights of the vehicles lit up an air strip where four huge globe masters rested in intimidating readiness. Their engines idling, their whine carried by the evening wind. The grunts were ordered to debark, form up and marched to the giant aircraft in single file. Leadened with gear they embarked into the huge fuselages. The hatches closed and the engines roared with a fury and the 8th Marines lifted into the night airborne with the twinkling stars to face and overcome another challenge on their path to the warrior's way. Fear and anticipation continued to be ever present among these young warriors but they knew that this is what they had trained for and were well prepared.

LeSage strolled over to Broken Rose as the plane's engines whistled and hummed their workings creating vibrations within their mammoth bodies which made it difficult to stand while the large craft was taxing down the runway. "So John, what do you think any thoughts?" The Rose, his amber eyes glistening in the darkened fuselage, smiled, "Lee, no need to think. We march to the beat of the drum and we answer to and obey the powers that be. We'll know soon enough what our objective is when we enlisted we traded our individuality to warrant the tittle Marines. So we obey and we follow and we answer to the call. It's as simple as that. You don't question, you don't object. We're America's guardians. Once you accept that status your spirit is free and steady. We answer to the Great One and each other. That's the measure of the true warrior." LeSage smiled, "yeah, John, guess you're right. No game of tag here. It's all about loyalty, devotion and faith in our leaders and our beliefs." The Rose blinked, settled back in his hard seat. Get some rest. No way of knowing when you get another moments reprieve." "Yes sir, Corporal sir. You're right on. Both laughed softly. LeSage turned and returned to his seat.

Striker sat facing his exec, Major Pezzone, speaking softly he asked, "Frank everything status quo. You checked on provisions? You know medical, ammo" "Yes sir, we're okay, Colonel any idea where we are headed?" "No Frank. Only the senior pilots know. They've been given landing coordinates and are held to strict secrecy. Who the hell cares where we're going. It's going to be hairy and a challenge. But this battalion is hard core. We've seen to that. There's a great opportunity here to work out and dissolve whatever kinks may exist. It is not for us to question but to lead our troops in whatever the issue is. This is the time, the moment it can't be later if we get in the shit." Pezzone stared into the night. "Yeah Eric, you're right. Mold em scold em. Only the bold survive. That putz on the other side, whoever he may be, won't show mercy or quarter. Striker's eyes twinkling, retorted, "No Frank, he won't and neither will we."

The great birds glide through the night sky and the world below them oblivious to their existence or destination while Americans asleep in their beds safe and secure uncaring that their men and women in the military marched into harm's way to ensure their peace and prosperity. The big bird's engines began to whine in the night as the engines coughing and belching black exhaust. Slowly they taxied down the runway gaining speed and momentum. The huge aircraft shuddered and shook. The men huddled in their seats and sat shock still as the huge craft vibrated and suddenly lifted into a moonlit sky. Airborne, the troops sat quiet thoughts of where they were destined filled their subconscious. One thought enveloped their minds, "what was their goal and objective when these huge birds landed and where?" Hours passed. Off in the distance the sun rose slowly painting the sky with its golden hue. The men gazed out at passing clouds. Light flooded the cabins. Men stirred from restless slumber. There was little conversation. Some spoke in hushed whispers. Others sat sullen and nervous.

The pilot's voice startled them as he ordered over the intercom fasten seat belts. The behemoth craft descended slowly ever so slowly. Then one by one nose down glided onto a large grassy meadow. The planes rolled to a stop. The grunts ordered to disembark the craft where they formed up in companies, they stared in awe. They were surrounded by jungle. The trees stood as huge sentinels. The sun shone bright overhead. Company Commander's took charge. The troops were ordered to lock and load. Striker was taking no chances. They'd landed in a foreign country. He had no idea where or if there were hostile adversaries in the area. Supplies were unloaded quickly. Once complete, their transport aircraft taxied down the meadow and with a thunderous roar lifted into the sky. The 8th Marines stood alone. Noncoms filtered up and down the squads and platoons ensuring weapons were locked and loaded. Striker and Pezzone watched the proceedings with keen interest. Standing on a small knoll, they watched as a small military patrol headed towards them. Both officers strolled off to greet them. The patrol halted directly in front of them. Their green uniforms blending with the foliage. A young lieutenant approached Striker, threw a crisp salute. "Colonel welcome. I'm Lieutenant Raoul Sanchez. I'm the officer in charge of this detail. We are to be your guides and assist you and your command. I am at your service sir." Striker rendered a snappy return salute. "Fine Lieutenant glad to have you with us now point us in the right direction and let's move out. I don't like being in the open." The Lieutenant chuckled. "Yes sir, if your form up your battalion, we'll lead the way."

The battalion in column snaked into the thick forest. A platoon from Able Company had been issued machetes and soon were hacking a trail that was covered with vines and heavy brush. Platoons would relieve each other taking their turn at this difficult tiresome task. Exotic birds cawed and screeched screaming their displeasure at this intrusion. Insects filled the air and ground critters scurried through and fro. Monkeys swung through tree tops chattering and observing them as they battled their way slowly through elephant grass and tangles of shrubbery that nature had formed into formidable green walls.

Progress was slow and painful with the grunts slapping at weird insects and suffering cuts and abrasions from the sharp grass and deep rooted underbrush. LeBron turned to LeSage, "Fuck we're in a large exotic zoo. Look at them funny looking fuckers hopping from tree to tree. They remind me of a Friday night in Brooklyn. LeSage laughed, "Yeah looks like this is going to be a real treat." "What the fuck man," retorted LeBron "Oh well, at least Gunny Burke can have a reunion. His kin are here up in the trees. Shit, look just like him only smaller and skinnier."

Four hours into their tortured march, they came to a clearing hosting a small spring. The battalion halted, cold rations consumed. They were instructed to drink to keep hydrated. They formed a semi-circle as their guides educated them on wildlife they would encounter and to boil water, then add purification tablets, as well as what snakes to watch for that could be lethal and the hazards of mosquitoes which the grunts had already encountered. They were shown certain moss that could be used for fuel. Instructed on what lairs and wild life to avoid, rule of thumb, avoid them all if you can. Broken Rose listened attentively and honed to the forest he felt comfortable but the words of Two Wolves were ever mindful. "Listen, watch, observe be quiet." Yes, this was forest but new and unknown creatures abounded here. He too would learn. They were shown what vines could be cut and used for rope. Here certain ground insects could be mashed and if need be eaten for their protein. How certain plants could be punctured and their moisture sucked down to quench thirst. They were advised and warned about forging ravines and streams for in this country piranha thrived and struck suddenly and without warning. They were taught the invaluable lesson of capturing live animals and throwing them down stream and once seeing the water boil from the attacking predators to run like hell across the waterway.

The jungles canopy was thick and heavy casting a surreal semi-darkness though. It was high noon. Here and there tongues of the sun's rays struggled to filter through to the ground below, but sunlight was sparse. Steam hissed from the ground wafts of white like vapor curling upwards disappearing into the thick foreboding canopy. Striker had decided they would camp here for the night ensuring Company Commanders posted pickets and sentries through the battalion's perimeter. He stalked the lines. Satisfied military procedure and protocol was enforced, he returned to his CP. A small tent erected yards from the stream bed. Darkness descended. The foreign cries and howls and screeches of the jungle inhabitants played with the men's nerves. On advice from their guides fires were lit and kept burning through the night. Jungle creatures usually withdrew from fire avoided it but the Marines could use their small fires for cooking and boiling water. It was imperative they maintain reserve supplies of this precious liquid. It fell on the individual to fend for himself and they were quick to realize this was what this exercise was about. Survival in the raw, learn here and absorb for it might save your ass somewhere, sometime, somehow.

After morning chow the troops sitting in a semi-circle were again educated in the use of various berries that when boiled and mashed could be used as camouflage paint. How roots from different trees could be boiled and used for medicinal purposes. Berries and plants were cut and put on display by their guides. They were also informed of the large gators that inhabited the forest and to be mindful that these huge creatures could propel out of water at 30 miles an hour. And were advised what to watch for as to their nests as well as their adeptness at camouflage. Lessons went on till noon after chow; the battalion secured the area and entered the dark foreboding jungle.

The grunts hacked and clawed their way through thick unforgiving jungle. The area host guides leading and cajoling in professional expertise. At times the column was forced to halt and detour once again through jungle which showed no mercy. The change in direction of travel necessitated due to the perils of quicksand. At intervals the jungle cleared allowing a free line of march. The Marines gazed in astonishment as a large anaconda slithered past its head the size of a large Rottweiler. It scurried by peacefully displaying no aggression. The grunts estimated its length between forty and fifty feet. They watched as the large predator twisted and slithered disappearing into the safety of the thick jungle. As the young Marines labored along their route of march, the constant cries and screeching of wild animals accompanied them. LeBron nudged LaPore "Damn I feel like I'm in a giant cage with wild creatures. Fuckers give me the creeps. UH oh here comes the devil, Gunny Burke cruised past constantly up and down the line, cajoling encouraging the troops. Soon they entered a meadow. The smell of decaying vegetation was overwhelming. Their boots sucked into wet muck. Their legs tired from the constant need to pull their feet step by step through the ooze and slimy watery mud. The battalion forced marched through haze and hissing steam, finally reaching dry ground by a murky river. It was piss color and slime coated it with a foreboding frosting. Striker called a halt. "We're camp here for the night. Post sentries and let's get campfires ignited." The grunts had been battling the jungle for four days and that night Doc Little and his band of Corpsmen were busy treating abrasions, insect bites, admonishing the men on the importance of foot care and to make certain the crotch and armpits were kept as clean as possible. Salves and injections of penicillin were administered the later to ward off signs of infection. As the men lolled about they were informed by NCO's that their evening chow was the last of their rations. From this point on they would forage from the jungle.

Broken Rose sat quiet by the small fire. Whittling away on long tree limbs obtained from the jungle floor. His squad watched quietly with interest. LeBron spoke up, "Hey Corporal Tonto, what's you making. The Rose continued at his labor. "Jake, I'm making spears. You heard the man, Now, we hunt for food. We are not allowed to use our weapons. So now we do it the Indian way." "Yeah, but what's out there Tonto?" "Lots of things, we will eat. What's the Corps saying, adapt, and overcome. This we shall do." The men gaped at his feet lie two very sharp spears. This is all I need whispered the Rose, this and my old buddy here. He held his knife high for all to see. This is what Striker brought us here for. To adapt, to overcome and to use mother earth and her gifts and survive. Now get some sleep. You'll need it." "Night Rose," the men uttered. He watched his squad bed down for the night. Smiling inwardly, "yes now Tonto will be Indian again and care for his white eyed brothers." LeBron couldn't sleep, sat up and watched Broken Rose. Scrambling to his feet, he approached and sat facing his bro. "Tonto, you really think those crude weapons will suffice?" The Rose gazed into the fire. "Yes Jake, I do. This is how I once lived. Jake, if there's one thing in life I have learned it's that a man has to be at his best when things are at their worst. Now hit the sack and so am I."

Sentries patrolling in silence around the perimeter while the men lay restless on the hard ground trying to find comfort in sleep, their senses constantly tuned to the cries and rustling of the jungles creatures. The Rose had remained staring into the fire. He loved the musical chorus emitting from the jungle. LeSage unable to sleep softly approached John. "Might I join you?" Broken Rose smiled "sure old friend. Welcome to my parlor." They sat talking quietly while the fire glowed warm and bright and the smoke curling into the night. They spoke of boyhood, family the Rose's amber eyes soft and bright, sighed. "You know Lee, I remember my grandfather Two Wolves told me once and once only about my grandmother. He said I was born when she kissed me; I died when she left me but in between I lived many years when she loved me. A tear coursed down his cheek. It is what it is Lee." "Yeah, John we're born, we live, and we die. It's what we do in between and leave behind that count. Good night old shoe."

LeSage returned to his small night refuge and took notice of sentries patrolling ever watchful all along the camps perimeter. He raised himself upon an elbow and stared at the silhouette of his Indian friend sitting motionlessly by the fire watched as the Rose stood abruptly and snaked into the jungle. LeSage set up quickly startled by the rustling approach of his two pals LaPore and LeBron. "Hey man," whispered LeBron. "You asleep" "No dip shit I'm flying a kite." Both grunts laughed nervously. "Shit," uttered LeBron. "Them jungle creatures noisy as hell, worst then a Brooklyn whore house on a Saturday night." "Fuck you guys did you see that big ass worm slither by?" "Naw, some night crawler, ain't a worm Jake, chortled LaPore. "That was an anaconda which will swallow you whole after mashing you into a syrup stew. Only thing is the poor bastard will get indigestion eating your black ass where it's been." "Fuck you whiteys, you all jealous because us brothers got bigger dicks." "Well yeah, he turned to LeBron, that's where your brains are." "Shit," admonished LeBron, "none of us got any brains wouldn't be here in this maggot infested hell hole, if we did." The camp was restless. The grunts edgy, alert, weird cries and screeches from the jungle kept them in alert mode. The rustle of small creatures propelling in an out of their sleep

Leo LePage

areas denied any chance of sleep. Their nerves frayed worried about poisonous snakes and other deadly fiends. The rain forest was new turf to them. The intent was to hardened the battalion so that in time, they would confront and ward off whatever adversaries, dangers of foreign lands and its inhabitants both man and beast.

As the sun peeked through openings in the thick vegetated canopy, the battalion broke camp. Sweaty, bruised, battalion swarms of insects that flew into ears bit at exposed flesh and feasted on open soars. The column trudged deeper into the immense jungle. They were in constant semi-darkness and a hard rain now struck and water pouring from the canopy drenching the area turning the ground into slushy dark brine. Foul odors rose from the jungle floor and boots sucked into the sinking earth works. They passed several native villages deviating away and beyond them. Striker wished to give them a wide berth. He had no intention of creating or confronting an international incident. The guides were professional taking pains to avoid the jungles inhabitants. Striker called a halt at noon. Tired men fell to the ground. Their uniforms covered with muck, leeches clung to boots, leggings trying to get to grunts flesh and blood. Supplies had dwindled and company commanders instructed to choose their best to accompany two guides in the hunt to forage food. Broken Rose had already befriended two guides and it was decided that he and the two foreign soldiers would be responsible for provisioning the battalion.

Broken Rose and his two new found friends clamored into the jungle. Their weapon's wooden spears and bow and arrows produced by the Rose. The men smoked and rested their eyes always peering into the foreboding unfriendly confines of the thick dark green jungle. Men were hungry. They'd exhausted their rations. They waited anxiously. Four hours later, the figures of Broken Rose and two guides emerged from the forest. The two guides one walking behind the other spears affixed to their shoulders carried a large dead boar dangling from their make shift shafts. The Rose trailed slowly

252

behind. In his hand hanging by his sides dangled the corpses of two large birds resembling turkeys. Wrapped around his waist were two large burlap bags when opened produced large quantities of wild onions and mushrooms and the stems of dandelions. The Rose was burdened but showed no signs of fatigue.

A huge spit was erected. The boar skinned and gutted. The men dug a deep circular hole which they filled with dry wood, twigs and moss. A fire was ignited and the spit now containing the butchered boar placed above. Men took turns rotating the carcass. The roasted met expelling in sweet odor causing saliva due to hunger to kick start growling stomachs of famished Marines.

The Rose had plucked and gutted the two birds and they two dangled from pits roasting over a separate fire. Several helmets were drafted from grunts and the steel pots filled with an Indian stew of wild onions, mushrooms and dandelions greens. The Rose had also added various roots like substances. That emitted a sweet acid odor. At dusk the meat and stew like concoction was dealt out equally to the troops who wolfed their fare greedily surprised at its goodness. The Rose cut thick slabs of meat from the remaining carcass roasting them almost black, then setting them on a flat rock by the fire. Jake asked "what's that Tonto?" The Rose laughed quietly "Indian Jerky." "Have no fear dark man, we will eat. Remember no one should go hungry or thirsty in the Great Spirits wonder garden."

The rain had tapered to a drizzle. The men tramped along in route step in columns. Flankers hacked their way through thick brush and their job to protect the battalions' flanks from unknown hostiles. Platoons took turns at this difficult exhausting responsibility. Soon they came to the banks of a dirty greenish river. Slime and dead carcasses of animals floated slowly by the bodies bloated and fly infested. Death was sudden and cruel in the animal world of the jungle. The guides halted the column. Their lieutenant dispatching two men to an out of the way village, shortly they reappeared driving a sickly undernourished cow before them. The officer conferred with his two subordinates who quickly headed down stream along the bank where they suddenly threw the cow into the murky water. Within moments the water boiled and hissed with swarms of piranha. The cow emitted sad squeals of terror. The officer pointed at Striker. The water is high, quick double time your troops across while those bastard fish feast on the cow. The Marines plunged into the chilled filthy river and double timed to the north bank. The last man stumbling safely just as the last remains of the doomed cow disappeared in a geyser of boiling disturbed water. The grunts were learning quickly to establish eatable plants. To hydrate and to recognize dangerous hazards that lay along their route of march. Bodies already steeled by Strikers intense training now hardened to the grinds of jungle conditions and the perils that could devour them. Now in their eighth day they bivouacked for the night. The Rose and the two guides continued to provide food. Sometimes snake, sometimes eggs of unknown origin, small like birds that were brothers to Cornish hens even alligator meat was devoured. It was eat or starve this was an exercise in survival. There was no time or patience for being squeamish. The Marine Corps had no tolerance for weakness. Adapt and overcome, those words repeated over and over and why? They meant survival.

Dark settled laying its black tarp on an unforgiving jungle, where death could leap at you in a second. The battalion had reversed direction. Now hell bent on heading to their pick up point where the Goliath Globe Masters would pluck them from this perilous unfriendly world. Campfires glowed bright red and orange. The groups were anxious to depart this world of growling, screeching, and foreboding atmosphere. Men were busy at cleaning weapons and equipment struggling to clean wounds with antiseptics provided by the Docs. Utilities were frayed and torn tarnished with muck and droppings of creatures. The men sponged and bathed out of helmets and donned their last pair of fresh utilities which emitted odors of mildew caused by the dew and wetness of the rain forest. Boots would have to be replaced once they returned to base. Broken Rose like his brother NCOs spent the night checking on his squad's welfare ensuring that proper foot care was in motion. As well as checking his squads bruises and abrasions. Fortunately the battalion had not seen or experienced crippling injuries. Striker consulted with Company Commanders digesting their reports as to their people's health both mentally and physically. It had been a tough row to hoe but now they were at termination status. He was determined to return with his battalion whole and admonished his officers to lean on non-coms in order to achieve success in a safe return. He turned to his exec Major Pezzone, one more day Frank and home. Pezzone stared at his commander. "Eric do you think this jungle foray was worth all the sweat?" "Yeah, Frank I do. Look at these kids. We've made Marines of them. I'm confident this battalion is ready and able to stand and pass any test. We've driven them hard. But the day may come when all this hardship will pay dividends. This is a combat unit Frank. Less you forget that's what we're all about. That's what the corps is about. We've got to be better than that other guy and I think we've taken leaps and bounds in order to accomplish just that."

The battalion had now reversed their line of march. Heading pell mell to their prearranged pick up point as the column snaked slowly through the thick uninviting jungle. Drizzle now their constant companion and nature playing havoc with weapons and gear. The slurp, slurp of boots sucking slimy mud as the men battled to push on. Still not a man had succumbed to the hardship. Forced to sponge bathe out of helmets with the use of slimy water which was scarce and when they were able to replenished canteens inserting purification tablets generously. Game had become difficult to locate, the creatures fleeing with the scent of man as though aware they were the hunted. The troops slept on spongy wet earth yet they persevered. Striker always in the lead and never wavering in leading his troops by disciplined example.

Broken Rose approached Gunny Burke. "Yes Tonto," uttered Burke. "Gunny, I think we have a potential problem. We are being stalked by a large contingent of native inhabitants armed with spears, long knives and blow guns." Burke stiffened, "you sure Tonto." "yes, Gunny I've been watching them the past three days. They creep ever closer day by day. I believe they're on the move during night hours too. They're approximately one mile to our rear. Appear to be dispatching flankers." "How many, Tonto?" "About 400 all warriors, painted themselves with multicolored paint." "Okay Corporal come with me, the Colonel needs to be informed."

The Rose and Burke stood at attention. "At ease men, what's up?" Striker stood appraising his two noncoms. The Gunny nodded to the Rose, who repeated his information to his Colonel. Striker frowned, "good job Corporal Rose. I want your eyes out there keep me informed." "Yes sir." "Corporal take two men with you." "Sir, I'd rather be alone. No offense white man emits odors." Striker smiled, "Yes I know, spirits, tobacco, spices, okay. But use caution. This battalion needs you." "Yes sir." "Very good carry on. Dismissed." Striker beckoned to his exec. "Yes sir, what's the scuttle butt?" Striker filled in his exec ending the conversation with. "Get me that in country Lieutenant. I want him here yesterday." "Yes sir. Pezzone about faced and stalked off quickly. The lieutenant approached Striker snapped off a sloppy salute. "Yes Colonel, what's your pleasure?" Striker fired up a Lucky, inhaled deeply. "Lieutenant, are you aware we are being stalked by a large force of native inhabitants?" "Yes sir, but I didn't think it warranted your immediate attention. I saw no reason to cause you undue concern." Striker stiffened. "I'll tell you this just one time Lieutenant. You're our lead guide. I don't get concerned just careful. Now here's the layout. You speak their dialect?" "Yes sir, I do." "Then you go tell those bastards to back off, to go away, and to disappear. If they refuse I'll order my boys to blow their fucking heads off. Leave carte blanch meals for the jungle creatures. Now we both know it'll cause an international firestorm. I'll get court marshaled But you being of this country, will probably be executed. Do I make myself clear? Never! Ever! Keep me in the dark again!" He advanced now eyeball to eyeball with the Lieutenant. You read me?!" "Yes Sir!" "Good! Now get out of here and send those stalkers on their way or I sure as hell will!"

As the Lieutenant turned to leave, Striker spoke up, "Lieutenant, you should have known I have my own eyes out there. We're Marines I will not jeopardize this command. Nor will I allow any of my troops to become casualties for no good reason. We came here in peace for training purposes up till now everything has been status quo. Our countries are at peace allies. It's up to men such as you and me to keep it that way. We don't need an incident here and this is a potential dangerous situation. You agree?" "Yes sir, Colonel I'll handle it. I made an error in judgment here. I under estimated your leadership and skill of your Marines. I stand corrected and apologize. I'll diffuse this situation." He turned and left quickly assembling his guides and marched into the foreboding jungle unaware that the eyes of Broken Rose would be ever watchful.

The battalion trudged on. Broken Rose continued to be their eyes and ears. Reporting the native threat had dissipated. They'd simply disappeared after the in country Lieutenant had spoken and met with their Chief. Once again they came to the banks of the Ominous River. They faced a dilemma here for there was no old cow to use as a diversion concerning the piranha. Striker ordered the use of grenades. Men at intervals heaving them into the murky waters explosion after explosion followed soon the waters were filled with the bodies of piranha floating to the surface. The men sprinted across the foul waters. Striker's decision paying dividends as the troops waded to the far bank unimpeded by assault from the predator fish.

257

The rain had ceased the sun battling to spread its comforting warmth through the thick jungle canopy. Striker stood on a knoll with his exec Major Pezzone, observing his command. He slapped Pezzone on his shoulder. "Take a look Frank. Look at these troops honed to a fine well-disciplined unit. Not a main fell out and no stragglers." "Yeah, they bitched, but a happy Marine is a bitching Marine and we made it. There's the field pick up point and we're early." "Post pickets and have the men rest easy till the birds arrive." Pezzone turned faced his Commander, "Yes sir, congratulations Colonel. Now you've the elite battalion in the Corps and it's an honor to serve with you." Pezzone strolled off to issue the proper orders for bivouac security.

The men smoked and lolled about leisurely. Happy their torment in the dark jungle was over. LeSage, Broken Rose, LeBron and LaPore sat at the base of a large purple heart tree. A soft rain began to pelt the area. LeBron uttering, "Fuck more rain. This sucks" Broken Rose placed a hand tenderly on LeBron's shoulder. "Jake, I've said it before and I'll say it again. Rain is the tears of those who have gone before us crying for us. Remember that their spirits roam free. Free from the trials of life. The hardship that plagues one's footsteps through the road of life. Having led the way, they worry for us and are saddened by life's errors and ineptness." Jake smiled softly, "Yeah, Tonto guess you're right. Wherever I go, whatever I do. I'll always recall what you said. Rain is the tears of the dead."

The sun glowed fiery red and its warmth comforting the troops. Welts and scratches and abrasions soaking taking pleasure in the warm rays. The drone of heavy engines filled the sky. The troops faced north and there they were. The large Goliath Globe Masters like majestic birds descending in the sky. They lined up in perfect formation as they made their final landing approach. As they swooped in their engines thrust in reverse to slow their advance. The troops rose gathering gear and slapping each other on the back. Happy this ordeal was at an end. The giant birds taxied on the meadow and came to rest. The troops responding to orders from officers and non-coms to embark. Collapsing in seats each filled with thoughts of going home to the USA.

Army Captain Ray Philips strolled quickly to the main mess where he again sought out the Master Sergeant in charge. Catching sight of him he beckoned, "Master Sergeant John Stebbins, newly assigned, sprinted to the officer. Threw a salute and ram rod straight asked, Sir, how can I help you?" The Captain smiled; look our adopted Marine battalion will be landing here at Benning in about four hour. They've been through an ordeal and in need of hot chow can we accommodate them?" The Master Sergeant rolled his eyes. "Yes sir, I'll dish out a hot stew and biscuits, coffee, milk, whatever. I'll have to keep my crew over their shift. No sweat we'll handle it sir." Captain Philips smiled, "very good Master Sergeant." He glanced at his watch, should arrive at 2300 hours. Thank you and thank your men." The Captain turned and strolled from the mess and headed directly to the reception center where he conferred with a young 2nd Lieutenant arranging that hot showers be available to the incoming Marines. Satisfied all was arranged, He returned to his office, picked up his phone and dialed extension 311. The tired voice of Colonel Arron Fitzsimons came on the line. "Sir, this is Captain Philips as to your orders. All set and in motion as to the welfare of the arriving Marines detail. Benning's Executive Officer sighed with relief. "Thank you, Captain. I'm sure our brothers with the motto Semper-Fi will be eternally grateful. Good job and good night." The Colonel disconnected

The loud hum of the Globe Masters engines lolled the Marines into an exhausting sleep. The men never noticing as the planes began their descent into Benning. Only when the large crafts engines roared into reverse trust did the grunts begin stirring. Darkness had spread its lonely tarp as the Marines debarked from the aircraft and formed into ranks. They marched to the reception center where they reveled in hot showers, scrubbing away muck and scabs of numerous cuts and abrasions. They donned fresh utilities and marched to the main mess where they began relishing the hot stew, coffee and cold milk and biscuits. Completing their meal they were marched to waiting trucks where the final leg of their journey would once again plant them in the bowels of Camp Lejeune. Like thieves in the night the convoy steered through the gates of Fort Benning. Under the camouflage of darkness only those who had a need to know were privy to the 8th Marines adventure.

The convoy roared through the gates of Benning. The troops content their stomachs full. Army mess had anticipated their hunger and had provided generous portions of chow. Their bodies' clean and donning fresh utilities. The grunts smoked and chattered excitably commenting and reminiscing over the events of the past ten days. They had seen and experienced the hardship of jungle life. Successful in their mission, they felt pride in themselves and their unit. Soon the trucks grew quiet the men nodding off and regressing into deep slumber.

The long convoy snaked through the gates of Camp Lejeune at 0400 hours. The base quiet in the darkness. The battalion came to a halt within its designated area. Companies formed up in formation where officers and noncoms informed them that they were free till 1400 hours that day. The battalion would assemble at that hour for a weapons and gear inspection. The command dismissed sent the grunts scurrying to their quarters and warm cots.

Lieutenant Colonel Striker had ordered his battalion officers and senior noncoms to his office. The small office cramped with bodies, Striker locked eyes with his top soldiers. "Okay you officers and noncoms check with logistics and get the troops resupplied with utilities, skivvies, and boots, whatever. Also set up a time with Doc Little and the medical boys. I want my Marines examined with a fine tooth comb. I rely on you to get it done. Now go get some rest. Inspection at 1400 hours. Then the troops will be rewarded with a ninety six hour pass. I've already cleared and received approval from the Regimental Commander Colonel Von Meer. You men know I insist that the welfare of the battalion be foremost in your minds. You all did a fine job in that forsaken jungle. We've got this battalion in top notch condition. Let's make damn sure it continues. Thank you gentlemen, any questions? No very good, you are hence with dismissed." The top soldiers filed from their commanders presence. Fatigued but proud.

As the battalion officers and senior officers dispersed to their respective quarters. They did so with pride and determination in their heart and souls. Why this fierce pride? It is easily explained. They served in an elite military institution. Renowned worldwide. They served their flag and country swearing to protect fellow Americans. Pride surged through their veins pumping furiously for hearts that swore to uphold a constitution that propelled America to the forefront of the world. They were men who excelled in their profession and while they stood on the wall, vowed nothing would hurt or threaten their native soil. Not on their watch.

The grunts were allowed to sleep in till 10:00 hours when NCO's stormed into their huts screaming, 'Up and at em! Get out of the racks! Shit, shower, and shave time!" Then square away your webb gear and weapons! Chow call at 12:00 and the skipper's inspection at 1400! Get you asses in gear!" The men shaking off cob webs slowly filtered to the head area. Once toilet necessities were complete they threw themselves into scrubbing webb gear. Spread same on the walkway allowing their ally the sun to bleach and dry their equipment. Then they attacked weapons with gun oil, lin seed oil, cotton swabs and oil cloths were used for the task. Chatter echoed in the huts as the troops labored at their task. They knew from experience their Colonel would inspect with microscopic eyes. He was a stickler for perfection. At 1200 hours they formed ranks and to the singsong cadence of Staff Sergeant Laurent marched to chow.

The battalion stood at parade rest. Rifles glinting under the strong sun light. Soon the figures of Colonel Striker along with his Exec and the Battalion Sergeant Major Hoved into view. Company Commanders called their units to attention. The commands resonating up and down the formation. As Striker inspected their units company commanders escorted him. Remaining slightly to his rear. Striker at intervals would address an individual Marine posing questions such as what is interlocking fire. You're a bar man, who's your assistant on and on. The men stood tall, sweat dotting their brows from the hot sun that beamed on them mercilessly. At last Striker marched to the front of his battalion. In a loud crisp voice bellowed, "8th Marines at ease!" Like a clap of thunder the men snapped to parade rest. Striker surveyed his pride and joy eyeing the guidon with its battle streamers. "Company Commanders, take charge. March your men to supply, where they will draw new gear to replenish what was damaged." He smiled, "tomorrow my Marines you will be given thorough exams by Corp's Men. Upon completion you will be granted a ninety six hour liberty. Semper-Fi!" He turned and with his small entourage marched briskly headed to regimental headquarters.

Broken Rose observed his squad rushing to prepare for liberty. Pulling out clean pressed class A's. He smiled inwardly. He knew and was proud his guys were well honed Marines. The hatch flew open and in strode the massive hulk of Gunny Burke. The grunts ceased activity. With eyes on their Gunny who's eyes shone with fire. Well, well, if it isn't my little girl scout troop seems like someone is quite the joker. A prankster incognito or maybe just a fucking asshole. Seems someone embossed a photo of my face onto a picture of a hairy ape holding its dick framed it and hung it on the bulk herd of the first shirts office. Children must play and maybe I'll get you a led box. "Whoa Gunny," uttered LeBron, "why you here hassling us?" Burke, a large bear like man, moved lie a cobra. He was on LeBron like a hawk mantling prey. You Fuck! I know it was you. Get this and get it right! If I find out for certain, I'll make a Hersey bar out of you! Stomp your black ass like a cockroach! Nobody else in the company would have the balls!" The squad stood transfixed stifling laughter. Burke eyeballed them one by one. "You fuckers' best know I'm on to your comic sense of humor. Be advised I'll be watching your putrid asses! Step out of line I'll mash you like the slimy maggots you are!" Looking around the hut he bellowed, "Enjoy your fucking liberty come Monday your asses belong to God again and I'm God! He stormed from the quonset hut the hatch slamming behind him.

The Rose stood and approached LeBron, "Jake why do you enjoy fucking with the Gunny?" Jake laughed softly "come on boss man it keeps the big bastard on his toes." "Yeah well don't let him catch you or you will be chocolate syrup." The grunts quickly dispersed streaming through the hatch each heading off to embrace their liberty. LeSage approached the Rose. "Old shoe what are your plans?" Broken Rose smiled, We'll see. Don't worry about this Indian remember we kicked Custer's ass. What about you? Headed to Fayetteville with LaPore. LeSage smiled sheepishly. "Yeah, met me a girl over there, nice kid, a little older but smart with life's road." "Have a good time, later." LeSage and LaPore strolled out the hatch. LeBron had long left headed to Brooklyn.

Broken Rose appraised the empty quonset hut and strolled to his locker and began donning his greens. Eyeing himself in the full length mirror he was satisfied his gig line and appearance was right on. Grabbing his overnight bag he exited the hut and marched briskly to Able Company's area, where he met up with Charlie White Cloud, an Indian from another company. They were brothers in the creed of the Great Spirit. Together they bordered a greyhound bus. Destination the Reservation of Red Hill Valley. The bus rumbled on its tires performing a musical chorus that lulled passengers to sleep. The Rose and White Cloud chattered quietly almost a whisper. Their objective lay fifty miles south of Lejeune, an hour's ride. Both looked forward to sharing time with the Great One's people.

The blue and white gray hound carrier dropped them at the mouth of a dirt road. A posted sign announcing Red Hill Valley Reservation, one mile a yellow arrow pointed down the dusty road. The bus roared away emitting a cloud of diesel black smoke. The two Marines hefted their overnight bags and walked casually down the dirt road. Their footsteps emitting small puffs of dust which covered their once highly spit shined shoes. They passed several Native Americans who gazed curiously at their uniforms not a word was exchanged. Suddenly the modest center of the reservation loomed before them. There was an antiquated general store and what appeared to be a small market. Fruits and vegetables piled in neat rows on a slanted table. A mangy dog announced their arrival. Yip yipping away. The sun was at its zenith high in the sky. Both glanced at their watches surprised that the noon hour was already upon them. White Cloud spoke softly. "We turn left here. This will bring us to the lodge of Chief Large Bear. He is old school and believes the Great One breathes life in to all living things. He leads his tribe with honor and courage. He has the respect of all. You'll like him. Broken Rose nodded waving to a young boy and girl who sat in front of their mud house eyeing them with sullen and suspicion. Yes, uniforms were rare and when seen raised fear and concern among the inhabitants. After a short walk they approached and stood before a modest lodge. Built of Pine with a clapboard roof. White Cloud whispered, "we are here, this is home to Large Bear."

A tall well-built man in his forties appeared at the door. "Charlie White Cloud it is good to see you once more. Come, the old one sits in his rocker. It will please him you have come. The three men entered a semi-dark interior, which appeared to be the living room. It took a few moments for the visitor's eyes to adjust but as vision heightened they found they stood face to face with the old Chief. His face was worn and chiseled from years under a hot sun. His eyes black that burned like coal embers. He had a sharp prominent nose and his eyes watered due to old age. He suffered from tremors, but sat erect and proud. "Charlie White Cloud, how good of you to come. Who is that who walks tall by your side?" "Ancient one, I am John Broken Rose. A son of the Great Spirit who's land is as far as the crow flies. I am honored to stand in your presence in the lodge of your ancestor." "Ah, muttered the old chief. Then sit and squat my young warriors. He stomped his foot on the floor which creaked from the assault. A young maiden flowed through the worn curtain that separated the two rooms. Broken Rose stared in awe. She wore a white buckskin dress which hung just below the knees. Her legs bronzed her calves muscular and strong. Her jet black hair hung in two braids down to her shoulders. She had thin surreal lips and her smile displayed even ivory teeth. She was burdened with two large bowls which she placed on a braided floor mat. The contents had fruit, berries and a sweet smelling corn bread. She quickly exited the room but returned almost at once carrying a water pitcher and a larger container which hosted chunks of a white meat floating in a thick syrupy sauce. "It's rabbit," spoke the Old Chief. "Eat; drink, then we will smoke the pipe of peace and friendship."

They ate in silence only the rustle of the curtain as the maiden returned to see to their needs. As he ordered the young girl to wait, He smiled, "This is my granddaughter Little Bird. This is Charlie White Cloud and John Broken Rose. They follow the ways of the ancients. They are warriors who serve their white chief in Washington. She bowed her voice soft and tantalizing. It is good to meet brave warriors. Welcome to our lodge. She flitted away brushing the curtain aside, as she exited again into the rear room. The men smoked and talked their voices low and respectful. The old chief relished telling them stories of his youth and listened attentively to their revelations of a world with iron horses and large birds that carried men in the sky, of ships the size of small cities that could carry off his entire tribe, and of concrete roads that traversed what was once virgin woodlands.

He marveled at their tales from time to time. Little Bird and Broken Rose's eyes locked. He'd caught her several times staring at him. A lump formed in his throat. He could feel his heart thumping and felt the pulse pounding in his veins. Her beauty mesmerized him. Never had he looked at a woman with such emotion.

The hours ticked away and White Cloud had long departed gone to his sisters. The Rose sat alone with the old one. The old chief was not immune to the exchanged looks between his granddaughter and his guest. He laughed inwardly at the discomfort the young warrior squatting before him must be feeling. Finally the Rose stood. "Wise chief, I wish to talk." "Speak young one." "I ask permission to walk with your granddaughter before the sun hides behind the clouds." "Ah, so that is why you've been itching. Well, my young warrior, if she agree, you have my blessing. But alas remember the Indian creed of honor and respect. He gazed at his granddaughter. "Are you agreed" "Oh yes, grandfather." "Then my young spirits go. Flow into the forest, sing with the birds, and walk with the Great One's creatures. Breath the fresh clean air. Listen to the wind. The voices of our ancestors can sometimes be heard. Finished he raised a trembling hand. "Go my children. The old one will rest now. You, Broken Rose, will spend your time here with us. We have an extra room in the back. The floor mat is dry and the hides of brave animals will provide warmth. When you sleep, pray for them and thank them." The old man sighed bowed his head in tranquil sleep.

Broken Rose and Little Bird took exit of the old chief. Walking slowly they left the lodge quietly and began their trek together. Their footsteps leading to a dirt trail that traversed into a wondrous woodlands. They marveled at nature in its natural origin and the chorus of the birds in their musical chants or chasing each other though the woodlands. Here and there humming birds fritted through and flow invading flowers for their sweet nectar. Rabbits scurried all about seeking cover from their human invaders. Squirrels ran helter skelter following natural instincts for food and survival. They approached a stream and its clear waters host to frogs who crocked to mates hoping to secure companionship. The babbling waters coursing through the forest. Here and there a fish would leap into the twilight then plunge into the security of his watery kingdom. Beavers, natures engineers, criss crossing the waterways building dams and homes for their young. Life abounded in the forest. The innocence of the creatures doing what nature intended As well as the screech of owls as a warning to sisters and brothers that man had infiltrated their sacred refuge.

Broken Rose marveled at natures creations. They walked slowly, delicately. The Rose had never socialized with a woman. Little Bird had been denied the companionship of a male for she was busy monitoring her grandfather for many moons. Their hearts pounded. Both experiencing emotions thus denied them. Butterflies churned through their stomachs as only the young experience. The sun settled in the sky and soon the forest insects raised a crescendo that orchestrate through the forest. It was time to reverse steps and head back to the lodge. They had shared few words content to be together. As night settled the lodge came into view. They locked eyes, under a glowing moon; they entered their humble dwelling each heading to their private quarters. But the darkness could not dampen their pounding hearts. Both knew and felt in their spirits that the vapor of life had breathed into their very souls.

The twill of birds rose him from his slumber. He strolled into the modest kitchen where the old chief and Little Bird already seated at the rough hew pine table sharing tea and kibitzing about world affairs. The reservation had for moons been immune to the cancerous words of the world, but modern technology had managed to reach into their peaceful existence with unmolested tentacles. The Rose approached quietly. "Good morning Old Chief, Little Bird." Both smiled and Little Bird pointed to a chair. She had already stationed a plate and cup. She poured him herbal tea and placed a plate of eggs as he sat. Their eyes locked for a moment. Little Bird's eyes twinkled and smiled, that pierced his heart. For the most part they breakfasted in quiet. The Old Chief occasionally questioning him as to his background, both as a child and now to his chosen profession in the warrior's way. Little Bird cleared the table. The Old Chief grunting as both the Rose and Little Bird sought his permission to once more walk in the forest. His smile was his approval and as the young warrior and his maiden granddaughter departed. He raised his hands in supplication. "Great One let your blessings and wisdom fills those two souls. It is my hope you breath into them the way of the ancients and bless the world with pure newborn spirits."

They spent the remaining days exploring the wonders of the green lush forest and walking the reservation chatting with its inhabitants. All knew who he a warrior and shared stories and tea. Both were welcomed and shown respect in the lodges of those honest simple people. The Rose reveling in reliving this pure simple way of life, but time has a way of never wavering and soon his last night was upon them. In their beloved forest sitting by the gurgling stream, they embraced. His lips sought hers. Tenderly and then hungrily, but he knew he must honor his pledge to the Old Chief to honor and respect the spirit of his granddaughter. His heart felt heavy. He'd never known the sweetness of a woman's lips and the comforting scent of her body as well as the warm softness and tenderness of her voice and hands that caressed him. An old owl screeched somewhere in the distance and both knew it was time to abandoned their private refuge. They strolled hand and hand returning deliberately to the humble lodge. As they stood staring at the door, both turned and gazed into each other's eyes. The Rose spoke, "Little Bird, I love you. One day I will share my lodge with you if you'll have me." Little Bird smiled, "yes my love, I will wait. I will be unmolested here my heart and spirit will be yours as one." The Rose kissed her and turned walking into an unknown destiny. For the first time since his loss of Two Wolves

Tears coursed down his cheeks. He'd found his mate, but was torn as to what fate had planned. Little Bird, hand to her head, watched as her warrior departed. She gazed at the now star lit sky. "Eiyah, Eiyah," she wailed, "Oh, Great One wrap your strong arms about him. Let your breath caress him and keep him safe so that his spirit returns to me." She was startled by the mournful wail of a morning dove calling to her mate. Yet she sat alone listening for her mates responding call. Little Bird stood quiet, while her heart pounded and her eyes full of tears. Then the rustle in the treetop as the doves reunited, cooing and pecking one another. "Ah, uttered Little Bird, "A good omen, my warrior shall return to me."

Broken Rose was quiet and the squad noticing that he was even more subdued than usual. Yes he performed his duties assuring his squad was up to snuff but during down times he sat alone often heading off for distant jogs. The men watching as his silhouette disappeared into the forest. It was raining the tattoo of the water creating a drum like beat on the tin quonset hut roof. LeSage ambled over to the Rose. "Hey, old buddy feel up to company?" The Rose stared at his friend, "yeah white eyes, pull up a seat, looks like my foot locker is beckoning." "What's up there Corporal? You've been real quiet almost snobby, unlike you." The Rose blushed, and then smiled, "Lee, I met someone, I mean it's real. All new to me and I don't know how to handle it." LeSage laughed softly, "Hey, old shoe good for you, look just ride the tide. Follow your heart; your instincts are second to none. Look John it's good for your soul to keep you on your toes. Look old boy, The Great Spirit breathes a fire in your heart and that's what it's all about. Run with it, but remembers this squad, this battalion needs your expertise. You're in love fantastic, but don't let that sensation cloud your warrior's mind. We need you and my gut tells me even more down the road. Broken Rose stared at his friend, broke into a smile, your right Lee." "Hey John you've got someone to hold onto, someone to return too. Embrace it, protect it, by staying sharp, adapt and overcome." "Thanks Lee Semper-Fi." "Yeah bro, Semper-Fi."

The battalion settled in after their ninety six. But Striker refused to ease off intensifying their training pushing them to their limits and beyond. They hooked up with armor, learning that an infantry man's role in defending these large mobile fortresses was imperative. Their task to eliminate enemy forces that could take out a steel monster at close range. Tank and foot soldier mirrored each other in defense and offense. They trained in close air support with corsairs flying at tree top level. Marines exchanging places as FTO's digesting the lingo and procedures years of practice has perfected. Each man learned the basic of the field radio mechanisms. As well as how to run wire and they were drilled endlessly in map reading and mastering the art of calling coordinates. Striker was adamant that his battalion be diversified. Driving his Company Commanders relentlessly but always stood tall in the lead for that was Striker's way.

He constantly had his field artillery buddy fire salvos over their advancing columns, insisting they experience outgoing, telling his Company Commanders, "they'll sure as shit learn the difference of incoming if we ever hit the shit." He insists his men practice high standards of personal hygiene that weapons and gear were kept in high readiness. He demanded pride and discipline knowing full well these were the ingredients that would not waver in the face of adversity. He had steeled their bodies and his goal to steel their minds and to mold them into a cohesive unit that would not falter. He knew the Hell of combat and spent fitful nights planning analyzing his strategies preparing them for the worst Hell could offer.

Gunny Burke approached the Rose. "Corporal!" "Yes Gunny." "Get your ass in gear!! Report to the battalion Commander's office forthwith the old man called ordered your Indian ass to meet with him post haste!" "Okay Gunny." "Your still here! God Damn it, Tonto!

Double time your ass out of here, should have already been there!"
The Rose laughed softly and flew out the hatch.

The Rose stood at ram rod attention. "Sir, Corporal Rose reporting
as ordered." Striker pushed back from his desk, stared at the young
Marine who stood lean and mean before him. "At ease, Corporal
Rose. I'll get right to the point. I want you to select several good
men. I want them to be extra eyes should the need arise." "You mean
scouts sir?" "Exactly, I know we have Recon Marines, but I want a
small unit that moves swift and stealthy. One that can mesh with the
landscape and I am aware of your expertise in this area. I leave the
selection process to you. No one will interfere, is that understood?
They will be acceptable to you." "Yes sir, White Cloud, from Able
Company and Johnny Two Toes from Charlie Company. Striker
gazed out his window overlooking the expansive parade ground.
"Both Indians thought so. I know the answer but I'll still ask why?
"Sir, in the forest, in heat, a white man's sweat will omit odors
of tobacco, spirits, spices; a good warrior would pounce on this
weakness." Striker half turned facing his newly appointed head scout,
"Yup heard that analogy before, as I said, your call Sergeant Rose."
The Rose stiffened, "Sir" "You heard me; you've just made Buck
Sergeant. Now get out of here and bump heads with your two Indians.
I'll clear it with their Company Commanders. The now Sergeant Rose
came to full attention. "Yes sir. Thank you, sir." About faced and
marched tall and proud through the hatch.

Striker fired up a Lucky exhaling a bluish plume of smoke towards
the ceiling, smiled inwardly. He felt satisfied and content in his mind's
eye. He'd just completed an end run comfortable in the thought his
battalion would have the eyes of eagles guiding them wherever and
whenever their march brought them. Lt. Colonel Striker and Don
Josephs sat before their Regimental Commander Colonel Von Meer.
They'd been summoned to regimental command at 0600 hours. Von
Meer sat erect flanked by old glory and the Marine Corps colors.

271

"Gentlemen, I won't dance around here." He stood and advanced to a large map of the world tacked to the north bulkhead. Picking up a pointer, he pointed to a location marked Middle East. There's a hot spot brewing here, a pot that's about to boil over. Using the stick He directed same to a country marked Lebanon. The capital is Beirut and rebels are raising hell and causing havoc. Washington has ordered that a regiment of Marines is to be dispatched and deployed to assist that government in its struggle. They have requested military aid from our government. You will assemble your battalions and be ready to roll out of here by 9000 hours this evening. You will travel by convoy trucking to Norfolk. Where you will embark on transports which are ready and waiting. You will sail forthwith. At sea your transports along with your escorts will meet up with the fourth and fifth Marines. The sixth fleet is in transit as we speak moving to support an amphibious landing. You haven't much time. So I won't weigh you down with rah rah, bullshit. Whether there's a fight or bloodshed only our landing will reveal an answer. I wish you both good luck and God speed. I know your troops are ready and capable. That's it gentlemen. Dismissed and again farewell, Semper-Fi." Both stood and came to attention. "Yes sir, thank you sir." About faced and sprinted to their commands. There was a ton to do and little time for small talk.

Striker headed to his office flew through the hatch and ordered his clerk to notify all Company Commanders to assemble in his office forthwith. Picking up his phone he called his Exec Major Pezzone, who was sitting sharing a coffee with his wife Joyce. She grabbed the land line, "oh, good morning Colonel, yes sir, he's right here." She handed the phone to her husband. "It's Colonel Striker." Pezzone took the phone smiling at his wife. "Morning Colonel, what's up?" "Frank, get your little boy's butt over here. Kiss your wife for you and me. Give her a big hug. We're being deployed. I'll fill you in when you get here. Don't dawdle, Frank, there isn't much time. Tell Joyce I'm sorry, but this is the Corps. Now we earn our pay." Pezzone frowned, "yes sir, on the way." He hung up and gazed at his wife whose eyes had clouded with worry. "Honey got to go, won't be home for a while. We're being deployed. Don't know where and you know the drill. I can't tell you anyway. Dumping his cup in the sink, man and wife embraced. This was the way of the warrior. Their world one minute peace and tranquility and then without warning the warrior must go to defend his country. Hearts would be separated. Tears will be shed. The faithful wife left to fend for herself and spend days in dread and loneliness. She'd known that when she'd married him as a young handsome First Lieutenant. Now she would live life in fear and loneliness until once more he came through the door. But that door was revolving and it would happen again and again. He was a Marine. A warrior and this was his calling. They embraced tightly and like a small loving bird, he disengaged and was gone. The door closed softly behind him. She pondered in her mind, "where was harm's way leading him." She uttered softy, "as tears coursed down her cheeks. "Farewell my Major, I love you, Frank. Oh God take care of him." She fled to the bedroom clutching a photo of them young and virile and happy. Her sobs shook the bed as she fell into a heart breaking sleep.

Striker addressed his Company Commanders informing them of their pending deployment. They were dismissed quickly and currently time was of the essence. The command was in disciplined chaos. Logistics is the major headache, ammunition and medical supplies and a thousand other matters. Drove officers and noncoms into a beehive frenzy. The grunts busy preparing weapons and gear. Ordered that silence was the golden rule and none of the troops were allowed to leave their quarters. Senior noncoms assuring that no leaks made to the world at the motor pool. Trucks were being gassed and oiled. Supplies loaded on to deuce and a half's. Doc Little and his entourage of Corpsmen drawing ample medical supplies. Company Commanders guiding their Senior NCO's who rode herd on Junior NCO'S. So it went. The 8th Marines were on the move.

Striker watched as logistics and men meshed and smiled his intensive training already paying dividends. Within four hours the battalion was ready. The 8th Marines drilled and trained prepared to sail into harm's way.

At 2000 hours under a light drizzle the convoy roared through the Gates of Lejeune into the chilly night. MP's held traffic stationary as the long envoy stretched onto the highway. Headlights glowing from the military vehicles lit up the night. The convoy stretched for miles carrying over two thousand men and supporting heavy weapons. Tanks secured to flat beds and supply trucks heading up the rear. Motorists formed to wait patiently as traffic snarled to a halt. No way could the convoy allow interruption. The 8th Marines had been summoned and answered the call with quick precision. State Police halted traffic at intersections. Exits and motorist gaped in awe as the seemingly endless convoy whizzed by.

As the miles clicked by Marines chattered all wondering where they were bound. No scuttle butt had reached their ears. Rumors were plentiful. The troops speculating. It was Taiwan, maybe the Philippines, maybe even Korea. Finally NCO's quieted the troops and admonishing them with phrases such as you'll get the word when the skipper feels the time is right. For now stand down and rest easy. Take advantage where ever the hell we're going it won't be a cake walk. The sound of the powerful engines and hum of tires on the concrete highway soon lulled the grunts into fit less sleep. Sitting on hard wooden benches was no comfort zone. Rain pelted the canvass roof tops and for the time of year a chill in the air kneaded their bones. Body heat their only source of warmth as the deuce and a half's lay open in the rear. Drivers shifted into gear as they occasionally climbed rolling hills. Here and there lights could be seen in nearby homes, other than that, little could be seen through the tarp of darkness. Men shifted trying to find comfort. Butts ached from the wooden benches. Legs cramped. There was no respite. There would be no halts in the military. Time is of the essence and there was a time table that had to be met. Town's people in small villages heard and felt the rumble as the mammoth convoy roared past their habitats. While America slept Marines were enroute to an unknown fate and destiny. Where they know not but history one day would point the way.

Through the long night the convoy snaked its way through the countryside. It had grown late and civilian traffic had long faded. Now and then a rig would pass headed in the opposite direction. Some drivers, hitting their air horns, throwing half salutes to the convoy. Men drank from canteen cups and if one had to piss he did so in an old c-ration can, which was passed to the rear and Marines who poured its contents over the rear tailgate. God help the poor jar-head who needed to shit. The gags and cat calls and disgust of his buddies would resound up and down the line. There were no head breaks. You relieved nature where you sat. Gears whined, engines coughed, fumes filled the night air, so much so that in low lands a vaporous like fog like a thin cake frosting enveloped the convoy. Cigarette smoke emitted clouds of a blue like haze filtering out the open bays. Soon large highway signs beckoned announcing Norfolk, VA. Five miles. The men gazed at the signs. Yeah, they whispered, Norfolk Naval Yard. Debarkation station.

The sun was just coming up with its face over the horizon greeting and blessing earth with her warm rays. That like tentacles found their way warming and lighting the world. The convoy haled. An eerie silence descended as engines were cut. But not for long. The authoritative voice of NCO's and Officers whipping their squads, platoons, companies into formation. Navy Stevedores descended on the convoy like a horde of locusts. Heavy equipment skidded to and fro. The troops marched and in single file climbed ramps into the two waiting transports and watched with interest as tanks and heavy artillery was hoisted and disappeared into the bowels of huge LST's. The Navy Yard was a beehive of activity and sailors gaped at the combat laden Marines as they disappeared into the holds of their transports. The men shuffled along lines of racks. There was no democracy here. One placed his gear where he stood and that was home for the next ten days. LeBron elbowed LeSage. "Fuck Lee, we're gonna be as tight in here as a virgin's pussy. God damn somebody farts we're all wasted." A passing sailor chortled, "Hey gyrenes pray we don't hit a storm or your ass will really be grass. "LeBron stared at the sailor, "Hey squid, how's the chow on this tub?" The sailor smiled, "Oh great, you'll be issued menus and you'll have several different choices every day." "No shit," "Hell no, we want you Marines to have all the comforts." He laughed quietly as he shuffled away. "Damn that's A-Okay," exclaimed LeBron. Gunny Burke standing by the hatch had overheard, "hey, LeBron!" He yelled, "yeah Gunny." "You fucking moron, you're an asshole. What the fuck you think this is the Queen Mary. Menus, he's fucking with you. That squid whipped the game on you, idiot." Burke in disgust turned and exited through the hatch seeking his Senior NCO's berth.

Striker met with his Company Commanders inquiring as to the welfare of his command and if the troops had settled in. He scanned their faces. Look, very soon we'll be deploying on the beaches of a country in turmoil. Well this is what we've trained long and had for. Now very possibly we'll be in a fire storm. It's imperative you keep the troops sharp and maintain discipline and I want them on deck if weather permits. Conduct inspections and physical exercise each and every day. Make sure your Noncoms keep on personal hygiene. I don't want this battalion just lolling below going soft. Make sure the Doc's keep a wary eye on the men's physical and mental health. Make damn certain discipline is maintained below deck in those holds. I won't tolerate any fool hardy incidents in those hellish confines. I hold you personally accountable. Your officers, Company commanders, you know how I stand and where I'm coming from. Now get it done. Look after your troops as a mother does her young, any questions, suggestions, bitches?" He looked around. "No Okay, go to it, dismissed!"

The troops driven by NCOs got busy setting in stashing gear. Attempts at neatness futile as quarters were cramped and crowded and the air heavy with the smell of oil and perspiring bodies. The ship a beehive of activity as sailors set about preparing their ship for sea. The sound of wenches hoisting equipment and supplies resonating throughout the navel yard while the grunts lay on their bunks or sat where ever there was space chattering about their destination and role they may play. Most nervous for they knew they were quartered in the bowels of this iron vessel located beneath the water line. Whoa, to the individual who suffered from claustrophobia for this was not the place to be for that phobia. NCO's neither would sit idle nor would they allow the troops to grow soft. They were always pushing them to check gear and weapons and even holding mini inspections. They would remind heir troops that this was no luxury liner and they were not on a Caribbean cruise. Most Senior Noncoms had experienced the tightness and foreboding existence on troop transports and kept the grunts busy doing their best to discourage one's head to fill with needless worry that could fray even the toughest nerves to the limit. The ship suddenly erupted into life. The whine and humming of the ships engines clamoring through the soul of the ship as the deck vibrated as the steel transport slowly ebbed from the dock picking up speed as it headed to open sea. The two transports were soon joined with three destroyers as well as a light and heavy cruiser. Water lapped at the gunwales and the ships plunged onward their wakes trailing in the early morning mist.

The small convoy now in open sea plunged ever forward. Now and then a rain squall would engulf them and as quick as it struck was gone. The ocean remained calm and on the second day, Striker ordered the battalion top side, where calisthenics and drills were held. Striker had told his Company Commander's to keep their troops loose and in condition. He was ruthless in that. He refused to allow his battalion to lose its edge. As the days flew in the open ocean, the grunts would be marched up the ladders for their daily ritual of exercise. There was no reprieve. Striker adamant that mental and physical condition be maintained to his satisfaction. His reason was sensible and it was twofold to allow the troops freedom for the tight confines of the holds and to bask in sun shine and fresh clean air. He knew what doldrums troops would experience in such condition only a troop transport afforded. Chow was okay, but no five star rating. Powdered eggs, potatoes, beans, sometimes a semblance of meat tossed on their trays. Coffee tasted like burnt toast and at intervals salt water showers allowed. One week at sea and as the troops stood in tight formation on the ship's deck, Striker gave his command the scuttle butt. "We the 8th Marines will be hooking up with the 4th, 5th, and 6th Marines very shortly. We will effect an amphibious landing on the beaches of Lebanon. Rebel factors are attempting to overthrow that government. What carnage occurs we'll know soon enough. Keep your equipment ready and your minds sharp. Dismissed"

The convoy plunged ever forward through the Atlantic at times clashing with several sea squalls. The Marines strapped to their bunks and locked in the hold beneath the sea line. They suffered untold agonies such as vomiting, the shits, and the dreaded sea sickness. The stench in the hold became unbearable, only those who experienced the discomfort of a troop transport would understand. The ship's sailed onward and the waves of the Atlantic lapping at their gunwales. Striker ever mind full of his troops duress. Constantly ingesting them exercise, discipline, onward they sailed. The ship's crew was doing their utmost to allow fresh air into the holds by keeping the hatches open when weather allowed. The convoy plowed ever forward through the Atlantic, at times clashing with several sea squalls. The Marines strapped to their bunks locked in the hold beneath the sea line suffered untold agonies. The troops continued vomiting and had the shits due to sea sickness and the stench in the hold unbearable.

As the convoy sailed forth in the early morning darkness it smiled and passed through the Straits of Gibraltar then entered the Adriatic Sea. It continued its endless journey. Soon entering the beautiful Mediterranean Sea, where on an early morning dawn, hooked up with its sister transport and its escorts. The second regiment of the 2nd Marine Division was now united. Four thousand combat ready Marines were now ready to follow their countries orders. The sea remained calm. The sun shone bright. America was peaceful and serene, but her warriors were headed in harm's way and while the nation slept, Marines were preparing to embark amphibiously unto amid east shore. In the holds, Marines sweated and the stench now unbearable. Hatches were opened but it would take muscle and gallons of disinfectant to erase the intolerable odor. This would be addressed only after the troops debarked. The troops lay in their racks, each with their own thoughts. Some prayed silently others chatted with buds; it was their way of camouflaging nervousness. Most were attired in just skivvies as the holds were like ovens. An individual sought what little comfort he could. A cool filter of air brought sighs of relief. The grunts antsy like a wild heard of cattle. They were ready to stampede. Climb the ladder and bolt once more into the world of sun and fresh air.

A hush fell on the holds. The ships had stopped and their engines winding down to a soft wine. Winches threw noise cascading over the water flew into action. Anchor chains rattled and crashed as the large ships anchored and came to rest. The light of a new dawn revealed the ships in battle array and the glow of the sun bouncing and glinting off the sleek gunwales. NCO's roamed the holds. Marines now in full battle gear stood waiting. Sweat forming in armpits with rivulets of perspiration coursing down young but determined faces. In the semi-darkness, an authoritative voice blared from the loud speakers. "Marines!! Man your debarkation stations!" Admonished by Noncoms, the grunts scrambled up the ladders. Lining up on transport decks. Here they were issued live ammo. The order lock and load resonated across the blue tranquil sea. Nets dropped over the sides. Landing craft bobbed up and down in the blue waters awaiting their cargo of warriors. Marine's clambered down the nets dropping into their amphibian carriers. Hearts pounding. Eyes flushed with excitement. Adrenalin coursing through youthful disciplined bodies. Yes, there was also the smell of fear. Fear of the unknown. But these were green warriors and the instincts of their training would kick in.

As the sun's rays burned through the tarp of darkness. Four thousand combat ready Marines hunched down in their landing craft which swept toward the white sandy beaches of Lebanon. Their goal to relieve and secure Beirut and to dispense rebels. Cutting the noose, they were attempting to wrap on the head of the legal authoritative government.

Gunny Burke stood to the front of his landing craft determined to be the first to step foot on white sands of Lebanon. He yelled over the roar of landing craft's engines. "Look to your rear girls, see what's backing us up. The men turned a loud gasp emitted from the packed troops. They stared in awe at a mighty powerful spectacle. The sixth fleet had come up in the night. It was a powerful sight. The battleship New Jersey was huge and threatening. The sound of her turrets turning pointing her large guns in land resonated across the water. Corsair fighters suddenly came in low and menacingly. The carrier Independence expelling fighters and observation aircraft. America had puffed up her chest. Those on shore waiting whatever their intent assured by such a show off force that this was no bluff. Colonel Von Meer elected to remain on the command ship in order to coordinate his battalion's movements. He'd already designated Striker's 8th Marines to take the lead. The regiment's battalion fanned out on the sandy beaches setting up perimeters. Striker's battalion hove to setting up recon patrols entering the capital city of Beirut and it's out skirts. Flushing out rebel infractions who it appeared had fled the area once observing the powerful force of the 6th fleet and the awesome landings of the Marines ready to dispel them whatever the cost. Patrols in combat force walked the streets. There was sporadic fire. Several Marines wounded but the combat landings as such was a marvel in success. Yes, there were injuries, broken ankles here and there, the result of climbing down ships nets. Abrasions due to various obstacles upon landing. All and all the landings were a text book success. The rebels had fled into the mountains and rural areas electing not to engage the massive landings and avoid a combat confrontation with such a show of force and discipline. The Marines setup perimeter defenses dispatched patrols in strength throughout the area. Resident's happy and content to embrace them. It was a successful exercise. Rebels had dispensed and the Marines had excelled and would affect security to the area.

Colonel Von Meer, the Regimental Commander, remained aboard the flag ship coordinating his battalion's as they deployed on the beaches. His objective to secure and drive the rebels from the heart of Beirut. He monitored the incoming radio messages sensing that the deployment had accomplished its objective. Rebel fractions observing the powerful force of the 6th fleet and the intimidating ground landings of Marines in combat array had driven them from the streets and byways of Beirut into the mountains and rural areas and outskirts. They simply vanished electing not to confront the landings of highly charged combat ready Marines. The Marine ground forces setup their perimeters digging in, prepared for the worst scenario. Officers and noncoms pushing their troops to the peak of readiness ever alert to the threat of counter attacks. As darkness descended on the area. An eerie quiet carpeted the beaches of Lebanon. There had been sporadic rifle fire. Several Marines fell wounded. The mission was accomplished with minimal casualties.

As the sun peeked over the horizon, Von Meer ordered Colonel Striker's 8th Marines to spearhead the incursion into Beirut. Recon Marines reconnoitered the city simultaneously to assist the march into the city following Marine protocol properly. Patrols fanned out in all directions as the Marines probing seeking an enemy which seemed to have simply disappeared. The troops spread out in the city proper encountering zero resistance. The American colors and that of the Marines were hoisted high in the sky in order for the eyes of the sixth fleet to observe. The Navy and Marines had effected a successful operation. The rebels had dispersed into the winter lands awestruck by the display of power and fortitude of American intervention.

The Marines like worker ants went about their duties with military precision establishing a strong perimeter. Colonel Von Meer came ashore and met with his battalion commanders and directed Striker's 8th Marines to take the point on entering the city proper as well as the outskirts. Platoon size patrols led the way eyes ever attentive to suspicious individuals or groups cautiously advancing ever mindful of booby traps or the perils of ambushes. Darting house to house hoping to flush out potential adversaries, two full battalions now snaked their way through the heart of the city. Two others patrolled and secured the outskirts. There was little resistance. Residents of the city stared in awe at these young American Warriors clapping and joyous at being rescued and free from rebel factions. Von Meer and other ranking officers along with State Department Officials met with local and governmental leaders establishing guide lines as to interaction by Marines with the local populace. A non-fraternization order restricted the Marines from interacting with residents. Officers and Noncoms quick to jump and enforce laid out orders. Thus limiting and controlling movements of the Marines with the native populace as to limit confrontation.

As days turned into weeks, calm enveloped the city. Residents went about their business of daily living. The Marines continued to patrol checking points established. A curfew had been in effect since day one when not on duty. The Marines remained within the confines of their perimeter. Most of the grunts board with little or no source of entertainment. NCO's kept them busy with rifle and equipment inspections, close order drill, and exercise for Von Meer was adamant that his Marines would not become lax or soft. Discipline within the racks was strictly enforced. These were tough times. No liberty and a foreign culture neither side understanding the other.

LeBron approached his three buds. "Fuck, this country is fucked up. I walked by that big ugly camel over there and the son of a bitch spit a honker at me the size of a grapefruit. Fucking thing was all slimy and stunk like an old unwashed pussy." LaPore stared at LeBron, "Poor fucking creature probably thought you were stalking him. Thought maybe you wanted to fuck." "Aw, fuck you LaPore! You know you guys are just wrong, always putting ol Jake down. Shit, I just wanted to look at him." "Why piped up LeSage, it doesn't have tits." "Aw fuck, that's it I'm outta here." He turned and stalked off leaving the Rose, LeSage and LaPore quivering with laughter.

LaPore and LeSage approached Mossad-Amman who stood 6'3 and in skivvies weighed in at 240 lbs. a wall of muscle. "Hey Mo, can we talk with you?" Busy cleaning his 30 Cal machine gun, he looked up at the pair, "Yeah, feather merchants, what's up?" "Well listen we want to fuck with LeBron. Will you go along and you know back us up?" "What's the plan?" They sat next to him and laid out their trap. PFC Amman laughed heartily. You go guys sure but on one condition." "Yeah Mo" "I get to scare the shit out of that Hershey Bar." "Hey right on Mo, even better."

The two conspirators sought and found LeBron sitting on a rock starring at Arab women. "Hey Jake what's up?" "Aw, fuck these broads, got their faces covered. They wear all those robes and shit. Can't tell if their ugly, got tits, or even an ass. This place sucks. Smells of camel shit. It's Hot! I hate it!" "Yeah ain't to good here, you know Jake piped up LeSage, these Arab women. They're different from white or black girls." "Yeah how so, questioned LeBron. "Well our women their pussies are straight up and down. "Yeah, Yeah, I know that." "Well Arab women pussy's are on a slant." "Say What? Fuck you, you're full of shit." "No, No Jake. Go ask Amman, he's an Arab, wife's Arab, if you don't believe us. Go ask Mo." Fucking right, I will. Shit that means a guy gotta fuck em on an angle. That's fucked up." "Hey Jake, there's Amman, Go ask him. Shit you think we're bullshiting. There he is, ask em." "Fucking A I will," LeBron ran over to Amman. "Hey Mo, you mind I ask you something personal." Amman stared down at LeBron. "Yeah okay, what's on your mind?" "Well, ah, ah, I heard Arab women. Uh, Uh, their thing you know, oh shit; well I heard their pussy's are on an angle. Shit man, if that's true how you fuck em?"

Amman took one step forward and snorting like an enraged bull, he pulled LeBron in close. "Why you little prick, what the fuck kind of question is that? You think we're defective people. Huh?! Probably think we stink too. I'll crush you like a bug. I'll maul and slam out your black ass. No, No, Mo, I meant no offense shit man. You're all wrong. I'd heard that scuttle butt. Only thought you could confirm its authenticity." "You maggot fuck! Now you're gonna use five dollar words with me. Get the fuck away from me. Grabbing his bayonet, he displayed a heinous smile. LeBron broke free and ran pell mell back to LaPore and LeSage. "Jake, what happened?" "Man that mother fucker be crazy. Thought he was gonna cut my throat." "What'd he tell you?" "Nothing never answered and threatened me with bodily harm. He crazy and they issue him a machine gun. I'm telling you the devil is all around us. He's everywhere. He's as crazy as Gunny Burke." LaPore and LeSage burst out laughing. LeBron flopped on his back and white sand spilling over his utilities. "You mother's, I've been had. Damn Mother fuckers! It ain't easy being me."

With little to do the men turned to playing soft ball on the soft white sand. The participants heckled and criticized by their Marine audience. Von Meer kept in constant contact with his commanders. On one occasion a regimental formation and inspection held minus one battalion deployed within the city limits. LaPore and the Rose walked by the beach talking quietly about life and their future. "Hey John, look at that." They'd come upon a washed up dead sand shark. Maybe six feet in length. Seaweed and flies enveloped its carcass. "John, you thinking what I am?" "Yeah, LeBron's asleep out like a dead dick. Both grinned yeah let's do it." They picked up the dead fish. Foul orders emitted from the slimy body. Carefully and quietly they carried it to the objective tent. It was evening and night was laying its tarp over the Marine's tent city. Using stealth and senses, they opened the tent flap quietly. LeBron lay on his back snoring loudly. For the moment at peace with the world. Gingerly they placed the soft squishy carcass on LeBron's chest. Then silently backed out through the tent flap closing same gently. LeBron stirred. His nostrils inhaling a sickening odor. He felt something wet and mushy on his face. His arms were wrapped in an embrace with something soft and slimy. He sat up right flicked on his flashlight. His eyes wide and white. He began to quiver and tremble he emitted a loud piercing scream that echoed in the night and thundered through the perimeter. He leaped from his cot. But the decaying carcass had adhered to his utilities. He flailed and jumped around ripping and tearing at this abomination. He couldn't dislodge the thing. Its wet slimy tongue kept lapping at his face. He ran from his tent. Marines had gathered outside curious as to what was occurring. Flashlights lit up LeBron's figure. Marines gaped in astonishment and then the night erupted in hysterical laughter. It looked as though LeBron was dancing with a lover who possessed a tail. "Hey LeBron did you get laid? Maybe some head? "Aw fuck you mothers. Get this fucker off of me! It stinks I'm getting sick!" The Marines still laughing filtered away. "Naw, no way Jake. We don't want to ruin your chances of getting laid." LeBron finally flung the ugly decaying fish at his departing brothers. "Fuck you mother's ol Jake one day gonna get even." His only response was the muted laughter of brothers returning to their own humble quarters.

As the Marines dispersed in the darkness a voice cried out "Hey Jake that's one ugly mermaid your fucken get her some make up." Jake lay in the sand. Ran to the water's edge scrubbing his hands. He stripped down in the water determined to cleanse himself of fish stink. As he splashed something banged his thigh. It was the dead shark. He fled back to his tent and vowed to get even with all of them.

Von Meer ordered his battalion commander's to intensify patrols after a squad of grunts observed a wiry Arab dart into a small residence carrying a rifle. They pursued the suspect into a dark apartment and ordered him to freeze. A sergeant relieved him of his German Mauser and a search of the premises revealed a cache of ammunition and fifteen additional rifles of various makes. Some German, others Russian and several Italian of poor quality. The suspect was taken into custody and questioned by 1st Lieutenant James Byrd and his partner Staff Sergeant Ralph Monroe. Both highly respected and experienced intelligence personnel. The man revealed, after intense questioning that, yes he was a member of the rebel forces but had refused to flee wishing to remain with his family. The interrogators pounced on this info. Won't your superiors take reprisal on you for this betrayal? The suspect merely shrugged his shoulders staring at the cold floor annoyed with the blaring lights that engulfed him. At this point he went cold silent refusing to respond to any additional questioning. Frustrated the Intel investigators simply handed him over to locale authorities. As he was whisked away, Byrd turned to Monroe, "you can bet Uncle Sam's sweet ass, they won't be as nice as we were." Monroe inhaled a strong pull on his Camel Cigarette and blew a large plume of grayish smoke towards the ceiling chuckling. He retorted, "No I strongly suspect they won't be."

The Marines now had been on station several weeks, continuing patrols and maintaining check points had rounded up dozens of suspected rebels. They'd confiscated numerous weapons and local authorities were kept busy with the stream of rebel supporters. In the darkness screams were heard coming from the local constable's headquarters. The Marines left it alone. They were here to offer security to a weak government. They minded their business.

Colonel Von Meer sat up right on a green 30 caliber ammo crate. He scanned his Battalion Commanders. "I want you men to know I'm damn proud of this regiment. You officers performed in exemplary fashion. We commandeered numerous weapons and incarcerated dozens of suspected rebels. In short, we severed the noose that was strangling this government. The regiment suffered thirty six casualties; three K.I.A's most injuries were due to accidents of various causes. I'm sorry for the K.I.A's but sad to say loss of that magnitude with a force of four thousand men is quite acceptable. We occupied foreign soil losses occur that's the business we're in. Have your Company Commanders hold intense inspections. Now the good news, this outfit is to be relieved by Army units on Monday next. A division size detachment is on its way as we speak. Keep the troop's alert we're still in the red zone. Good job and thank you. Dismissed Oh and Semper-Fi."

Lieutenant Colonel Striker sat in a small field canvass chair. He'd made himself a makeshift desk using a crate of motor rounds. He was perusing field reports from his Company Commanders. A voice from outside his tent flap bellowed, "Sir, Petty Officer Little reporting as ordered!" "Come Doc." Doc Little entered the humble command tent. "Grab a seat, Doc. Welcome to the Statler. There drop your butt on that box of 30 calibers." "Morning Colonel." Striker chortled, "Yeah it is that. Look Doc I summoned you here because I want your honest input as to the battalion's physical and mental welfare." Little gazed at a weird insect crawling on the tent's dirt floor stalling determined to pick his words carefully. Clearing his throat he looked his boss in the eye. "Well Sir, there's the usual medical problems, dysentery, rashes, abrasions. There have been some cases of dehydration. The water as you are aware isn't the best quality. We've encouraged the troops to hydrate and to bath as much as possible. Your Officers and Noncoms have cooperated fully and pushed grunts to maintain their personal hygiene. As to the mental conditioning, well they're Marines, The Corps prides itself on strict discipline and thus far it has proven its effective value. But Colonel these men are constantly in harm's way. Nerves frayed adrenaline pumping with no chance to vent but to each other. No liberty, confined to tent city, nothing to offer some type of relaxation. I'm not being critical Sir, don't mean to come across in that manner with all respect you asked and I'm being as honest and up front with you as I can." Striker smiled, "I know that Doc. Look you and your entourages of Corpsmen have performed in the highest standards. I've watched you and your boys ministering not only to my Marines but sick kid's mothers, elderly, the list is endless and I want to both thank you and commend you. I agree one hundred percent that the troops need relief. An unfortunately the 3.5 beer rations we're allotted falls far short." He raised his hand alerting the Doc he was not through cutting Little off as he began to respond. Doc, the good news is on Monday next, we're to be relieved by the Army. That's only five days from now. I've issued orders to my Company Commanders to ease off on inspections and drill sessions. I believe the troops when completing their patrol tours should be allowed a least some semblance of down time a chance to unwind in their own way." "Colonel, may I interject here?" "Go to it Doc." "Well Sir there have been fights among the troops. Tempers have grown short. All under the gun have developed short fuses." "I know Doc. My Officers have kept me informed. Thank God there's been no major incident. The Corporals and Sergeants are cognizant of these isolated episodes and on top of the issue, Doc any advice or any ideas that we can implement for these issues?" Doc Little smiled, "no sir. Like you I'm well aware we're in a combat situation. Your Marines have been trained vigorously and discipline will prevail as it always has and always will." Striker smiled, "Doc you're a good man. This battalion is damn fortunate to have you and your fellow docs. Just be careful when ministering to the locale populace, we don't know who they are, but they sure as hell know who we are." "Yes sir, but as you we also have our creed and code. We live and die with it." Striker looked past Little, "Yeah Doc your right and its one hell of an honorable creed and code. Thank God for it and for men like you. Thanks for your input Doc. Now get the hell out of here and for Christ sake's, be careful. Petty Officer 1st Class Little rose, smiling he uttered "Aye, aye sir, Semper-Fi." Striker whispered softly, "Do or Die."

Little stepped into the morning sun and headed towards the sickbay dispensary. Striker rose from his seat and stepped into the hot sunlight watching the form of Doc Little disappear towards his objective. What makes men like them? What drives them to expose themselves to help others who burrow for cover? What makes Marines or any warrior, who suffered degradation, discipline, loneliness, and fear, with a chance of dying alone in agony on a foreign soil. Gazing at passing cumulus clouds the answer came. Love of country, dedication, pride. "Yeah," he thought returning to his crude desk, as long as we hold on to that analogy and belief we'll be okay.

The 2nd Marine Regiment continued its aggressive security patrols. Its battalions leap frogging relieving each other to maintain its high standards of manning check points and reconnoitering the out shirts and the heart of Beirut. The troop's anxiously awaiting their relief from their Army Brothers. On Sunday the transports and their escorts hove into view adding to the mammoth armada of vessels that stood off the shores of Lebanon. Colonel Von Meer in a small motor vessel made his way to the flagship, Once negotiating the ladders; they headed to the quarters of the Army Commander. He entered the comfortable quarters and came to attention and under arms saluted and reported to Major General Ray Mueller, commander of the Army expeditionary force. "Sir Colonel Von Meer, 2nd Regiment Commander U.S.M.C. reporting as ordered." Mueller smiled, "as ease Colonel pull up a seat. There are fresh coffee and sweet breads. Help yourself." "No thank you, General. Had a fine breakfast." "Glad you're here and I'm at your personal service, sir." "Ah, well Colonel your Marines have done a hell of a job. Now it's up to my boys to keep things tight. How do you wish to proceed too effect the relief of this battalion?" "Well sir, here are the coordinates of where my one remaining battalion people are located. I feel this will be the most effective transaction. I certainly hope you agree." Mueller studied the coordinates. "Makes sense Colonel. We can't leave the city naked. I'll pass these coordinates down to my Regimental Commanders where you posted battalions in line. I fortunately will be able to assign regiments. My division will be going ashore at 0400 hours. Your people should be ready to stand down by 0900. I commend you Colonel on a job well done. At the effected hour the Army will assume all responsibility as to defense and security of this nation. Thank you Colonel and I wish you and your Marines a safe voyage home." Von Meer stood and came to a rigid attention, "thank you sir and good luck to you and your command." Mueller Rose, "Colonel it's always a pleasure to deal with the Marines. Good luck to you and if I may Semper-Fi." Von Meer smiled, "Semper Fi, General." Negotiated an about face and exited the hatch for he was in a hurry to return to his command and oversee the relief process.

At 0500 hours, The Army came ashore on beaches secured by the Marines. They roared into Beirut with heavy armor and weaponry and massive manpower. Striker's battalion was relieved piece meal by Army Contingents. Once the relief process was complete, the 8th Marines marched to the sea and boarded landing craft and headed toward their waiting transports while the packed amphibious craft bobbed and weaved on pasty turbulent swells scrapping alongside the armor plates of the transports. Marines scrambled up the netting where they formed up in the ships decks. Once again they were herded into the holds, chose their berths and relieved themselves of heavy equipment. The ships engines shook and groaned. The rattle of anchor chains loud and wrenching as the mammoth ships weighed anchor and set course for the U.S.A.

Again the noncoms and officers set to assuring that discipline and personal hygiene was enforced as well as calisthenics and close order drill was the order of the day on the decks of the transports. The voyage was made with little disturbance from mother sea. Nature was kind and seemed to bless the small armada on its journey home. In time the shores of the U.S.A. hove into view. The transports glided into their berths in Norfolk guided by the skill of their captains and crew. The Marines debarked and boarded the endless array of waiting deuce an a half's and with a roar of numerous engines and the expelling of exhaust fumes the convoy roared off destination Camp Lejeune. There was no band or fanfare and like thieves in the night the 2^(nd) Marine regiment united had returned home. Mission and objective accomplished. The world now breathed easier. The Army was on station and would ensure peace and security in that torn nation of Lebanon.

The regiment powered through the gates of Lejeune in the wee hours of the morning with the tarp of darkness masking its arrival. The troops were quickly assembled and dismissed to their respective areas. There the grunts settled in happy and content to be in humble and familiar surroundings. For this had become their current comfort zone. They cleared and honed equipment fine tuning the tools of their trade as well preparing for the 1300 hour inspection. Chatter among the troops soft and low key. Men mostly deep within themselves mainly with thoughts of what they'd been through and home occupied their minds.

The regiment stood in crisp formation in the warm North Carolina sun with an awesome array of four thousand combat laden troops. Guidon and flags rippled in the soft breeze. A Marine band stood off in the distance. The beat of the Marine Corps hymn wafted across the parade ground as Colonel Von Meer marched alongside his Division Commander, Major General Marcus Greene, who came to review and welcome his 2nd regiment back to the confines of Camp Lejeune. The Marines stood erect and proud with their weapons glinting in the sun. The Major General was a no nonsense officer. He stood in the front and bellowed "WELL DONE, MY MARINES, WELCOME HOME!" Turned briskly and sauntered away followed by his entourage, the review was over. The grunts dismissed after being told the battalions would be granted fifteen day leave, piecemeal, one battalion at a time.

The battalion had been granted a fifteen day leave. Striker stood staring out his office window watching as his men dispersed heading home to love ones. Family maybe sweethearts, wives, kids who knows. He felt content for them for they performed brilliantly in Lebanon. He walked away from the window pulled on his blouse and looking in his small mirror he placed his piss cover at just the right angle. He took a last look around his small office and exited through the hatch. He walked briskly to his white fifty five Ford. Threw his luggage in the truck and watched bemused as a company of grunts ran by chanting loudly in Marine sing song, the lyrics questionable. He entered the Ford turned the ignition and the engine exploded into life and in a grayish plume of smoke. He headed out to a deserved R&R. Heading down the highway soft music wafted from the car radio. He hummed to the tune recognized it as a current top ten. He inhaled the cool fresh air and basked in the beauty of rolling hills and scenic tree lines. He had mixed emotions and knew he needed time to unwind, down size so to speak but hated the thought of being separated from his battalion. He felt naked and insecure in the civilian world. He loved the discipline and camaraderie of the Corps. Out here in the world, people were growing soft and greedy. "Yeah," he thought they depend on their warriors to protect the soft life they've chosen and relish. "Oh well," he uttered job security. The Ford rolled along. Its tires humming softly on the concrete highway and traffic moved steadily and the sun shone bright with a clean blue sky. Striker didn't feel nor want the stares or share in small talk with civilians who stand in awe at his green uniform adorned with the ribbons earned in the warrior's way. He gulped down a burger with fries washing them down with a black coffee. He completed his last gulps of coffee enjoying the taste of a Lucky Strike. Igniting the engine and roared out of the parking lot continuing on his journey.

Within hours he was traveling in the beauty of the rolling hills of Maryland. He marveled at the massive dairy and vegetable farms and fathomed how much work it took to maintain them as he passed them. His heart beat hard in his chest and a sour taste in his mouth came up to haunt him. His mind in grief mold for his objective had loomed into view. He turned right onto a graveled road and a large sign greeted visitors, "Holy Name Cemetery." Cruising slowly he perused the headstones noting the names, noting that the souls lying in repose beneath were authors of life time stories which always ended incomplete. Never follow the script intended. How many hopes and dreams had gone awry? How many tears, laughs, and disappointments? Had they passed in anger or peace? Did they die hard? Were they loved in life and their memories treasured in death? Did loved ones come and share their worries? The individual graves gave mute testimony to his thoughts, some neat and groomed while others disheveled and in disarray. He moved slowly noting the tall pines as sentinels lining the roadway. He came to a small knoll located between two maples which stood as guards and housed singing birds that emitted sweet tunes comforting the dead.

He exited the vehicle and walked slowly. His feet leaving small prints on the dew wet grass. Tears coursed down his cheeks. He halted three headstones lay at his feet. He removed his cover, knelt and like a burst dam tears gushed forth. The names jumped at him their embossed lettering on black granite reaching to him.

Coleen Donovan Striker
Born: February 1st, 1927
Died: April 19th 1954

Elizabeth Striker
Born: July 10th 1944
Died: April 19th 1954

Eric Striker Jr.
Born: May 10th 1947
Died: April 19, 1954

His heart ached. His stomach churned with nausea as the tragic horrific memory enveloped his soul. How on a rainy day and an out of control eighteen-wheeler had slammed into their Volkswagen head on. How his family, his life, had been torn in a heartbeat. He walked life byways with a deep quilt. His spirit covered in a tarp of darkness for his soul had died with them. "Oh honey," he whispered if only I'd been here. Maybe I'd still have you and our two little ones. He felt bitter. He was in Pendleton at the time and had just made Major. She'd never known. The news of their deaths delivered moments after his promotion. Reaching in his side pocket, he pulled out his old gold oak leaves and gently and tenderly placed them on the grave. He stood gazed off into the distance. He'd vowed the day of their burial that the Corps would be his only living family. He vowed to his dead wife and children that he, Eric Striker, would throw his whole being into the making of Marines and train them vigorously so that if they saw combat his teaching and leadership would save more then was lost. He bent and kissed the grave stones and heart heavy turned. Broken hearted and without looking back left this place of sorrow that housed his soul. The oak leaves glistened in the sun, a gift to his loving wife and children.

LeSage had hitched a ride with LeBron who had borrowed an old beat up Ford from a brother in the 6th Marines who also hailed from Brooklyn. The floor boards were all but gone, rotted and what remained were covered with pieces of plywood and old U.S.M.C blankets. But at least the windshield wipers functioned and hell it was transportation home. The miles flitted by as the pair bitched and gossiped about the Corps, life, politics and just every day bullshit. "Hey Lee piped up LeBron, "What'd you think about the fucked up Lebanon?" "Fucked up country and people, shit the only thing we could identify with were them ugly fucking camels. Damn I'll bet Gunny Burke fucked one." LeSage chuckled. "You and Burke someday that monster gonna kick your ass Jake." "Naw, I keeps my distance. He be alright really doing his business, shit ain't no telling what kind of shit we gonna get into next. My mom-ma she always told me don't throw corn in the snow. "Hey what you got planned, man?" "Dun no Jake, see the family, some friends, got no girl waiting, who knows just chill I guess. What about you? LeBron laughed. "Shit got all kind of poo tang waiting. Gonna dine, drink and fuck. Lot's going on in old Brooklyn. Want to come?" "Shit Jake, my white ass. They'll fry me for sure." "Hell no honky not if your with ol Jake. Naw, I'll pass my brother, gotta see the folks but thanks." "Okay Lee, I be dropping you off at Grand Central and I'll meet you there for the return trip. He pulled to a stop and LeSage exited hefting his heavy barracks bag. "See you Jake, watch your ass." "Yeah my man, don't choke your chicken too much." He roared with laughter, raising his fist as he pulled into ongoing traffic.

LeSage caught his train to Hartford. It stood hissing steam on track no ten. He grabbed a window seat and sat back with his heart pounding with the excitement of coming home. It'd been eighteen months and he was anxious to get to the old homestead and the comfort and security of his room. The smell of home and mom's cooking. The stale odor's that lingered from dad's black cigars. The train had lurched slowly pulled hard gaining momentum and speed.

Soon it plunged into sun light. He closed his eyes the clacky clack, clacky clack of the wheels on the track lulling him into sleep.

"Tickets, tickets please," the conductor strolled down the aisle collecting tickets. Tearing them, he kept half and the passenger the other. His eyes met LeSage's, "on leave son, going home' "Yes sir." "Well that's good. No place like home. Hope you enjoy and God bless." He moved on down the aisle his voice echoing through the passenger car. "Tickets please, Tickets please." He smiled with contentment as the train's whistle announced its behemoth presence. They'd entered Connecticut soil and his heart beat pounded as the miles faded away. Bringing him ever closer to home and forgotten memories of his boyhood. He began recognizing landmarks and soon the conductor returned winking at LeSage a broad smile on his face. "Hartford next stop! Hartford five minutes." The train slowed came to a crawl and then halted and stopped discharging passengers within Union Station. He was home.

He hoisted his barrack's bag over his right shoulder. As he stepped on to Union Place where he hooked a right. He knew his dad was working and mom didn't drive. He elected to walk up Asylum to Main Street where he could catch the Hillside Ave bus, which would bring him home to Amherst Street. He walked briskly. People smiling and staring at him. His greens crisp and neat. Four ribbons adorned his breast, along with weapons badges he knew he looked sharp. He'd better or Gunny Burke would have his ass. LeSage smiled at the thought. He stopped at a hot dog wagon. Realizing he was hungry and without much deliberation had a dog and a Coke then moved off briskly. Arriving at Main and Asylum, he crossed Main Street to the old state house and stood at the bus shack. Luck was with him within minutes #16 blue and white transit bus he sought hove into view. The huge letters above the windshield announcing Hillside Avenue.

He reveled in seeing old landmarks. The White Tower, The Traveler's, The Wadsworth, Traveling South on Main than West on Park Street, The Old Frog Hollow, The French Quarters, Saint Ann's, the church where his folks had married. South on Zion St, then west on Hamilton and then a left and south on Hillside. He exited at Hillside and Yale. Hoisted his bag and walked slowly. He could see his home, a modest red cape. His eyes brimmed with wetness. There was mom hanging cloths. He crossed the street; she turned her eyes locked on the green moving figure. Her small hands flew to her face. She dropped her clothes basket and as a little bird flew towards him. He dropped his bag. She jumped into his arms. Hugging him as only a mother hugs. Oh my son, Oh my God, your home you're here. Oh, how I missed you. Tears rolled down her cheeks spilling onto his uniform. She was a little petite woman. He swung her around and she giggled. "Stop that you'll drop me." "Mom, I love you." "Come son into the house, I've just made tea and cookies. Why didn't you let us know you were coming." "Ma, isn't it a nice surprise." "Well yes." "Then enjoy, you always loved surprises." He stood in the kitchen surveying the interior feeling the love and warmth that only a loving home can offer. He was back in the nest and for the first time in months, felt secure and safe.

The elder LeSage pulled into his driveway. It was a warm night. The air clean and fresh so he didn't bother to park his car in the garage. He exited the vehicle and entered his home. He'd had a taxing day in the office and was content to return to his refuge. His wife, Marie was busy at the stove stirring a large pot of stew humming happily to herself. "Hey lady," he uttered "Why so happy?" "Hi, my husband, go peek in the den. There's a nice surprise waiting." Grunting, he moved to the door and peered inside and gasped as his son rose to greet him. "Hi dad, what's happening?" Son and father melted in each others arms. "My God boy, where have you been? Damn, but you filled out, lean and strong hard as a rock. Welcome home son. We've been

297

praying and thinking of you." The father stepped back appraising his on. "You look good, lean and mean looking. The Marines obviously have whipped you into shape." Tears welled in the old man's eyes. "Are they treating you alright? Aw, what do I say? What do I know, you didn't write much. We've been worried. Where you been? What's with your life?" Lee laughed softly, "it's okay dad. I'm fine and I took a little trip to the Middle East and saw a different part of the world." The old man inhaled deeply, the Middle East, were you part of those Lebanon Landings?" "Yes sir, I was." "God son, that was all over the news. We watched those Marine's landing not realizing our son was among them. Thank God your safe. How long are you home for?" "Fifteen days, dad." Fifteen days of paradise. I've missed you and mom and my siblings so much. It's heaven to be home." Once more they embraced. A call form the kitchen that supper was ready separating them arm in arm. They entered the small kitchen greeted by the smiling face of little Marie. The elder LeSage turned to his son, "see little Napoleon awaits us."

The next day was Saturday so he called his boyhood pal of years Paul LeBrick. "Hey old shoe, this is Lee I'm home on leave. What's on the agenda for tonight?" "Oh, shit Lee, I'm going to a house party. Damn, how about tomorrow for a get to?" "Hell Paul you haven' seen me in almost two years and you put me off for a party, that's just wrong. Fuck a duck, wait, wait Lee, let me call the girl who's hosting this shing ding. See if I can't bring you along. I'll call you right back." Within 10 minute the phone rang. He grabbed the receiver on the second ring. "Lee, its Paul. All set I'll pick you up at six sharp. Be ready." "Okay, anybody else at this thing I'll know?" "Don't think so, but don't sweat it. They're nice kids told her you were in the Marines and just back from Lebanon. You'll be well received." "Okay short change, see you at six." "Roger that, buddy see ya."

He donned a pair of faded pair of jeans and a v neck aqua sweater. He found an old pair of loafers took a shower and waited. At six on the dot a horn blared in the driveway. He kissed his mom, hugged his dad and fled through the door anxious to mingle with new people that didn't wear green.

Paul pulled up and parked in front of a modest green colored cape with several vehicles already lining the street. They climbed three stairs an after two knocks, the door swung open. "Hi, Mrs. Granato." "Hi, Paul, this is my friend Lee, he is on leave from the Marines." "Oh hello, well come on in. The gang and party are down stairs. Have a good time. Nice meeting you Lee and welcome home." "Thank you, ma'am."

The cellar was compact but clean and cheerful. Several couples sat on couches and chairs. Soft music wafted from a corner record player. Paul with Lee in tow headed to the girl playing DJ. She turned as they approached. "Hi Jo, this is my friend Lee I called about." She cocked her head, a smile played on her face. "Why thank you for coming." She extended a small feminine hand. He grasped it and held it maybe a minute to long. But for some reason he was reluctant to release his grip. Her fingers warm and soft and her friendly smile that displayed even white teeth sent a tingling sensation coursing through his very being. Her dark almond eyes bore into his as though reading his mind. She wore dark slacks and a loose fitting knit sweater attempting to mask her ample figure. It failed to do so. "I hope you have a nice time and welcome home." The soft tones of "In the Still of the Night" filtered through the room. He stepped in close, "Can I have this dance?" She blushed but stepped into his arms and they spun off into a dark corner. It set the stage as they continued to whirl to the tunes of "Come Softly, Dream, Dream, Dream, Earth Angel, Little Darling, Etc." It was as though they floated through air and that only they existed. The night flew and soon the festivities ended. As he stood at the door in parting, he inhaled deeply. "Jo, can I see you again, maybe tomorrow?" Her perfect lips parted in a little girls smile. "Well, I've church in the morning, maybe." He interrupted her, "Church, that sound's fantastic. Could I take you?" Well it's at 10:00 am at St. Lawrence. No, no, no, Jo you're an old Parkville girl. Just like me. Let's go to Our Lady of Sorrows. They have a beautiful mass at 11:00 but damn I've no car or license for that matter." She grinned, wait here. She returned shortly. "My dad says I can take his car. Be here at 10:30. His heart skipped a beat. "Yes ma'am, 10:30 it is."

He walked on air to Paul's car, he had been waiting patiently. "Well old shoe, you two sure as hell hit it off." "Yeah Paul, I like her, like her a lot." They rode to Lee's home in silence.

Sunday morning he rose early, shaved, showered and feverishly spit shined his shoes, He donned his forest greens. Kissed his mom goodbye and skipped out the door walking briskly to what he hoped was a new found lady friend. Her home was located a block from his parents residence. Both sat in a modest blue collar neighborhood. Approaching the door, he noted the sun was shining. Birds were chirping and his heart was pounding on the second knock he door opened and his pounding heart skipped a beat. Jo stood there in a black velvet dress which clung to her ample body like a stamp on an envelope. Her eyes were aglow and her perfect white teeth shone in as lovely a smile which shone like the early morning sun. His mouth dry and he was able to mutter, "Morning Jo." "Hi Lee I'm all set. It's about a twenty minute ride to Sorrow's so we've got to go." "Sure I just wanted permission from your folks to take you to lunch after mass." Both parents had come up behind her. Her father uttered, "sure and be careful." Her mother interjected, "don't eat big; I'm making pasta for supper. We hope you'll join us." "Yes ma'am, and thank you."

They spent the ride to church engrossed in idle chatter. Gossiping about the old neighborhood and mutual people both knew. They'd grown up under the spires of our Lady of Sorrows but had never known each other. He'd been half way around the world and only then had their spirits connected. The church was packed. The organist and choir meshed to a beautiful crescendo as they departed the beautiful Gothic structure which had honored their dead and hosted family weddings as well as where they both had made first communion and confirmation. They were greeted by old school chums. Laughter and high spirits filled the air. Finally they broke away and drove to the A&W for burgers and an icy glass of root beer. Their eyes locked and they knew they were parrying one another and getting to look into each others souls. The ride home was subdued they'd had a nice time and both were reluctant to see the time pass so quickly. He returned to share supper with her family. They queried him as to his time in the Corps. Interested in what he relayed to them. Then the two retreated to the cellar where they danced slowly to the wonders of 50's music. He pulled her close and gazed into her dark glowing eyes. His lips found hers. Gently and tenderly they swayed to the music and then he kissed her long and hard. She broke away. "Wow she said. Okay Marine, at ease." He laughed, "Yeah, but damn Jo that was heaven." She smiled "Yeah Lee, it was and can be."

They spent the evenings together. Dancing or walking in the neighborhood. Several times they jumped into her dad's car and headed to A&W. One night she drove into Goodwin Park. They kissed and caressed and whispering sweet endearments. There is nothing in the world like new found young love. One's heart sings and jumps with joy. The soul is aglow and the stomach full of butterflies. The world ceases to exist and you walk on air not a care in the world. Days passed quickly. It was Friday and he had two days of leave left. He'd talked her into taking the day off. Donning his greens he quick stepped to her house. She was waiting. They left in a light drizzle catching the transit bus to downtown. Her head on his shoulder she whispered, "Where are we going?" He chuckled softly, "Be patience my little girl, you'll see."

They exited the bus at the old state house. Hand and hand they crossed Main Street to Asylum. Halting in front of Savitt's Jewelers, with a grin on his face, he gently pulled her inside where he headed to a glass display of rings. The owner Bill Savitt stood smiling. "Good morning, good people. Can I help you?" Jo looked bewildered, confused, "I don't know?" She stared at Lee; who suddenly fell to one knee. "Jo I love you. I know it's not fair I've still two years to go in the corps. Don't know what's hidden behind the mountain but, I want you as mine. I want to get engaged. On lookers gazed in fascination while some cheered and many clapped. Here this Marine was proposing to his lady on his knee in public. Bill Savitt stood smiling and basking in the scent of young love. Jo's eyes filled with tears. "Oh yes Lee and I'll wait for you forever if need be." She chose a modest diamond and he placed it on her small finger. A voice form the gathering spectators shouted, "Kiss her you damn fool!" He chuckled and pulled her close. Their lips entwined. They'd committed to each other. He paid the bill with his back pay. Savitt had given a modest discount and now the young couple souls enriched exited the store hand and hand. She held on to his strong arm. Now honey I'm your finance. "Yeah babe and one day you'll be my wife, my soul mate."

That night they dined with his parents. Both ecstatic on the engagement. It was a quiet evening spent in small conversation each attempting to get to know one another. The hour grew late and hand in hand he walked her home. Shivers ran up and down his spine as they strolled under a starlit sky. Young love like a beautiful rose blossoming in the spring. He held her close as they stood at her door and he kissed her long and hard and then she was gone sprinting into the sanctuary of her home. His heart heavy as he reversed direction and headed home. Emotions never experienced coursed through his veins. His time was short and he was in love. He was experiencing what millions before had gone through. Falling in love and then the forlorn doom of separation.

Saturday they drove to Elizabeth Park where they marveled at the rose garden. They walked slowly hearts throbbing wishing they could hold back the hands of time. They sat by the pond watching as a family of ducks swam by honking their songs of love for family. That night they went to a bean supper at St. Ann's Hall hosted by his aunt where he was proud to introduce his love to family members. She basked in the attention and they danced to the music rendered by a DJ. The night slithered by and soon they took leave of the festivities. They'd had a wonderful evening. They cruised through the streets slowly not wanting this cherished night to end. But it was late and being an Italian girl she could not and would not violate the trust of her upbringing. She pulled into his driveway and they embraced and kissed for the thousand time. He watched as she drove off. His loins on fire and desire overwhelmed him but he knew he'd had to practice restraint. This was the 50's and one displayed love with respect and trust.

Sunday they attended the ten am mass at St. Lawrence. The couple had a simple lunch at A&W and drove to his home. He packed his barracks bag and gazed around his small room noting various artifacts of his days as an athlete. His heart was anchored with nostalgia. The hands of time refuse to stand still. It was that hour. Time to depart. He hugged his mother long and hard. Tears welled in her eyes. "Take care my son, come home to us." He bolted out the door. His dad and Jo were waiting. He sat next to her inhaling her scent not knowing when he'd see her again. The ride to the train station was subdued. Father worried about his son and Jo in love with her Marine and Lee heavy hearted in leaving this quiet wonderful world of love.

Union Station was packed they sat quietly on a long wooden bench. Then the words they dreaded blared over the speaker. "Attention, train for New York, stopping at Berlin, Meriden, New Haven, Stamford, Rye New York, 125th Street, Grand Central Station, departing in five minutes. All-Aboard, They stood by the track, steam hissing and curling upward from the passenger cars. He shook his dad's hand and then embraced. "Take care son, God be with you." He stared into Jo's eyes. Tears coursed down her checks. I love you Lee. Please, please come back to me. He pulled her close and tight. He kissed her long and hard. Pulled back, "take care of mom and my girl, dad. I'll be back." Hosting his barracks bag the hauled himself into the waiting passenger car. "All aboard, All aboard!" The passing conductor signaled he train lurched then slowly pulled away. He stared long and hard at his dad and lady holding hands and waving. He sat back in the seat his mind had photographed that picture. He would carry it in his soul where ever he went.

The clacky clack of the train's wheels on the track lulled him into a restless sleep. Nostalgia gripped his consciousness. Dreams returned him back through time. He was once again a young boy carousing with boyhood friends. A whirlwind stew of past love and warmth and the security of youth meshed in his brain. Seeing old friendly faces stirred emotions he thought were long past. He could hear the voices of youthful pals as they played ball in Old Pope Park. The old black ball, identified by its electrical tape wrappings, and whizz-whizz as it came at you. Ah yes, youth is fleeting he'd turned his back on a life full of love and caring and now encroached in the harsh discipline and demands of the Corps. His heart stirred heavy with love and fear. Fear that his lady would fail in her vow to wait for him. Had he asked to much, expected to much only the mischievous hand of time would reveal its answer. As he slept the iron wheels churned ever forward leading him to what or where. Would he see home again and return whole? For sure he would not be the same in spirit. He'd enlisted as a confused boy. One way or another he'd return a man.

A loud voice roused him from his slumber. "Grand Central Grand Central Station, next stop in five minutes!" He stirred and was looking into crystal blue eyes. He bolted upright. He'd had fallen asleep on the shoulder of a lovely petite blond. "Oh God, I'm so sorry ma'am," he mumbled. She smiled sheepishly, "It's okay Marine it was interesting listening as you talked in your sleep." "No, no, I'm so sorry. Embarrassed really." "It's okay Marine, My husband is a Captain in the 101st Airborne. I understand believe me." "Damn not only did I fall asleep on a woman's shoulder, but an officer's wife. Hell's bells, what can I say?" "You say nothing it's okay, tough returning from leave. I've been that route." The train lurched to a stop. He reached up tackling his barrack's bag. She held out a small hand. He grasped it smartly. "Good luck Marine." "Yes ma'am, good luck to you and your captain." They drifted away in separate directions. He watched as she was swept away by the hurrying crowd and was gone.

He turned and strolled through the crowded terminal. Hoisting his barracks bag, he found his way to the street. He placed his bag by his feet and waited for the arrival of LeBron. Within minutes the old Ford chug a lug smoke billowing from its exhaust to where he stood waiting. Gabbing hi bag, he flung it into the rear seat and quickly entered the passenger side of the tired old Ford. LeBron ever smiling stated "Semper-Fi old man. How was your leave?" They crawled through New York traffic and eventually reaching the Jersey Turnpike where the old Ford coughed and hissed trying its best to keep up with turnpike traffic. "Well Lee, How did it go?" "Great Jake, spent time with the family, old friends and got my ass engaged." LeBron his white teeth displayed in a wide smirk spouted saying, "What you got your ass hooked? You got your dick contracted to one pussy. Are you crazy? Damn Lee, there's all kinds of women out there wanting your dick. Are you locale, gone south, under a rock? Shit man you got at least two years more in the crotch. You gonna masturbate. You think that chick ain't gonna get the crotch itches and fuck some civilian prick. Boy you fucked up, old Jake his dick meant to fuck em all. That bull in the field, he doesn't look at one cow. He looks at em all and wants to fuck em all. Damn Lee you lost your head on me." "Jake, can it. She's a nice girl and I love her." Jake smiled "Yeah I know. Really congratulations. Hope you don't get hurt. Me I ain't ready for that serious shit, too much pussy and fun out there. But I respect your decision, hope all goes well."

The rest of the ride was spent in idle chatter regarding their leave. A small drizzle had appeared from nowhere. The miles clicked by and soon the gates of Lejeune loomed bright and forlorn before them. Jake pulled the old Ford to a predesignated parking area. Both hoisted their barracks bags and entered the huge base. Their hearts heavy and sad at what they'd left behind. The mighty hand of the Corps would soon swoop over them and ease and tighten their soul nostalgia. They were green warriors and the Corps would quickly shed them of their recent caress of love and softness.

Both hoisted their barrack bags and approached the main gate where they displayed leave papers and waved through by the on duty sentry. Slowly they approached their assigned quonset hut. An eerie stillness carpeted their area. Moonlight guided them as their humble quarters hove into view.

They entered through the hatchway quietly. There positioned in the squat position sat Broken Rose. The hour was late. Most if not all of those on leave had long since returned. The musical chorus of snores blanketed the interior. "Hey John," whispered LeSage, "how was your leave?" The Rose smiled softly. His voice like the wind smooth and quiet. "The Rose is never alone," he uttered. "He walks always with the creatures of the forest. The soul of the wind and the spirit of his ancestors. Welcome home my brothers. Go rest your selves. Tomorrow we once again begin the rigors of true warriors. You are the last to arrive safely. Now my spirit will rest and gaze into the future. Prepare your mind and spirit for what lies ahead."

"I want them back in fighting readiness, that's our job. Set things in motion Frank, like yesterday." "Yes sir, Colonel, consider it done." Striker strolled quickly from his knoll, disgusted. "Now heads will roll and quickly. There was no time for games." "You know Erick sometimes the men don't know when your acting." Striker stared off into the distance. "I don't act Frank. There's no time for that shit. I want this battalion back in tip top condition and remember to insist some of those fat ass officers to shed weight or their asses will belong to me. Carry on." Striker took off at a run into the nearby forest determined he vowed to return his battalion to its original battle hardened conditioning.

True to his word, Striker conducted a full weapons and equipment inspection that very day. The battalion stood in a torrid sun for four hours. But Striker displayed little or no sympathy. He had a battalion to get back into shape and drove his officers and noncoms relentless. His personal vow of having a razor tough outfit would never leave nor would it soften his blitz on having a smooth running engine.

The next day a 20 mile hike in a soft drizzle commenced. Striker set the pace and men double timed at the quick to keep pace. The next day a repeat. There would be no reprieve. He was obsessed with melting down fat calories and getting his warriors back on track. He pushed and cajoled his officers. Roared at his NCO's time was of the essence. This was a combat unit and by God he'd place it back at the head of the other battalions with blood, sweat and tears. Already he unit was falling into shape. Leg muscles and flat stomachs now the order of the day. Striker knew from experience that at any moment in time his battalion would be called to arms. H was obsessed they be ready and he was merciless in his pursuit to drive his troops to the limit and already signs of success deployed through the companies. He stood on his knoll as his troops returned from a forced march nodding his head in approval. A grin on his face, yes, they were looking like Marines once again. And he'd stay on their asses and keep it that way. There was no time for games. His was a world of the old warrior leadership and he would guard that thought with his very soul. His blood, hard training saved lives and he would and had lived by this code.

Von Meer sat in his office steadily gazing out of his window bemused by the hard training Striker driving his battalion. But there were other thoughts occupying his brain. He spun around in his swivel chair and gazed at the large wall map that adorned a large portion of wall space. He zoned in on the area of The Philippines sighed and picked up an order from his desk top stamped confidential. It was an order from headquarters Marines Corps advising, no ordering him to choose an elite battalion which would be deployed to The Philippines, as that government had requested assistance. Embroiled with the Huds, a large bandito force. Its small military was no match and The Huds were busy dismantling that country piecemeal. The commandant was aware of the 8th Marines successful jungle training and so had directed Von Meer that Striker's outfit would deploy in full to assist the Filipino's, hunt down The Huds in their own yard and destroy them.

As Striker stood tall serving his troops a runner appeared at his side. "Sir you're wanted in the regimental commander's office, forth wit." Striker eyeballed the young Corporal waved at Pezzone to take charge and hopped in the passenger seat of the jeep sent as a transport. Ten minutes and he entered his CO's office. "Sir Lieutenant Colonel Striker reporting as ordered." Von Meer exhaled smoke from a fingertip Lucky. "Sit Colonel, sit. Smoke if you like." Striker chose a seat to the right of the huge desk and fired up a Lucky Strike. Sat back and waited. He knew by the stern look on his commander's face that this was no social visit. Von Meer rose from his seat and beckoned Strikre to the wall map and informed him of the circumstances spreading as a cancer throughout their allied country. X's and O's marked hot spots around the Manila area. Old man Von Meer sneered if you haven't figured it out your battalion has been fingered for this job. You're more than ready and I know your willing. Have your battalion at Cheery Point by 1600 hours tomorrow. There they're be flown to Pendleton where your truck down to San Diego and board the transport ship, Guardian Angel for the cruise to the Philippines. Your orders are sealed in this envelope. But you have the discretion and backing to take whatever action you determine to destroy this herd of goats, understood?" "Yes sir." "Then by God Eric, get the hell out of here. You've got work to do and in a hurry. No time to waste." "Yes sir. My boys are ready." "I know that otherwise someone else would be sharing stale smoke with me. Good sailing Eric and good luck. The eyes and backing of The Corps are with you." "Yes sir." Striker came to attention and about faced and flew out the door. His heart pounding with excitement for his battalion was being deployed to a hot spot. This was what it was all about. The hard training and the discipline soon they would see action and hunt a formidable prey.

Jungle trained well-tuned his Marines should and would be up to the task.

Striker had his jeep transport driver put the petal to the medal. He was in a frenzy to return to his command. The jeep roared to a stop and Striker in leaps and bounds stormed into his office. He beckoned the Sergeant Major into his inner sanctuary. Sergeant Major, he began, have all company officers and senior noncoms assembled here at 1400 hours. I want no Johnny come lately's." "But sir the battalion is out on training tactics." "I don't give a shit Sergeant Major. Send out the Marines. Have them here at the designated time and have the battalion march back to our area. Give the order to clean weapons and gear and await further orders. Do I make myself clear?" "Yes sir, I'll dispatch every available vehicles we have in the motor pool to lasso your officers. I'll even form a posse if need be." "Good show Sergeant Major. Start the ball rolling. There's heat in the wind and this unit is going to put out the fire. Now hop to. Designate all your clerks to spread out and get my boys back here post haste." "Yes sir, any further orders?" "You just got them. Get it done, clean and fast. I want no scuttlebutt. Just inform them of their orders." "Aye, Aye, sir." The Sergeant Major flew out the hatch at the double quick.

Every available mode of transport was rounded up and secured by the 8th Marines. Deuce and a halves, large cattle trucks which once literally transported cattle were sent head long and screeching into the boon docks to round up the 8th battalion busy at battle tactics. The convoy of vehicles came roaring into the area. Large clouds of dust and the smell of diesel fuel announced their arrival. The grunts were ordered into the vehicles and whisked away at high speed to their home area. There they fell into formation and informed by Platoon Sergeants to remain in quarters cleaning and checking equipment. "Chow call at 16:30 hours," bellowed Staff Sergeant Laurent. Then showers and some leisure time. You'll be informed in due time as to what's up. For now no questions just get your asses in motion and in shape. Dismissed!"

The grunts disappeared to their respective quarters. Once housed within their hut, LeBron uttered, to no one in particular, "anyone noticed none of the officers or senior noncoms were in that fucked up truck convoy. What the hell is happening?" Ray Phillips chortled, "Jake probably the end of the world is your black ass ready to meet its maker?" "Oh, fuck you. Really, don't you guys think it's weird? Only platoon Sergeants acted as our chaperons. Somethings up. Gotta be." Broken Rose stood in the center of the quonset hut. "Yes something up. That's obvious in the meantime. Hit those weapons and gear. We'll get the word when the boss says so. Enough bullshiting! Get your asses prepared. I've a feeling there's not much time."

Striker eyeballed his officers and senior noncoms for a full minute. Before his voice cut through the silence. "Listen up and listen good. This outfit is on a deployed assignment. You'll get the word as to where and when once we have boarded ship in Diego. I want no rumors or false scuttle butt filtering through the ranks. You commanders make damn sure your units are ready both physical and emotionally. Doc Little here has already scheduled up for oriental shots. Seems where we'll be going other types of bugs will be like gnats. So we'll immunize for those fuck a duck critters. Your companies must and will be fit and ready to go at 1400 hours tomorrow. We need not pack logistics or ammo. We'll pick that good stuff up in San Diego. Ask me no questions and I'll tell you no lies. You'll get the word and be informed once we're at sea. For now I strongly suggest you push and ride hard on our outfits. We're not going to a church social. That you've already figured I'm sure. Make sure your troops have evening and morning chow. I want them clean and sharp when we march off this base. Okay that's it for now. Get moving. You've little time for tit and tat. Your Dismissed!" "Aye, Aye sir." As chairs and feet scurried about the small command office. In seconds Striker sat alone with his Exec Major Pezzone. "Well Frank, I guess we're about to earn those fat pay checks." "Yeah Eric, we're on the move again. I will say this you keep it very interesting for this battalion." Striker laughed softly, "Yeah Frank, but that's how we earn our living. We train to be warriors and now it's time to heft spear and shield." "Yes sir Colonel, and again I'll say this. The battalion is ready and honed to the bone. You've seen to that afternoon sir." Pezzone turned and exited through the open hatch.

The grunts settled into cleaning weapons and checking and repairing defective gear. They took showers and lounged about their quarters. Some wrote letters or reread over and over those received from home or sweethearts. Others sat in groups discussing what was in the wind. Rumors ricocheted about the huts. It was Taiwan, maybe the Middle East again, perhaps Korea had exploded. Young men with their minds in over drive looked to relax but nerves and excitement obstructed their desire to unwind. At 16:30 hours they marched to chow. Then to a large medical dispensary where Doc Little and his small Corps of Corpsmen dispensed added shots of who knew what into young muscular arms. The return to quarters was subdued. Men crawled into their cots with the sad melody of taps A reminder that soon they would be headed into harm's way somewhere in a world gone mad. In the dark young boys now in a warrior's world, Reflecting on their lives. What they'd left behind and for what? And where were they going? Would they return? Would they share the embrace and warmth of loved ones again?

Throughout the night bodies tossed and turned. Restless unable to obtain the comfort of sleep. Hearts pounding, they groped in the dark seeking answers to questions they could not ask. Men whispered in the night seeking to gain strength and courage from their buddies. Crunch time was once again at their doorstep and they realized all they had at this moment was each other. Yes, they felt confident, somewhat cocky but each in his own way felt that tinge of fear in their souls. Fear of the unknown, perhaps perishing in a hostile foreign land or whether they would ever again look into the eyes of loved ones. All had knots in their stomachs. Deployment was a warning chime to a warrior. They'd been trained and driven hard, so in their young trusting hearts knew they were headed to a hot spot somewhere on this God's earth. Most prayed and sought peace in the quiet and solitude of the night. Some shed quiet tears, only those who have experienced the fear of the unknown can accept this. But it is there embedded in the deep recesses of a warriors soul. That one horrendous thought, where ever he was going. Would he return, would he be whole and as he was or would his soul and body lie bleaching in the sun of some unfriendly land?

Reveille sounded at 05:30. The men bolted out of racks and headed to the head where they shaved and performed their morning constitution. Then marched to morning chow. Gunny Burke in his deep raspy voice calling Marine cadence as they returned to quarters. "Okay girls!" Bellowed Burke. "Get your gear in order. Make damn sure your weapons are clean and in working order. Your young shiny asses may damn well depend on them. Formation at 14:00 hours. Full packs and weapons at the ready. Don't fret about ammo. It will be dispensed to you at the right time. Those who wish get your letters to the clerk's office to be mailed home. All your personal gear will be stowed in the battalion's storage shed. Now we go earn our pay. You've been trained well and if you paid attention and digested what you've been instructed should fare well. Look to your buddies, all we have from this moment on is guts, honor, integrity and each other. Watch your backs and depend on your Brother Marines. I'll say this only once, wherever we're going good luck and Semper-Fi. You've four hours to relax. Dismissed!"

1400 hours, The battalion stood tall and proud in battle formation. Colonel Striker stood to the front enthralled with the appearance of his troops. He was momentarily distracted as Colonel Von Meer; the Regimental Commander was seen marching towards him in the lead of two sister companies. As they approached both companies broke off and took position to the left of the 8th Marines on a line with the battalion. Von Meer approached Striker and exchanged salutes. Von Meer in a hoarse voice, "Striker, I've added Echo Company from the 5th Marines and Helo Company from the 4th to your command. You now have a reinforced battalion. This should and will add strength and fire power and hopefully assist in destroying those goats in their lair. Do you need anything more from me or the division?" Striker eyed the two new companies, "No sir, I thank you for the additional support. Are they up to my standards, sir?" "Yes Colonel or they wouldn't be here. Well Striker it's time. I wish you God speed and a successful expedition and safe return." "Thank you, sir." Striker saluted smartly, turned faced his command. Columns of young hardened faces stared straight ahead. Striker bellowed, "battalion left face!"

As thunder the battalion's boots exploded on asphalt as the battalion executed the command, "battalion forward march!" The thump, thump of 1400 pairs of boots echoed across the base and the soft wind carrying the soft whispers of marching boots throughout Camp Lejeune. Most of the base had stood silent as spectators watching their brother battalion march towards idling truck transports. The 8th Marines guide arm and colors flapping in the breeze marched brisk and sharp toward waiting transport vehicles. Cries of "Semper Fi" and kick ass rocked the base as thousands of brother Marines applauded and screamed encouragement to the deployed battalion. The 8th Marines embarked into the huge vehicles as the base band struck up the Marine Hymn. Then with a roar and a cloud of black diesel fuel, the battalion departed to its unknown destiny. A Chaplin stood saluting and uttered softly, "May the hand of God lay on your shoulder and return you safely to home and loved ones." The base stood silent as Marines watched the convoy disappear. They skittered away quietly and some in despair and some ecstatic that they were not in the hot seat. But as one, all worried and prayed the 8th Marines would suffer little and affect a great victory.

At 1600 hours sharp four behemoth aircraft lumbered down the runway at Cherry Point. Manned by skillful pilots who's experience showed there was little or no room for error on takeoff from such a short runway. The huge craft roaring in the night lifted into the starlet sky carrying the reinforced 8th Marines to a destination yet unknown to them. The grunts settled in knowing they'd get the word on their objective in due course. Men whispered in the reddish hue within the interior of their aircraft. Below America slept unaware that once again husbands, sons, brothers, sweet hearts were being ferried to an unknown objective going in harm's way to preserve, protect and secure freedom for an oppressed people. The red, white, and blue of Old Glory, stars glittering would lead the way. Unfurled in the wind of a strange land, she would rally her young warriors to support and protect those who clambered and stood for freedom.

LeBron sat in the eerie glow of the planes interior gossiping with his buds. "You know I don't understand people mostly broads." "Why, Jake?" queried LeSage. "Well shit, when I was home on leave me and one of my close bro's met this honey of a creature, a real yum, yum. So we ply the bitch with drink and some green tobacco, white teeth gleaming in the dark, you could tell he was smiling. So we rent this cheap hotel room planning to pork this prime meat all night long. I'd been drinking weird shit all day and ate some sick chicken. Maybe it was pigeon for all I know. It really sucked. Anyway we rented the room and Wing Ding, that's my bro, and I flip a coin to see who goes first. Well luck was with ole Jake and I get heads. I guide the bitch up the stairs to room 3B cause she's stone fucked up. I got a hard on the size of a healthy ass cucumber and can't wait to get into the chicks ass. As we enter the room. My stomach is doing flip flops and I mean there was rumbling tumbling. I'm passing silent gas like a leaking gas tank but trying like hell to camouflage the stink and the passing of wind. The broad gets bare ass on the bed tits like large onions. A fantastic bush garden and I'm as horny as a lonely bull isolated in a pent up stall. I rip off my clothes and jump on her bones and begin playing with those you yum tits and ram my shaft into her cunt. As I begin pumping away, I feel this explosion occurring in the bowels of my gut. Ignore it thinking it's only a large trapped fart. But oh no suddenly a swishing sound like the wind in a tunnel emits from my asshole. A geyser of brownish fluid gushes high in the air. God damn it hit the ceiling then this same brown wet sickening shit with a stench like the devil in heat rains down on me and the yum, yum chick. Shit was everywhere, on the wall, ceiling, and drops rolled down her cheeks. It ran like rivulets down my back side. The sheet and pillow no longer white but now a deep brownish tint. The chick looks at me in astonishment, says nothing, gets out from beneath me and sprints for the shower gagging. I follow suit when she finished. When I came out the yum, yum is long gone. I head down the stairs and Wing Ding is waiting, horny as the devil himself, with a big grin on his face. "Ah finally my turn and it's about time." "Before I can speak he flies up the stairs two at a time. He's after some ass. He storms into the room and seconds later he's at the top of the stairs screaming and cursing ol Jake." "What the fuck happened? What the hell did you do? Where's the chick? You fuck! The room looks and stinks like a condemned outhouse. You're an asshole, and a fucking moron." "I say nothing; Wing Ding flips me the bird and storms out of the flea bag hotel. I'm devastated, I stink like shit and my hard on is gone and the yum, yum disappeared into the night and Wind Ding and I have obviously parted ways. Anyhow, two days later I call the bitch and you know to apologize, but she's an unforgiving cunt and hangs up. I try to explain to Wing Ding before my leave expired but he wouldn't talk to me. Fucker's, I don't understand people, no compassion." Broken Rose, LaPore and LeSage laughing hysterically uttered as one, "No shit Jake, I wonder why. You get the trophy as the biggest fuck up of the month." Jake sat back in deep thought unable to comprehend an unforgiving world.

The huge birds rode the winds, powerful engines discharging contrails in their wake. The hum of the motors and props lulled most of the grunts into a semblance of sleep. bullshiting had ceased and eyes closed lost in their own private thoughts. Warriors always psych themselves like a prize fighter and those young Marines were in that mode. It's unnerving to have little or no knowledge of where you're going or why or who but the Corps whose backbone is discipline and grunts would react and follow orders without question. The sun was just rousing from its slumber as the big birds began their descent. Once more the experience of the pilots displayed itself as they were professional and there was no margin for error in landing on the short runways of Pendleton. One by one the huge craft bumped and thumped on their meeting with asphalt. The roar of engines in reverse and the familiar smell of brakes applied roused the sleeping grunts. Slowly the aircraft approached their assigned area. And suddenly all was quiet. The engines shut down.

The 8th Marines had landed and ordered into formation. They marched ¾ of a mile to a snake like convoy waiting in the distance. By platoons they embarked into the rear of the waiting transport

317

vehicles. Officers and noncoms shouting orders, they were intent on control and purpose.

The long convoy roared into the early morning sun, then screeched to a halt in front of a large mess hall. Their cooks had been waiting and preparing a meal of spam, fried potatoes, corn, and thick bread and as always the perennial tart hot coffee. The men ate in quiet solitude. Oh soft monotones of conversation could be heard but mostly from the officers and senior noncoms section, busy discussing their upcoming assignment. The men were once again formed into a tight formation, and then reordered to enter the waiting transports operated by impatient drivers. The command go and the huge convoy roared off speeding through the main gate and hit the highway and pointed its way to San Diego some miles away. The ride was spent in small talk or gazing at the sights of the California landscape. There were eastern boys and most if any had never traversed the countryside of the western half of their great nation.

Within two hours the convoy slowed as they crawled through the gates of San Diego. The vehicles negotiated a turn here, a turn there and soon the docks stood before them. The troops were ordered out of the trucks and the Marines in disciplined formation gazed at their sea going transports. Two shiny transports stood waiting, The USS Integrity and USS Courageous, with their gun whales clean and sparkling, lay at anchor already supplies were being leaded into the bowels of the ships by sweating stevedores. Sailors on the decks busy with various tasks, took a moment to stare at the formidable aray of battle ready Marines. Striker strode up the gangway, saluting the ensign and officer of the day, handed over his orders and stated, "Captain my Marines are in your hands and ready to embark." The captain smiled, "Very good Colonel, embark your troops. We're set to sail in approximately forty five minutes. All your logistics are already loaded." "Yes sir, Thank you sir." Striker turned and waved to his Exec Major Pezzone who saluted, turned smartly. "Okay Marines embark on the ships, Companies, Alfa, Bravo, Charlie, Delta to the Integrity and Companies, Helo, and Echo and supporting weapons crews to the Courageous. Move out at route step."

The long line of grunts moved steadily up the gangway. They were being directed below into the holds of the ships. LeBron uttered, "To no one in particular, "move over rats The Corps is here." Men chose their shanty spaces. Once again living conditions would be tight. Once again the NCO's would enforce discipline and hygiene. This was not new to the 8th Marines. They knew the drill. At 1900 hours, bells sounded. The ships shuddered and quivered and as their engines sprang to life. Slowly the two transports departed the docks and added speed which kicked up wakes as they passed. As the Integrity and Courageous exited the port heading to open sea, waiting were a heavy cruiser and two destroyers, their escort to destiny.

The small armada plowed on through the blue Pacific waters. The grunts kept busy and in shape with daily calisthenics and repetition with the manual of arms. NCO's kept a watchful eye below decks as such close quarters could develop into heated exchanges and Colonel Striker was adamant that strict discipline be maintained at all times. They were three days at sea and land birds had long disappeared and still the troops had not been given the word. Sailors went about their duties bemused by the constant training Marines performed on deck. The sea was calm and a soft clean breeze filtered through the open hatches allowing the holds to store fresh air thus keeping the grunts below with some semblance of comfort.

"Colonel Striker" a young ensign approached quietly as he was studying a map of The Philippines with his Company Commanders. "Yes ensign. What's up?" "Sir the ship's captain requests your presence in his quarters A.S.A.P." "Very good ensign, thank you. I'll be there directly."

Striker knocked twice on the captain's hatch. "Come," was the loud response. Striker entered quickly, "Good morning Captain." "Good morning Colonel. Have a seat. The smoking lamp is lit if you like." The captain was old school and stood 6 ft. with broad shoulders and his face a golden hue with lines from years at sea. Behind his desk hung a large wall map of the orient and circled in red marking, was the area of Indochina now called Vietnam.

"Colonel, I've received new orders from Washington. Your assignment has changed drastically in the last four hours. Your unit is canceled out from The Philippines. You've been ordered to the shores of Vietnam, formally Indochina. A Special Forces camp within the interior has been on the receiving end of mortar attacks and reported a huge buildup of NVA troops to their front. Their Commander, a Major Hecker, reports he has twenty five troops and if attacked will be flanked and overrun. It's his deep belief that an attack is imminent. Your unit has been designated to enter by landing craft, at Vinh and force march at the quick to DeLong where the special camp is operating, maybe 50 miles inland. The carrier Independence battle group will be joining us within hours. I know this throws a wrench in your previous plan but you Marines are known to adapt and overcome. I'll do everything in my power to ensure your battle group has back up at its disposal, any questions?"

Striker lit up a Lucky. "Indochina, shit that's where the French got their asses kicked." "You're right on Colonel. Hopefully you can get in quickly, rescue those GI's and get the hell out without a fight." Striker grunted, "that's a dream world Captain. My gut tells me they'll be a hell of a fight." "Oh Hell, that's why Uncle Sam pays us. Striker keep in mind that the battleship New Jersey is among that battle group and her guns can give you plenty of support, within twenty miles. Your orders are to spearhead a quick drive to DeLong. Discretion is the better part of valor is how the orders end. But you have command and authorized to react to the situation as you determine best of luck, Colonel. I've order our armada to change course. We'll meet up with the battle group approximately 150 nautical miles from here. Your troops will be landing on Vinh's Beaches in about three days. I've been authorized to inform you that your unit was chosen. One because of its intense training and two its discipline and three because we're the closet that can possibly avoid a tragic confrontation. Good luck Colonel. I know you've lots of work to do with your Commanders. Dismissed and please feel free to contact me should you feel the need for further information or any assistance we can deliver or offer." "Thank you Captain."

Striker rose from his seat and quickly exited through the hatch. He beckoned to his Exec Major Pezzone. "Yes sir," uttered Pezzone as he responded. "Frank, have all Company Commanders and Senior Noncoms assemble in the mess a 1400 hours." "What' up, Eric?" "A change in venue looks bad. I can feel a fight in my gut. I'll explain further at the briefing. Make God damn sure those people are punctual and on time." "Aye, aye, sir, consider it done."

Signal lamps now blinked from ship to ship and the great ships revved up their engines and were able to push the groaning craft to 40 knots. Time was of the essence. American Soldiers were in a periless situation and the small armada drove hard to connect with the 7th fleet and land the Marines, hopefully in time. The ships plowed ahead and large wakes left to their rear. In the holds, the grunts felt the vibrations and knew they had gained speed. Belted in their racks, they lay staring at anything. Minds full of wonder as to what the Hell was happening.

In the mess, Striker briefed his Company Commanders. A map of Vietnam laid spread on a mess table. The officers took turns studying its contours, rivers, mountain ranges etc., etc. They knew they were to land on the beaches of Vinh and decided dawn would be the perfect setting. Striker gazed at Lieutenant Sisco, Bravo Companies skipper. "I'll want eyes out there, Lieutenant. So here's the scoop. You'll put Tonto and his Indian Friends out front. Way out front of recon. They can communicate with them and they'll pass the word along to me. I want no surprises. Delta Company you'll be responsible in protecting our flanks in platoon. This will be our strength when we hit the beach we move and move quick and fast. Get our troops into the brush before roving eyes can observe. Then we spearhead into DeLong. We'll try to avoid any confrontation. Our job is to get those troopers to hell out of there. Some of you are thinking will there be a fight. God damn right there will. Those fuckers are unfriendlies and we're unwelcomed quests. Make sure your troops have plenty of ammo and water and rations for three days. Bravo Company will be in the lead. Echo Company will trail in the rear of the main body keeping 500 yards apart thus ensuring we don't get hit from behind. He locked eyes with his officers. "You all are well aware that chances of getting into the shitter are probable so keep your discipline and remember firepower will be the deciding factor. At this point we have little info as to how large a force is out there. Only that the green berets have radioed it's a large buildup. We'll leave it to Tonto and his Indian Brothers to inform us as to what's really out there. Those fucks are mystical and I am most confident they will ascertain what or how many hostiles we may or may not face. You Senior Noncoms make certain squad leaders and fire teams are set and ready to go. This is no waltz in the park. My gut tells me this unit is headed into one hell of a fight. You officers meet with your troops and spread the word. Pay day is upon us. We've trained long and hard. Now let's hope it pays dividends. Also make damn sure our Corpsmen have ample supplies. Check all radios and be certain they're in working order. I will be in the lead with Bravo Company. Major Pezzone, you will command Delta for obvious reasons. Should I get hit the command is yours. Okay, your good officers now it's time to lead and I mean by example."

At 0200, the transports found the 7th fleet. The ships were two on a line and the huge flettala drove toward the beach of Vinh. As the sun peeked over the treetops, the white sandy beach came into view. The loud speakers in the holds blared, "All Marines report to your debarkation stations!" The Marines galloped up and out of the hatches and clambered over the sides and slowly but surely descended the nets to the bobbing landing craft below. Within 40 minutes 1400 Marines were in landing craft. With the sting of water spray hitting their eyes as they headed in land. Operation rescue of our own had commenced. In the semi darkness green clad. Marines stormed onto the beach and set up quick defensive perimeters and then the faith full command was bellowed by Colonel Striker. "8th MARINES ASSUME YOUR ASSIGNED POSITIONS AND MOVE OUT!!!"

They spread out in company formation. Platoons were in a column with Lieutenant Connoles for they would be leading the way with 10 to 15 yards between each man. Good dispersion and good coverage plodded through the country side under a blazing sun in a cloudless sky. Long low ridge lines covered with vegetation gave way to grass covered knolls interspersed with expanses of lush green rice paddy.

The heat was stifling. The heat intensified and so did fatigue. Slowly they moved along the tree line angling north and west. Further and further into the heart of this unknown province a remote zone, farther and farther from help.

The battalion halted and reconnaissance had found a good bivouac which was easily defensible. The warriors dug in and grabbed some chow. Night set in and the night passed quiet and uneventful. Roused at dawn, the grunts limited themselves to C ration delicacies then the order of move out passed down the line. Fifteen minutes into the stifling heat of the march, Bravo Company reported that they'd made contact with the objective. The battalion was ordered to surround it. Lay down recon and be advised came the directive form the Co. All males are considered suspect. 1st platoon led the way moving slowly forward on a line. They passed two deserted hamlets as they entered the Special Forces camp. They were edgy. It was to quiet. Smoke and several fires raged within the camp. As they came around the outside of a hooch Lieutenant Connole with a raised hand, halted his platoon. Before them was a glimpse into Dante's Inferno. American soldiers lay in various grotesque positions within their defensive perimeter. The platoon gaped in horror. Hundreds of dead NVA lie intermingled with American dead. There were no Special Forces survivors. They died where they stood. Retreat was not in their manual.

Suddenly the air exploded with the pop, pop, pop of incoming fire rounds of machine guns. Whacked the dirt and stumps where Marines dove for cover. "Shit!" exclaimed Connole we should have known the bastards were there. How stupid can you be? There could be hundreds, maybe more. Larry Burns crouched by the radio informing battalion in an excited voice. That they'd taken fire and relayed the situation as to what the platoon had stumbled into. Marines were returning fire and as suddenly as it had started firing came to an abrupt halt. Luckily, no one had been hit. On command the battalion formed up and swept out of the tree line into the adjoining village advancing unopposed through the carnage and devastation brought about in the Special Forces last stand. Marines stepped in and around and on bodies. The ground littered with dead. On inspection it was noted that all 25 Special Forces had defended their camp to a man. The NVA had paid dearly. 450 enemy dead were counted and blood trails leading into the tree line hinted there were more. The real victims of the NVA's savage assault had been helpless unarmed civilians, for three bodies of two women and one man lie twisted and lifeless under the side of a smoldering hooch. Other villagers were wandering around dazed. Mumbling incoherently and in shock and all were crying.

Captain Hopkins, the Company K Commander, hooked up with Lieutenant Connole. "What a bloody mess, what a stinking God awful bloody fucking mess, the fucks kill even their own." "Yeah," Captain whispered Connole, "but why did they stay?" "Shit Lieutenant, the attack came too sudden on the Forces camp. It makes no sense. These guys were here for humanitarian purposes and attempting to render medical assistance mostly. Jesus H Christ, damn good soldiers. Gone to a man and for what? Now the shit's really going to hit the fan." Corpsmen were busy checking bodies and ministering to civilians, mostly children.

Private First Class John Ritter, Captain Hopkins radio operator, approached on the run. "Sir, Colonel Striker is on the horn." "Yes sir," Hopkins spoke hoarsely. "Captain form a burial detail to work on those dead troopers. Post haste. Then get your company back here upon the knoll. Form up with the rest of the battalion. The order of the day just came from the top pursue and destroy."

Striker approached Lieutenant Sisco, "How the hell come we didn't hear from Broken Rose?" "Sir, he'd notified recon that he and his buds have continued on. They are observing enemy forces as we speak. States he'll return shortly to fill you in on what we're up against. His last words tell Colonel Striker, many, many NVA like sand in a wind storm. Reported they are regrouping in large strength.

The Marines respectfully and anguished rendered a military burial to the twenty five dead Special Forces. Wrapped in blankets they were gingerly placed in a large common grave which was well marked to be exploited at a later date. ID tags were strung and handed over to Colonel Striker who in tuned placed them in the outstretched hands of his Sergeant Major for safe keeping. Then Striker walked the perimeter his trained eyes inhaling every detail of the battle field and landscape. He had his company's dig and dig deep, creating a formidable defensive perimeter. His right flank had natural protection from a cliff which nosed into the sky. But just in case, he had a squad scale the cliff side and placed a 50 caliber to discourage hostiles in attempts to scale from the other side. He ordered his fire team to embrace the interlocking fire mode and had mortars placed in strategic positions. His corpsmen were kept busy treating wounded civilians. But he reminded Doc Little on several occasions to go easy with what medical supplies were available. He stood on a knoll overlooking his position. It stretched long and in a horseshoe. His concern was to prevent the enemy from flanking the extreme end of the horseshoe. That area he peppered with mines and antipersonnel weaponry and bouncing Bettys. He directed several mortars to zero in on the area that would be their direct responsibility.

He roved the lines, suggesting gun emplacements and fields of fire. He was in a quandary for he really had no concrete info as to how large or aggressive an opponent he was facing. He ordered several patrols to reconnoiter the bush that surrounded his position. He directed fires be used to burn and limit the use of tall elephant grass which threatened close to his line. Several patrols reported discovering additional dead NVA but no wounded that could be interrogated. He turned to Lieutenant Sisco. "I want recon out there deep Lieutenant. God damn it, we've got to know what's gonna hit us. The brass commands at sea have ordered that we pursue. But I'm not rushing into a repeat of Custer." "Colonel, Broken Rose and his Indians are on it, sir. Moments ago they radioed in they're in sight of the enemy. Reporting a very large well-armed opponent, he states they've I.D. at least three separate regiments and suspect a fourth lies somewhere to the rear." "Eric looks like we're tackling a division, not good boss, not good." Pezzone stood to his Colonel's left. "Well Eric, what are you orders?" Striker snorted, "Orders? Hell, we hold right here till I know for fucking sure what's ahead of us. The patrols in our rear report all is clear. So for now our escape route back is secure. I've notified the fleet of the demise of the Special Forces and that we came under sporadic fire. They're probably playing with their balls wondering where this is going to take us. The entire perimeter has anti personal mines strung 300 yards to their front. If we get hit tonight, we'll God damn know it but those fuckers will suffer. Captain Hopkins make damn certain we have ample flares. You Company Commanders check and recheck your positions. I want no gaps and keep the troops down. I want little movement. I'm sure we're under observation and any doubts or confusion we can lay on the fucks is a plus for us. They're unsure at this time as to our strength. Best you believe they're be some probing come dark. Expect it and prepare for it. Lieutenant Sisco order Broker Rose back. I need that information and quick. I know the brass is skeptical but well, we're old pros and we'll shove that skeptical shit up their asses and it won't be long in coming."

Fifty miles east the 7th fleet steamed slowly back and forth in the flag ship aboard the New Jersey. Major General Tom Waller had listened and dissected Striker's latest radio message. His dark eyes studied the map and then analyzed every bit of the radio communication. He rose and approached Admiral Ted Tedone. He advised him as to what appeared to be a major enemy element obstructing his thin line of Marines. The admiral requested and was given the coordinates of the Marine position. The Admiral picked up the phone and rang the bridge asked for and was immediately putt in communication with the ship's Captain. "Captain signals the fleet to form in a line. "Have them elevate their guns to these coordinates. Have the carrier place their corsairs in the ready mode. I won't let those Marines be slaughtered."

In the ready room pilots were advised over the loud speaker, "B-1, stand by." The fleet displayed a formidable armada and it deployed on line. The New Jersey, her huge super structure towering into the semi-darkness turned her large guns inland with the churning of the turrets rumbling across the open water, the Navy was ready and prepared to unleash Hell. While the Nay was flexing its muscles, the Marines had instilled order in the abused camp. Civilians along with their wounded were dispatched to the rear escorted by a squad from Helo Company with orders to quick back to their command. Striker continued to prowl the perimeter with his trained eye denoting and correcting the holes in the perimeter. The grunts manned their positions in quiet solitude with their eyes scanning the bush that surrounded their horse shoe perimeter. Trip wire and flares were placed in strategic locations. Small patrols darted in and around the camp. They were Striker's eyes to avoid any uninvited surprises. He'd grown impatient waiting for Broken Rose to report in. I gnawed at his gut that in all probability, he was facing an entire NVA Division. He needed confirmation and quick. Returning to his knoll he scanned his defenses and was satisfied he and his officers had erected a formidable defense. His only concern that of the open end of the horseshoe. But he had that well marked with mortars and a 50 caliber. It was imperative the opening be kept secure. It was their only escape route should retreat become paramount.

The enemy was within five miles of his command and at last radio contact were staging in heavy strength between a small mountain and heavy brush in line with the center of his defensive perimeter. He dispatched a listening post 1000 yards to his front. Corporal L LeSage and Private First Class L. LaPore were ordered to this assignment and entering thick bush surrounded by elephant grass. They dug a deep hole and placed fallen logs to their front and flanks and as the sun slowly descended, they lay in their hole at the ready. Their radio cradled between them kept at low pitch. Night birds screeched and squawked adding to their nervousness. Slowly light faded and a grunts fear of the dark settled about them. They dared not smoke or even talk and continued straining their hearing for any warning signs. They breathed deeply in hopes they could inhale the smell of the rice and fish NVA soldiers were known to carry in pouches. They were alone and on their own sweat soaked their utilities. Bowels churned with fear. The two buds knew there were many bad guys to their front and that they could easily be flanked and they were a thousand yards from their own lines. It might as well have been a million. Both prayed peered into the dark and listened, listened to sounds in the night. LeSage nudged LaPore whispered, "you hear that?" Both strained to hear in the pitch darkness. There was no mistaken the sound of snap twigs or the soft crunch of feet meeting the ground. They'd set up three claymores 30 yards from their hole. LaPore activated the mines which exploded in a fury cries of anguish and pain like a horrific musical chorus washed over them. Enemy soldiers had been blown to mush and their wounded twisted and rolled on the ground in agony. LeSage grabbed the radio whispered, "Red fox to lair. Red Fox to lair," no response. "Shit Lance the batteries dead. God damn it! Lee squabble your butt out of here and get one quick." "You'll be okay?" "Who the fuck knows, we know they're out there. Just go and bring back the Calvary."

LeSage pushed out of the hole and had crawled maybe 15 yards when the explosion lifted him inches from the ground. Debris and dirt rained down over him. With his ears ringing, he turned and where his hole had been small fires danced around ignited by dry grass. Smoke wisped from the interior. LeSage heart pounding with fear for his friend. He crawled back to the smoking hole where he peered in and there was LaPore. His body twisted and quivering. His right leg lay at the top of the hole. His left leg severed at the knee and lay somewhere beneath his torso. His right arm, hung by a thread and where his manhood once stood there was only a bleeding gaping wound. LeSage slid into the hole. LaPore was gasping for breath and groaning in pain. Smoke wafted from his utilities. His eyes wide in shock and he gazed into LeSage's eyes. "Lee, I am in agony and I'm a goner anyway so finish it and get the hell out of here. "No Lance! I'll bring you out!" "Don't be an asshole. I don't want to go back to the world like this. Won't make it 10 yards anyway. Ease my pain if your my friend do it." LeSage, tears rolling down his checks saw the large piece of shrapnel protruding from LaPore's chest. "Please Lee I can't stand the pain. Be a fucking man and a fucking Marine! DO IT!" LeSage without a word slammed the metal projectile with his palm. The force driving the object deep into LaPore's chest. It's pierced his heart. LaPore gasped and took one breath then fell back in total silence. His pain ceased and he died in the midst of blood gore and horror. LeSage wept unashamedly; suddenly a strong hand had him by the collar pulling him out of the hole. It was Gunny Burke. "That was a tough brave thing to do for there was no option. Let's go LeSage. They're all round us." "Go where Gunny?" "We'll be going to Hell if we don't get back to the MLR. Now move it!" "But he was my pal, we just can't leave him." "That's just what we're going to do. He' gone and he belongs to the ages. Move your ass and I mean pronto!" With a last glimpse at his friend, LeSage and the Gunny sprinted into the night. LaPore's last words forever branded in LeSage's Heart. "Tell Jeanne, I love her."

The night lit up like a Christmas Tree as flares whooshed into the sky. Their eerie red and green hue lighting a scene from Hell. NVA soldiers charged head long belting into the string of claymores when activated blew bodies parts in all directions. Men were decapitated, torso's torn in half, legs and arms flew and tumbled through the air. The scream and cries of anguish competing with the sounds of Hell. 75 NVA soldiers were instantly eliminated. The devastation inflicted on the probing force quickly demoralized them. The night went quiet there were no more probing attempts only the smell of cordite along with the moans of the dying and the sweet syrupy smell of blood, shit, and urine pierced the stillness. Marines lay in their defenses anticipating a stronger attack that never came. As the sun rose and lit the field, dead NVA were observed in groups. Limbs hung from trees and heads rolled along the ground fueled by the morning's soft wind. The field was littered with helmets, weapons and viscera. It was a sight young Marines would carry with them forever.

In the meanwhile Gunny Burke and LeSage had approached the MLR. A young deep voice challenged, "Halt who goes there?" "Gunny Burke and a maggot." "Advance and be recognized and give the password." "Always." "The retort faithful was returned." Burke's huge bulk stepped through the brush followed by LeSage. Burke slapped the Marines helmet, "Good job! Shit for brains. If you hadn't done that I'd would of tied your balls in your asshole." As the two blackened Marines entered the perimeter, Burke stopped short and grabbed LeSage's arm. "Look kid, what you did took guts. You saved your buddy hours of agony. He would have never made it out of there. You know that. Fuck for sure it'll be stamped on your soul for the rest of your fucked up life. You'll have to reach down into yourself and adapt and overcome. There's your other pal LeBron, get by his side and vomit all that shit your carrying inside. You have my respect kid, good luck."

The sun rose quickly hordes of flies hovered around and on the dead NVA. Already the repulsive stench of dead carcasses filled the air. The Marines waited and kept watch knowing this was not over. Burke sprinted to Striker's C.P. and filled him in on the early explosion which had placed the MLR on full alert. "Shit, that's tough on those kids," muttered Striker, "but fuck we're in a fight and shit happens. Gunny, where the fuck is Tonto and his tribe? Now I'm worried, maybe the fucks got em!" Burke smiled, "no way Colonel there, they're coming now." Striker turned half right and there walking shirtless and barefoot came Broken Rose and Charlie White Cloud. They approached their commander nonchalantly with smirks adorning their faces. "Well Happy New Year!" exclaimed Striker. "Where the fuck, have you been?" "Nice to see you Colonel, good morning, been on an adventure skipper. Lot's going on out there." "Well, how about sharing those goings-on with me." "Yes sir." Striker sat on an ammo box and Burke remained standing. The two Indians sat in the squat position. "Colonel we've definitely identified four separate regiments headed this way. They have ample mortars and it appeared an artillery battalion was marching several miles in the rear of the main body. They're not running Colonel; they've regrouped and are on the way here. They've scrimmaged leading the way out front." Striker gazed off into the distance. How many you estimate Tonto?" Broken Rose dug both hands into the ground and lifted mounds of grainy sand. Letting it slide slowly to the ground, "this many. Sir you've got to turn us around or in due course hey will out flank us and overrun us with shear manpower." Striker lit a Lucky and exhaled loudly. "Fuck, we're in the shit for sure. How much time before they're main body arrives?" "Well sir, there's a good size force setting up to hit you sometime today. That's to test your strength and defenses. The main elements are about 10 miles back and could be here tonight if they move well. Oh and Colonel, they had four Russian Officer Advisors in their midst." "What'd you mean had?" Broken Rose threw a damp smelly pouch on the ground and tilted it upside down where four ears and four metal ID tags tumbled onto the ground. Burke fingered an ear. "Good cut job Tonto." Striker unamused fingered the ID's gazing at Russian names, three Lieutenant Colonels and a Major. Striker locked eyes with the

Rose. "How the fuck did you take these guys out?" The Rose laughed, "Piece of cake, sir. Lot's of elephant grass encircled their camp and years ago sister snake taught the Rose and his brother White Cloud how to slither quietly through such vegetation."

Gunny Burke chortled, "what about guards?" "Oh Gunny, no offense, they give off stink worse than the white eyes. Their fish and rice and garlic carry on the wind. We just let them pass and found the officers quarter and waited till the moon slipped behind the clouds. These officers were fast asleep with vodka, so without resistance the event took place, sir." Striker smiled, "good job Staff Sergeant, now get some hot chow and rest while you can." Turning to Burke, "Gunny, have all Company Commanders and Senior Noncoms report here in one hour. Inform them if we get hit before that time to belay the order till they hear from me." "Aye, sir, got a plan Colonel?" "Hope so Gunny, otherwise we're all be dispatched to Hell."

Lady luck smiled on Striker, all was quiet. His officers and Senior Noncoms sat in a semi-circle. "Okay here's the scoop. We're gonna get hit anytime soon by a strong probing force. I'm not going to waste time. There is an itinerary. All I am going to tell you there is a full division is at this moment marching to have our heads. We'll have to stand fast for the moment and beat off the coming attack. Once that's accomplished we will then begin to play leap frog with the fucks. Gunny Burke is handing you slips of paper with marked coordinates. Make fucking sure you don't lose them. If you're hit or in danger of being overrun eat them, understood?" "Yes sir, came the response." Okay on our route step bringing us to this Hell hole we passed a medium size mountain about 35 miles to our rear. That would place us in a position where the New Jersey's fire power could help save our asses. In order to reach that mountain, where we will dig in, we've got to slow the gooks advances and can't and must not, let them flank us. On your paper you see the coordinates with the company to be assigned to each area. In other words Bravo Company will remain here for half an hour pinning down and slowing their momentum. Then Bravo will disengage and bypass the next coordinate where Delta will be positioned. Now it's Delta's turn to hold back the Hun. Again after a half hour of fighting, Delta will pell mell through the next coordinates where Charlie Company will satisfy its lust for blood. You've got the picture? We'll continue this maneuver till we reach the mountain. I've already contacted fleet command and they are dispatching corsairs to snipe and harass the enemy columns. Once we set up defenses on the mountain, the New Jersey will fill the airways with tons of metal. And air power will hit them with napalm and anything else they have in their lunch pail. Now be it understood, you can't fuck up on the leap frogging maneuvers. You must hold at each position at least one half hour thus ensuring the other companies have ample time to set up their positions to cover those units scurrying rearward it's our only chance. We can't out run them and we can't let them flank us or we're dead meat. Oh and I don't want to hear from a Company Commander that he can't hold. You've got to stand fast and I don't care if Hell unleashes its legions or you. You hold or you die it's that simple, any questions?"

The Company Commanders had listened attentively digesting every word from their CO. They had complete confidence in his decision and knew he was right on. As they stalked off returning to their companies, each knew in his heart, chances were high they'd never embrace loved ones or see home again.

Striker sat in his command post on the knoll flanked on either side of him was Gunny Burke and Major Pezzone. Suddenly Striker laughed softly. You know what the Rose and his bud did and had to fuck up their command structures heads. They'll probably going ape shit wondering how the fuck such an operation could unfold amidst thousands of their troops, quite an accomplishment, one for the text books.

All three, as well as the Marines, on the line watched the tree line intently. A soft breeze had leaves dancing in the tree tops. They knew the NVA was near for birds had swarmed into the sky. Ground creatures scurried here and there as though to give way to an oncoming adversary. Suddenly whistles began blowing. There was yelling and screaming as green clad NVA troops burst from the tree line. They came on a line three deep with bayonets fixed they advanced slowly. Then began to trot all the while screaming attempting to psych themselves and intimidate the Marines. Their trot escalated into a hard charge. "Must be four to five hundred," muttered Burke. The Marines held their fire waiting patiently each sighting down on his personal target of choice. Within 200 yards, Striker gave the anticipated command. "Commence fire! Commence Firing!"

The line exploded with the roar of 1400 weapons. 50 Caliber's chattered, their brother the 30 caliber joined in the orchestrated heat of awesome devastating fire. The NVA soldiers crumbled in droves. Rifles flung into the air as they fell. Screams off horror and the guttural sounds of dying men filled the air. Smoke and cordite caused men's eyes to tear and cough. Tracers pointed the way. NVA wounded tried to crawl back to the tree line and were cut down by continuous and merciless fire power. The field was obscured by smoke. Some NVA soldiers had returned fire. But fear and the apparition of so many comrades flailing and fallen detracted them from their aim. After an intense twenty minutes of pouring lead and steel into the advancing NVA attackers, Striker ordered, "Cease fire! Cease Fire!" As the smoke drifted off, the Marines gaped in horror. In the field before them lay the bodies of dead or dying NVA soldiers. Hundreds of green clad bodies lay strewn in grotesque positions. The attackers had been decimated and only several survivors were observed running into the tree line. Reports from the Marine line informed Striker C.P. that fourteen Marines had been hit and eight K.I.A. and six wounded three critically. Striker accepted the report quietly and then turned to Pezzone. "Okay now they know our position and approximate strength. Those poor slobs were sacrificed so they could hone in on us with mortars and eventually artillery. It's time to start the game of leap frog. Signal the Company Commanders to get the troops moving. Do it with discipline and smartly. Let's get it done. They'll hit us next with artillery. We've some time. Their artillery battalion hasn't arrived as yet, but I'm sure we're feel the sting of mortars real soon."

Striker had coordinated with fleet command to dispatch corsairs at precisely 1200 hours and on the dot the drone of the engines roared overhead at treetop level. Six corsairs had come in low strafing the tree line and beyond. Four more followed suit but laid down canisters of Napalm. The jungle exploded in huge jellied fire balls. NVA troops could be heard screaming. Bodies danced out of the tree line in flames, charred and twisted. Some broke in half falling to the ground while others knelt charred never to move again. The corsairs were like bees stinging and stinging again. The attack was coordinated with the intent of keeping the NVA down masking the movement of the Marines from the camp. Bravo CO stood alone spacing men 4 feet apart giving the appearance that a formidable foe laid before the advancing NVA, now cowering in stream beds and deep holes to avoid the lead of bullets and fire bombing. Their casualties were heavy as they'd been caught in the open. The advance came to an abrupt halt still the corsairs like gnats continued to effect successful strafing runs. Bodies lay everywhere. Trees and brush in flames. The elephant grass smoldered and as the wind gained in strength it burst into flames. NVA Companies fled to the rear seeking refuge from the Hell above. Striker's plan had worked. His companies at the quick exited from the rear of the camp. Bravo would have to hold and hold fast and tight for at least 30 minutes to some it would feel like 30 hours. Smoke and fire obscured any observation of the tree line. But the offensive odor from burned bodies told them that the air attack had been a rousing success. The NVA never expected an attack from the air. Pilots reported many, many K.I.A's below and that the main body had halted and began digging in. Bravo braced itself as the corsairs rocked their wings and flew back to the Independence.

Gunny Burke had elected to remain with Bravo Company. He knew if Bravo was hot that the shit would hit the fan. Captain Hopkins beckoned to Burke. Burke sprinted to his side. "Yes sir, Gunny, see that little dirt path that winds up and around the cliff." "Yes sir, it's got me shaky." "Have a squad check it out. Let's make damn sure there's no gook heads up there in the dark for they could really raise Hell with us. Give the job to LeSage for it may help him deal with that LaPore tragedy." "Yes sir." Burke crawled to LeSage and relayed their skipper's orders. LeSage chose 2nd squad and crawled to the edge of the path. Keeping low so as not to be observed by enemy observers. Slowly they ascended the path. It was quite a challenge. Their left flank was a 500 foot fall into the jungle. Their right flank overgrown with bramble bush and thick brush. They cautiously climbed the path and found all was quite. Birds and wood creatures had long departed due to the Napalm and smoke and horrific sounds of the fire fight. LeBron was two yards to the rear of LeSage. As they came to a sharp bend on the path, rifle fire exploded from a well concealed hooch. Three Marines gasped and hit the ground hard and quick. Their Brother Marines fell to the prone position and laid down intense fire at the hooch. LeBron crawled close using the brush as concealment and lobbed three grenades into the hooch. The explosions caused the roof and east wall of the hooch to collapse and small fires were ignited. Smoke bellowed from the interior. The Marines lay as they were in a defensive mode. All was quiet and there was no return fire. LeSage ordered his men to advance slowly. Trees and thick brush served as allies in allowing them to get within 5 feet of the smoldering hooch. Finally after a five minute interval, LeSage and three men entered the hooch from the rear. As their eyes adjusted to the semi-darkness, they gasped at what lay before them. Three NVA soldiers lie dead by the front door and window but in the center of the structure lying and twisted in grotesque positions were the bodies of three women and nine children. One mother was cradled a torn baby to her crushed chest. Another had her arms around two little girls with their heads split in half from the immense fire that poured into the hooch. There were no survivors. LeSage locked eyes with LeBron. "Yeah, Jake I'm one Hell of an NCO. Get LaPore killed now this. Fuck it, Fuck it, fuck it!" "Hey Lee," Jake spoke softly, "it ain't nothing man. Nothing. Ain't your fault. Look there, there's smashed radios. These fucks were observers. Had us on the radio. You, we did what we had to do. No way we knew civilians were in here. Would of made no never mind anyway. We still had to take these fucks out. These people may have been friends or family. Forget it Lee. War is Hell."

They returned to the downed Marines. Doc Lawson gazed at LeSage shook his head. In his right hand he'd already retrieved their dog tags. They lay still and ashen and each had been shot through the face and never knew what hit' em. "Lee," uttered Lawson. "Just as well, no pain, no agony." LeSage shaken gave the order to make certain their job was complete. Then ordered the remainder of his squad to return to the company area. As the squad shuffled off slowly, they gazed sadly at the still forms of PFC Rob Mullen, PFC Todd Jones and Private Larry Wilkins, in compliance with orders the bodies would lie where they fell. There was no time or resources to remove them. Flies were already nosing and the grief stricken Marines knew their buds would be devoured in hours by hordes of the ugly creatures that lived in the forest. LeSage made his report to Captain Hopkins, who nodded, "sorry LeSage but you did a good job and took out as observation post. Have a smoke and a java. This is war kid and some choices are not left to us."

As LeSage walked away with his head bowed, a strong hand grasped his shoulder. He straightened and looked into the tough hardened eyes of Gunny Burke. "Look kid, those fucks were using those civilians as shields. In an hour or come sunset, we'd a been creamed by motor fire. You did a hell of a job. Either way you would have had to destroy that position. You've had a rough go. But always remember only the dead see the end of the war. You'll go through a lot more by-ways of hell before this is over and so will many thousands more Marines. Don't let this shit fuck you up. You need to stay sharp, alert, or you'll end up fly bait. We're in a tough situation a rough business. But remember we chose it. Steel yourself. You've got to get hard." "Yes Gunny, I know. Now I understand why you were always hard on us." "Been there done that. Know what this show is all about." "Thanks Gunny, It's men like you that make the Corps." "Get out of here kid. Go flop with Tonto and LeBron. Watch your backs. This fucking shit is only beginning. They're been many a taps played. Many a horseless rider and reservoirs of tears. Arlington will fill before whatever mess is building gets vacuumed clean.

"Striker One to Bravo One." "Bravo One go ahead." "What's the activity down there? We've heard gunfire from our position on the ridge." "Aye, I'd discovered a concealed path that wound its way up and around the cliff. Corporal LeSage led a squad to reconnoiter and ran into an observation post. End result 3 dead NVA and 12 civilians used as shields. We had three KIA. Any further instructions?" "Bravo One be advised your position probably zeroed in. Delta Company had reached their position. Charlie Co., Alpha, Helo and Echo are still marching to theirs. If your concerned move your company at the quick. Delta is positioned approximately 3 miles to your rear. You have the coordinates and still have enough day light to locate their perimeter. I say move and move now. I believe you've been compromised." "Aye, aye, sir. Bravo off." Hopkin's signaled to Burke pointing towards the troops and then to the rear. Burke nodded affirmative and one by one Bravo's Marines at double time headed rearward. There was no confusion. Hopkin's knew the skipper was right. They'd probably would have received a full attack at dusk.

Boots crunching in the ground. The grunts ran for their lives. Keeping three yards apart, Burke stood to the rear watching the tree line with a 50 Caliber which he held in his right hand. He scanned deep and long, nothing but a whisper, not yet anyway. The elephant grass slowed their pace. The company spread out across an open field. The air still and unbearable and hot even though the sun was descending below the tops of the trees that flanked them. Legs tired and with rifles cradled in arms felt heavier with each step. Without warning PFC Phillip's body suddenly catapulted into the air. The womp, womp, thump, thump of mortars filled the airway. You could feel the concussions of the explosions rippling against your face. Throwing men to the ground like rag dolls. The deafening noise swept across the open field and all around bodies rocketed out of the ground in twisted impossible poses. A grotesque ballet. Heat and pressure from the explosions permeated the air. Arms, legs, fingers, bones, bits of flesh, pieces of brain, muscle and gore sprayed the field with a sickening aroma. A crimson mist fills the air carried by the soft wind. Blood, sticky to the touch, coats the field with an iodine smell. The grass glistens with the gore and thickness of blood. You could hear the screams and anguish of the dying men with stomachs torn open, viscera falling about striking one in the face or careening off a helmet. Calls for Corpsmen eco up and down the line to no avail. Wounded and dying men lay in heaps. Fear knots the stomach yet Bravo Company pushed on. Its life and soul at stake.

The NVA had observed Bravos quick departure. Their gun commander waited patiently and was familiar with the terrain. He waited till the Marines had stalled in the elephant grass and knew they'd be sitting ducks. His patience and decision had paid a huge dividend. Bravo Company had 27 KIA and 16 wounded. The battered company sought refuge in the opposite tree line. Mortar shells screeching and detonating all the while. Once within the security of the trees, Hopkins stood mute. His company had been mauled and there were wounded he could not reach. He turned to Burke, "have the men continue the march. Leave several to assure NVA infantry aren't in pursuit. Let's Move!" "Captain, the wounded?" whispered

Burke. Hopkins, with tears in eyes "expendable Gunny. They're expendable, God have mercy on them and me. We can't risk more casualties. Move Gunny! Get your people moving!"

"Striker One to Bravo One." "Aye sir, Bravos on." "What the fuck happened?" "Sir elephant grass. They marked us in the elephant grass and ambushed us with mortars. Bravo suffered 43 casualties sir. There are wounded we can't reach." Striker sighed audibly. "Roger that Bravo. Continue your march to Delta's coordinated position, Striker out." "Roger sir, Bravo out." "Striker turned to Pezzone and cursed softly. "Bravo Company has already lost 55, Fuck!!" Pezzone didn't respond. Both commanders knew they had a long way to go and now knew the NVA was all to familiar with the landscape. "Its gonna be Hell Frank, gonna be Hell." "Yeah Colonel, but we'll make those Hell devils pay dearly. They've already felt our muscle and there's a Hell of a lot of pop to come. We'll suffer Eric no doubt but your leadership will salvage most of this battalion. Sure Bravo got hurt in that open field of elephant grass, but if you hadn't ordered them out when you did, they'd be massacred. You know that." Striker nodded, "Yeah Frank, that's all well and good, think 55 mothers, fathers, sisters, sweethearts would understand." He turned and walked off electing a lonely private solitude.

Gunny Burke selected Broken Rose squad to rain in the rear and observe what tactics the NVA would now exploit. He chuckled to himself. He was only obeying orders wasn't he. He hefted a 50 caliber on his shoulder and had confiscated five belts and had ordered Tonto's squad to rig more or steal automatic weapons. He knew the NVA would rush from the tree line thinking Bravo Co had speedily departed the area. He knew the pricks would come to exploit their spoils of war and he wanted to lay down a small surprise. He positioned the squad near the edge of the tree line concealed by brush and elephant grass. All 12 men carried either Bar's 30 caliber machine guns and a modest supply of grenades begged from fellow

Marines. They lay silent 6 feet apart. Watching, ever watchful. They agonized over the cries of their wounded buddies. Dug deep to anchor themselves at their position. "Ah," Burke whispered. "Here they come approximately 300 NVA soldiers swept out of the tree line.

They advanced in a skirmish line. Bayonets a fixed to their weapons. The field covered in smoke and the stench of dead and decaying bodies was quiet as the NVA neared the area where most Marines had fallen. Nine wounded Marines suddenly stood. They were arm and arm. They faced their enemy with pride and silence. Then they knelt still arm and arm and the squad burst into tears as the soft chorus of "Nearer My God" began to waft through the tree tops being carried by the wind. They were singing knowing and awaiting their fate. It didn't take long. The NVA pounced on the singing Marines. Bayonets, their steel glistening in the sun plunged downward into soft flesh. Dozens of NVA joined in the fray of stabbing, spearing, bludgeoning the nine wounded into silence. Blood and brain matter and viscera spewed into the air. Unarmed men wounded had been brutally executed. Burke roared with anger and aimed his 50 caliber at a sword carrying officer and fired an intense burst that stitched him form head to toe. The officer head exploded like a melon. His chest disintegrated, his bowls, spewed from his stomach. His legs were cut in half and severed from his torso and then his body split in half as he fell heart, lungs, liver, kidneys tumbling to the ground. The NVA in their frenzy had bunched up all wanting their piece of meat. The squad opened fire with devastating effects. NVA fell by threes, fours, fives. Bodies flung backwards and upwards. Geysers of blood spewed into the air. They had no cover. Bodies of soldiers appeared to be dancing as armor piercing bullets tore into them. They fell in droves. Legs kicking in the air. Arms flailing. Screams of horror echoed throughout the field. The squad continued this intense firing for 15 minutes. Smoke and cordite enveloped their position. Brass shelling lay in heaps. Burke firmly yelled, "CEASE FIRE! Lets get the hell out of here! They'll soon lob mortars this way!" The squad weapons hot and in hand began a quick run to join their CO. One look back revealed the smoldering twisted babbling bodies of at least 100 NVA. Most were running back into the tree line. A few fired their weapons but where and at who?

Hopkins met Burke. "What the fuck did you do?" "Followed orders Captain. We kept watch as the what the rice worms were going to do. So we gave them a Bravo surprise and send off. At least 100 of the cocksuckers will join Buddha tonight." Hopkins smiled, "Well I really didn't want you to expose yourself Gunny, we need you. But your actions and that of this squad definitely will halt their movement for the night. This will give all the companies time to dig in and time for us to meet the defenses perimeters. Good Job. I am recommending all of you for a Bronze Star. Well deserved. Now fall in with the rest of the company."

Burke filled his captain in on the actions of the singing Marines as they died. The word would filter through the ranks and in effect fill the troops with a fierce determination to enact as much revenge on those butchers as possible. There's no meaner weapon in the world then a pissed off nineteen year old Marine.

Burke suddenly let out a low "er-rra." As the familiar womp, womp, thump, thump struck the position his squad had shortly vacated. "Go ahead fuck heads waste ammo on land crabs and dead brush. Hopkins stared at Burke, "You just made it Gunny. Don't push your luck. Those lousy bastards are everywhere like a disturbed ants nest. We're gonna be in a running fight all the way to sea." "Yup your right Captain. That will give us plenty of opportunity to hurt em."

Bravo moved steadily up the slope fatigue taking its toll. The grunts dug deep for every ounce of strength. One foot down and one foot up. Brush and bramble bush created havoc. Men suffered deep welts and scratches. Mosquitoes feasted and men had to slap flies from open wounds. Soon they approached a semi-rounded knoll. A guttural voice challenged, "Halt who goes there?" Sentry, it's Captain

Hopkins with Bravo Co." "Password please." "Semper." The retort Fi allowed those to pass on in to Delta's perimeter. Hopkins trained eyes could see they were well entrenched with weapons in strategic positions. Once Bravo had entered the perimeter, two men were dispatched from Delta to man a listing post 300 yards out. LeSage, standing near by gave a nod of sympathy, for he had to erase the awful memory of his LP. The Delta Company commander, Captain Ray Reynolds, met briefly with Hopkins. "Got hit pretty hard, huh? Bob." "Yeah Ray and they're coming. They're hit you tonight. I'd say around 0300. They don't like those corsairs fucking with em. So I'm sure they'll choose darkness for a fight. We're ready after your people are armed. I've troops stringing claymores and other goodies, about 200 yards out, that'll stall em then we'll mortar the shit out of em. Those that get through the grunts will handle. Oh and Striker, relayed to me to keep your company on the move till you hit Charlie's perimeter. About another 5 miles. "Okay Ray, good luck." "Bravo Company on your feet saddle up we're moving out!"

Three NVA Battalions moved quickly in a skirmish line. Bayonets fixed, their faces contorted in determination. They'd witnessed the slaughter of Brothers from the corsairs and as they prodded on, they tried not to look at charred twisted corpses. They moved quick hoping to catch the remnants of Bravo Company. Frustration set in when they failed in that quest. They spread out further as they began ascending the slope. They suffered the same fate as Bravo, bramble bush and mosquito and flies. They trudged on, skirmishers lead the way. All was quiet. The jungle dark and foreboding. Trees created a natural canopy so it was close to pitch black. As they continued their march suddenly bright flash of light and explosions enveloped the skirmish line. NVA soldiers flew through the air. Helmets, weapons, torsos, clothing back packs reined down on the lines. Moving forward, they hit the dirt. But to no avail. Soon the womp, womp and thump, thump of mortars landed in their midst. Groans and cries of agony as the defenseless ranks were torn by hot flying shrapnel. The Marine mortars were right on target. They had zeroed in just yards in front of the line of claymours. The Marines had called it right in where the main body would be. Steel whistled through the trees and brush. Wounded lie everywhere. Heaps of dead bodies lying in grotesque rows hampered the remaining NVA troops to move forward quickly. Officers and Noncoms tried to rally confused soldiers. Finally a major screamed, "Charge!" Three hundred and fifty NVA soldiers joined in the frenzy and charged running over the dead and dying. As they neared the knoll red and white flares popped in the night. They froze for a moment fully exposed.

The knoll exploded in a horrific devastating fire. Red tracers pointing the way. NVA fell in drones. The gaggle of dying frightened men filled the night. They tried to fire back from the prone position or from behind rocks or tree stumps, but the enemy was laying down superior fire power and their mortars were lobbed into their exposed positions. Bodies both dead and alive leaped into the air. Wounded were hit again and again. Bullets whizzed through the trees and brush. The night, now a grayish black, due to so much firing. The Nam commander dug in a hole. Shocked to realize that almost two full battalions had been hacked to pieces. He blew his whistle and what remained of his command turned tail running down the slope.

When the sun peaked over the tree tops, the men of Delta Co gazed into the sight of massacre its count revealed over 220 dead NVA and only 9 Marines had been hit on the line and 5 KIA. An NVA regimental commander on watching the remains of a slaughtered battalion was heard to say "Our general is over zealous. He should just let them go. He'll have our division decimated." After all, they're running and are damn good soldiers. Why pursue? Let them return to their ships and be done with it." He bowed his head and knew his general was egotistical and wanted the heads of those intruders. He whispered to himself, "but at cost now general? What cost?"

Broken Rose and Charlie White Cloud had shadowed the retreating NVA. Well camouflaged, they kept watch and observed every movement. It soon became apparent the NVA were about to throw an entire regiment with mortar fire as back up at Delta perimeter. Four thousand plus die hard NVA were forming for the attack. Their commander determined to crush those devils on the knoll. The Rose and White backed out of their concealment and on the fly returned to Delta's position. They reported their observations to Captain Reynolds who in turn got on the horn with Striker. Informed of the huge impending attack. Striker ordered Bravo Company to return and hook up with Delta's Company. "That perimeter could not be over run. Reynolds," he bellowed on the horn. "You must hold at all cost, You understand?" "Aye, Colonel, I understand. We're hold on or die. Its that simple out."

The Rose meanwhile had gathered several other Indians. They confiscated several cans of black powder and gasoline. They zigzagged through the elephant grass who's tentacles reached towards the MLR and poured black powder and gasoline throughout the tall brutal grass. A natural enemy to foot soldiers. They returned to the MLR and fastened crude bows and arrows with cloth soaked in oil on their tips. They took position in high trees and waited.

Bravo Company had since filtered into the MLR and took positions along with the Delta Brothers. It wasn't long. Soon whistles and the crunching of thousands of feet could be heard as they, the horde of NVA infantry streamed out of tree line. "Whoosh, whoosh, womp, womp, enemy mortars fired away and walked their hits into the MLR. Several direct hits flung a dozen Marines through the air. The gaps were plugged but other grunts were blown out of their position. The screams pierced one's heart. The NVA charged bayonets gleaming and screaming hell bent on revenge. The line fired. Dozens of NVA collapsed, but onward they came paying no attention to their losses. Now they were bunched in the elephant grass where machine guns and barbed wire which was cutting them to pieces, still they ran ever forward. There was no disclaiming their bravery. Packed now, unable to move quickly, Broken Rose fired up his arrow as did Charlie White Cloud. They fired their arrows. Both struck in the center. Suddenly a large whoosh and fire ball engulfed the elephant grass. NVA ran on fire screaming. It was hell in action. They bumped and crashed into each other. Bodies peeling fully engulfed in flame. Some broke in half. Ammo exploded. They died in horror by hundreds. Yet continued the charge using smoldering smoking dead bodies as stepping stones. They reached the MLR and breached through gaps made in the line. Hand to hand combat came into play. One young Marine was bayoneted by three NVA screaming for his mother. Another was hacked to death by an NVA hefting a huge sword. Marines fought furiously. LeBron had his knife twisting back and forth in an NVA's chest. LeSage lay on top of an NVA and bludgeoning him with his helmet. Smashing, smashing, you could here the head bones and check bones cracking. Blood and brain matter spewed into LeSage's face. Burke pulled him off, "he's dead, God damn. Find another one, there's plenty to go around." An NVA Major came at Burke, he side stepped grabbed the officer by his throat and crushed his larynx. He smashed another solder in the face driving the nose bone into the brain. An instant death.

The battle raged for two hours. There was no quarter and none was given. These were warriors who had turned animalistic and fought to survive. Bodies lay everywhere. The dark green of the NVA mingled with that of Marine utilities. The Marines never let up on their firing and as the smoke and stench of death grew in proportion. It was apparent this battle could go either way. The Marines badly outnumbered held their ground. Burke held a 50 caliber and quickly blew 10 NVA off the wall yelling, "Buddha awaits you!" Men crawled on the ground vomiting. Others dazed were shot down like ducks in a pond. Three hours later an NVA whistle blew and the remnants of their unit retreated over the hundred of dead bodies in the charred elephant grass. Striker had arrived on scene as the battle ended. He walked the field with his two Company Commanders, Reynolds and Hopkins. Dead lay everywhere in grotesque impossible positions. Knives protruding through chests. Rifle bayonets a fixed stuck in the backs of a dead Marines. Blood ran in rivulets and the stench of shit, urine and sweat permeated the air. Men lay on the ground convulsing gasping for that last breath. Some lay eyes wide open seeing nothing. Arms, hands and legs lay scattered in the brush, on the ground, even hanging from the tree lines. Striker uttered, "there is no hell we've just walked through it." The line had held but at a terrible cost of 76 Marines died at their positions. There were no wounded. They were quickly dispatched by the NVA diehards. 556 NVA died in the assault. The Marines licked their chops and rolled up their sleeves. Striker turned to his officers, "saddle up your troops quickly. We move to Charlie's perimeter at the double." "Aye, aye sir!" Striker gazed at the field covered with debris. Bodies, viscera, stomachs, guts hanging and hugging the ground. He watched as the black flies made their appearance. Tears welled in his eyes. Once again the dead would lie where they fell. Their bones bleaching in the sun. "Semper-Fi," he whispered, Semper, fucking Fi."

General Li Chi Min, Commander of the People's Army 15th Division, was both perplexed and frustrated. Seething with anger, he'd thrown his aide and groom out of his command post. Boots off, he sat back in a high wicker chair studying a large wall map. He felt anger and frustrated because he had a superior force in number and in his pursuit of these ignorant intruders perplexed because in his chase of these so called Marines his division had suffered unacceptable casualties. Some of his ranking officers had tried to persuade him to let them go after all they were running, no? His temper had exploded like a volcano. "No, No!" he screamed. "I want their heads dangling on poles in the streets of Hanoi. We far out man them and outgun them, I, your general, has figured out what their commander is up to. He pulls back slowly but has defensive barriers in place but then he ambushes and rakes us with high casualties. He will continue this method in hopes of reaching the sea and safety from naval vessels. Well, we will through a wrench n his plan. Here are my orders. The first regiment will continue to pursuit and engage the Americans in those harassing fire fights. The 2nd regiment will head north. Five miles then turn and march east. The 3rd regiment will head south five miles turn and march east. A three pronged attack. We will move fast and surround them before they can reach the mountain. That is the 1st objective. He plans to move his troops through the gap in the mountain and thus succeed n salvaging his unit. But now the 2nd and 3rd regiments will flank him as he continues to wage his hop and scoot battles with the 1st and what is left of the 4th regiment. Our brave soldiers will slip around his battlements and annihilate him, do you understand my order?" His senior officers all nodded in the affirmative. Then issue the command and commence the operation as I've explained immediately. His commanders gone, he sat back smiling in the semi-darkness. "Now I've got you. You American pig and I'll roast you in oil." He lit a cigarette and sat perfectly still staring into the darkness. The cries of orders and the crunch, crunch of thousands of feet told him his plan was being implemented.

Striker sat with his Delta and Bravo Commanders. "That division commander can't be the dumb ass I think he is. I believe by now he's figured out our plan of defensive actions and will race to flank us thus cutting off our drive to the mountain." He grabbed the radio. "Striker to Charlie CO Commander" "Sir I'm on, go ahead." "Desert your defensive perimeter. Head pell mell to the mountain and erect defenses approximately 500 yards high on the mountain. Ask no questions get it done. Do it now!" "Aye sir, understood." He repeated this message to the commanders of both Helo and Echo companies. He spoke to a Lieutenant Frank Hissels, a navel FTO. Mark coordinates at the base of the mountains 500 yards distant. Make sure you get it right. Then call those coordinates to the commander of the fleet. Understood?" "Yes sir." "Then get on it like yesterday, Striker out."

349

He turned to Hopkins and Reynolds. "We have to push hard to reach that mountain. Those fucks are not far behind us. I know the troops are fucking exhausted, but it's live or die. So ditty bop out of here at the double quick. Get your companies up and moving and I mean moving!" "Yes sir."

Striker stood tall as the remnants of Bravo Company and Delta Company marched into the night. The moon was low so visibility would be minimal good fortune for his grunts. The grunts in combat mode moved off. They were tired, they stunk. In battle men shit or urinate in their pants unknowingly. They carried the stench of sweat caused by the tension and horror of battle. They were filthy. Many suffered numerous abrasions and yet they marched off like Marines, disciplined and proud. It was going to be a race against time. He had to get these good troops to that mountain before the NVA could affect the jaws of a pincher movement slamming the door to safety. He'd run his Marines all night. He left Broken Rose and White Cloud behind knowing they could and would easily elude the enemy. He needed eyes behind him and they accepted the assignment without comment for their job was to eyeball the pursuing NVA, and alert Striker as to their location. Striker figured he'd had a good jump on his pursuers and he was right. They were marching toward him but in a cautious route step. His men were running and continued to run till they reached the mountain and united with their sister companies. The battalion would be whole once again and if they dug in deep enough into the soul of that mountain, navel gunfire and air power would be there savor.

Bravo and Delta Companies drove hard through the brush. They passed several hamlets and its occupants asleep oblivious as to what was occurring in their home inhabitant. It had begun to rain. The grunts turned their faces upwards basking letting the pure clean water wash grim and blood from their faces.

Broken Rose and White Cloud had hung back. They'd obtained a dozen claymores and chose strategic locations in placing them. As the NVA columns approached they would activate two at a time. Dozens of NVA infantry collapsed causing the rest to deploy and fire randomly and wildly into the brush. Hitting noting but trees and dirt as the Rose and White Cloud as mystics had slithered quickly and quietly into the comfort and protection of the jungle. Their actions were repeated over and over slowing the NVA's advance and creating psychological havoc as well as numerous casualties. At last their regimental commanders put a plan in action by dispatching twelve man patrols ahead of the main body. Broken Rose and White Cloud concealed in mud and waited. Then they would strike as a snake taking out the last two members of the patrol and then on to the next two members of the patrol with their knives slashing the enemies throats causing quick and silent death. They stalked the patrol and within the hour the twelve men patrol lay sprawled and dead alongside the dirt trail. They were silent and quick death from the dark was the thought of the NVA troops who stumbled on to the grotesque fly infested bodies. NVA soldiers peered into the night weapons always set to the ready. Nerves were frayed, who were these silent killers who they could not see or hear. A Major strode up to observe the carnage rendered to the patrol. He gagged and grabbed his throat as an arrow whooshed into his neck. Soldiers knelt and fired in all directions, but once again the ghost killers had burrowed into the darkness. The NVA spread into the brush determined to butcher those adversaries. Boom, blam another claymore spewed hot deadly metal in all directions anther dozen NVA were blown into oblivion. Legs and torsos cut into ribbons. Fear spread through the ranks. Another major ordered the troops forward, but the advance had slowed to a crawl. Along the march the NVA had lost 75 men but to whom and how many were there? Broken Rose and White Cloud sprinted through the dark rainy night. These actions had allowed Bravo and Delta Companies to forge far ahead of their pursuers. The NVA at last deployed long lines of skirmishers' to no avail and too late. The Rose and White Cloud like the creatures in the forest had long disappeared.

Charlie Company had reached the mountain and immediately began digging in. Heavy weapons were emplaced in positions which offered open fields of fie. They were soon joined by Helo and Echo Companies and a formidable defense perimeter was in the making. The navel FTO had marked his coordinates. Double and tripling his calculations, satisfied, he radio the information to the fleet. The huge structure of the New Jersey moved closer to shore her guns programmed with the coordinates called in by the FTO. Two heavy cruisers also moved into better firing position. On the Independence corsairs were like worker bees. Loaded and ready to expend fiery death on the approaching NVA columns.

Four hours and shortly before dawn, Bravo and Delta Companies hooked up with, Charlie, Helo, Eco and Alfa Companies in their mountain refuge. They'd won the race with their NVA pursuers. Now the NVA would have to confront their prey in a brutal frontal assault. What they didn't know was that 16 inch and 8 inch guns were programmed, locked and loaded, to deliver Hell when they chose to attack. Striker walked the defenses pointing out several weak areas. He was suggesting various weapons be set up in positions suited to inflect heavy damage on his future attackers. The Marines labored through the night and rain. Striker took one last inspection tour. Satisfied he collapsed in his command foxhole. The grunts locked and loaded and waited for the action to begin.

General Min was seated at his small field desk enjoying a hot cup of tea and steaming bowl of fresh rice and native vegetables. He was startled by his aide outside his door requesting permission to enter. "Yes, yes enter Major. Would you care for some hot tea?" "No sir, sir bad news from the front." "Well get it out major, tell me." "Sir, the Americans succeeded in reaching the mountain and as we speak are fortifying with strong entrenchments." Min banged the table. His rice and tea spilling onto the dirt floor. Scowling and cursing he stood. "How can that be? What shit do I have for commanders? Have a runner bring back that regimental commander who was in pursuit. I'll hang the godless son of a bitch!" "Sir can't be done. He's dead. Shot in the neck by an arrow." "A what?" "An arrow, sir." ""What the fuck kind of demons are we fighting? Who or what is out there?" "Sir a patrol of twelve men were found butchered. Their throats cut so deep their heads lobbed side to side. Also the pursuing regiment suffered the loss of 75 men due to claymore traps." The General kicked his chair across the room. "What about the other two regiment?" "Sir, they are within striking distance of the enemy." Min Growled, "striking distance. Have the artillery and mortar crews lay down an intense barrage. I'll make a salt pile of that mountain. They're animal demons from Hell and I want them destroyed! Is that understood, Major? I want their heads! There is to be no quarter. They are to be annihilated to every last man. I want their commander's heads. He's a two headed pig. Now go issue my orders and inform my commanders they either succeed or die in battle. For if they fail they will die by my own hand." "Yes sir." "Then get out of my sight and your next report better be good or I'll hang your ugly oriental ass. Go, and go now!" The Major bowed and sprinted out of the structure. Calling for a car to bring him to the front.

The mountain had been turned into a fortress with mortar emplacements and machine guns programmed to lay down intense fire. Broken Rose and White Cloud on arrival were summoned to Striker's CP where they filled him in on their nights activity and that the NVA columns were now setting up in the adjacent tree line. They were preparing for an all-out attack. The Marines were facing a formidable foe, approximately 18,000 NVA troops were posed to spring into action. Striker nodded, "good job you two rate the Silver Star and I'll see that you get it. Now grab some chow and java while you can. And again great job. I can't thank you enough. Go and relax before the shit hits the fan." "Yes sir, thank you sir. The two warriors strolled off slowly seeking a hot meal.

The rain had stopped and a haze covered the field and formed a Helo effect around the mountain's top. The sun rose slowly as if trying to avoid the coming event. At 0630, the first salvo of military rounds roared into the mountain. Dirt and debris flew in all directions. Several Marines bodies catapulted in the air minus arms and legs. The concussion from the explosions were causing temporary deafness to many. The grunts burrowed deeper into their holes. Many prayed and all sweated anticipating instant death by the numerous projectiles peppering their perimeter. There was no respite. NVA artillery continued to fire salvo after salvo, then the womp, womp of mortars. Geysers of dirt and brush flew into the air and the cries for Corpsmen could be heard up and down the line. Striker held his breath. He knew casualties were mounting. But held off calling for naval gunfire. He wanted the NVA to commit infantry then he would unleash Hell.

LeBron, LeSage and John Gerry were moving towards a fire pit. LeSage uttered, "Hold on I've got to piss." He stepped out of formation to urinate when the explosion occurred. He was thrown into the air crashing face first into the side of a tree. LeBron and Gerry took the bulk off the shell. They lay sprawled on the wet ground. Their uniforms smoldering and small fire danced along the brush. LeBron had been blown in half. His legs detached from his torso lay approximately four feet to his rear. His right arm dangled helplessly from a tree limb. He lay face downward blood and viscera left a hideous trail. Gerry was decapitated. His boots, feet still intact, landed in brush 15 feet away. They died instantly. LeSage lay at the base of the tree. Shock set in, then darkness, as he lost consciousness. His right arm laid twisted and only ligaments and muscle had kept it intact to his shoulder. The tree gleamed with several teeth sucked from his mouth. Smoke and fires covered the area. LeSage at one point felt strong arms lifting him and heard muted voices and then complete blackness.

A whistle blew. The barrage had lifted and suddenly a horde of NVA troops stormed out of the tree line. Thousands with fixed bayonets screaming and in a frenzy, charged at the Marine positions. The Marines laid down a withering fire. The first line of attacking NVA collapsed but the maddening charge continued. As well as the mortars, machine guns, bars and M1's, spit fire and steel into the on rushing horde. The field was covered with bodies yet still they continued to advance. Soldiers, many lay on the ground wounded. They were seeking the safety of the tree line but armor piercing bullets found soft flesh and bodies twisted and screams of agony resonated throughout the small valley. Arms flew unmolested through the air. Headless torso's, their momentum carrying them a few feet and collapsed. The field turned crimson. Blood mingled and embedding itself in the wet earth. Men knelt in attempts to hold their intestines in place where stomachs had been torn open. The stench of death and blood and fear knotted ones nostrils. Gun barrels grew hot and shell casings filled the landscape and the smell of cordite and smoke tearing one's eyes. The field was covered in a thick layer of grayish smoke. Dead Marines lay in their positions with their eyes open but unseeing. The NVA line drew closer. Striker grabbed the handset. "Striker to big guy, (the code for the New Jersey) NOW! Commence your firing now! They've reach the marked coordinates. The Jersey was ready. Her large guns roared, which caused the big ship to tilt. Huge shells the size of a Volkswagen flew through the air. The noise was frightening. It was as though the heavens had disintegrated. The shells found their mark ripping huge gaps in the advancing NVA. Bodies and body parts flew in all directions, helmets and pieces of weapons creating a field of debris. The NVA ranks shuddered and stalled. Then turned and fled toward the tree line. But the New Jersey and cruisers walked their fire into the tree line continuing to dis-interject bodies. They found the artillery emplacements and field pieces were blown into useless metal. Their crews incinerated. Wheels and the barrels of cannon lay in heaps. Bodies intermingled with steel and armor. The mortar pits were found. Huge mounds of earth and hundreds of up rooted trees rafted down on the crews along with the deadly crash of shells landing and dancing within them. In moments the mortar crews were nothing but crushed and torn pieces of meat. Flesh hung in the trees and in the brush. Blood pooled and rivulets ran into the gullies and fox holes and what were once gun emplacements, the big shells screeched and howled as they struck dry dirt. The slaughter continued for two hours. Every inch of the field was covered with bodies or body parts. The tree line had been decimated. Now the bees swept in. Corsairs at tree top level staffed and dropped canisters of Napalm. The brush exploded into a fire storm. NVA troops incinerated and those that were not were burned beyond recognition. Bodies lay in grotesque positions. Some died charred sitting or kneeling some ran hysterically in all directions in flames. Some Marines with compassion shot them dead, others cursing said, "fuck'em, let em burn."

The corsairs took turns in their runs. There was no respite. The entire tree line and for hundreds of yards further in were in flames. The heat turned the defending Marines faces red. They watched in horror even with some compassion for they were witnessing Hell in all its fury. The NVA attach faltered then fully collapsed. They ran retreating from Dante's Inferno. The bee's chasing and pursuing all the while thousands lay dead, crushed by the shells of the New Jersey and cruisers. They'd been mauled. Thousands died the horrific death by fire. The stench of dead and cooked bodies had some grunts vomiting. But the attack had been a slaughter and came to an abrupt halt. The NVA pulled back, way back to lick their wounds and attempt to regroup. They'd been repulsed by the horror of navel gun fire. And their ranks had reduced by at least 5,000. When General Min received this news, he sat at his desk in the dark, drew his revolver and then blew his brains out spraying them all over his field desk. As the smoke cleared and bellowed into the sky, the Marines gazed into the after math of Hell. The ground before them lay littered with dead and equipment. It was a sight none would forget, bodies smoldering and falling apart before their eyes.

Striker radioed the fleet to cease fire and then requested a report of Marine casualties. He sighed audibly when told 66 Marines were KIA by the artillery and another 54 wounded. But those wounded would be brought down the savior path to awaiting hospital ship. These wounded would not be expendable. For the moment the battle had ceased, now Striker had to get his command to the sea and the waiting safety of rescue ships two miles away.

Major Pezzone approached Striker, "well Colonel that was a turkey shoot, but you can believe this is only the beginning and we'll be back." Striker turned faced his exec, "Major don't look over the horizon that's the Lord's business.

"Well Colonel, it was a wise decision on your part that you had Broken Rose recon this mountain and thus discovering this escape route." "Yeah, lucky hunch I guess. Anyway get the troops saddle up. It's time to head for the goal line. They've still got a formidable force and we've dead and wounded to remove." 'Two jeeps were brought in and are transporting the wounded. They've laid stretchers across the rear. "It'll take us the rest of the day to affect our escape and there's not a hell of a lot of daylight left. Move em out." "Aye, Colonel." Pezzone headed off in the direction of the company commanders and orders were given and burial details were kept busy burying dead comrades. Wounded were being ferried by jeep, but progress was slow as each jeep held but two litters. The hours passed and soon the sun ducked behind the tree line. The mountain was now in shadow and still wounded were being taxied to the landing craft waiting two miles below.

Broken Rose and White Cloud sprinted up to Striker. "Colonel, the NVA are on the move." "Yeah Sarge, I'm not surprised they're going to hit us in the dark." Striker bellowed to Captain Hopkins. "Bob, how many wounded remain?" "Twenty- two sir," came the reply. He turned to the Rose, "where are they?" "They're creeping out of the brush on all fours, well camouflaged. He radioed the fleet whose cruisers fired flares into the night sky. But in the eerie haze little or nothing could be seen. The New Jersey fired several salvos that no doubt rendered casualties; but the human eye could not decipher its extent.

Striker strolled to where a pile of weapons lay waiting to be extracted. He picked up a 50 caliber with 7 belts. He scanned the entrance to the path and honed on two boulders which set to the right of the entrance. Perfect he walked over and placed the 50 caliber in a small opening between the rocks and locked and loaded. He then jogged over to his Exec Major Pezzone. "Listen Frank, there's no time to argue. Ride hard on the troops and get their asses moving. Have some of the wounded carried if need be. Those little yellow fuckers are close. Probably at the mountain's base I can smell em. The big ships can't depress those guns to reach them so it's on us to cover our pull out. I've set up a 50 caliber, he pointed to its location. I'm going to man that monster and keep those fuckers off your back. Hopefully long enough to effect a complete withdrawal. "But Colonel you could position a squad here. You're the CO. Come on, don't be foolish. You know they'll eventually overrun you." Striker stared off into the night. "Frank these are my boys. I trained them and rode them hard. You might say I'm the father of this battalion and a father looks after his boys. Enough tears will be shed by wives, mother, children, sweet hearts, for those I already lost. I won't order any other Marines to die in this shit hole. Looks like you're going to inherit a battalion." "But Eric" "But shit Frank, you have your orders, carry them out. You're a good officer Frank. You'll make a damn fine Commander. Pezzone embraced his Colonel, "Eric it was an honor and priVillege to serve under your command. Someday, somewhere, somehow, we'll meet again." "Yeah in Hell, Marines don't die they just go to Hell and regroup. Now move out Major and good luck." "Good Luck Colonel, maybe your still make it out." Striker gave a sad smile. "It's okay Frank, my wife and daughters are waiting for me." Pezzone spun around hiding his tears and sprinted toward the laboring troops.

NVA sappers had indeed reached the base of the mountain 200 strong. They fumbled their way upwards slowly and quietly. They were intent on cutting the Marines exposed on the path and small beachhead. It was now completely dark. Striker sat behind the 50 straining his and ears, nothing, nothing yet, as he lay there reflecting, he felt a presence come up behind him. The huge bulk of Gunny Burke positioned beside him. Another sound and the figure of 1st Sergeant Donald Gates lay in the prone position to his right. "Eric smiled your orders were to withdraw, were they not?" Gunny Burke chortled, "Yeah Colonel, I guess you'll court martial us in Hell." "Anyway we're here spoke up Gates and we're staying. You forget those are our boys too. Minutes ticked by, Striker whispered, "here it?" Small rocks were falling and disturbed as NVA hands groped for grips. Striker fired a flare. Three NVA soldiers were already standing feet away. Burke squeezed off a burst and all three screaming tumbled over and off the mountain. But dozens more came running the three Marines fired at will. Bodies crumpled and fell hundreds of feet to the abyss below. NVA soldiers returned fire ricochets, zing and zinging along the rocks. More NVA appeared another flare then more firing. Striker, Burke and Gates held the attackers at bay for over an hour. The last remnants of the 8th Marines heard the intense firing as the last grunt entered the waiting landing craft. Those who could stood and saluted the mountain top, they screamed, "Lieutenant Colonel Striker, 1st Sergeant Gates and Gunny Burke, Semper-Fi from your sons, The 8th Marines."

The landing craft gunned their engines. They roared into life leaving large wakes as they headed to the big ships. On the mountain, Striker and Burke and Gates continued to hold the NVA at bay. Suddenly a flash and explosion struck their position followed by three more. The NVA had drawn near enough to lob grenades into their position. Burke was killed instantly his head blown from his shoulders. Striker fell back in shock. Half his face was gone and his chest lay open to the elements, pierced by dozens of pieces of shrapnel. He gasped, struggling for breath gurgled once and whispered, "mommy, daughters, I'm on my way and he fell back with the USMC on his utility jacket bracketed by starlight. Gates stood and continued firing when he felt a terrific jolt to the chest. Then two more and NVA with an automatic ended the small but fierce fire fight. The Marines enroute to the waiting ships listened. The firing had ceased and in their hearts they knew that the men who had led and molded them were finished. The interior of the landing crafts went silent only the muffled sounds of crying men sighed softly in the night.

Two destroyers moved close to shore. Their spot light flares exposing the path to freedom in brilliant harsh light catching hundreds of NVA clamoring downwards toward the beach. Their 51 inch guns took aim and fired crashing into the crowded troops. Again bodies were flung upwards, sideways, tumbling, arms, legs, heads, equipment, torsos, being tossed as by a horrific windstorm. Bodies lay in clumps. The 51 inchers could not miss. The expedition's final good-by was the death of another 250 NVA, who never made it to the beach and planted in the sand, was a huge sign placed by the grunts which said, "Semper-Fi from the 8th Marines!"

Exhausted Marines climbed the netting and hauled themselves aboard the waiting transports. Sailors stood by with hot coffee and even cold cokes. The troops were directed into the holds where noncoms headed them into hot showers. The Navy had reserved a generous amount of hot fresh water and the grunts delighted in scrubbing grim, shit, urine, blood and sweat from their abused bodies. When complete they threw themselves on the small cots and fell into coma like sleep. Weapons and gear could wait till tomorrow. The wounded were hoisted up into the hospital ship decks. A triage nurse assigned each man to various wards according to his wounds. They were treated with tenderness and respect and stripped naked then wounds were checked and if called for emergency surgery was performed immediately. Bodies were washed and wounds treated throughout the night. The operating rooms lights burned bright and hot. The fleet remained anchored in no hurry to depart. At intervals the New Jersey would fire salvos into the open field and tree line. The NVA fell into a disorganized retreat. Their division had been decimated and it would take time even months for it to heal and replenish their horrendous losses.

Two silent figures emerged from the brush in the tarp of night concealing their movements. Broken Rose and White Cloud slithered like sister snake slowly along the path. Skittering by the decaying bodies of NVA infantry where one was found to be wounded and alive he was quickly dispatched to Buddha Land by the sharp knives of the two warriors. Finally they arrived at the opening of the freedom path located the bodies of Striker, Burke and Gates. Gingerly and respectfully committed the carcasses to the base of a large tree where they already opened a wide deep hole. Wrapping the dead Marines in blankets they lowered them slowly into the ground and then with amazing energy commenced to bury them. An American flag covered all three bodies. Once the grave site was complete, Broken Rose and Charlie White Cloud in guttural voices chanted old warrior prayers. Ole Great Spirit's welcome these brave warriors into the new life. Open your hearts and receive them so that their spirits may sit in peace with their warriors of old. Let their spirits flow free. Let their eyes and ears see and hear the peace of your lounge. Let them mingle with the old ones warriors lastly bless their spirits with joy and peace. Both men saluted, lingered a short time, and then leaped into the sea. They would swim to the anchored transports.

The 8th Marines battle flag would yet add another streamer but the price was high. The ghosts of 145 KIA would forever peer down on that forsaken land. No one knew at that time 5 years hence, a full scale war would escalate and ravage that country. All to no avail only the dead know the end of war.

For those that gave their all.
Lieutenant Colonel Striker
1st Sergeant Gates
Gunny Burke
All the KIA Grunts

"Semper-Fi"

The wounded would forever have horror branded on their souls.

LeSage had no recollection of the hit. Slowly he regained consciousness and in the semi-darkness, he saw that he was in a large ward housing numerous beds. Many were empty but scores full of writhing groaning figures. He awoke several times during the night. His arm throbbing terribly, but he was safe and that's what mattered. Early in the morning LeSage received a visitor, a Lieutenant Commander something or other. He was dressed in green surgical garb and told that he was going to perform surgery on his arm, explaining where shrapnel had hit and the extensive damage caused to ligaments, tendons, muscles and nerves. Shortly afterward two orderlies in green appeared. LeSage was placed on a gurney and wheeled a short distance through green lit hallways. One whistled softly as he was wheeled through sliding doors where a table lay in the middle of the room. Several huge lights peered down showering the room in bright garnish light. Naked he was lifted gently and placed on the table on his back. He felt nauseous and the pain in his arm was excruciating. LeSage felt a slight breeze and then a chill.

The room was air conditioned and suddenly a female's voice came wafting over his shoulder. "What's your serial number corporal?" Her voice husky pleasant almost playful and LeSage struggled to look behind him. She was a woman, all right. A round eyed American female, most likely a nurse. She was dressed in green garb and had reddish hair and a cream like complexion and a clipboard in her hand filling out forms.

LeSage chilled gave her his serial number and other essentials. Not thinking twice that he was lying there spread eagle naked and almost freezing to death. After Florence Nightingale had finished another nurse entered. LeSage muttered, "Jeez I'm so cold and the nurse retrieved a gray navy blanket and gently covered him. She then skillfully inserted an intravenous into the vein on top of the left hand tapping it to a brace to keep it secure. Another nurse entered and attached a plasma bottle to an overhead hanger and plugged LeSage into the drip. The nurse then injected something into the IV tube. Stating it would help him to relax and maybe a little sleepy. Lieutenant Commander something or other appeared now masked and gloved. "Son we're going to do our best to save that arm, okay." All LeSage could do was nod in the affirmative. Drowsiness now covered his body. A short while later the anesthesiologist appeared. "Roll over on your left side. Now bring your knees up to your chin. You'll feel a little bee sing. Okay, roll over on your back now." Settling back comfortable the nurse to his left adjusted the IV. LeSage fell into a deep black void.

He had no idea how long he'd been on the operating table. But when he broke into semi consciousness, the doctor was saying he was debriding the wound and cleaning out all the grim that had gotten into it as well as the dirt, grit, mud. Then once again he fell back into the black void. Once he came to, LeSage was told later that some of the shrapnel would be left where it was that they'd cause more damage attempting to get it out then leaving it in. LeSage mumbled, "You're the doc." And fell asleep again.

LeSage woke bleary eyed and could see gray walls and white painted ceilings float by. And it was swaying to rhythm to a clean plasma bottle dangling over his chest. Someone was holding the bottle. She was a nurse. A beautiful blonde in green utilities, her hair short, complexion flawless and her eyes kind and gentle and was absolutely beautiful. Like an angel. "Looks like you're going to smile," she said. How could he not. He'd just fallen in love. The gurney took a sharp left turn and stopped momentarily, then turned into a dimly lit room with printed gray walls. To the calm quiet commands of his new blood compadras, LeSage was maneuvered to the left again. Lifted off the gurney and placed in a bed, a real hospital bed with clean white sheets. LeSage had been placed in the bed nearest the hatch. He tried to lift his head. "Oh no, no," said the blonde. She was a nurse, Lieutenant JG, Her name tag read, Brady. "You've got to lie flat otherwise you'll get a terrible headache." LeSage felt terror, he couldn't feel his arm. Would the feeling come back? Yes, it would. His new blonde friend was attaching the IV to a hanger in back of the bed. Admiring her soft curves, she suddenly leaned over him checking the IV lines with a smile she looked down. "Is there anything I can get for you?" "Will the feeling come back in my arm?" "Yes but it will take time. It required hours of surgery to repair the massive damage to that arm. She pointed. LeSage followed her eyes and was startled to see his right arm casted and held in an upright position by several wires attached to some type of pole. "I'd love a smoke." "Sorry. No smoking in the ICU." "Damn how am I gonna survive." "Hey Marine, you'll be fine. You'll only be here 24 hours. We want to be sure there's enough blood flow to that arm. Keep your head flat on that bed and don't move that arm and get some sleep, okay! Oh, remember if you need something for pain just yell, you're going to need it.

LeSage looked to his left. A figure was in a bed near him. He could sense beds beyond it all the way to the far grayish wall lots of them many full. Turning back, Lieutenant JG Brady was staring down at him. "Where am I?" He whispered. She smiled an angelic smile, "why, you're a guest of the hospital ship Hope!!" She turned and sauntered off. LeSage saw a nurse's station to his right and his eyes followed several nurses in green utilities ministering to other wounded. "Ah," he was safe and it was wonderful. He finally fell into a deep sleep.

Fitful sleep ruled the ward LeSage listened in silence to the groans and moans of men in agony all about him. Screams would jolt one out of a sound sleep and on occasion a gurney bearing a draped figure would be wheeled by and exit through the hatch, never to return. LeSage recollections of that ward were hazy, but mostly comfortable. After a day or two the doctor who'd done his surgery came by to examine his handiwork. Cautiously removing the cast and he showed it to LeSage. He showed LeSage that there was a four inch gash on the bicep of the right arm where you could see exposed bone and torn cut flesh. With a mirror he showed LeSage the six inch gash where metal had penetrated under the armpit and its force ripping muscles, severed tenders, ligaments and bone. They'd stitched up only the armpit allowing the bicep cut to drain. Gauze packing needed to be changed daily which caused extreme pain when withdrawn. The arm remained up- right and gradually some healing began. But the doctor warned that further surgery would more than likely be necessary back in the states and much rehab to regain use of the arm.

As the wound slowly healed and the shock of battle wore off, LeSage grew angry questioning why a single battalion was sent in harm's way where large forces of enemy lay waiting and penetrated the Marines line of march. They had been zoned in by enemy artillery and mortars. He wondered if an honest answer would ever be forth coming.

His days and nights were spent in fitful rest. He wondered and asked doctors, nurses, orderlies and other wounded how his unit had fared. He received silent stares and shaking of heads. He had recognized few of the ward occupants. They were from other companies and were either to wounded or out of it to talk. He resigned himself to the worst and constantly being injected with morphine to ease his pain. His sleep filled with nightmares as he relived the battle and screams over and over. The dark eyes of LaPore penetrated his soul. He begged for forgiveness. His soul lingered in clutches of Hell and the devil. Only the merciful efforts of the drugs gave him reprieved sleep. Slowly the hospital ship Hope plowed toward the U.S.A. While in her wake, the cries of anguished men whose tears, grief, horror, screamed, but why?

He'd gone to Vietnam more or less completely unaware of his capabilities and unaware of everything in life. Because he was very young and also straight out of a background that was repressed and conducted in a quiet vacuum that held no scope for anything much in the way of experience. He knew Nam had changed him and could have broken him. It broke plenty of other guys all around him guys were going to pieces not just the kids like him but older guys too. The long service professionals who'd been in for years, Nam fell on people like a weight and some cracked and some didn't. He hadn't he looked around and knew he had changed and needed to adapt, listen and learn. Killing was easy and he was a guy who'd never seen anything dead before apart from road kills the chipmunks, squirrels and the rabbits and even the occasional stinky skunk.

First day in country he saw twenty five dead Green Berets and hundreds of slain NVA. The burn twisted grotesque corpses of children and elderly as well as pieces of bodies everywhere some of them large, clearly a defining moment. His buddies had gone quiet and throwing up and groaning in sheer object miserable disbelief. He lay quiet and still in the dark. The words change and adapt stamped on his soul as he drifted into a restless sleep.

As he lay quiet in his bed clothed in semi-darkness, all about him the muffled sounds of men in spiritual and physical agony. Like him they struggled to mute their sobs and groans, hoping, praying that others would not hear and struggling to conceal their private suffering. LeSage was restless, afraid because he wanted to crawl under the earth. Within his heart he felt his soul had left his body. Try as he may the word why would not separate from his mind. Why, why, why Green Berets envoys of mercy were attacked and overcome only because of superior numbers. Sleep was futile and his subconscious in chaos. His soul in the deep dark abyss agonizing over what fate had dealt to his battalion.

The dark horrific look on his friend LaPore's face as he gasped in his death knoll and the Hell of those final moments together will never leave LeSage's tortured mind and soul for it is branded forever. He would have to live with that horrific decision made now and in even into eternity for it was made in the clutches of Hell. He knew that only God would rule and judge that terrifying choice made in a blink to be right or wrong. He shivered, trembled, would Hell be his reward? No he thought I'm already in its grasp now and forever. His mind continued to whirl in over drive. Weird he thought man enters life in partnership with his mother but enters that deep unknown dark void alone. Tears coursed down his cheeks. LeSage knew his youth had been lost in that fiery Hell in a land he knew nothing about. That a large part of him and so many others had dissipated in the mud and gore in that foreign land called Vietnam. Like good men before and after, he'd face life differently from those who had not been, nor seen the face of Hell. Muting his sobs, the images of his comrades flashed before him. They'd followed the flag as young men and now they could not age peacefully for their souls and hearts were forever stamped with images of horror, death, and agony that the subconscious could never, never erase.

He lay on his back on his bed with an IV needle taped into a vein in his left hand. The IV was a square polyethylene bag hanging off a curled steep stand behind him. The bag contained liquid and he could feel the pressure as it seeped down into his hand. He could feel it pushing his blood pressure higher than usual. There was hissing in his temples and he could feel the pulses behind his ears. The liquid in the bag was clear an d like thick water but it was doing the job. His arm had stopped hurting and the pain fading away leaving him calm and sleepy. He tried to giggle at the confusion in his mind but his breathing was to slow to get much of a sound out. So he just smiled to himself and closed his eyes and swam down into the warm depths of his bed. Peaceful sleep continued to elude him. Pain signaling tremors and chills coursing through his body which caused his brain to go in overdrive. Anxiety mixed with grief causing blood pressure to rise along with nausea and the sweats harried not only physical components but spiritual as well. He gazed at his right arm in the semi-darkness. Its form standing straight upwards casted and held aloft by wires and cables and held taut by poles overhead. He'd suffered through three surgeries to repair torn tendons, muscle and ligaments needed to reattach his humorous, all but destroyed, shattered. Surgeons had labored to preserve what they could and hoped for the best.

Morphine dulled the brain and so relieved physical pain but its tentacles could not reach into the soul. He groaned softly as the image of that tragic patrol gnawed at his subconscious. He could still recount the moment deep in his heart. The screams of the three Marines shocked as they fell mortally wounded. How his squad had returned devastating fire into the offending hooch. The scene as they entered mimicked that of Dante's Inferno. Three dead NVA lay sprawled on the floor by the window opening that was okay that the enemy was dead but it was the horror of three young mothers who'd tried to shield their children which caused him and his squad to vomit and piss themselves. Body parts lay everywhere with a baby minus its head. There were two toddlers cut in half. Here a mother eyes open in shock staring at nothing clutching two children to her breast. Their blood, intestines, brain matter mingling together formed a river of blood flowing dripping through cracks to the earth below. Over here three children lay behind the dead form of their mother. Their bodies torn and ripped, arms and legs twisted detached from their bodies. There in the night the screams came involuntary and the shakes and sweat pouring as an open faucet spilling onto the floor. He screamed in unashamed anguish. God, if you're there you'd pull down the shade, for you wouldn't give a damn. Corpsmen rushed to his side and injected him with heavy sedatives. Blissful darkness overcame him. For now the demons would elude him. His form lay still but like so many he would always walk he fringes of Hell.

The huge ship cruised across the Pacific gently along the oceans swells. Now and then passing threw a squall of little impact. Like those around him, he lay still in his cot reflecting and failing to block out the screams of men in the night relieving the terror and Hell they'd experienced.

Fourteen days at sea and the huge ship slipped and secured to a dock in San Francisco, the tarp of darkness masking her arrival. gray ambulances marked with U.S.N lettering stood by. Wounded were quietly transferred into the mobile carriers, which quickly and quietly passed in the night. LeSage and Fourteen other' were driven to a nearby airport to groggy he knew not where. They were loaded on a large silver winged bird with the marking Marines embossed on the fuselage. Secured in cots, the aircraft engines roaring lifted into the starlit sky. Sedated the wounded warriors slept peacefully unaware of their destination.

He awoke with the sound of wheels hitting pavement and the roar of engines in reverse thrust. "Oh hell," he thought, "Where the hell, are we?" Then once more drifted into slumber getting no answer to his question.

When LeSage awoke, he was in a fresh clean hospital bed. He opened his eyes and a figure in white stood over him. It was a female who was quite attractive. On her collar hung the gold bars identifying her as an ensign. He croaked, "Where am I?" Adjusting his IV, she smiled, Well welcome to the world Marine. You're a quest of Saint Albans Naval Hospital. You're in Jamaica, New York, near to home warrior and rest assured we'll take good care of you. He raised his head and saw that he was in a long clean ward. The bulkheads painted hospital blue. There were about 20 beds all occupied. He lay back content. Home wasn't all that far. He was safe, being cared for and hoped to see loved ones soon. The ringing in his ears had diminished and blood from his eyes slowly dissolving. His vision was clearing and he'd been told by a nurse that the concussion of the explosion had created havoc with his ears and eyes. But that would pass and she'd been right, it wasn't quick but the effects were slowly healing.

The next morning an entourage of doctors entered the ward. A tall dignified figure wearing a white smock stood at the foot of each rack studying clip boards and conversing with its occupants. He would issue orders to the nurses assisting him. He stood at the foot of LeSage's rack, "morning Marine, How goes it, this morning?" His collar bore the silver oak leaves of a commander. "Not bad sir." "You were asleep when I examined your arm. It's healing well. We're going to begin adjusting our harness. Lowering it an inch a day so that when we succeed in leveling it, it won't be frozen, you understand?" "Yes sir." "Good, there will be several more sessions of debriding your wound. But everything seems to be progressing better than expected. Whoever performed the surgery did an excellent job. It's my belief that he or she saved your arm. Get some rest and make certain you hydrate and eat as best you can. Your IV's have been removed. And in a few days your arm will be resting by your side. Then we'll begin finger exercises, okay with that?" "Yes sir." He patted the bed, "Okay Marine, see you tomorrow. Try not to move around too much, not just yet." He moved away to the next rack.

Sunday was a day spent in heaven. The door to the ward burst open and loving and concerned family members poured down the aisle. Tears mixed with laughter and hugs as well as words of endearments as those who had waited at home welcomed their sons back to the world and their lives.

Napping he sensed a presence by the foot of his bed through sleepy eyes; he gazed upon the tear streamed faces of his mother and girl Joey. His father stood to their rear. His fingers on his chin and with a concerned saddened look on his face. The reunion was food for his soul. He was smothered n hugs and kisses from his mother and fiancee. He shook hands left handed with his dad who squeezed with a firm grip. Tears trickled down his cheeks. Them he loved and cherished the most and whom he thought he would never see again surrounded him rendering comfort and encouragement. Visiting hours passed quickly as do all good times and loved one's filed slowly out of the ward reluctant to leave, but with promises of quick returns. As the ward emptied the muffled sobs of wounded grunts piqued the floor. Men crying in happiness and gratitude and thanking whatever God they prayed to for stretching out his fiery hand and sparing them.

It is said that all events in life are part of God's plan. As he lay back on his pillow he thought, but how? And what is the overall plan for men who are incinerated and blown to pieces? He gazed at the white tiled ceiling and knew there were no answers. Once a wise man had told him that every man has free will, and that he and he alone is the sculpture to tragic events. But this could not and was not a satisfactory answer to his tortured soul.

Days turned into weeks, weeks into months and the healing process to LeSage had gone well. He was able to squeeze a small rubber ball. His arm was still mounted in a cast from his shoulder to wrist with a window where the wound was located. Doctors had been slowly closing the area with silver nitrates. Sundays continued to be scenes played from heaven with loved ones fussing and doting on wounded sons, brothers, sweethearts and husbands. The ward had thinned as men were discharged either back o duty or the world.

It was a Thursday and Dr. McDermott stood smiling at the end of LeSage's rack. "Well gyrene, I think you're doing quite well. What do you think, ready for some liberty to step back into the world?" LeSage felt a shiver up his spine. "Why yes sir, I'd like that." "Would you like to go home son?" "Oh, yes sir." "Get yourself squared away and pick up a liberty card at the nurses station. You can leave today. Report back next Wednesday, how's that?" "Oh sir, thank you sir." "There is also a pay chit containing back pay with your freedom card, enough there for a nice liberty. Enjoy your visit home but be careful of that arm. We really don't want a setback." "Yes sir, thank you sir." The doctor waved and smiling moved on to his next patient.

His liberty at home was paradise. The feel of his old room gave him a sense of security. His family could not do enough for him. Friends came to visit but of course the bulk of his time was spent with his sweetheart Joey. They took walks, took in a movie, inexpensive dinners but mostly sat in her cellar necking and listening to current hit records. All too soon his liberty ended. On the train ride back to New York, he felt at peace and relaxed. His arm was healing and he had a great girl waiting for him. He had 36 days left and counting.

Dr. McDermott examines the wound. "Well son, it's pretty closed up and has mended well. I'm not going to recommend rehab. I want you to work through the pain in your own way. You've been told and shown what to do. Do this and your arm should eventually function at least 90-95 percent. Tomorrow I'm discharging you from the hospital and you'll be sent to the Brooklyn Navy Yard. There you'll be assigned to casual company where your duties are nil. You sleep, eat and just lounge around. No one bothers you and you've only 20 days to go. So you might want to rest and very cautiously get some work going on your arm in the Marine's gym. I've had orders sent to the VA Hospital in Newington, Connecticut. They will take it from here and keep a close watch on that arm of yours. Thanks for being a model patient and for the service you rendered. You've a lot to be proud of. I wish you the best." The doc extended his hand smiling and said "Use your right Marine." They shook hands and Doc McDermott moved off. "God speed and good luck Corporal." LeSage whispered, "Thanks Doc."

He moved into Casual Company and chose a rack by the far wall in the NCO's Section. He looked around only two other Noncoms were habitants, a buck sergeant and another Corporal. They nodded to each other. But none spoke. LeSage, using his left, and squared away his locker. Lit up a Lucky and crawled onto his rack. The squad bay was quiet. Most of its occupants had opted to take liberty that day. All were short timers waiting for their discharge day. Most were quiet men lost in the terror they'd left behind. Struggling with nightmares and how they would soon cope in the world. Oh there were conversation but all avoided discussing their personal encounter with the Hell they'd been through. Small card games and a few beers in the base GI Dunk. The Garrison Marines gave them a wide berth not wishing to disturb them. A staff sergeant named Muffet had instructed them as to their functions. There would be no duty assignments. All that was expected of them was to keep their area and personal hygiene spotless. They could retrieve liberty cards on any given day. They knew the chow schedule and it was left to them whether they ate or not. There was no reveille for them. They could sleep their lives away if they so choose. They had the freedom of the base, but must be in uniform at all times. For them the uniform of the day was utilities. "Your still Marines remember that!" Muffet screamed. "You did well, so don't go south now. You're in the home stretch. Soon you'll be back in the world and if you need anything in the way of gear, utilities, socks etc., etc. the supply room is one floor below and we have cleaners and a tailor two doors east of here. Enjoy your private R&R here guys, you've earned it. The GI dunk opens at 10:00 hours and taps out at 300. Pitchers of beer are 50 cents and it's not bad for 3.5. Okay, that's it if you need me for anything my room is through that north hatch 2nd door on your right. He strolled out the hatch. The grunts in causal now no longer boys but men before their years, smoked, read, frequented the GI Dunk and attempted to clean their minds of the images of Hell. They counted the days longing for home and loved ones.

LeSage spent his day inspected the huge shipyard. He sat for hours watching yard workers lay the keel to the U.S.S. Constitution, a mammoth air craft carrier. Two weekends he went home but mostly had spent his final days at the Corp's base just strolling the Navy Yard. He had his arm checked daily by the dispensing Corpsmen in keeping with orders. He enjoyed a few beers and then would hit the sack savoring in undisturbed sleep.

Finally the day came he was summoned to the commander's officer's compound. A corporal pointed to a hard chair by his desk. LeSage sat quietly. The Corporal named Kelly, then asked his name, rank and serial number, blood type, religion. He typed all this information on a single paper. Placed same in LeSage's service record and then handed him a 3-5 plastic card with his photo worth its weight in gold with the words United States Marine Corps Honorable Discharge. He would not receive his discharge certificate till years later when he was discharged from the inactive reserves. But this little card was his key to the world. The Corporal stood shook his hand and said "good luck brother. You can leave today and Semper-Fi" He was handed his final pay envelope and dismissed. That was it all the blood, sweat, tears, horror, agony, ended with a few typed words. But as he would soon see those fears and horrors would shadow him all of his days.

He raced to his locker and filled his duffel bag with his belongings and donned a cleaned tailored well press set of dress greens. He shook hands with several by standers and hefted his duffel bag on his left shoulder, heart pounding he headed to the Sand Street Gate and displayed his discharge card to the sentry who uttered, "lucky you" and waved him through.

He exited the gate and strolled up the steep hill to the subway station. Once he reached the top he turned and observed the sentry walking his post in a crisp military bearing. He stared long and hard mindful this would be the final time he would don his beloved greens. His ribbons gleamed in the sunlight. His red corporal chevrons bursting from the forest green.

As he stood at the top of the hill he imagined the faces of comrades gesticulating and smiling at him from an ivory cumulus cloud. Ah yes, the grand reunion one day all would be reunited. Gazing at the heavenly image, he was frozen in time, imprisoned by the moment. A tear trickled down his check as he reflected of his service. He knew it would be scrutinized by his maker. This thought in mind, he took comfort in old Gunny Burke's words. He'd said, "when our time comes we simply march to the pearly gates, salute and say another Marine reporting sir. We've served our time in Hell."

He turned and whispered, "Yes John, it was the Mountain of Tears." He entered the subway which would bring him to the huge highway of life where he would forge his destiny.

DEDICATION

Dedicated to all veterans
Living and Dead

"All gave some, some gave all"
Only the dead have seen the end of war.
Words of a lonely, confused vet!!!
A day came when I should have died
And after that nothing seemed very important.
So I have stayed as I am without regret separated from
The normal human condition
Newly minted Marines, Fresh from basic training
Find civilian life contemptibly lacking
One Marine commented,
"This place makes no sense
People are too fat
I hate the rudeness,
The chaos"
Life is completely weird
a person lives 60 years
Does all kinds of things
Then its over
Just like that
Built like a condom full of walnuts
How a combat vet feels
You want to crawl under the earth
It's like your soul left your body

In Memory of Corporal Charlie Bloom WWII
Picture on the Wall
I asked a little boy to see his father
He said he couldn't and sighed and when
I asked him what was wrong.
Here's what the boy replied.
My daddy is only a picture in a frame that hangs on the wall.
Each day I talk to my daddy but he doesn't talk at all.
I tell him all of my secrets and all my little plans.
And from the way he smiles at me I know he understands.
The angels took daddy to heaven when I was just going on three.
But I'll bet they never told him how lonely and sad it can be.
I try to cheer up my mommy when the tears flow down her face.
My daddy is only a picture,
but I'm trying to take his place.

The Supreme Sacrifice

In Memory of all servicemen who
Made the supreme sacrifice

His eyes are dark waters that flow through flowered lands.
His smile the morning sun beams that dance the river sands
His mind the sharp island cliffs cut by the floods of time
And his goal a distant mountain peak that only the brave can climb
His voice the hush of evening when the western sky grows red
It was just at day break they said our son was dead

In Memory of Corporal Lance LaPore

Still nests the mall and in the spring
And still the dogwoods blow
But the river winds are sighing things of long ago.
The trout lilies have opened unfurled the sand ferns grow
But the waters whisper things of long ago
Yesterday, I took the wreaths that stood the winter's snow
And placed spring flowers here
I wanted you to know.

Marine Creed

Before God, I swear this creed.
My rifle and myself are the defenders of my country.
We're the saviors of my life. So be it.
Until victory is America's and there is no enemy, but peace!

In Honor of Navy Corpsmen

Sailors Creed

To represent the fighting spirit of the Navy
And those who have gone before me
To defend freedom and democracy around the world
I proudly serve my country's Navy combat team
With honor, courage and commitment

EPILOGUE

Four old vets sat in the corner of the American Legion Hall seated in an out of the way booth. Soft country music wafted through the interior with the low husky voice of the female singer cooing "Why not me." The walls were adorned with numerous photos of men in uniform posed in various military regalia when they were young and virile. Now most were bent and twisted with age. Many had passed to the other side. The hall was quiet it was a rainy Wednesday morning and few patrons were about. The old men chattered about various occurrences occurring internally and internationally. It was Ron Lagasse who pushed open the forbidden door. Few vets ever discussed what demon's lurked in their souls or how they'd locked eyes with the face of Hell.

He spoke softly in a gravelly voice sipping his beer. He posed a question. "Do you guys believe in the NAM?" John LeClaire gazed back in time and spoke for all of them. "Back then, we were boys. It was a different time. A different generation we were compelled to serve and so we followed the flag and did so with honor and integrity. Now aged, we can look back and see it for what it was. "The Big Lie" It was the wrong place, wrong time, wrong reasons, wrong methods, wrong approach, wrong leadership, no real backing, no real will to win, no coherent strategy.

It's the way it is. Politicians throughout the world forge decisions that ultimately spread death suffering and devastation to millions of innocents and then simply walk away and fade into oblivion and never held accountable. Such loss of life, men, women, and children disabled souls scared forever because of that raging hell hole. The carnage that occurred and the millions who perished is unfathomable. I don't know about you, but sometimes I want to crawl under the ground that my soul has left my body. If it were left to soldiers, truly they would seek peace. No words describe the horrors of war. You and I are in the winter of life, yet still headlines reek of savagery, killing, carnage. Until the hand of God falls like a sickle peace will elude the world. We remember our fallen brothers and sisters and honor them. But it is far short of an exampling of what they stood for. To the glory of the political leaders who connive and propel youth into such horror be advised there will be a reckoning. You will somewhere, sometime, someday have to ante up with tears in his eyes; he raised his glass in a solemn gesture, "To all who served then, before, and now, God speed. In a nearby darkened corner "Old Glory" stood as a sentinel. With a slight breeze coming from a nearby window supplying a ripple of movement as though blessing those who honor her. The four old vets strolled out the door greeted by a soft rain and behind them the words of the female vocalist fading, "Why not me?"

PLATOON 75

FIRST RECRUIT BATTALION
S.SGT.M.L.BAKER   SGT.W.G.HANDSCHUMACHER
JUNE 6ᵀᴴ 1957

M.C.R.D., PARRIS ISLAND, S.C.
SGT.R.A.MANUEL   SGT.B.W.DANIELS
PHOTO BY, MAAG

War drew us from our homeland
In the sunlit spring time of our youth.
Those who did not come back alive--
remain in perpetual spring time
forever young
and a part of them is with us always.

Author Unknown

Printed in the United States
By Bookmasters